Identifying Pattern Glass Reproductions

Identifying
PATTERN GLASS
Reproductions

BILL JENKS ◊ **JERRY LUNA** ◊ **DARRYL REILLY**

WALLACE-HOMESTEAD BOOK COMPANY   *Radnor, Pennsylvania*

Dedicated to the memory of HARRY J. ROBINSON
(1921–1991)
Educator, Collector, Dealer, and Friend

Copyright © 1993 by Bill Jenks, Jerry Luna, and Darryl Reilly
All Rights Reserved
Published in Radnor, Pennsylvania 19089, by Wallace-Homestead,
a division of Chilton Book Company

On the cover: Dakota pitchers (reproduction
on left, original on right).

Designed by Adrianne Onderdonk Dudden
Manufactured in the United States of America

Library of Congress Cataloging-in-Publication Data

Jenks, Bill
    Identifying pattern glass reproductions / Bill Jenks, Jerry Luna,
Darryl Reilly.
        p.   cm.
    Includes bibliographical references and index.
    ISBN 0-87069-642-4
    1. Pattern glass—Reproduction.   I. Luna, Jerry.   II. Reilly,
Darryl.   III. Title.
NK5439.P36J46   1993
748.2913—dc20   92-50676
                                                         CIP

1 2 3 4 5 6 7 8 9 0   2 1 0 9 8 7 6 5 4 3

Contents

Acknowledgments

The most enjoyable part of writing a book is listing the credits of all who helped. It is not the easiest part, though, because it is so easy to overlook a name or a place. However, acknowledging those who helped is important because, without the sharing of knowledge, we might not have any books at all.

Although this book is the culmination of the advice and help of many individuals, a special thank you is extended to Harry J. Rinker, consulting editor for the Wallace-Homestead Book Company and executive director of the Institute for the Study of Antiques and Collectibles. Harry's continued encouragement and support are deeply appreciated. Without his personal commitment to fair play, we would all live in a lesser world.

We will remain forever indebted to Frank Fenton and the Fenton Art Glass Co. of Williamstown, West Virginia. Not only did Mr. Fenton unselfishly share his knowledge and time, but he also provided insight into imitation glassware, which otherwise would remain unknown.

Once again, we would like to thank the entire staff of Chilton Book Company. In particular, we extend our deep appreciation to Chris Kuppig (general manager), Edna Jones (managing editor), Susan Clarey (acquisitions editor), and Troy Vozzella (developmental editor). Without their belief in and dedication to this project, this book would not have come to fruition.

We also extend our thanks to a very special friend and incredibly talented lady, Marilyn Shattuck, who not only read, reread, and edited our entire manuscript but also caught many editorial lapses and errors in grammar. In her Yoda-like wisdom, only she will truly know the importance and significance of her participation in this book from its inception.

Special acknowledgment is made to the following collectors and dealers who have graciously provided us with information and examples of reproduction glassware from their study collections: John and Alice Ahlfeld, Don and Lois Bailey, Roger Benett, Keith and Cathy Bergey, Elizabeth Bixby, Donald Bankert, Rachael Bowers, Scott Brown, Irene Cain, Dolly Councilman, Tom Eiserlahr, Howard L. Glatfelter, Jr., Al and Grace Guido, Katelyn and Kylah Hartford, Ruth S. Hickey, the Hodgkins, Nellie and Charlie Huttunen, Robert and Marilyn Jackson, Andrea and Allan Koppel, Robert Lucas, George Mazeika, Jim and Birdie McGee, Lillian Morin, Hal and Shirley Olsen, Joan Pappas, Jacqueline Reilly, Virginia Renschen, Chris and Rena Reynolds, the late Harry J. Robinson, the Sanfords, Shirley Shattuck, Chub and Bette Wicker, Pam Wuth, and Audrey Yerger.

The following institutions proved invaluable in their assistance and cooperation: Bennington Museum, Bennington, VT; Commissioner of Patents & Trademarks, Washington, DC; Corning Museum of Glass, Corning, NY; Henry Ford Museum, Dearborn, MI; Metropolitan Museum of Art, New York, NY; National Archives & Records Services, Washington, DC; Rakow Library, Corning, NY; Sandwich Glass Museum, Sandwich, MA; Smithsonian Institution, Washington, DC; State Museum of Pa., Harrisburg, PA; Sturbridge Village Museum, Sturbridge, MA.

We would also like to thank Norma P.H. Jenkins (Head Librarian), Elizabeth Hylen (Acquisition Librarian), and Virginia L. Wright (Associate Librarian) of the Rakow Library in Corning, New York.

To those we may have unintentionally overlooked, we extend our sincerest gratitude.

Introduction

BEGINNINGS

While we continued work in 1989 on *Early American Pattern Glass—Major Table Settings,* the need for a book devoted exclusively to reproduction Pattern glass had already become apparent. Before then, little new research had been published in the field of imitation glass. Articles appeared occasionally, but the dissemination of information remained limited. As we accumulated data, we wanted to organize and share our findings.

In early 1991, we discussed the proposal for a book on Pattern glass reproductions with Harry L. Rinker, consulting editor of the Wallace-Homestead Book Company. Harry had been conducting seminars on reproductions for a number of years and was well aware of the need-to-know premise we presented. Supporting our interest in this field, he presented our views to Chilton Book Company and, after numerous deliberations and meetings, plans were made to produce this volume.

From the outset, it had been our desire to illustrate *Identifying Pattern Glass Reproductions* with original catalog reprints. Because so many contemporary glass factories produced imitation glassware, using original illustrations seemed logical as well as educational. Certainly, the abundance of catalogs seemed endless. However, to our dismay, problems quickly arose. Copyright laws prohibited us from using any illustrations published after 1985 without the express written consent of the copyright owners. Compounding our problems, private collectors were often reluctant to share illustrations, while the ability to locate examples of reproductions frequently became more difficult than finding original glassware.

In New York, the Rakow Library at Corning always proved to be an invaluable source for research. Here, on microfilm and in original form, is perhaps the largest available collection of original contemporary glass materials. The addition of the J. Stanley Brothers research papers to the museum's archives proved to be yet another treasure trove. However, after months of commuting to Corning, our research came to an end.

THE FENTON CONNECTION

At Corning, we had often heard of the Fenton collection of contemporary catalogs and of the mild-mannered Frank Fenton. Until this time, we had gathered a wealth of information but had little pictorial proof. On the day we returned home from our last visit to Corning, we sent a letter to the Fenton factory.

In May 1991, encouraging news arrived from Mr. Fenton, who welcomed us to the Fenton factory. After several telephone conversations and a number of preemptive starts, we arrived at the factory on what seemed to be the hottest day in July. On the second floor of the factory site, tucked far away from the maddening rush of daily affairs, the tall, lanky Frank Fenton smiled at us as we entered his office.

From our first meeting, Frank Fenton was a gentleman, readily willing to share his great joy of glassmaking. As he spoke, his reminiscences flowed like schoolroom text—infallible and to the point. As minutes turned into hours, we were eloquently led by this master glassman through the history of the Fenton factory and his views on imitation glassware. With no hesitation, he recalled the lean years and his association with Lawrence G. Wright of the L.G. Wright Glass Company.

Wright's relationship with the Fenton Art Glass Company began when business in general was at an all-time low. Precipitated by the fall of the stock market in 1929, by the mid-1930s many factories remained idle. Like other industries, the glass market wavered in the midst of an economic slump. While many closed, those factories fortunate enough to garner work operated from only one to perhaps three days a week. It was at this time that Wright approached the struggling Fenton factory.

Interestingly, the motivating factor behind Mr. Fenton's decision to provide private pot-work for Wright lay in Fenton's concern for its employees—not in reproducing glassware. According to Mr. Fenton, work would clothe and feed hungry employees and their families, pay overdue bills, and provide at least the bare necessities in an otherwise devastated economy. Because many of the designs Wright proposed to produce were only twenty to thirty years out of production, Mr. Fenton always considered Wright's proposal the lesser of two evils: employment versus ruin.

The most significant decision made regarding the production of glassware from original molds, however, was Mr. Fenton's insistence that existing trademarks be altered in such a manner as to designate each new item as a recast. A classic example of this policy centers around Fenton's reissue of the Argonaut Shell design. Unless Wright agreed to alter the original Northwood signature, Fenton refused to produce copies. This resulted in the creation of an entirely new mark: the Northwood underlined "N" joined to the radius of an outer circle by a diagonal line. As Mr. Fenton pointed out, at no time did the Fenton factory create new molds for Wright, although old and worn molds were often repaired and retooled at the factory to keep them in working order.

Because Wright remained in full control, he could usually choose where, when, or what glass would be produced. He was an astute businessman and entrepreneur and, characteristically, would arrive at the factory in an old pickup truck loaded down with molds. In later years, he did this usually during the summer season, when the factory was idle and the company needed work. After agreeing upon the colors that would be used, Wright would wait while only the number of items made within a single turn were produced. When the cost of producing a particular item exceeded his expectations, he removed the molds and carted them to Imperial, Paden City, L.E. Smith, Westmoreland, and other factories, where he might strike a better deal. By selectively producing glassware by item and company, and by transporting the molds and the finished product, Wright was able to minimize costs and become the largest distributor of early American Pattern glass reproductions.

THE OTHER SIDE OF THE STORY

As he reminisced, Mr. Fenton also spoke of his own love of, and fascination with, classic patterns and the challenges he encountered in presenting them in contemporary shapes and colors. With a smile, he fondly recalled bringing to the factory pieces of glass he had purchased from antiques shops and shows. In a small storage area several rooms down from his office, we walked between ceiling-high shelves of glassware. Inspirational or dysfunctional, each item had become an integral part of the Fenton story. Among numerous antiques was a multitude of experimental pieces of new glassware produced at the factory.

As Mr. Fenton explained, it had always been his intention to adapt old designs to contemporary shapes and colors. When original shapes and colors were put into production (as with the Cactus pattern), contemporary colors were employed.

As Mr. Fenton knew, we had come in search of original contemporary catalogs. Perhaps because of our apparent anticipation, Fenton led us across the hall and into a small, narrow room. Here, neatly stored in box upon box were antique and contemporary company catalogs, price lists, and sales brochures. Here, too, were mounds of company diaries, records, and the minutes of meetings that the American Flint Glass Workers' Union had entrusted to Fenton's care. And here, he quietly left us to wander back through time in search of imitation glass.

A HISTORY OF REPRODUCTIONS

Little is known of when or where the first reproductions of early American pressed glass appeared. Even less is known of its manufacture, although it is safe to assume that the earliest items were imported. As early as 1924, The Hamilton Shops of New York City advertised in *The Magazine Antiques* reproductions of the famed Boston and Sandwich Glass Company's dolphin candlestick and compote in solid amber, blue, clear, and combination colors. Before this time, literally no reproductions of pressed-glass table patterns existed because consumer interest in pressed wares had steadily decreased in favor of blown and cut glass. By 1929, however, The Period Shop, Inc. (also of New York City), ran an interesting ad in *Antiques* illustrating a new, clear Horn of Plenty tumbler and advised patrons that reproductions could be purchased directly from stock or made to order. This was the first time a popular pressed-glass tableware pattern had been reproduced. With this reproduction, the era of imitation early American Pattern glass had begun.

Without question, the era of imitation Pattern glass was as misunderstood as its meager beginnings. In the early 1930s, such pioneer glass researchers as Ruth Webb Lee stimulated an interest in, and a demand for, early Pattern glass. Sparked by the findings of factory excavations and original company records, a new collector emerged who hungered for information. Unfortunately, the same forces that made Pattern glass collectible also created some fears—a fact confirmed by Mrs. Lee's own hasty decision to sell her collection of Horn of Plenty (a decision she later regretted).

Looking back upon the years since 1930, one is immediately overwhelmed by the attitude of early glass authors. Purveyors of glassware vaguely resembling reproductions were portrayed as fakers and forgers motivated by deceit, greed, and profit. Manufacturers willing to reproduce glassware were depicted as men of questionable character, while both maker and seller were seen as foes deliberately willing to defraud the unwary buyer. Throughout these early years, this theme was propounded by Ruth Webb Lee, Kenneth Cooper, Alice Hulett Metz, and others in lavish editorials. The mere thought of producing and distributing any early pattern was viewed as part of a deliberate master plan launched in deceptive phases. Various areas were rumored to be seeded with suspect glassware, and accounts abounded of dealings with unscrupulous dealers. Exposés in *The American*

Collector, Hobbies, Old Glass, Spinning Wheel, and other leading trade publications expounded the injustices of imitation glassware. Rumors and allegations contributed to what has been termed the "reproduction craze." In the August 1938 issue of *Antiques,* the Boston-based Early American Glass Club itself cautioned against "the purchase of pressed glass as genuine until careful examination could be made."

As accurate as these accusations may seem, nothing could be farther from the truth. Unlike the incredible accounts of fakers producing pattern glass under the secrecy of night, the simple truth is that from the early 1930s until America's entry into World War II (an action that caused cast iron for mold making to become all but extinct), a number of the leading glasshouses already had been producing imitation glassware. By the time Ruth Webb Lee published her book on reproductions, imitation glassware had become a part of American life. For years, copies of antique Pattern glass adorned the showrooms and display windows of many leading department stores. As early as 1932, advertisements for milk-white Lacy Dewdrop were carried by *Good Housekeeping* magazine. In 1933, the L.G. Wright Glass Company, in conjunction with the Fenton Art Glass Company, reissued the Hobb's Hobnail barber bottle, and in July 1936 copies of Westmoreland's clear Westward Ho goblet were advertised by Paul Thomas of Berks County, Pennsylvania. In subsequent years, myriad advertisements appeared in *China and Lamps, The Crockery and Glass Journal, The Gift and Art Buyer,* and *Gifts and Decorative Accessories.* For the "lady of the house," advertisements in *Ladies Home Journal, House Beautiful,* and other magazines regularly brought the latest glass offerings into the American home.

In the early 1960s and 1970s, the growing interest in reproduction glassware was heightened by major exhibits at the Detroit Institute of Arts (1953), the Corning Museum of Glass (1954), and the Henry Ford Museum (1963), as well as the Toledo Museum's exhibition of nineteenth-century American glassware (1963). This revived interest prompted many contemporary glass manufacturers to produce a large variety of classic antique patterns. A number of institutions began to reproduce glassware by granting a particular glasshouse exclusive rights to reproduce patterns from the museums' collections. The Henry Ford Museum (Dearborn, Michigan), the Metropolitan Museum of Art (New York City), the Sandwich Glass Museum (Sandwich, Massachusetts), and the Smithsonian Institution (Washington, D.C.) each granted reproduction rights to appointed glass houses, then sold the glassware through museum mail-order catalogs and gift shops. Advertised as authentic copies of original glassware, items were produced in both flint and nonflint glass. Copies were permanently marked and gift boxed and often included elaborate histories of each item. As an added means of promoting sales, the Metropolitan Museum produced numerous limited-edition copies, often to commemorate museum events.

IMITATION GLASSWARE

Imitation Pattern glass can be divided into three distinct categories: reproductions, reissues, and look-alikes.

Reproductions are copies or images of original items. Because they are produced from new molds, reproductions vary in detail, size, and weight. Examples of reproductions are Girl with Fan, Lion, Morning Glory, Three Face, and Westward Ho.

In contrast, reissues are produced from original molds and are exact duplicates of the original in design, form, and shape. Examples of reissues are Imperial's Atterbury Lion, United States Glass Company's Knobby Bull's Eye punch bowl set, and Duncan's Palm Beach. Items in each of these patterns were produced from the original mold as exact copies.

Unlike reproductions (produced from new molds and resembling originals in design and form) and reissues (produced from original molds as exact duplicates), a look-alike is an item that merely *imitates* the original. Examples of look-alikes are the Artichoke goblet, King's Crown iced-tea tumbler, Three Face sugar shaker, and the U.S. Coin four-footed spoonholder.

As you can see, imitation pressed glass can, at first, seem quite convincing. However, when compared to antique glassware, all new glass shares a number of subtle discrepancies:

1. Because old glass has survived the trials of time and use, the contour of edges will appear blunt or dull, not crisp or sharp.

2. Imitations are usually heavy and thick-walled. Although these are not always a sign of newness, any excessively heavy item should be evaluated upon its overall likeness to a known original in appearance, detail, and weight.

3. Cheaply produced imitation glassware feels oily or slick. Because the glass contains a high sodium content, the sodium attracts dust and moisture, producing a greasy film.

4. Unlike the soft, clear nature of old glass, imitations are too bright and shiny and the glass is often tinged with blue, gray, green, or yellow. New colors are also artificial and harsh instead of mellow or pale, while both clear and colored reproductions are often muddy or streaked. Of course, any contemporary color (dark brown, ruby, etc.) is obviously new.

5. Any item having a contemporary shape or form may be considered suspect. However, it is always prudent to compare unknown forms and shapes against a reliable reference.

6. Unlike the soft, grayish-white frosting of old glass, the frosting on imitation glassware is chalky, coarse, and entirely too white.

7. Although reissues usually present a good likeness of the original design, the pattern on reproductions and look-alikes characteristically lacks fine detail and workmanship.

THE VALUE OF REPRODUCTIONS

Contrary to popular belief, imitation glassware serves a valued purpose in collecting. As escalating costs continue to put items out of reach of collectors, reproductions can provide collectors with a means of adding otherwise unattainable examples to their collections. Interest is also enhanced by the addition of new colors and forms, such as the Artichoke goblet, Paneled Thistle sugar shaker, and Westward Ho oil lamp. The most valued aspect of imitation glassware, however, can be found in using reproductions as educational tools. Only by holding, studying, and touching imitations can you gain a true knowledge of the differences between old and new glass.

One of the most common questions we hear is, "What is the monetary value of a reproduction?" This is probably the hardest question to answer. Like all collectibles, reproductions are worth only what someone is willing to pay. And, as with all antiques, collectibility, condition, form, and quality must be considered. Today, many reproductions (Westmoreland's milk-white Heavy Paneled Grape, for example) have become highly collectible in their own right. Because many of these items are permanently marked, their value has escalated far beyond the worth of older, comparative items.

As a general rule, most collectors establish the value of reproductions as a percentage of an original item. This percentage usually ranges from 5 to 50 percent, but we feel this figure should fall on the low end—from 5 to 10 percent. Value, however, is inevitably influenced by demand, desirability, and rarity.

A WORD OF CAUTION

Unfortunately, there will always be someone willing to gain at another's expense. The allure of quick profit has established itself so rapidly that, today, no facet of the collectibles field can be deemed immune. Even sadder is the fact that, as collectors and dealers, we continue to permit ourselves to be deceived. However, as easy as it may seem, there is no better weapon for combating deception than knowledge.

As any well-informed collector will admit, there is no easy road to knowledge. Reading is certainly the most logical start, and Chilton publishes an outstanding selection of books covering every conceivable collectible. But reading alone will not protect you against every pitfall. To be well informed, you must supplement what you read with what you see. By holding, feeling, and touching an item, you gain valuable experience as well as understanding.

At a recent antiques show in Indiana, a young couple queried us about the authenticity of a Klondike bowl. Although the bowl was correct in color, shape, and weight, rumors of items newly stained with color easily removable with acetone or alcohol prompted these collectors to request a quick test, assuring both buyer and seller of the item's authenticity.

Never let embarrassment prevent you from asking if you may handle an item. Whenever possible, carefully examine each potential purchase under direct, strong light, noting any defects or discrepancies. Reputable dealers do not knowingly carry reproductions and they will gladly stand accountable to reasonable questions and requests. If they do not, it is better to abstain from making a purchase that will later end in disappointment.

Repair (Grinding and Polishing)

Ethically, there is nothing wrong with an item that has been repaired. Antiques of every conceivable nature are refurbished. Silver plate is resilvered, textiles are rewoven, furniture is refinished, and fine art is restored. Entire volumes have been written covering each subject, while self-help articles appear frequently in many of the well-known trade journals. Today, bestowing original beauty to our treasured heritage has become an accepted way of collecting.

Because it can be easily ground and polished, pressed glass is no exception to repair. Many authentic pieces of pressed glass possess blemishes or imperfections. Known as manufacturer's flaws, many of these imperfections are so insignificant that manufacturers still sold the items as first-quality. However, when blemishes diminished an item's overall appearance, the item was repaired. An example is using gilding or enamel to hide imperfections. Imperfections were also concealed by etching and copper-wheel engraving. When more extreme measures were required, grinding wheels were employed. By removing small amounts of glass from deformed or misshapen bases, objects were prevented from tilting or wobbling.

Today, when chips or flakes are removed from a treasured glass item in the hope of enhancing its aesthetic appeal, restoration has fulfilled its purpose. However, repair turns into deceit when any item is deliberately altered for the sole purpose of enhancing its monetary worth. It is also fraud when an item's original form is altered in any way and offered as a rarity. Examples of this are the removal of a small rose bowl's rim in the hope of creating a more valuable master salt, or the reduction of the size and shape of a goblet, thus producing a more desirable champagne.

Like grinding, polishing pressed glass has also become popular. Cake stands, plates, and other flat items are especially vulnerable to scratches and daily wear. Buffing or polishing the surface of these items with an abrasive such as pumice often conceals or removes these blemishes. Unlike grinding, polishing does not appreciably change an article's form or shape.

Fortunately, ground and polished glass can be detected easily. Telltale signs are flat, sharp surfaces that usually display small abrasion marks; bases or rims that are too small; misproportioned sizes; and indentations where chips had once occurred. In addition, ground glass is noticeably gray-colored unless polished, in which case the area appears overly shiny and smooth. Although repaired items should be plainly marked as such, collectors and dealers should never hesitate to inquire about the condition of any suspect item.

Stain

Originally devised as a more economical method of decorating glassware, clear (and rarely colored) items were coated with a heat-sensitive liquid paint. Under temperatures in excess of 1,000 degrees, the color of this paint would develop or mature and become permanently embedded in the outer surface of the glass. Depending upon the ingredients, varying shades of amber, blue, green, pink, purple, ruby, and other colors could be produced.

Because excessive heat is required to produce this color effect, you will often find stained pieces with standards or stems that are crooked or tilted. The reason for this is simple: while the temperature needed to affix stain was not high enough to melt glass, the glass did become malleable, causing the standard or stem to bend under the object's weight.

Today, relatively few patterns have been reissued or reproduced with stain. On those that have, the color is entirely too light (ranging from pale amethyst to cranberry) and the surface scratches easily. New, plastic-based glass stain, available at craft and hobby shops, is, unlike the original, easily scratched and removable with acetone, alcohol, or hot water. We have also encountered a number of old items that were painted with fingernail polish—also removable by the same techniques.

Sales Slips as Guarantees

When making any purchase, always request a sales slip. For your protection, this slip should contain: (1) the dealer's name, address, and telephone number; (2) a brief description of each item purchased; and (3) the sum paid. Sales slips should also note all "as is" and "repaired" merchandise.

When you have a valid reason for returning any item, return it in its original purchase condition with the sales slip and the seller's original unaltered label.

A FINAL NOTE

Regrettably, the words *look-alike, reissue,* and *reproduction* have become synonymous with the words *deceit, fake,* and *fraud.* For more than fifty years, collectors and dealers have shunned numerous pressed-glass patterns, which has resulted in a dramatic decline in their collectibility because of outdated beliefs or erroneous information.

In *Identifying Pattern Glass Reproductions,* we attempt to present a broader understanding of imitation glassware. Due to space limitations, it was impossible to include every reproduction. However, you will find that we have included the more troublesome patterns. As you read through this book, it is our hope that you will realize there is no reason to fear imitation glassware.

Comments and suggestions are always appreciated and can be sent to the authors at: The Antique Research Center, P.O. Box 1964, Kingston, PA, 18704.

How to Use this Book

Entire volumes could be written on the many glasshouses, both large and small, that have continually reissued and reproduced antique pressed glass throughout the twentieth century. It was neither our desire nor our intention to present their stories in total. Factory or production histories can be found under each pattern and in the Appendix at the back of the book. For clarity, we have eliminated abbreviations from the general text.

CHARTS

The larger, more widely known or popular patterns are accompanied with charts. Each chart is arranged alphabetically by manufacturer, and then alphabetically and numerically by item, and contains the following information:

1. The pattern name as well as the original pattern name.

2. The contemporary manufacturer or institution producing the pattern.

3. CMN denotes the contemporary manufacturer's name for the pattern.

4. Mark. Indicates whether items are permanently marked, signed with a paper label, or are unmarked.

Each chart has further been divided into columns which include:

▫ a description of the item

▫ the color in which each item has been produced

▫ the year in which a particular color was produced as documented by contemporary catalogs, price listings, and sales brochures

▫ a designation *(Orig.)* which indicates that the form corresponds to an original shape

▫ a designation *(New)* which indicates that the form is strictly contemporary in shape

COLOR CODES

In most instances, we list color codes as they originally appeared in order to maintain the integrity of original materials. In instances where different manufacturers used the same color code, or when codes were not used, we created simple letter codes.

HINTS AND REPRODUCTIONS

Two additional features follow the description and history of each pattern: information on reproduced items and how to spot them. Hints provide a brief description of the reproduced pattern, followed by a list of the reproduced items described in the chart(s). For the benefit of the reader, a Glossary and Bibliography are provided at the back of the book.

GUIDELINES FOR SPOTTING REPRODUCTIONS

Does the item have
- a crimped, flared, or ruffled rim
- excess glass
- a thick stem
- an unusual thickness
- an unconventional base, finial, handle, or stem

Is the glass
- crinkled or wavy
- exceptionally heavy
- glossy, oily, or slick
- nonflint with no belltone
- off-colored (clear glass only)
- of poor quality

Are colors
- brash and harsh
- contemporary
- weak or artificial

Is the pattern
- blunt or smooth
- exaggerated
- poorly detailed
- poorly pressed

Do applied decorations
- chip or peel
- wear easily

Are shapes
- contemporary in form

Pattern Glass
Reproductions

ACORN

No one knows who originally produced this well-defined pattern. Natural-looking acorns and leaves lying against a plain background create the basic design element. The finials are clusters of well-molded acorns and handles are applied. Acorn was produced in clear nonflint glass in the 1870s.

Originally produced in a limited number of table forms, new 6$\frac{1}{16}$-inch-high goblets appeared in the early 1950s. These may be found in amber, blue, clear, and vaseline and are heavier than the originals. Typical of most reproductions created from new molds, the fine detailing of the old glass is absent and, at times, the acorns look like clear distorted blotches. The same holds true for the detailing of the leaves, which is intricately fashioned in the old glass and poorly executed in the new.

In 1969, the L.G. Wright Glass Company of New Martinsville, West Virginia, offered the new No.77-17 Acorn goblet in clear and amber, as illustrated in Fig. 1. As in its predecessor, the same discrepancies are apparent. Although neither goblet is permanently marked, the weight and detail of design make it possible to determine the reproduction.

Fig. 1. Reproduction No.77-17 Acorn amber goblet. L.G. Wright Glass Co. Circa 1969. Unmarked.

Hint: Look for intricate veining on the leaves to be sure of an original; any colored goblet is new.
Reproduced items: Goblet.

ACTRESS

The designer and producer of the original Actress pattern is not known. A highly collectible pattern that portrays a number of well-known actresses from the Victorian Era, Actress was produced in an extended table service in a good-quality clear and clear and frosted combination glass. Dating from the early 1880s, through the years it has also become known as Annie, Jenny Lind, Pinafore, and Theatrical.

Fig. 2. New amber Actress relish dish. Imperial Glass Corp. Circa 1957. Embossed "IG." (Note the hobnails on the rim, which do not appear on the original.)

The only authenticated reproduction in this pattern is the relish dish made from a new mold by the Imperial Glass Corporation of Bellaire, Ohio. Produced as part of the Americana Series of Glassware Items, the new relish was introduced by Imperial in 1957. As part of the Collector's Cupboard 4-Color Assortment, the new dish comes in honey amber, midwest rue, Stiegel green, and Wistar purple (Fig. 3). Like the original, the new relish is embossed on the inside base with "Love's Request Is Pickles" and carries the basic Actress design. However, it is exceptionally thick and heavy,

Fig. 3. Reprint of circa 1957 Imperial Glass Corp. ad featuring reproductions from the Collectors Cupboard of Americana Glassware, including Actress and Hobbs' Hobnail.

measuring $9\frac{1}{8} \times 5\frac{1}{8}$ inches, while the original is $9 \times 5\frac{1}{4}$ inches.

Although similar in design, the reproduction relish lacks the detail of the original. This is apparent in the figure's face, which is lifeless and undefined; most notably the eyes lack pupils. Reproductions feel slick or oily, and due to poor pressing techniques, a pronounced waviness appears in the glass near the base of each item.

The distinguishing design of the Actress pattern, the familiar crossed shell and leaf motif, appears in the border at the ends of the original relish. On reproductions, however, this design appears inside the bowl. On the original, the rim is smooth; on the reproduction, 42 pointed hobnails (readily seen in Fig. 2) have been added to the overall border design.

It is interesting to note that in 1957 Imperial illustrated this new relish without the hobnail border. In 1966, the same relish appeared with a hobnail border as part of the "Stamm House Dewdrop Opalescent" collection. This suggests that Imperial may have retooled the mold to the Actress relish to be included in this new hobnail collection (see Dewdrop).

In recent years, relish dishes have been seen in solid amethyst, blue, clear, and vaseline and in opalescent green, purple, and vaseline. The same discrepancies can be noted in all colors.

Each Imperial issue is permanently embossed with that company's "IG" insignia on the bottom of the base and originally carried a paper label.

Hint: Any color other than clear or clear with frosting is new; beware of the hobnailed rim.

Reproduced items: Relish dish.

ARGONAUT SHELL

First issued around 1900, Argonaut Shell was a product of the genius of Harry Northwood. His Northwood Glass Company of Indiana, Pennsylvania, originally produced this fussy pattern, comprised primarily of shell and seaweed motifs, illustrated in the catalog reprint in Fig. 4. The moderate table service includes the basic four-piece table set, water set, and a master berry bowl with matching sauce dishes.

These pieces came in clear, custard, and the opalescent colors of blue, white, and

CHART 1 ARGONAUT SHELL. L.G. Wright Glass Company, New Martinsville, West Virginia.
CMN: Argonaut Shell.
Mark: Unmarked or embossed misshapen underlined "W" in a circle.
Color Code: BO Blue Opalescent, C Clear, CUS Custard (plain or decorated).

ITEM	COLOR(S)	YEAR	ORIG	NEW
Bowl. #911. Master berry, open, low footed. 11" oval.	BO	1970	X	
	C, CUS	1969	X	
Butter dish. #921. Covered, footed.	BO, C, CUS	1970	X	
Compote. #924. Jelly, open, high standard.	BO, C, CUS	1970	X	
Creamer. #922. 5"h.	BO, C, CUS	1970	X	
Salt and Pepper shakers. #927.	BO, C, CUS	1970	X	
Sauce dish. #910. Footed, 5" oval.	BO	1970	X	
	C, CUS	1969	X	
Sugar bowl. #923. Covered.	BO, C, CUS	1970	X	
Toothpick holder. #925.*	BO, C, CUS	1970	X	
Tumbler. #926. Water 6 oz.	BO, C, CUS	1970	X	

*Never originally produced in clear or blue opalescence.

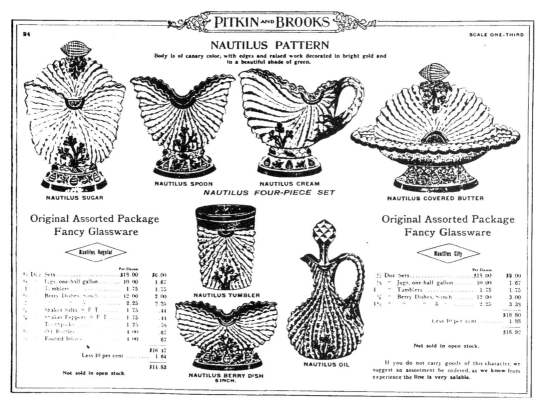

Fig. 4. Pitkin and Brooks circa 1900 catalog reprint of Argonaut Shell. (Note the shape of the finials on the covered butter dish and sugar bowl.)

vaseline, with or without gold. On custard items, the seaweed motif may be decorated in green, while the remainder of the piece is trimmed in gold.

Throughout the years, the L.G. Wright Glass Company of New Martinsville, West Virginia, purchased more than one thousand original pattern-glass molds as they be-

came available. These molds were worked through such factories as Fenton, Paden City, and Westmoreland Glass. In 1969, Wright issued copies of the Argonaut Shell 11-inch oval master berry bowl (Fig. 5) and the 5-inch footed sauce dish in plain and decorated custard. In the following year, Wright produced these and seven additional items (enumerated in Chart 1) in plain and

Fig. 5. Reproduction Argonaut Shell blue opalescent oval master berry bowl. L.G. Wright Glass Co. Circa 1970. Embossed mark.

Fig. 6. New Argonaut Shell No.927 salt and pepper shakers and No.925 toothpick holder in undecorated custard. L.G. Wright Glass Co. Circa 1971. Unmarked.

Fig. 7. Closeup of L.G. Wright Glass Co. mark embossed on the base of the Argonaut Shell master berry bowl.

blue opalescence simply look new; the blue is light, washed out, and has very little opalescence, while the custard is really a pale yellow or off-white. Wright used a cold-paint process to decorate items, replacing the more expensive process of permanently firing gold or enamel to the glass surface.

Allegedly produced from original molds, the pattern appears flat and lifeless. This is especially true of the seaweed motif, which appears crisply molded and vibrantly detailed on originals. The most obvious difference, however, is the treatment of the finial on the covered butter lid. On originals, the finial is a finely detailed seashell. On reproductions, it is a round, blunt shell of solid glass.

Widely available through a network of authorized distributors tightly controlled by Wright, many Argonaut Shell reproductions are embossed on the bottom of the base with an underlined "N" joined to the radius of the circle by an additional line creating a misshapen "W" (Fig 7).

decorated custard and blue opalescence (Fig. 6).

The easiest way to detect Wright reproductions in Argonaut Shell is by color and detail. The items that Wright produced in

Hint: Items marked with a "W," cold-painted items, and pale blue items with little opalescence are new.

ARGUS

Among the elite patterns in early flint is Argus. Christened Concave Ashburton, it has also been referred to as Argus-Creased, Argus-Faceted Stem, Argus-Five Row, Barrel

Argus, Hotel Argus, Master Argus, Tall Argus with Bulbous Stem, and Thumbprint. First introduced in about 1859 by McKee & Brothers of Pittsburgh, Pennsylvania, the pattern quickly found favor with a number of glass houses, including Bakewell, Pears

CHART 2   ARGUS. Fostoria Glass Company, Fostoria, Ohio.
CMN: Fostoria's No.2770, Argus
Mark: Unmarked, embossed "HFM" or paper label.
Color Code: A Amber, B Blue, C Clear, CB Cobalt Blue, G Green, GR Gray, OG Olive Green, RBY Ruby.

ITEM	COLOR(S)	YEAR	ORIG	NEW
Compote. #2770/386. Covered, low footed, 5½"d., 8"h.	C, CB, OG, RBY	1964	X	
Creamer. #2770/682. Footed, pressed handle. 6"h., 8½ oz.	C, CB, OG, RBY	1964	X	
Dessert dish.	C	1963		X
	CB, OG, RBY	1967		X
Goblet. #2770/2. 6½"h. 10½ oz.	A, B, G	1982	X	
	C, CB, OG, RBY	1964	X	
	GR	1974	X	
13 oz.	CB, OG, RBY	1967	X	

ITEM	COLOR(S)	YEAR	ORIG	NEW
Plate. #2770/5.	C, CB, OG	1963		X
	RBY	1964		X
Sauce dish. #2770/421. Flat, round, scalloped rim, 5"d., 2⅛"h.	C, CB, OG, RBY	1964		X
Sherbert. #2770/7. 5"h., 8 oz.	A, B	1982		X
	C	1972		X
	CB, OG, RBY	1967		X
	GR	1974		X
Sugar bowl. #2770/682. Covered, footed, double pressed handles, 6⅛"h.	C, CB, OG, RBY	1964		X
Tumbler.				
#2770/63. Iced tea, 6¾"h., 13 oz.	C, CB, OG, RBY	1964		X
	GR	1974		X
#2770/64. Highball, 6¾"h., 12 oz.	C	1963		X
	CB, OG, RBY	1964		X
#2770/73. Old-fashioned, 5¼"h., 10 oz.	C	1963	X	
	CB, OG, RBY	1964	X	
#2770/89. Juice or cocktail. 3⅞"h., 4½ oz.	C	1963	X	
	CB, OG, RBY	1982	X	
Wine. #2770/26. 4 oz., 4¾"h.	A, B	1982	X	
	C	1972	X	
	CB, OG, RBY	1967	X	
	GR	1974	X	

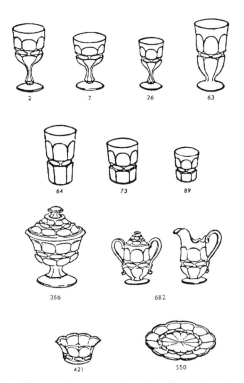

Fig. 8. An interesting group of new Argus by the Fostoria Glass Co. Circa 1964. Embossed "HFM."

and Company and King, Son & Company, both from the Pittsburgh area.

Argus was originally issued in a heavy, brilliant, clear flint glass. An extended table service was produced that included such necessities as ale, beer, and jelly glasses, bitters bottles, and an array of flat and footed tumblers. Typical of their time, the applied handles are gracefully fashioned. Any original item in colored flint is rare.

As interest in reproduction glassware increased throughout the early 1960s, the Henry Ford Museum in Dearborn, Michigan, appointed the Fostoria Glass Company of

Fig. 9. Reproduction assortment of Argus No.2770 goblets. Fostoria Glass Co. for the Henry Ford Museum. Circa 1964. Embossed "HFM."

Fostoria, Ohio, exclusive license to reproduce items in the Argus pattern (see Chart 2). The Fostoria Glass Company issued non-flint reproductions in clear and a number of contemporary colors from new molds that were fashioned from original pieces in the museum's collection.

Fig. 8 shows an interesting group of Fostoria's Argus. You can readily see from the illustration that Fostoria reproductions capture the look and feel of the original ware. These reproductions are produced from a good-quality glass and are available in both antique and contemporary shapes. Although handles are pressed instead of applied, finials run true to conventional styles. The glass is heavy but lacks the belltone of old flint. The contemporary forms distinguish many of these as look-alike items from true reproductions.

Fostoria's reproductions for the Henry Ford Museum are permanently embossed with the "HFM" monogram. Additionally, each item carried a tag depicting a tall building, a Model "T" Ford, and the words "The Henry Ford Museum, Greenfield Village, Dearborn, MI." Items produced for distribution and sale by Fostoria carried a paper label but were not marked (Fig. 9).

Hint: Reproductions are embossed with the "HFM" monogram and made from nonflint glass.

ART

Adams & Company of Pittsburgh, Pennsylvania, first introduced Art in 1889, with continued production by the United States Glass Company at Factory "A" in Pittsburgh. It is also known as Jacob's Tears, Job's Tears, and Teardrop and Diamond Block.

A rather heavy pattern, Art was originally produced for more than a decade in a large and extended table service. Both a regular and hotel or extra-heavy form were available in a brilliant clear and clear with ruby stained nonflint glass.

Like a majority of early American pressed-glass designs, Art is a safe pattern to collect. The only reproduction authenticated thus far is the milk-white 6-inch × 9½-inch-high covered compote illustrated in Fig. 10. For many years this compote has caused much confusion and concern among collectors. Fortunately, a 1961 advertisement identifies it as a product of the L.E. Smith Glass Company of Mount Pleasant, Pennsylvania. Originally called Teardrop, the compote is typical of most reproductions created from new molds. It is thicker and heavier than the old glass, and the standard, clearly seen in the illustration, is lower and wider than any known original.

Fig. 10. Reproduction milk-white Art covered compote. L.E. Smith Glass Co. Circa 1961. Unmarked.

Hint: The original Art was never produced in milk white.

Reproduced items: Compote.

ARTICHOKE

A popular pattern for many years has been that known to collectors and dealers as Artichoke. Often referred to as Frosted Artichoke, it was produced by the Fostoria Glass Company of Fostoria, Ohio, which called it No.205 or Valencia. Fostoria originally issued Artichoke in an extended table service in a good-quality nonflint glass. Clear, clear with acid finish, and limited production in clear opalescent and satin-finished colors complement the basic design of this pattern.

In 1969, the L.G. Wright Glass Company of New Martinsville, West Virginia, produced the only known copy of Artichoke, a goblet. Fig. 11 shows the new goblet known as Wright's No.77-18 or Artichoke. As you can see from the illustration, this clear and frosted nonflint goblet contains all the original basic design elements of the original pattern.

Artichoke goblets are not permanently marked. Distributed for many years by Jenning's Red Barn of New Martinsville, West Virginia, and Carl Forslund of Grand Rapids, Michigan, these goblets may often fool beginning collectors and dealers. Although the newness of the glass is self-apparent, you must only remember that goblets are always reproductions.

Fig. 11. New look-alike Artichoke No.77-18 clear and frosted goblet. L.G. Wright Glass Co. Circa 1969. Unmarked.

Reproduction goblets are not permanently marked.

Hint: A goblet was never made in the original Artichoke pattern.
Reproduced items: Goblet.

ASHBURTON

For more than three-quarters of a century, Ashburton has been avidly sought by collectors of fine early American pressed glass. Many of the leading manufacturers of pressed-glass tableware produced Ashburton from the late 1840s to 1891. The major producer was the New England Glass Company of East Cambridge, Massachusetts.

Originally called Ashburton and Ovington's Double Flute, this pattern has acquired myriad names throughout the years. These include Barrel Ashburton, Choked Ashburton, Dillaway, Double Knob Stem Ashburton, Flaring Top Ashburton, Giant Straight-Stemmed Ashburton, Large

Thumbprint, Near Slim Ashburton, Proxy Ashburton, Semi-Squared Ashburton, Short Ashburton, Slim Ashburton, and Talisman Ashburton.

Ashburton was extensively produced in

Fig. 12. New Ashburton assortment by the Westmoreland Glass Co. Circa 1974. (Both the iced tea and sherbert are strictly contemporary.) Embossed "WG."

CHART 3 ASHBURTON. Libbey Glass Company, Toledo, Ohio.
CMN: Ashburton.
Mark: Unmarked or paper label.
Color Code: C Clear, G Gold (amber).

ITEM	COLOR(S)	YEAR	ORIG	NEW
Ashtray, round, flat.				
4"d.	C, G	1981		X
6"d.	C, G	1981		X
8"d.	C, G	1981		X
Bowl. #5233. Flat, low, smooth rim.	C	1981		X
Goblet.				
#5225. 10 oz.	C, G	1981	X	
#5226. 12 oz.	C, G	1981	X	
Salt shaker. #5221. Footed, tall, 1¼ oz.	C, G	1981		X
Sherbert. #5222. Footed, 6½ oz.	C, G	1981		X
Tumbler.				
#5227. Low, footed, 8½ oz.	C, G	1981		X
#5229. Tall, footed, 10 oz.	C, G	1981		X
#5230. Tall, footed, 12 oz.	C, G	1981		X
Wine. #5223. 6 oz.	C, G	1981	X	

varying qualities of clear flint and nonflint glass. Collectors may occasionally find pieces enameled or engraved. Any colored item in flint is a rarity (Fig. 12).

The renewed interest in reproduction glassware during the 1960s and 1970s prompted many contemporary glass manufacturers to produce a large variety of classic antique patterns. A number of museums granted particular glasshouses exclusive rights to reproduce patterns from their collections. The Metropolitan Museum of Art in New York City, the Smithsonian Institution in Washington, D.C., the Henry Ford Museum in Dearborn, Michigan, and the Sandwich Glass Museum in Sandwich, Massachusetts each gave reproduction rights to glasshouses, then sold the glassware through the museums' mail-order catalogs and gift shops.

The glasshouses produced items in both flint and nonflint glass, which they advertised as direct copies of original glassware. These copies were permanently marked and gift boxed and often included elaborate

Fig. 13. Ashburton reproduction clear ship's tumbler. Non-flint. Imperial Glass Corp. for the Metropolitan Museum of Art. Circa 1981. Embossed "MMA."

CHART 4   ASHBURTON. Westmoreland Glass Company, Grapeville, Pennsylvania.
CMN: Line #1855, Ashburton.
Mark: Unmarked, embossed "WG," or paper label.
Color Code: A Amber, BB Bermuda Blue, BR Brown, C Clear, F Flame, MW Milk White, MWD Milk White Decorated (Roses & Bows), OG Olive Green, P Pink.

ITEM	COLOR(S)	YEAR	ORIG	NEW
Ashtray.	F, OG	1967		X
Cake stand, low footed.	A, BB, OG	1967		X
	C	1983		X
Candlestick.	A, BB, OG	1967		X
	C	1983		X
Claret.	A, BB, C, OG	1966	X	
Compote.				
Covered, high standard, 7½"h.	A, BB, C, OG	1966		X
	F, MW, MWD	1967		X
Open, high standard.				
Flared rim.	A, BB, OG, MW	1967	X	
	C	1983	X	
Lipped rim.	A, BB, OG	1967		X
	C	1983		X
Creamer, footed, pressed handle.	A, BB, OG	1967	X	
	C	1983	X	
Goblet.	A, BB, C, OG	1966	X	
	BR	1974	X	
	P	1977	X	
Pitcher, water, footed. Pressed handle.	A, BB, OG	1967		X
	C	1983		X
Sherbert.	A, BB, C, OG	1966		X
	BB, BR	1967		X
	P	1977		X
Sugar bowl, covered.	A, BB, C, OG	1966	X	
	MW, MWD	1967	X	
Tumbler.				
Iced tea, straight-sided.				
Flat.	A, BB, C, OG	1966		X
	BR	1974		X
Footed.	A, BB, C, OG	1966		X
	BR	1974		X
	P	1977		X
Old-fashioned, flat.	A, BB, C, OG	1966	X	
	BR	1974	X	
	P	1977	X	
Wine.	A, BB, C, OG	1966	X	
	BR	1974	X	
	P	1977	X	

histories of each item. The Metropolitan Museum of Art produced numerous limited-edition copies (Fig. 13).

As early as 1960, reproductions in Ashburton appeared in a number of original and contemporary colors and forms. Produced from new molds and under varying condi-tions, reproductions exhibit notable vari-ations in shape and quality.

By 1966, the Westmoreland Glass Company of Grapeville, Pennsylvania, had is-sued five items in the pattern. Advertised as Westmoreland's No.1855 or Ashburton, each was produced from a new mold in quality nonflint in amber, Bermuda blue, brown, clear, and olive green. In 1967, nine additional forms and two new colors, blue and pink, were added to the line (see Chart 4).

Characteristics that distinguish Westmoreland's reproductions from the original Ashburton are (1) pressed, flat-sided handles, (2) larger finials that stand on a higher, narrower shaft, (3) large knobs on the stems, just above the base, of the goblet, claret, and sherbert, and (4) ovals that are generally much squarer. Westmoreland reproductions are permanently embossed with the firm's familiar "WG" insignia (Fig. 14).

In 1981, the Libbey Glass Company of Toledo, Ohio, produced a line similar to Westmoreland's. Libbey created forms that

Historic "Ashburton" Handfashioned by Skilled Craftsmen

1855 Goblet	1855 Claret	1855 Sherbet	1855 Ice Tea, Fld.	1855 Ice Tea, Str.	1855 Old Fashion

1855 Sugar/Cream

1855 Compote

1855 Candy

1855 Jug

1855 Candlestick

1855 Bowl, Flared

1855 Candlestick

1855 Bowl, Lipped

1855 Cake Salver

Fig. 14. New Ashburton assortment by the Westmoreland Glass Co. Circa 1967. Embossed "WG."

used the basic Ashburton design (see Chart 3). But, unlike Westmoreland, Libbey issued its reproductions only in clear and gold (amber). Libbey reproductions were not permanently marked but may often be found with a paper label.

Both Westmoreland and Libbey reproductions are convincing. As you can see in Fig. 12, stemware and tumblers (in particular the "old-fashioned") may prove most troublesome. Goblets, wines, and "old-fashioned" tumblers are excellent copies and can easily be mistaken for originals.

The Imperial Glass Corporation of Bellaire, Ohio, also produced two items, the goblet and champagne, for the Henry Ford Museum. These are good copies made from a new mold in clear flint glass, and both are embossed with the museum's "HFM" logo.

Another outstanding reproduction made by Imperial is the ship's tumbler offered by the Metropolitan Museum of Art. Illustrated in Fig. 13, this new tumbler was introduced in 1981 in a high-quality clear flint glass. This tumbler has been faithfully reproduced from a new mold. The newness of the glass and the embossed "MMA" insignia of the Metropolitan Museum of Art are the only two clues pointing to its contemporary origin.

The easiest way to determine reproductions is by form. By acquainting yourself with the number of original shapes produced, you will quickly recognize the contemporary look of reproductions.

Hint: Reproductions are lighter than originals, do not ring, and have pressed handles and a smooth design.

ATLANTA

Throughout the era of early American pattern glass, manufacturers employed many decorative techniques and designs to capture consumer interest. Designed for the Victorian housewife, tableware was offered in a vast array of patterns that included animals, birds, flowers, and geometric motifs. One such pattern has become known to collectors and dealers as Atlanta.

Also known as Clear Lion Head, Frosted Atlanta, Late Lion, Square Lion, and Square Lion Heads, Atlanta was originally produced by the Fostoria Glass Company of Fostoria, Ohio, as pattern No.500. Fostoria issued Atlanta in an extended table service from about 1895 through 1900 in a brilliant nonflint glass. The company offered complete table sets in clear and clear with frosting (plain or copper-wheel engraved). Although you may find odd pieces in camphor, clear with amber or ruby stain, and milk white, these are considered rare.

Only the goblet has been reproduced in Atlanta (Figs. 15 and 16), appearing prior to 1964 in clear nonflint glass. Produced from a new mold, this goblet is larger and heavier than the original; the bowl is longer and the stem is shorter. Unlike the origi-

Fig. 15. Original clear Atlanta goblet. Fostoria Glass Co. Circa 1895.

Fig. 16. Reproduction Atlanta clear goblet. Circa 1960. Unmarked.

nals, which are crisply molded, the lion's face on the reproduction goblet is blurred and lifeless, especially around the eyes and mouth, which are so poorly pressed they appear to be missing. Also poorly pressed is the decorative band that connects each lion head. The glass is heavy and has a distinct light yellow cast best seen under strong light. Along the base of the bowl, the glass often appears wavy or crinkled. New goblets are not marked as to manufacturer or place of origin. However, weight and lack of detail make it relatively easy to distinguish the new from the old.

Hint: The goblet is the only Atlanta reproduction.

Reproduced items: Goblet.

ATTERBURY LION

Among the diverse pressed animal designs produced in Victorian America, none can compare to the covered pieces of Atterbury & Company of Pittsburgh, Pennsylvania. Atterbury is unequaled in the production of this type of glassware. Today its covered dishes are regarded as classic examples of the designer's art. One such item, highly regarded by the ardent collector of milk-white glass, is the Atterbury Lion.

Although the most common Atterbury base for this dish has a lacy border, you may also find original specimens with a ribbed base that matches the ribbing on the cover. Produced from the finest milk-white glass, originals are permanently

Fig. 17. Reproduction Atterbury Lion amber covered dish with lacy base. Imperial Glass Corp. Circa 1967. Embossed "IG."

dated "Pat'd Aug.6. 1889" inside the cover.

There are at least two reproductions of the Atterbury covered lion dish. The first was produced in the early 1950s by the Imperial Glass Corporation of Bellaire, Ohio. Known as Imperial's No.51873, this new covered 7½-inch-long dish was made from the original Atterbury mold and carries the old patent date (Fig. 17).

The dish was first issued in blue mist and flask brown. By 1967 the mold was worked in amber, clear/frosted, milk-white, peacock carnival, purple slag, and ruby gold carnival glass. Because Carl Gustkey (president of Imperial from 1940 until his death in 1967) demanded that all reproductions be permanently marked, you will find the familiar Imperial "IG" logo pressed deep inside the head and upon the lacy-edged base of each Imperial Atterbury Lion reproduction.

When Imperial became a part of the Lenox Corporation, they began producing this covered dish for the Metropolitan Museum of Art in New York City as part of its "Exclusive Reproductions of Early American Glass from the Metropolitan Museum of Art." Each piece was permanently marked "MMA" and was accompanied by a certificate of authenticity guaranteeing that each item was an authorized copy of the original in the museum's collection.

As late as 1959, the Westmoreland Glass Company of Grapeville, Pennsylvania, issued a second version of the Atterbury Lion covered dish. Known as Westmoreland's Lion on a Nest, this reproduction was offered in brown marble slag, milk white, and purple marble slag. Westmoreland also produced this dish for the Levay Distributing Company of Edwardsville, Illinois, in blue milk, electric blue carnival, and turquoise carnival glass.

Unlike Imperial reproductions, the Westmoreland Lion on a Nest was not produced from the original Atterbury mold. This fact is verified by the measurements of the covers. While the original lion top measures 6⅜ inches, Westmoreland's top measures

159 "Lion"
Box and Cover

Fig. 18. Reproduction purple slag Atterbury Lion covered dish with lacy base. Imperial Glass Corp. Circa 1967. Embossed "IG."

6½ inches, making it impossible to place a new top on an old base. Moreover, Westmoreland copies are not dated inside the lid. They were produced with either a diamond basketweave or lacy-edged base and were permanently embossed from about 1960 onward with Westmoreland's familiar hallmark.

As you can see from Figs. 17 and 18, reproductions may seem quite convincing. Although any item in color is strictly contemporary, new covered dishes in milk white may prove more troublesome to collectors and dealers. Perhaps the easiest way to detect a new covered dish in milk white is by comparing the quality of the glass. New items are heavier and thicker than the originals and the glass is glossy and ricey in appearance.

Hint: Reproductions are permanently marked either with Imperial's "IG" or Westmoreland's "WG" logo.

Reproduced items: Covered dish.

AZTEC

One of many early American designs that can be classified as geometric is the Aztec pattern. Referred to as New Mexico by Julia Magee Hartley and Mary Magee Cobb in their work on states patterns, Aztec is a fussy design reminiscent of cut glass. Dominating the basic design are large pinwheels and other cut-glass motifs. McKee & Brothers of Pittsburgh, Pennsylvania, originally issued Aztec in an extended table service in a medium-grade nonflint glass in clear and milk white. Dating between 1894 and 1915, most items are marked with "Pres-Cut" in a circle pressed into the base.

At least three reissues of the Aztec punch-bowl set are known. As early as 1955, the Tiffin Glass Company of Tiffin, Ohio, reissued the Aztec punch-bowl set. The bowl is made from the original McKee mold in clear nonflint glass and has the original McKee trademark on the base. The punch cups are produced from a new mold and, unlike the originals, do not flare at the rim.

In 1966, the Jeannette Glass Company of Jeannette, Pennsylvania, reissued two additional versions of the Aztec punch set—Aztec or Jeannette No.924(TP) and No.926(BT). Set No.924 has a two-piece punch bowl, while set No.926 has a one-piece punch bowl. Both versions of this 26-piece set consist of a 10-quart punch bowl, twelve 5-ounce punch cups, and twelve nickel-plated hooks. Produced in clear nonflint glass, both Jeannette punch sets allegedly have been reissued from original molds.

In 1981, the L.E. Smith Glass Company of Mount Pleasant, Pennsylvania, reissued a third version of the punch-bowl set. Illustrated in Figs. 19 and 20, this set, too, was allegedly produced from the original mold in clear nonflint glass. Consisting of the two-piece punch bowl, twelve punch cups, and ladle, Smith's punch set is not permanently embossed with the original "Pres-Cut" trademark.

In 1987, the Fenton Art Glass Company of Williamstown, West Virginia, reissued the clear Aztec toothpick holder from the origi-

Fig. 19. Butler Brothers 1907 catalog reprint of the Aztec punch-bowl set.

Fig. 20. Reproduction clear Aztec punch-bowl set by the L.E. Smith Glass Co. Circa 1981. Unmarked.

nal McKee mold. Produced as a limited edition exclusively for the Fenton Art Glass Collectors of America 1987 convention, the original McKee mark was replaced with the familiar Fenton logo.

Both the John E. Kemple Glass Works and the Summit Art Glass Company also reproduced items in Aztec, offering them as its own Whirling Star design in amethyst and other contemporary colors. An example of this is the amethyst creamer by Kemple produced from the original mold.

Recently, a new unmarked 7½″ diameter

covered butter dish has been reported in clear and contemporary colors.

Hint: Original punch-bowl sets are clear and crisply molded, although the McKee

mark does not always indicate an original piece.

Reproduced items: Butter dish, creamer, punch bowl, punch cup, toothpick holder.

BABY FACE

A figural design popular in early American pressed glass is Baby Face (Fig. 21). Originally named Cupid, this pattern was produced in the early 1880s by McKee & Brothers of Pittsburgh, Pennsylvania. The limited table service was clear with an acid finish. Characteristic of the pattern, the finely detailed cherub faces appear almost lifelike on stems and finials.

To date, four known reproductions exist in Baby Face. The small covered compote, goblet, covered sugar bowl, and wine have each been issued in clear and frosted glass. Although reproductions have been noted since the late 1950s, the manufacturer is not known, as none of the pieces is permanently marked with either a paper label or embossed logo.

Contrary to popular belief, you can easily detect reproductions in this pattern. Compared to originals, reproductions are heavier, the finials and stems are squat and poorly molded, and the frosting is satin-like and uneven. Lacking the refined workmanship apparent in originals, the eyes and hair of the baby's face are distorted and lifeless.

During the 1980s, an electric lamp with matching ball shade was produced in clear and frosted glass. Unlike any known original form, it is strictly a contemporary form.

Hint: Pieces with scowling or distorted faces are new.

Reproduced items: Compote, goblet, lamp, sugar bowl, wine.

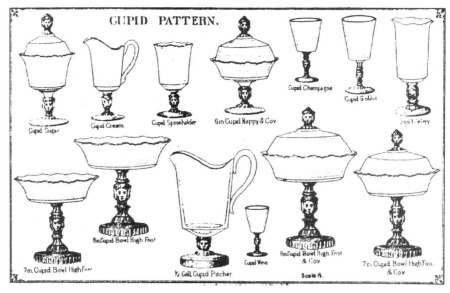

Fig. 21. Reprint of the circa 1888 McKee Brothers catalog illustrating Baby Face (originally known as McKee's Cupid pattern).

BALL AND BAR

Ball and Bar is one of the many patterns that comprise the geometric group of pressed glass. This pattern was first issued by the Westmoreland Specialty Glass Company of Grapeville, Pennsylvania, circa 1896. Produced in a medium-grade clear nonflint glass, Ball and Bar was originally available in an extended table service. Typical of the geometric series, the main design element consists of a band of vertical bars, the tops and bottoms of which are notched or pointed. Above and below this vertical bar is a single band of balls that forms small diamonds where each ball and bar touch.

Ball and Bar is a safe pattern to collect. The only known reproduction is a reissue of the 5-inch-high creamer. Allegedly reissued from original Westmoreland molds as item No.1950/980 by the Imperial Glass Corporation of Bellaire, Ohio, this creamer appeared as early as 1960 (Fig. 22). Unlike originals, which were produced only in clear, the creamer may be amethyst or milk white. Each element of the original design was carefully molded to produce an exact likeness of the original. However, because Ball and Bar was never originally produced in color, there should be no confusion about these new creamers.

Although reproduction creamers are not

Fig. 22. Reproduction Ball and Bar clear creamer. Imperial Glass Corp. Circa 1960.

permanently marked, they originally carried a paper label.

Hint: Any color other than clear is contemporary.

Reproduced items: Creamer.

BALL AND SWIRL

The original name of this quaint, old pattern is Ray. Also known as Swirl and Ball, this design was originally made by McKee & Brothers of Pittsburgh, Pennsylvania, in 1894 and was issued in a good-quality clear nonflint glass. Like many patterns produced during the last decade of the nineteenth century, Ball and Swirl was available in an extended table service.

In the late 1940s, the Westmoreland Glass Company of Grapeville, Pennsylvania, reproduced this pattern as a complete table service (see Chart 5). Known as Westmoreland's No.1842 or Ball and Swirl, this table

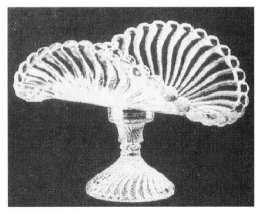

Fig. 23. Reproduction Ball and Swirl clear high-standard banana stand (made by folding the rim of the cake stand). Westmoreland Glass Co. Circa 1974. Embossed "WG."

CHART 5   BALL AND SWIRL. Westmoreland Glass Company, Grapeville, Pennsylvania.
CMN: Ball and Swirl or No.1842.
Mark: Unmarked, embossed "WG," or paper label.
Color Code: A Amber, AM Amethyst, B Blue, C Clear, CE Cerise, CMP Crimson Mother of Pearl, GM Green
Marble Slag, MW Milk White, PC Purple Carnival, PM Purple Marble Slag.

ITEM	COLOR(S)	YEAR	ORIG	NEW
Ashtray, square, flat, 4".	C	1940s		X
	GM, PM	1970s		X
Banana stand, high standard.	C	1974	X	
	MW	1950s	X	
Basket, handled.				
5½"d. Triple-handled.	C	1940s		X
7"d.	C	1940s		X
Bowl.				
6½"d.	C	1940s	X	
10"d.	C	1940s	X	
Cake stand, high standard.				
Large, 10"d.	C	1974	X	
	MW	1950s	X	
Small, 6"d.	C	1940s	X	
Candlelabra, two-light.	C	1940s		X
Candlestick, 4"h.	C	1940s		X
Candy dish, covered.	A, AM, B	1971		X
	C	1940s		X
	GM, PM	1970s		X
	MW	1955		X
Compote.				
Covered.				
7"d.	C	1940s	X	
Open.				
7"d. Flared.	C	1940s	X	
7½"d. Turned edge.	C	1940s		X
Creamer, footed, small.	C	1940s		X
Cruet, oil, 2 oz.	C	1940s		X
Decanter, wine.	C	1940s		X
Goblet, 8 oz.	C	1940s		X
Mayonnaise, footed.	C	1940s		X
Nappy, handled.				
5"l. Heart-shaped.	C	1940s		X
5½"d. Flared.	C	1940s		X
5½"d. Plain rim.	C	1940s		X
Pitcher, water, applied handle.	C	1940s	X	
	CE, CMP, PC*	1970s	X	
Plate.				
6½"d., Underplate for nappy.	C	1940s		X
8"d. Luncheon.	C	1940s	X	
10"d. Turned-up edges.	C	1940s		X
12"d. Dinner.	C	1940s		X
18"d. Torte.	C	1940s		X
Relish, three-part, 9"d., round.	C	1940s		X
Rose bowl, 5"d.	C	1940s	X	

ITEM	COLOR(S)	YEAR	ORIG	NEW
Sherbert.				
High standard.	C	1940s		X
Low standard.	C	1940s		X
Sugar bowl, double-handled, footed.	C	1940s		X
Tumbler.				
Iced tea.				
10 oz.	C	1940s		X
12 oz.	C	1940s		X
Water, 8 oz.	C	1940s	X	
	CE, CMP, PC*	1970s	X	
Vase, footed.				
Fan-shaped.	C	1940s		X
Flared, 9"h.	A, AM, B	1971	X	
	C	1940s	X	
	GM, PM	1970s	X	
	MW	1967	X	
Straight-sided, 9"h.	C	1940s	X	
Wine, 2 oz.	C	1940s		X

*Made exclusively by Westmoreland for Levay Distributing Company in 1970s.

service was made in both original and contemporary shapes from clear nonflint glass. Westmoreland later produced several items from this service in golden sunset crystal (amber), green marble, milk white, and purple marble slag.

In the late 1970s, Westmoreland also produced an exclusive, limited-edition water set for the Levay Distributing Company of Edwardsville, Illinois. This set consists of a pitcher and 8-ounce water tumbler in cerise,

Fig. 24. Reproduction Ball and Swirl amethyst covered candy dish. Westmoreland Glass Co. Circa mid-1960s. Embossed "WG."

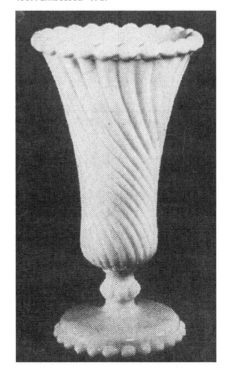

Fig. 25. Reproduction No.1842 Ball and Swirl 9-inch-high milk-white footed vase. Westmoreland Glass Co. Circa 1967. Embossed "WG."

crimson mother-of-pearl, and purple carnival.

As you can see from Figs. 23, 24, and 25, reproductions can be quite convincing. Although any color other than clear is contemporary, antique forms in clear may often prove confusing. Although these reproductions are generally heavier than the originals, you can easily detect new items by carefully examining the pattern. The design of original pieces runs from right to left; on both the tops and the bases, the design on reproductions runs from left to right.

Westmoreland reproductions, prior to 1949, are not permanently marked.

Hint: Reproductions are heavier than originals and the design runs left to right.

BALTIMORE PEAR

One of many members of the fruit series of pressed glass, Baltimore Pear has enjoyed a long and well-deserved popularity. Produced by Adams & Company of Pittsburgh, Pennsylvania, about 1874, this pattern was later reissued by the United States Glass Company at Factory "A" (Adams) in about 1891. Originally known as Gipsy, Baltimore Pear was made in a good-quality clear non-flint glass in a large and extended table service. Also known as Double Pear, Fig, Maryland Pear, and Twin Pear, it is a simple design of single or double clear pears in high relief against a stippled background (Fig. 26).

The first reproductions in Baltimore Pear appeared in the late 1930s. Clear goblets, 9-inch and 10-inch plates, sauce dishes, and covered sugar bowls were produced from new molds. Slightly yellowed in color, these reproductions are not marked with the maker's name or place of origin. By 1955, a number of contemporary glass houses, including Imperial, Jeannette, and Westmoreland Glass, issued a limited number of items from new molds in clear and contemporary colors. Enumerated in the following charts, each contemporary item is a good copy of the original.

Fig. 26. Reprint of circa 1891 United States Glass Co. catalog illustrating an interesting group of Baltimore Pear.

CHART 6   BALTIMORE PEAR. Jeannette Glass Company, Jeannette, Pennsylvania.
CMN: Baltimore Pear.
Mark: Unmarked.
Color Code: C Clear, MW Milk White, SP Shell Pink.

ITEM	COLOR(S)	YEAR	ORIG	NEW
Butter dish, covered, flat.	C	1956	X	
Chip and dip set. #3759/4. Master bowl 9"d., plated frame, dip bowl 4¾"d.	C	1966		X
Creamer. #3711. Footed, 6½ oz.	C	1966	X	
	MW	1955	X	
	SP	1956	X	
Sauce dish, round, flat, 4¾"d.	C	1966	X	
Sugar bowl. #3710. Covered, footed, table size, 10 oz.	C, SP	1956	X	
	MW	1955	X	
Tray, serving, double-handled, 12⅜" × 10½".	C	1966	X	

CHART 7   BALTIMORE PEAR. Other Reproductions prior to 1975.
Maker: Unknown.
Mark: Unmarked.
Color Code: C Clear.

ITEM	COLOR(S)	YEAR	ORIG	NEW
Cake stand, high standard.	C		X	
Celery vase.	C		X	
Goblet.	C		X	
Pitcher, water, pressed handle.	C		X	
Plate.				
9"d.	C		X	
10"d.	C		X	

Illustrated in the 1955 "Handmade Reproductions of choice pieces of Early American Glass" catalog of the Westmoreland Glass Company of Grapeville, Pennsylvania, are the reproduction Baltimore Pear covered sugar bowl and creamer. Known as Westmoreland's line No.1869 or Baltimore Pear, each of these items was made from a new mold and is permanently embossed with the company's "WG" logo. Unlike original items, these were made in milk white.

At the same time, the Jeannette Glass Company of Jeannette, Pennsylvania, offered a similar covered sugar and creamer (see Chart 6). This, too, was produced in milk white. In 1956, both reproductions were also offered in shell pink, and a clear covered butter dish was added. By 1966, this line was expanded to six items. All were produced from new molds and are not permanently marked.

Another version of the Baltimore Pear covered sugar bowl was produced by the Imperial Glass Corporation of Bellaire, Ohio. Illustrated in its undated catalog No.62 as line No.974 (Fig. 27), this new sugar bowl was made from a new mold in clear glass as late as 1960. In 1962, reproduction sugar bowls were available in clear with cranberry stain, doeskin (clear frosted), golden orange, and ruby decorated, and, in 1976, verde.

Fig. 27. Reproduction clear with cranberry stain Baltimore Pear covered sugar bowl. Imperial Glass Corp. Circa 1962. Embossed "IG."

Fig. 28. Closeup of original Baltimore Pear pattern. (Notice the fine detailing, which does not appear in reproductions.)

Once you take time to consider quality and workmanship, you will realize that Baltimore Pear is a safe pattern to collect. Original pieces are finely detailed, with heavily stippled and intricately veined leaves. The pears are natural looking, and the entire design is in high relief (Fig. 28). In comparison, reproductions are poorly detailed. Leaves are inadequately stippled and lack the intricate veining found on originals. Unlike the old, the pears on reproductions are misshapen, flat, and lifeless.

Hint: Items with poorly detailed leaves, and misshapen fruit are reproductions.

BARRED OVAL(S)

Barred Ovals is a favored pattern among collectors of ruby stained glass. This well-documented pattern is often referred to by early glass authorities as Banded Portland, Banded Portland-Frosted, Buckle, Frosted Banded Portland, Oval and Crossbar, and Purple Block. Originally produced by George Duncan & Sons of Pittsburgh, Pennsylvania, about 1892, it was reissued by the United States Glass Company at its Factory "D" as pattern No.15004.

The original Barred Oval(s) is a high-grade nonflint glass. It was made in clear, clear and frosted (the frosting was ground on a machine rather than by acid), and clear with ruby stain (plain or copper-wheel engraved). Complete table services were produced in both clear and clear with ruby stain. No doubt, with some effort, you can assemble a complete set in clear with frosting.

In 1985, the Fenton Art Glass Company of Williamstown, West Virginia, produced a number of items in Barred Oval(s) (see Chart 8) from new molds created at its factory. Issued in contemporary colors, these reproductions are a fine-quality nonflint glass. Fig. 29 is an interesting grouping of Fenton's Barred Oval. As you can see from the illustration, the only item

CHART 8 BARRED OVAL(S). Fenton Art Glass Company, Williamstown, West Virginia.
CMN: Barred Oval(s).
Mark: Embossed Fenton logo.
Color Code: NK Carnival, PW Periwinkle Blue, RU Ruby.

ITEM	COLOR(S)	YEAR	ORIG	NEW
Basket, applied clear handle.				
#8332. Low.	PW, RU	1985		X
#8333. Small, 6″h.	PW, RU	1985		X
#8361. Tall, 6″h.	PW, RU	1985		X
Bell. #8361.	NK	1986		X
	PW, RU	1985		X
Bowl, open, round.				
#8321. 6½″d.	PW, RU	1985	X	
#8322. 8½″d.	PW, RU	1985	X	
Candleholder. #8372. 6″h.	PW, RU	1985		X
Light. #8371. Votive, 3½″h.	PW, RU	1985		X
Sugar bowl. #8388. Covered, 7½″h.	PW, RU	1985	X	
Vase. #8351. Swung, 8½″h.	PW, RU	1985		X

8388 PW
Cov. Candy, 7½″ h.

Fig. 29. An interesting group of contemporary Barred Ovals. Fenton Art Glass Co. Circa 1983–84. Embossed Fenton logo. Only the covered sugar bowl (illustrated as the covered candy) emulates a known antique form.

that might cause confusion is the covered candy box, which is a direct copy of the original sugar bowl. However, this piece is thicker and heavier than the original. Each item in the line is permanently embossed with the familiar Fenton logo in the base.

Hint: The Barred Ovals pattern was never originally made in solid colors.

BASKETWEAVE

Little is known of the history of Basketweave. Appropriately named, the design resembles the weave found on handmade
baskets (Fig. 30). Although the date and
manufacturer of the original are not known,
design characteristics date the pattern to
the mid-1880s. Collectors can still assemble
an extended table service in a good-quality
nonflint glass in amber, apple green, blue,
clear, and vaseline.

The history of Basketweave reproductions is as elusive as the originals. New goblets, water pitchers, water tumblers, and
water trays first appeared in the late
1930s. Found in all original colors, they
were made from new molds and are unmarked.

The easiest way to detect Basketweave
reproductions is by design and color. The
weave on original pieces always looks
crisp, neatly pressed, and natural. The
color is always even, with a soft mel-
lowness that cannot be duplicated by today's methods. In contrast, the weave on
reproductions is weak, often blurred, and
exaggerated. Colors are harsh, artificial,
and washed out. Unlike a majority of
reproductions, those in Basketweave

Fig. 30. Original Basketweave water pitcher. Circa 1880s.

are smaller and lighter in weight than originals.

Hint: Unlike originals, the weave on repro-
    ductions is blurred and weak.
Reproduced items: Goblet, water
    pitcher, water tray, tumbler.

BEADED GRAPE MEDALLION

A charming old pattern of the grape family
of pattern glass, Beaded Grape Medallion
was designed and patented by Alonzo C.
Young on May 11, 1869 (mechanical patent
#90040). The Boston Silver Glass Company
of East Cambridge, Massachusetts, produced this highly collectible pattern in a medium-sized table service in a good-grade
clear flint and nonflint glass (Fig. 31).

The design consists of clusters of grapes
within large, clear, beaded ovals upon a
finely stippled background. Handles are applied, and finials are well-defined acorns. Interestingly, goblets appear in three different
base treatments: (1) stippled, (2) stippled
with three beaded ovals and grape clusters,

and (3) stippled with three small clear
beaded ovals.

Only the goblet (with three beaded ovals
and grape clusters on a stippled base) has
been reproduced. The new goblet (produced from a new mold) is 6¾ inches high
and is an excellent copy of the original. Collectors can find reproduction goblets in
clear, clear with light amber-stained rims,
or clear with cranberry-stained rims (Fig.
32). Unlike the original, the reproduction
goblet is exceptionally heavy nonflint glass,
the stippling is coarse and uneven, and the
stem is too thin. On many new goblets,
large indentations, hidden by the stippling,
are on either side of the central medallion.
These indentations are most evident when
you feel the inside of the bowl.

Fig. 31. Original clear Beaded Grape Medallion goblet. Boston Silver Glass Co. Circa 1869.

Fig. 32. Reproduction Beaded Grape Medallion goblet with amber stained rim. Maker unknown. Embossed mark.

New goblets are embossed under the base with an "R" and three stars within a shield.

Hint: Clear goblets with any color stain are contemporary.
Reproduced items: Goblet.

BEADED ROSETTE

Beaded Rosette is one of numerous patterns in which only goblets were produced. This pattern was originally issued by the Bellaire Goblet Company of Findlay, Ohio, as late as 1888. Bellaire excelled in manufacturing stem and barware, and during the 1880s made more than 7,500 sets of goblets each week. Production continued after Bellaire joined the United States Glass Company as Factory "M" in July 1891. Both Bellaire and the Columbia Glass Company

of Findlay, Ohio (Factory "J"), ceased operations in December 1892 after a dispute with the Findlay Gas trustees. By mid-January 1893, U.S. Glass had removed all equipment, including the mixing house, and transferred it to the new factory under construction at Gas City, Indiana (Factory "U").

The basic design of Beaded Rosette consists of large and small rayed and beaded circles separated by a star motif. The stem of the goblet is knobbed at the center and the rosette design is repeated. An original goblet is illustrated in Fig. 33.

Fig. 33. Closeup of original clear Beaded Rosette goblet. Bellaire Goblet Co. Circa 1888.

Fig. 34. Closeup of reproduction clear Beaded Rosette goblet. Unmarked.

Reproduction goblets appeared as late as 1970. As you can see in Fig. 34, there is a noticeable difference between this reproduction and the original. The beads and rays on reproduction goblets are smaller and more weakly impressed than those on the originals. The most noticeable difference, however, is the size and design of the star motif between the rosettes. Original goblets have large stars with elongated points. Stars on reproduction goblets are smaller and resemble a Maltese cross. More-over, new goblets are heavy and have a slightly bluish tint.

Reproduction goblets are not permanently marked. It is our opinion that they may be a product of the L.G. Wright Glass Company of New Martinsville, West Virginia.

Hint: Reproduction goblets have smaller star designs between the rosettes than the originals.

Reproduced items: Goblet.

BEATTY HONEYCOMB

On April 3, 1888, William Henry Barr of Steubenville, Ohio, was granted the mechanical patent for the process of creating opalescent glassware. By adding calcium phosphate or bone ash to the glass mix, then reheating portions of an article to a cherry red, glassmakers could control the way glass opalesces. Today, Beatty Honeycomb is a popular pattern in opalescent glassware.

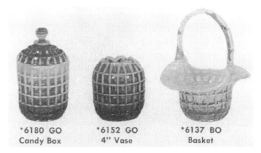

*6180 GO
Candy Box

*6152 GO
4" Vase

*6137 BO
Basket

Fig. 35. Assortment of new Beatty Honeycomb. Fenton Art Glass Co. Circa 1960. Unmarked. (Only the No.6180 candy box corresponds to an original form.)

Also known as Beatty Waffle, Checkered Bar, and Crossbar Opal, Beatty Honeycomb was produced by A.J. Beatty & Sons of Steubenville, Ohio, in 1888. When Beatty became a member of the United States Glass Company in Pittsburgh, production was continued by that company. Issued in a limited table service, the pattern was originally produced in blue and white opalescence with limited production in canary or yellow.

In 1960, the Fenton Art Glass Company of Williamstown, West Virginia, issued four items in the Beatty Honeycomb design. Fig. 35 illustrates the covered candy box (No.6180), a 4-inch-high vase (No.6152), and a basket with applied handle (No.6137). At the same time Fenton also produced the No.6158 9- to 11-inch-high swung vase. Each of these items was made in the opalescent colors of blue or green.

Although the covered candy box is an exact copy of the original covered sugar bowl, both the vase and the basket are typical examples of Fenton's innovative translation of antique designs into contemporary shapes. You will see from the illustration that the vase and the basket are both made from the sugar-bowl base. Fenton made the vase by crimping the rim of the sugar bowl; the basket was made by folding the rim of the sugar bowl slightly and applying a handle.

Unlike originals, Fenton's blue opalescence is deeper than any known original, while the green is strictly contemporary. Produced from new molds created by Fenton, each item is thick and heavy and permanently embossed with the familiar Fenton logo.

In 1976, the Westmoreland Glass Company of Grapeville, Pennsylvania, produced

Fig. 36. Reproduction milk-white Beatty Honeycomb covered sugar bowl. Westmoreland Glass Co. Circa 1976. Embossed "WG."

a similar version of the Beatty Honeycomb covered sugar bowl from a new mold (as shown in Fig. 36). Referred to as item No.339, the Westmoreland covered sugar bowl is a dense milk white. Characteristic of Westmoreland glassware, examples are embossed "WG" on the base.

Reproductions should fool no one. In general, they are heavy, colors are harsh and artificial, and the design is too sharp.

Hint: Green opalescence and milk white are contemporary colors.
Reproduced items: Basket, sugar bowl, vase.

BEATTY RIB

A companion design to Beatty Honeycomb, Beatty Rib was covered by the patent granted to William Henry Barr on April 3, 1888. This patent covered the mechanical process of creating opalescent glassware (see Beatty Honeycomb). A product of A.J.

Beatty & Sons of Tiffin, Ohio, Beatty Rib, like its contemporaries Beatty Honeycomb, Beatty Swirl, and Zig Zag, was produced about 1888 in a limited table service. Originally available in blue and white opalescence, sets included two sizes of toothpick holders and the rarely seen covered cracker jar.

Fig. 37. Reproduction milk-white Beatty Rib covered sugar bowl. Fenton Art Glass Co. Circa 1958. Unmarked.

background. On those items that are covered, the same design appears on finials.

Fig. 37 illustrates the reproduction covered sugar bowl. The Fenton Art Glass Company of Williamstown, West Virginia, began producing this excellent copy (item No.6601) from a newly created Fenton mold, about 1958. Known as Rib, the new unmarked covered sugar bowl is typical of Fenton craftsmanship. However, unlike the original, which was produced in opalescent colors, Fenton's copy is milk white. It is also thicker and heavier than the original, and the finial feels sharp.

At the same time Fenton was producing the covered sugar bowl, it advertised a matching covered butter dish in the February 1958 issue of *China, Glass and Tablewares.* Produced from a new mold in milk white, the new unmarked butter dish is also an excellent copy. It, too, is thicker and heavier than the original and feels sharper to the touch.

Hint: Items in milk white are strictly contemporary.
Reproduced items: Butter dish, sugar bowl.

Unlike Beatty Honeycomb, which traces its origins to the older Honeycomb design, Beatty Rib consists of vertical opalescent ribs protruding from a clear or colored

BELLFLOWER

Bellflower is one of the top ten patterns in early American pattern glass. Also known as Ribbed Bellflower, Ribbed Leaf, and the R.L. pattern, it is one of the earliest pressed patterns to be found in a complete table setting. Bellflower was first produced prior to 1840 by a number of glass manufacturers, including the Boston and Sandwich Glass Company of Sandwich, Massachusetts, and, later, McKee & Brothers of Pittsburgh, Pennsylvania, which produced the largest variety of table forms.

Produced in flint, the quality of original items in Bellflower varies from a fine silverlike luster to a crude, dull surface. Although the vast majority of these items were pressed in clear, rarities are known in amber, cobalt blue, fiery opalescent, green,

milk white, opaque blue, and sapphire blue.

Interestingly, this pattern was originally produced by two different methods. Earliest items were blown in a mold. A gather of glass, placed on the end of the blowpipe, was blown and expanded within a mold in which the design was cut, producing a finished, patterned item. Early items are crudely fashioned and pontil-marked or scarred where the blowpipe was removed. As the glass industry became mechanized, items were pressed in a full-sized mold, guaranteeing a more uniform quality.

Because so many glass houses produced Bellflower, there are a number of design variations. These variations have been classified as Single Vine–Fine Rib, Double Vine–Fine Rib, Single Vine–Coarse Rib, and Double Vine–Coarse Rib. Another interesting variation consists of the bellflower de-

CHART 9 BELLFLOWER. Imperial Glass Corporation, Bellaire, Ohio.
  CMN: Bellflower. (Single vine).
  Mark: "MMA" embossed.
  Color Code: C Clear, CY Canary, EG Emerald Green, SAB Sapphire Blue, PB Peacock Blue.

ITEM	COLOR(S)	YEAR	ORIG	NEW
Creamer, footed, applied handle.	C	1972	X	
Goblet. #F2035. Hexagonal stem, 6"h., 8 oz., single vine.	C	1979	X	
Pitcher, milk. 8"h., 1 quart.*	(1) C, SAB	1970	X	
	(2) EG	1971	X	
	(3) CY	1972	X	
	(4) SAB	1970	X	
	(5) PB	1977	X	
Sugar bowl, covered, footed.	C	1972	X	
Tumbler, water, 8 oz., 3½"h.	C	1979	X	

*Issued in a limited edition of: (1) 1,970 copies to commemorate the museum's 100th anniversary, (2) 2,500 copies produced to commemorate the museum's 101st anniversary, (3) 1,600 copies, (4) 2,000 copies, (5) 1,500 copies.

sign, which is cut rather than pressed into the ribbed background. In each variation, the resonance of the lead glass is notable.

Only the Single Vine–Fine Rib variety of Bellflower has been reproduced. The first reproduction, about 1938, was the water tumbler. This tumbler is unmarked, and its maker and origin remain a mystery. Unlike the original, the new tumbler is greenish-

yellow. Produced from a new mold in non-flint glass, it is quite heavy, and the thickness of the glass exaggerates the design. When viewed from the side, the base is large and thick.

In 1970, the Metropolitan Museum of Art in New York City appointed the Imperial Glass Corporation of Bellaire, Ohio, exclusive license to issue reproductions on its behalf (see Chart 9). Produced from new molds that were based on original items in the museum's collection, these reproductions are permanently embossed with the museum's "MMA" insignia. Each item was

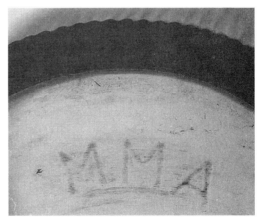

Fig. 38. Reproduction Metropolitan Museum of Art clear Bellflower milk pitcher with applied clear handle. Circa 1981. Embossed "MMA."

Fig. 39. Closeup of the "MMA" hallmark and pressed pontil mark found on the base of the Metropolitan Museum of Art reproduction Bellflower milk pitcher.

Fig. 40. Reproduction clear flint Bellflower tumbler and goblet. Imperial Glass Corp. for the Metropolitan Museum of Art. Circa 1979. Embossed "MMA."

Fig. 41. Sapphire blue reproduction milk pitcher with clear applied handle. Metropolitan Museum of Art. Circa 1970. Embossed "MMA."

gift boxed and accompanied by a paper tag bearing the name and brief history of the pattern (Figs. 38 and 39).

Advertised as exact copies, Metropolitan Museum of Art reproductions are, ironically, too perfect (Fig. 40). Produced in lead-quality glass, both the bellflower and vine designs are pressed too deeply, appearing outlined against the ribbed background, which is too evenly spaced. On the milk pitcher, in particular, the ribbing fades toward the rim and becomes completely lost (Fig. 41). On the bottom of the tumbler and milk pitcher, depressions resembling pontil marks have been added. These are perfectly round and smooth and, like the bellflower motif, appear too accurate.

In 1979, the Smithsonian Institution in Washington, D.C., issued its own version of the Bellflower Single Vine–Fine Rib tumbler. Produced from a new mold and available in clear nonflint glass, this tumbler is 3¼ inches high with an 8-ounce capacity and shares the same discrepancies as other reproductions in the pattern. Each Smithsonian tumbler is permanently embossed with "SI."

In addition to these museum reproductions, a new decanter is available. A single-vine variety in nonflint glass, it shades from blue to green and has a blue stopper. Although research is pending as to maker and year of production, judging from its general characteristics and make, this decanter appears to be a product of the mid-1980s.

Hint: Pontil marks are always ground, never pressed.

BIRD AND STRAWBERRY

A popular member of the figural family of pressed glass is the pattern today known as Bird and Strawberry. Also known as Blue Bird, Flying Bird and Strawberry, and Strawberry and Bird, its original name was simply Indiana's No.157. The Indiana Glass Company of Dunkirk, Indiana, produced this pat-

tern about 1914 in a medium-grade nonflint glass. The pattern included the more common table pieces, in clear, and clear with blue, green, and red stain (both with or without gilt trim).

Unlike many designs that gain high popularity and thus are extensively reproduced, to date only two items have been copied in the Bird and Strawberry pattern. Produced

Fig. 42. Reproduction Bird and Strawberry pale blue oval relish. Indiana Glass Co. for Tiara Exclusives. Circa 1978. Unmarked.

Fig. 43. Closeup of the Bird and Strawberry reproduction oval relish. (Unlike originals, the design on reproductions is blurred and poorly pressed.)

as item No.10103, Tiara Exclusives of Dunkirk, Indiana, issued the flat, oval relish dish from a new mold in 1978 (Fig. 42). Known as the "Blue Bird Bowl," this dish was made for Tiara by the Indiana Glass Company. Ranging in color from clear to a pale blue that often appears turquoise, the new relish is 8⅜ inches long and 1⅞ inches high. The second reproduction in the pattern is the 6½-inch-diameter, high-standard, covered compote, manufacturer unknown. This compote is clear but often tinged with gray, green, or yellow.

On original pieces of Bird and Strawberry, the feathers on the bird's body, wings, and tail are finely molded; the berries are natural and well developed; the leaves and branches are well defined; and the overall design is crisp and clear and molded in high relief against a clear background.

Both reproductions have an overall pattern that is terribly blurred. And, upon close examination, the design elements suffer from poor workmanship. As you can see in Fig. 43, on new reproductions, the feathers are all but nonexistent. Both the berry and leaf motifs lack detail and are often clear. The glass is overly heavy and extremely smooth and oily.

Although neither copy is permanently marked, there should be no confusion in detecting the reproduction from the original when you consider quality and detail.

Hint: The original Bird and Strawberry was never produced in blue or green.
Reproduced items: Compote, relish dish.

BLACKBERRY

Blackberry is one of the more popular patterns of the fruit series. This pattern was designed and patented by John H. Hobbs on February 1, 1870 (design patent No.3829) and produced in clear and milk-white non-flint glass by Hobbs, Brockunier & Company of Wheeling, West Virginia. More widely collected in milk white than clear, Blackberry was first issued in a small table service that included the standard table pieces, as well as the rare celery vase, the syrup, and the water pitcher.

As its name implies, the basic design consists of well-molded clusters of large blackberries and leaves set against a smooth background. Characteristic of the Victorian Era's fondness for fanciful detail, both berry and leaf are so well executed as to appear lifelike. Handles may be applied or pressed, and finials are either (1) a large natural blackberry, or (2) a round medallion ornament with a blackberry center. Milk white items are dead white, never opaline or translucent.

Misconceptions concerning Blackberry reproductions have been perpetuated by so many well-meaning authorities that, today, collectors and dealers tend to shy away from this pattern (see Dewberry). However, Blackberry is a safe pattern to collect. To date, only four items have been authenticated as reproductions. As early as 1940, new goblets appeared, followed later by creamers. Unmarked, both forms were produced in clear and milk-white glass from new molds. Unlike originals, early reproductions are poorly pressed, blurred, dull, and lifeless. New goblets and creamers in clear glass are distinctively yellow with a wavy, somewhat pebbled surface, whereas those made in milk white are pearl-like in color and translucent when held up to strong light. Early reproductions were most likely produced by the Westmoreland Glass Company of Grapeville, Pennsylvania.

The goblet illustrated in Fig. 44 is an interesting Blackberry reproduction. Unmarked, it is in a unique teal color, a color

characteristically Westmoreland's. While original catalog or advertising illustrations have yet to surface, the pattern on this goblet is identical to that found on authenticated Westmoreland reproductions of the Blackberry creamer, the spoonholder, and the covered sugar bowl. This strongly suggests that Westmoreland also produced goblets in this color. Whether production was based on a limited run, or whether the color itself proved unsuccessful, is not known. More likely, these goblets were exclusively made for an independent jobber and not as part of Westmoreland's regular Blackberry line.

In the February 1950 issue of *China, Glass and Decorative Accessories*, Westmoreland advertised its new No.1833 or Blackberry pattern goblet in milk white. By 1954, creamers, spoonholders, and covered sugar bowls (all in milk white) were added to this line. Although all items were ordinarily offered in milk white, by 1964 goblets were also produced in Brandywine blue, golden sunset, and laurel green.

Contrary to popular belief, Westmoreland reproductions have been produced from new molds. This is apparent when you consider the shape, size, and overall design of new pieces. As a general rule, reproductions are squat and decisively smaller than originals. Unlike the flat rims on original items, rims on new items are noticeably round. As you can see in Fig. 45, handles and shapes also differ; although pressed on both old and new creamers, each handle differs in shape. Original Blackberry pieces always have small indentations inside the bowls of creamers, spoonholders, and sugar

Fig. 44. Reproduction teal Blackberry goblet. Westmoreland Glass Co. Unmarked.

Fig. 45. Original and reproduction milk-white Blackberry creamers. (The original is on the right.)

bowls where handles are attached. These indentations are never present on reproductions.

The most interesting discrepancies on reproductions, however, are those in the overall design. On old items, although the design is uneven, the berries are round, large, and distinctly molded in high relief. In contrast, the design on reproductions is disproportionate, while the berries are flat, oval, smaller, and less detailed. New milk-white items are also translucent and have a pearl-like finish, unlike the dead white look of originals (Fig. 46).

Prior to 1949, Westmoreland reproductions were marked with only a paper label. Beginning in 1949, reproductions were permanently marked with the "WG" logo.

Fig. 46. Original and reproduction milk-white Blackberry spoonholders. (The original is on the right.)

Hint: The blackberries on reproductions are flat and oval-shaped.
Reproduced items: Creamer, goblet, spoonholder, sugar bowl.

BRADFORD BLACKBERRY

Bradford Blackberry, often referred to as Bradford Grape, is one of the many fruit patterns that captivated the designer's imagination in nineteenth-century America. This pattern, made about 1860, was a product of the Boston and Sandwich Glass Company of Sandwich, Massachusetts. Originally made in a limited number of table pieces, items are clear and of a good-quality glass that exhibits the fine belltone of flint. As its name implies, the design consists of nicely sculpted clusters of blackberries and leaves. Highly embossed upon a brilliant, clear background, one can trace the intricate details of both fruit and leaf.

On May 1, 1978, the Metropolitan Museum of Art in New York City introduced the No.G2015A 3¾-inch-high, flat Blackberry water tumbler. This reproduction tumbler was produced from a new mold for the Metropolitan by the Pairpoint Glass Company of Sagamore, Massachusetts. The glass is bright and clear and displays some resemblance to original flint glass. Three years later, the Metropolitan, in conjunction with the Fostoria Glass Company of Fostoria, Ohio, issued the No.G2031A 6-inch-high

Blackberry goblet. Advertised as authentic reproductions made in a limited pressing from new molds cut to exact specifications from original items in the museum's collection, each was "produced in clear, lead crystal to duplicate the weight and bell-like resonance of early American flint glass. In order to avoid confusion with the original, a slight variation has been added to the cutting of the decoration." To bolster consumer appeal, items were neatly gift boxed and accompanied by a short printed history that included the pattern's name and origin. Goblets produced by Fostoria are permanently embossed with the museum's "MMA" insignia.

New goblets and tumblers (Figs. 47 and 48) can be deceiving. Both originals and reproductions are heavy, finely molded, and produce a distinct resonance when gently tapped. However, upon close examination, you can easily detect a number of subtle discrepancies. Reproductions simply look new, shine with a glossy texture not apparent on originals, and differ in the basic pattern design. You can see this difference in the tendrils, leaves, and shape of the berry clusters. On reproductions, the tendril motif loops downward; on originals, it loops upward. In addition, the leaves on new

Fig. 47. Reproduction Bradford Blackberry goblets in clear flint glass. Circa 1982. Embossed "MMA."

Fig. 48. Reproduction clear flint Bradford Blackberry tumblers. Fostoria Glass Corp. for the Metropolitan Museum of Art. Embossed "MMA."

items more closely resemble those in a bunch of grapes, while those on original items look like blackberry leaves. More-over, the shape of each fruit cluster on authentic pieces is triangular, while on re-productions it is oval.

Hint: Reproduction items by Fostoria are permanently embossed "MMA."
Reproduced items: Goblet, tumbler.

BRIDAL ROSETTE(S)

Bridal Rosette(s) is one of the late imita-tion cut-glass patterns popular throughout the early 1900s (Fig. 49). It is also known as Checkerboard, Block and Fan Variant, Old Quilt, and Square Block. Originally known as No.500, this line was produced in an extended table service by the West-moreland Glass Company of Grapeville, Pennsylvania, about 1910. Typical of many later pressed-glass patterns, these sets were made from a mediocre nonflint glass.

Bridal Rosette(s) is often mistaken for Cambridge Ribbon, an entirely dif-ferent pattern, in which the forms are thinner, shorter, and often marked "Near Cut."

Beginning in the 1940s, Westmoreland reintroduced a number of milk-white items

Fig. 49. Reprint of 1914 Butler Brothers catalog illustrating an assortment of Bridal Rosette in clear glass.

Fig. 50. Reprint of Westmoreland Glass Co. 1955 catalog page illustrating an assortment of milk-white Bridal Rosette.

Fig. 51. Reproduction milk-white Bridal Rosette(s) high-standard true open compote. Westmoreland Glass Co. Circa 1955. Unmarked.

in Bridal Rosette(s), illustrated in Fig. 50 and enumerated in Chart 10. These items were either iridized, undecorated, or trimmed in 22-karat gold with enamel decoration. In the years that followed, an impressive number of articles was produced in both antique and contemporary forms. While milk white remained in continuous production (Fig. 51), a limited number of shapes was produced in various contemporary colors.

In 1961, the L.E. Smith Glass Company of Mount Pleasant, Pennsylvania, introduced No.8000, a covered compote. This item was 4¾ inches square and 6½ inches high and was available only in milk white. You can sometimes find this compote with a paper label; however, it is not permanently marked.

In 1983, Levay Distributing Company of Edwardsville, Illinois, offered both the seven-piece water set and four-piece table set in Ruby Mother of Pearl (red carnival). These two sets were made exclusively for Levay by Westmoreland in a limited edition of 500 sets each.

In 1988 the Plum Glass Company of Pittsburgh issued the low-standard, cupped bowl compote from the original Westmoreland mold. This reproduction, which is a contemporary shape, was available in black, blue, blue frosted, clear, cobalt blue, and milk white. You can find this compote permanently embossed with a "PG" in a keystone. Interestingly, the "WG" logo of Westmoreland is also on these pieces. Plum bought many molds from the closed Westmoreland factory, including Beaded Grape, Bridal Rosette(s), English Hobnail, Paneled Grape, and others. It is not known at this time whether Plum owns other molds for Bridal Rosette(s).

Bridal Rosette(s) is a relatively safe pattern to collect. Unlike the originals, in which the stars in the blocks are sharp and well defined, reproductions have stars that are smooth and blurred. This pattern was originally made only in clear glass. Reproductions are heavier than originals and have a new glossy look to the glass.

CHART 10   BRIDAL ROSETTE(S). Westmoreland Glass Company, Grapeville, Pennsylvania.
CMN: Westmoreland's No.500, Old Quilt Pattern.
Mark: Unmarked, embossed "WG," or paper label.
Color Code: ABC Aurora Blue Carnival, ABM Antique Blue Milk, B Blue, BB Brandywine Blue, BC Black Carnival, GM Green Milk, GS Golden Sunset, HAC Honey Amber Carnival, IBC Ice Blue Carnival, LG Laurel Green, LGC Lime Green Carnival, MW Milk White, MWD Milk White Decorated (Roses & Bows), MWG Milk White Gold, MWI Milk White Iridized, PSI Purple Slag Iridized, RMP Ruby Mother of Pearl, SB Softmist Brown.

ITEM	COLOR(S)	YEAR	ORIG	NEW
Ashtray, flat.				
4"sq.	MW	1950s		X
6½"sq.	MW	1950s		X
Banana stand, 11"h.	MW	1950s	X	
Bottle, toilet, patterned stopper. 5 oz.	MW	1955		X
Bowl, open.				
Flat.				
8"d.	MW	1955	X	
9"d., 2¼"h., Shallow.	MW	1950s		X
10½"d., 4¼"h.	MW	1955	X	
12"d., 4"h., Lipped.	MW	1950s		X
Footed.				
6"d., Cupped.	MW	1983		X
7"d., Cupped.	MW	1950s		X
7½"d., Flared.	MW	1950s		X
9"d., Bell-shaped.	MW	1950s		X
9"d., Crimped.	MW	1955		X
9"d., Shallow, plain rim.	MW	1950s		X
Box, covered.				
Cigarette, 5" × 4".	MW	1955		X
Puff or powder.				
Round, 4½"d.	MW	1955		X
Square, 5½"h.	MW	1955		X
Butter dish, covered.				
Rectangular, ¼ Lb.	MW	1955		X
Round, flat, flanged, 4½"h.	MW	1955	X	
	RMP*	1983	X	
Cake stand or salver, footed.				
11"d., Plain rim.	MW	1950s		X
12"d., Skirted.	MW	1950s		X
Candlestick, 4"h.	MW	1955		X
Celery vase, ruffled rim, footed. 6½"h.	HAC, IBC	1976	X	
	MW	1955	X	
Compote.				
Covered.				
High standard.				
6"h., Sweetmeat, plain stem.	MW	1955		X
6½"h.	MW	1955	X	
Low standard.				
5"sq.	MW	1955	X	
7½"h.	MW	1983	X	
Open.				
High standard.				
Crimped rim, patterned base.	MW	1967		X
Crimped rim, plain base.	MW*	1983		X
Low standard.				
6"h., cupped rim.	MW	1955		X
6"h., 9"d., shallow bowl.	MW	1960	X	

ITEM	COLOR(S)	YEAR	ORIG	NEW
Console bowl, flared, 13"d.	MW	1950s		X
Creamer.				
Individual.				
3½"h., Tankard.	MW	1955		X
4"h.	MW	1955		X
Table size, pressed handle.				
4½"h.	MW	1955		X
6½"h.	IBC	1976	X	
	MW	1955	X	
	RMP*	1983	X	
Cruet, patterned stopper, 6 oz.	MW	1955	X	
Cup.				
Flared bowl.	MW	1955		X
Straight sided, punch.	MW	1955		X
Dish, round.				
Flat, sauce.				
4½"d.	MW	1955	X	
5½"d.	MW	1955	X	
Footed.				
Fruit cocktail, scalloped rim, 3½"d.	MW	1955		X
Goblet, 8 oz.	BB, GS, LG	1964	X	
	MW	1955	X	
Honey dish, covered, low-footed, nonpatterned cover,				
5"sq.	MW	1955		X
Jar, cracker, low circular foot, bulbous.	ABM, MW	1938	X	
Jardiniere, footed.				
Cupped, 6½"h.	MW	1950s		X
Straight-sided, 6½"h.	MW	1950s		X
Mayonnaise, footed.				
Bell-shaped, 5"l.	MW	1950s		X
Round, 4½"d.	MW	1955		X
Nappy, flat.				
Bell-shaped, 5½"l.	MW	1950s		X
Round.				
4"d.	MW	1955	X	
4½"d.	MW	1955	X	
Pickle dish, flat, 10"l.	MW	1955	X	
Pitcher, pressed handle.				
Juice, 7½"h., 16 oz.	MW	1955	X	
Water, 48 oz.	ABC, BC, LGC, PSI	1970s	X	
	B, GM, MWD, MWG, MWI, P, SB	1960s	X	
	HAC, IBC	1976	X	
	MW	1955	X	
	RMP*	1983	X	
Plate.				
Bread and butter, 6"d.	MW	1955	X	
Dinner, 10½"d.	MW	1955	X	
Salad, 8½"d.	MW	1955	X	
Punch bowl, two-piece. 8 qt., 11"d.	MW	1955		X
Relish dish, three-part, round, flat, 9"l.	MW	1955		X
Salt shaker, flat, chrome top.	MW	1955	X	

ITEM	COLOR(S)	YEAR	ORIG	NEW
Saucer.	MW	1955		X
Sherbert, low, footed.	MW	1955		X
Spoonholder.	MW	1955	X	
	RMP*	1983	X	
Sugar bowl.				
Covered.				
6½"h., Bulbous, flat.	IBC	1976	X	
	MW, MWD	1955	X	
	RMP*	1983	X	
Open.				
3½"h.	MW	1955		X
4"h., Handled.	MW	1955		X
4½"h.	MW	1967		X
Syrup, individual, 3¼"h., 3 oz.	MW	1955		X
Tray, vanity or dresser, 6" × 13".	MW	1955		X
Tumbler.				
Bar, 7 oz.	MW	1955	X	
Iced tea, 11 oz.	MW	1955	X	
	RMP*	1983	X	
Juice, 5 oz.	MW	1955		X
Water, 9 oz.	ABC, BC, LGC, PSI	1970s	X	
	B, GM, MWD, MWG, MWI, P, SB	1960s	X	
	HAC, IBC	1976	X	
	MW	1955	X	
Vase.				
Flat.				
Bell-shaped, 9"h.	MW	1950s		X
Swung, 14"h.	MW	1950s		X
Footed.				
Bell-shaped, 9"h.	MW	1950s		X
Fan-shaped, 9"h.	MW	1955		X
Wine, 2 oz.	MW	1955	X	

*Distributed by Levay Distributing Company, Edwardsville, Illinois.

Westmoreland items, when marked, can be found permanently embossed with the familiar "WG" logo. Plum items are permanently embossed with a "PG" in a keystone and the familiar Westmoreland "WG" logo.

Smith items are sometimes found with a paper label.

Hint: Any color other than clear is a reproduction.

BROKEN COLUMN

Originally known as the United States Glass Company's No.15021, Broken Column was first produced by the Columbia Glass Company of Findlay, Ohio, in a brilliant, clear nonflint glass about 1888. When the Columbia Glass Company became part of the United States Glass Company in 1891, the pattern was manufactured at both the Richards & Hartley Glass Company, of Tarentum, Pennsylvania (known as Factory "E"), and at the Columbia Glass Company of Findlay, Ohio (known as Factory "J").

CHART 11 BROKEN COLUMN. Imperial Glass Corporation, Bellaire, Ohio.
CMN: Broken Column.
Mark: "SI" Embossed Monogram.
Color Code: C Clear.

ITEM	COLOR(S)	YEAR	ORIG	NEW
Bowl, flat, open.				
8"d.	C	1980	X	
8½"d.	C	1978	X	
Creamer, 4¼"h., 10 oz., pressed handle.	C	1978	X	
Goblet, 6"h.	C	1982	X	
Pitcher, water, 9"h., 40 oz.	C	1979	X	
Plate, round, 8"d.	C	1973	X	
Sauce dish, flat, round.				
4½"d.	C	1973	X	
4⅝"d.	C	1978	X	
Spoonholder, 4½"h.	C	1973	X	
Sugar bowl, covered, 5¼"h., lid does not have a finial.	C	1978	X	
Tumbler, water, flat, 3¾"h.	C	1979	X	

The pattern was produced in an extended table service in clear, clear with ruby stain, and experimental cobalt blue (punch cup). As in the majority of early pressed-glass patterns, Broken Column is known by a number of different names: Broken Irish Column, Irish Column, Notched Rib, Rattan, and Ribbed Fingerprint.

As consumer interest in reproduction glassware rose throughout the 1950s, reproductions in Broken Column began to appear. As late as 1954, the L.E. Smith Glass Company of Mount Pleasant, Pennsylvania, issued the familiar high-standard, square covered compote. This compote made from a new mold is unmarked and readily found in clear nonflint glass. Because original compotes were not made in this shape, no one should be fooled into believing that this compote is old.

In the early 1960s, the L.G. Wright Glass Company of New Martinsville, West Virginia, reproduced the goblet in clear nonflint glass from a new mold. Unsigned, it is 5⅞ inches high, smaller and heavier than the original. Wright goblets look new due to the glossiness of the glass. Examples may also appear slightly yellow when viewed under a strong light.

As early as 1972, the Smithsonian Institution in Washington, D.C., authorized the Imperial Glass Corporation of Bellaire, Ohio, to reproduce a number of items in

Fig. 52. Reproduction Broken Column clear goblets. Imperial Glass Corp. for the Smithsonian. Circa 1982. Embossed "SI."

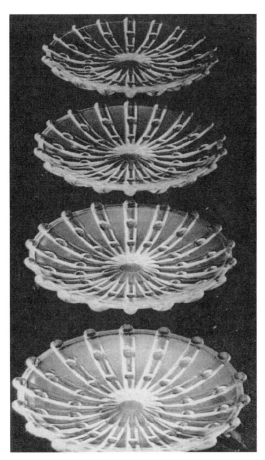

Fig. 53. Reproduction Broken Column clear 8-inch plates. Imperial Glass Corp. for the Smithsonian. Circa 1973. Embossed "SI."

Fig. 54. Reproduction clear Broken Column goblet. L.G. Wright Glass Co. Circa 1971. Unmarked.

Broken Column in a clear nonflint glass (see Chart 11). Produced from new molds created by the Island Mold and Machine Company of Wheeling, West Virginia, the Smithsonian reproductions faithfully follow originals in design and measurements (Fig. 52).

Reproductions in Broken Column are convincing. As you can see in Figs. 53 and 54, those of the Smithsonian are exact copies of originals and excellent examples of contemporary mold-making techniques. Unlike more fanciful patterns that inevitably display discrepancies in design, in this case it is the glass and not the pattern on reproductions that you must consider. While the surface of original pieces is soft and mellowed through age, reproductions look new. They are glossy and often oily or slick to the touch. Produced from new molds, they are also heavier than the originals. At one time, an infallible test for detecting reproduction goblets was thought to be the presence of a fake water line on the bottom of the bowl. This line was produced by elongating the bowl's inner base. However, as reproduction goblets were made from at least two known contemporary molds, this test is not always true.

Unlike earlier Wright goblets, Smithsonian reproductions are permanently embossed with the institution's "SI" insignia and carry stretch tags designating the name and a brief history of the pattern.

Hint: Broken Column reproductions offered by the Smithsonian Institution are permanently embossed "SI."

Reproduced items: Bowl, compote, creamer, goblet, pitcher, plate, sauce dish, spoonholder, sugar bowl, tumbler.

BUCKINGHAM

This imitation cut-glass design was first issued in 1907 as No.15106 by the United States Glass Company of Pittsburgh at its Factory "O" located in Glassport, Pennsylvania.

Buckingham was originally made from a good-quality clear nonflint glass in an extended table service that was often decorated with green and pink stain and trimmed in gold. Finials are mushroom-shaped and handles are pressed.

This is a safe pattern to collect because only the basket has been reproduced. As late as 1982, the Westmoreland Glass Company of Grapeville, Pennsylvania, issued this new basket in clear, nonflint glass. Known as Westmoreland's No.YC0806, this reproduction is 6½ inches high and has an applied, twisted handle.

As you can see from Fig. 55, new Buckingham baskets are good copies. Like most reproductions, however, the glass is thick and heavy, feels oily and slick, and has a distinct yellow cast. More important, baskets were never originally made in this pattern.

New Buckingham baskets are permanently marked with Westmoreland's familiar "WG" logo.

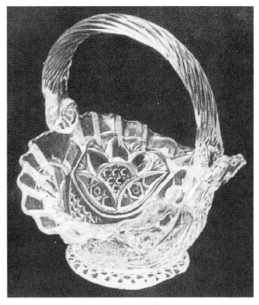

Fig. 55. Reproduction Buckingham clear nonflint basket with applied twisted handle. Westmoreland Glass Co. Circa 1982. Embossed "WG." (This form is not original to the pattern.)

Hint: The only reproduction in Buckingham is the basket.
Reproduced items: Basket.

BULL'S EYE AND DAISY(IES)

The geometric motif of this design reveals that it is a late pattern. The United States Glass Company of Pittsburgh, Pennsylvania, produced this pattern—No.15117 or Newport—about 1910. Made from nonflint glass, it was issued in a medium-sized table service in clear, clear with amethyst-, blue-, green-, and pink-stained eyes, emerald green, and clear with ruby stain (plain or with gold highlights).

The 9-ounce goblet is the only known true reproduction in Bull's Eye and Daisy (Fig. 56). Also made from this new mold is the swung, footed vase, which is a contemporary form (Fig. 57). Produced prior to

Fig. 56. Excerpt from circa 1910 United States Glass Co. catalog illustrating the original Bull's Eye and Daisy goblet.

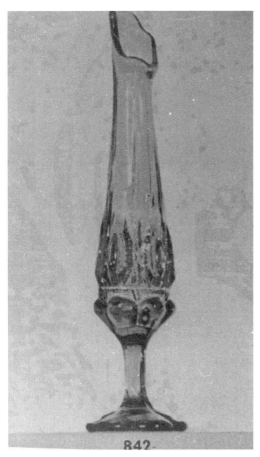

Fig. 57. Reproduction Bull's Eye and Daisy swung, footed vase made from the goblet mold. Kanawha Glass Co. Circa 1963. Unmarked.

Fig. 58. Reproduction Bull's Eye and Daisy clear goblet. Kanawha Glass Co. Circa 1974. Unmarked.

1974 by Kanawha Glass of Kanawha, West Virginia, from new molds, examples may be found in amber, blue, canary yellow, milk white, and sapphire blue.

As you can see in Fig. 58, each design element is skillfully applied to produce a convincing reproduction of a Bull's Eye and Daisy goblet. Upon close observation, however, subtle discrepancies between old and new goblets are apparent. The thickness of the glass used in new goblets makes them heavier than the originals. The roundness of the pattern from the new mold produces a smooth, slick feeling that is not found in the old goblet. Whereas the old goblet may show signs of gilding, new goblets are never decorated.

When signed, new goblets are embossed under the base with "Red Cliff" printed in half-circle above a blocked letter "R" within a circle, or carry a Red Cliff paper label.

Hint: Vases made from the goblet mold are new.

Reproduced items: Goblet, vase.

BUTTON ARCHES

Seaside or souvenir glass had been a staple item for glass manufacturers throughout the late nineteenth and early twentieth centuries. Characteristically stained in amber or ruby (although other colors were used), items were etched through the coloring with dates, names, and places (Fig. 59). Button Arches, also known as Scalloped Diamond, Scalloped Diamond–Red Top, and Scalloped Daisy–

Fig. 59. Reproduction clear with ruby stain Button Arches toothpick holder etched "Mt. Vernon." Westlake Ruby Glass Works. Circa 1970s. Unmarked.

Fig. 60. Reproduction Button Arches covered butter dish in chocolate glass. Fenton Art Glass Co. for the Levay Distributing Co. Circa 1982. Unmarked.

Fig. 61. Reproduction Button Arches No.9524 clear round sauce dish. Fenton Art Glass Co. Circa 1982. Embossed Fenton logo.

Red Top, is one of many patterns used for the souvenir trade.

Originally known as pattern No. 39, Button Arches was a product of George Duncan & Sons Company of Washington, Pennsylvania. This pattern was later produced by the Duncan & Miller Glass Company about 1900 after the company changed its name. Like a majority of late designs, the pattern was produced in an extended table service in both clear and clear with ruby stain (plain, frosted, or gold-trimmed). Although odd pieces may be found in clambroth and opaque white, complete table settings were not produced in these colors.

A number of reproductions have been made in Button Arches. In 1982, the Fenton Art Glass Company of Williamstown, West Virginia, reproduced the No.9580 covered butter dish (Fig. 60), the No.9525 high-standard, true open compote with smooth rim, and the No.9524 round, flat sauce dish (Fig. 61). Produced from new molds, each piece is an exact copy of the original pattern and can be found in a good-quality clear nonflint glass. Only the No.9580 covered butter dish (Fig. 60), exclusively produced by Fenton for the Levay Distributing

Company of Edwardsville, Illinois, can be found in deep, rich chocolate. In 1983, the No.9524 sauce dish also appeared in federal blue, and by 1986 the No.9292 mug with a pressed handle had become available in carnival glass.

Unlike original items, Fenton's Button Arches pattern is not ruby-stained. However, pieces are crystal clear, heavy, and

CHART 12   BUTTON ARCHES. Westlake Ruby Glass Works, Columbus, Ohio.
CMN: Button Arch.
Mark: Unmarked or paper label.
Color Code: CR Clear with ruby stain.

ITEM	COLOR(S)	YEAR	ORIG	NEW
Butter dish, covered.	CR	1971	X	
Cordial.	CR	1971	X	
Creamer.				
Individual.	CR	1971	X	
Table-size.	CR	1971	X	
Goblet.	CR	1971	X	
Spoonholder.	CR	1971	X	
Sugar bowl, covered.	CR	1971	X	
Toothpick holder.	CR	1971	X	

look new. Each new item is permanently embossed with the familiar Fenton logo.

Throughout the early 1970s, the Westlake Ruby Glass Works of Columbus, Ohio, reproduced the eight items enumerated in Chart 12. Also known as Button Arch, each is in clear and clear with ruby stain nonflint glass. Issued from new molds, Westlake reproductions closely follow original forms. However, unlike the light, airy look of originals, reproductions are of a much thicker glass, producing a distinct weightiness. Poorly impressed, the pattern is too smooth. As you can see in Fig. 59, unlike the cathedral-shaped arch of the original pattern, the arch on Westlake reproduc-

tions is an elongated oval. The most notable difference is in the color of the stain. Original items are stained a deep, rich ruby. The ruby on reproductions is, however, a pale cranberry, which is often blotchy and poorly applied. To date, stained reproductions of the pattern with gold trim have not surfaced.

Westlake reproductions are not marked.

Hint: Pieces with elongated ovals and cranberry stain are new.
Reproduced items: Butter dish, cordial, small and large creamer, goblet, mug, sauce dish, spoonholder, sugar bowl, toothpick holder.

CABBAGE LEAF

Some of the most highly collectible patterns in early American pressed glass are those depicting animals. One such pattern is Cabbage Leaf, or Frosted Cabbage Leaf, as it is often called. No one knows who originally produced this charming old design, although quality and workmanship suggest it is a product of the late 1870s or early 1880s.

As Ruth Webb Lee describes this design in her book *Early American Pressed Glass,* Cabbage Leaf is "a most amusing

and unique pattern" (p. 435). The body of each item is formed by large, heavily stippled or frosted cabbage leaves, and finials are molded rabbit heads. This pattern was originally produced in a good-quality, clear, and combination clear and frosted, nonflint glass in a limited table service that includes the four-piece table set, the water set, and a few accessory items. Although items are known in amber and blue, any color is rare.

Reproductions in Cabbage Leaf appeared as late as 1968. At that time, the L.G. Wright Glass Company of New Martinsville,

CHART 13 CABBAGE LEAF. L.G. Wright Glass Company, New Martinsville, West Virginia.
CMN: Cabbage Leaf.
Mark: Unmarked.
Color Code: A Amber, AF Amber Frosted, B Blue, BF Blue Frosted, C Clear, CF Clear Frosted.

ITEM	COLOR(S)	YEAR	ORIG	NEW
Butter dish, covered.	C, CF	1970	X	
Celery vase.	C, CF	1970	X	
Compote, covered, high standard.	C, CF	1970	X	
Creamer.	C, CF	1970	X	
Goblet. #77-19. 6⅛″h.	A, B, C, CF	1968		X
Pitcher, water.	C, CF	1970	X	
Plate, rabbit-head center.	C, CF	1970	X	
Sauce dish, round, flat, 3½″d.	C, CF	1970	X	
Spoonholder.	C, CF	1970	X	
Sugar bowl, covered.	C, CF	1970	X	
Wine. #77-70. 5″h., 5 oz.	A, B, C, CF	1968		X
	AF, BF	1969		X

West Virginia, issued the No.77-19 6⅛-inch-high goblet and the No.77-70 5-ounce, 5-inch-high wine in amber, blue, clear, and clear and frosted glass. In 1970, Wright issued nine additional forms in original shapes and colors (see Chart 13). Like Wright's goblet and wine, these were also produced from new molds in original and contemporary colors.

Reproductions in Cabbage Leaf are thick, heavy, and poorly pressed. Unlike original items, the stippling on reproductions is light and blotchy, and the veining on the leaves is faint, smooth, and deformed. Lacking in detail, items are lifeless. This flaw is most obvious on the rabbit-head motif, which is distorted and exaggerated. Items in clear and in clear and frosted glass are whiter with a softer satin-like finish than original pieces.

The most obvious use of the Cabbage Leaf pattern appears in the form of the goblet. As you can see in Fig 62, new goblets may be quite convincing, especially in combination clear and frosted glass. However, goblets are strictly modern in form, as an original goblet was never made.

L.G. Wright reproductions are not marked.

Fig. 62. New clear and frosted Cabbage Leaf goblet. L.G. Wright Glass Co. Circa 1971. (Goblets were never made originally in this pattern.) Unmarked.

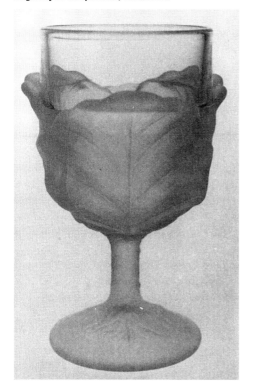

Hint: Stippling on reproductions is light and blotchy, and the veining on the leaves is faint, smooth, and deformed.

CABBAGE ROSE

Central's No.140, or Rose, is the original name for this attractive floral design. This pattern was designed by John Oesterling, who patented it on July 26, 1870 (design patent No. 4263). Later that year, the Central Glass Company of Wheeling, West Virginia, produced an extended table service that included more than twenty-five covered and open compotes from a good-quality clear nonflint glass.

This design consists of a large floral cluster composed of a single clear rose amid clear leaves. Both design elements are embossed in high relief on a plain background, tightly sculpted, natural, and well detailed (see Fig. 63). In addition, handles are beautifully applied and crimped, and finials are stylized acorns.

Cabbage Rose is one of the many patterns you can collect safely. Unfortunately, reports of unaccounted reproductions have frightened collectors and dealers for many years. Supposedly, new, unmarked goblets in clear and color were produced from new molds in nonflint glass in the early 1970s. We believe that they were most likely confused by early authors for the Open Rose reproduction goblet. However, without positive catalog identification, this theory is impossible to confirm.

A prudent approach to purchasing a sus-

Fig. 63. Original clear Cabbage Rose goblet. Central Glass Co. Circa 1870.

pect item is to compare its detail, quality, and weight to an authentic piece.

Hint: Cabbage Rose reproductions are unconfirmed; examine suspect items carefully.
Reproduced items: Goblet.

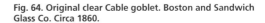

Fig. 64. Original clear Cable goblet. Boston and Sandwich Glass Co. Circa 1860.

CABLE

Cable is a member of the flint family that has, rightly, remained popular (see Fig. 64). Also known as Atlantic Cable, Cable Cord, and Early Cable, this design was first issued about 1859 in a medium-sized table service from a good-quality clear flint glass by the Boston and Sandwich Glass Company of Sandwich, Massachusetts. Although you may find odd pieces in clear with amber stain, jade green, opalescent, opaque green, blue, white, and translucent turquoise, any color is rare.

This lovely pattern consists of a row of clear vertical panels. Each panel is separated by a clear, thin, vertical cable design. On such pieces as the celery vase and the creamer, you will also find a fan-shaped or-

nament pressed into the upper portion of each clear panel. The glass is brilliant and heavy and produces a fine belltone resonance when gently tapped. In addition, handles are beautifully applied and crimped at the base.

Cable remains a safe pattern to collect because only the goblet has been reproduced. New, unmarked goblets made from a new mold in clear and colored nonflint glass entered the market as late as 1990. These gob-

lets are lighter than originals and the glass has an oily or greasy sheen. Clear reproductions exhibit a slight yellowish cast. When you examine a new goblet in strong light, you will also notice that the foot has the distinct waviness commonly found on reproductions.

Hint: Cable reproductions are nonflint and do not resonate when tapped.
Reproduced items: Goblet.

CACTUS

The Cactus pattern is well known among collectors of chocolate glass. This pattern was originally produced in about 1900 by the Indiana Tumbler and Goblet Company of Greentown, Indiana, in an extended table service made from a medium-quality nonflint glass. Primarily issued in chocolate, rare examples are known in clear, canary yellow, Nile green, and semi-opaque blue glass.

In 1959, the Fenton Art Glass Company of Williamstown, West Virginia, introduced a number of items in Cactus in contemporary and original forms from new molds made at its factory. These are enumerated in Chart 14. This line was issued in 1959–60 in topaz opalescent and milk white. Unknowingly, Cactus would be a poor seller. By July 1960, Fenton had discon-

3436 RN
7½" Double Crimped Basket with ribbed looped handle.

Fig. 65. New Cactus 7½-inch-high handled basket in red sunset carnival. Fenton Art Glass Co. for Levay Distributing Co. Circa 1982.

3480 CK
Cactus Covered Cracker Jar

Fig. 66. Reproduction Cactus covered cracker jar in chocolate glass. Exclusively made by the Fenton Art Glass co. for Levay Distributing Co. Circa 1982.

CHART 14   CACTUS. Fenton Art Glass Company, Williamstown, West Virginia.
CMN: Cactus, Desert Tree (OV line only).
Mark: Unmarked, paper label, or embossed mark (see notes below).
Color Code: BO Blue Opalescent, CA Colonial Amber, CB Colonial Blue, CH Chocolate, CP Colonial Pink,
IO Aqua Opal Carnival, CU Custard Satin, MI Milk White, RSC Red Sunset Carnival, TO Topaz opalescent.

ITEM	COLOR(S)	YEAR	ORIG	NEW
Banana dish, #3425. Low.	MI, TO	1959		X
Basket, applied handle.				
#3430. 10"h.**	CA	1967		X
	MI, TO	1959		X
#3432. Banana, folded sides, pie-crust rim.	RSC*	1982		X
#3433. 10"h., Low, double crimped rim.	RSC*	1982		X
#3436. 7½"h., Crimped rim.	RSC*	1982		X
#3437. 7"h., Scalloped rim.	CA	1967		X
	BO, IO*	1979		X
	CH	1981		X
	MI, TO	1959		X
#3439. 9"h., Deep, flared rim.	CH, IO*	1981		X
	MI, TO	1959		X
Bonbon dish. #3435. Triangular, single handled.**	CA	1967	X	
	MI, TO	1959	X	
Bowl, footed, open.				
8"d.	CH, IO*	1981		X
	MI	1960		X
9"d.	MI, TO	1959		X
10"d. #3420.**	CA, MI	1967		X
#3423. Fluted rim.	BO, IO*	1979		X
Butter dish. #3477. Flat, oval, ¼ lb.**	CA	1967		X
	CH, IO*	1981		X
	CU	1974		X
	MI, TO	1959		X
Cake stand, footed, 11"d.	MI, TO	1959	X	
Candleholder. #3474.**	CA	1967		X
	CH, IO*	1981		X
	MI, TO	1959		X
Candy box.	MI, TO	1962		X
Candy jar.**	CA	1967		X
	MI, TO	1961		X
Compote. #3429. Open, scalloped rim, high standard.**	BO, IO*	1979		X
	CA, MI	1967		X
	MI, TO	1959		X
	RSC*	1982		X
Cracker Jar. #3480. Covered.	CH, RSC*	1982	X	
Creamer. #3468. Pressed handle.**	BO, IO*	1979	X	
	CA	1967	X	
	CU	1974	X	
	MI, TO	1959	X	
	RSC*	1982	X	
Cruet. #3463. Original stopper.	BO, IO*	1979	X	
	CH	1981	X	
	MI, TO	1959	X	
	RSC*	1982	X	
Cuspidor, bulbous, short neck.				
#3426. Ladies, squatty, crimped rim.	RSC*	1982		X
#3427. Gentlemens', tall, ruffled rim.	RSC*	1982		X

ITEM	COLOR(S)	YEAR	ORIG	NEW
Dish. #3428. Nut, high standard, smooth rim.	MI, TO	1959		X
Epergne. #3401. Single lily.	CH, IO*	1981		X
	MI, TO	1959		X
Goblet. #3445. 10 oz.	CA, CB, CP	1962		X
	CH, IO*	1981		X
	MI, TO	1959		X
	RSC*	1982		X
Pitcher. #3407. Water, swung rim, applied ribbed handle.	RSC*	1982		X
Plate, round, flat, 11"d.	MI, TO	1959		X
Rose bowl, footed.				
#3420. 10"d.	BO, IO*	1979		X
#3453. 7"d.	BO, IO*	1979		X
Salt shaker. #3406.**	CA	1967	X	
	CU	1974	X	
	MI, TO	1959	X	
Sugar bowl.				
#3488. Covered, round, squatty.**	BO, IO*	1979	X	
	CA	1967	X	
	CU	1974	X	
	MI, TO	1959	X	
	RSC*	1982	X	
Open.	MI, TO	1959	X	
Toothpick holder. #3495.	BO, IO*	1979		X
	RSC*	1982		X
Vase.				
5"h.	CH, IO*	1981		X
	MI, TO	1959		X
6"h. #3459. Fan shape.**	CA	1967		X
	CH, IO*	1981		X
	MI, TO	1959		X
7"h. #3457. Ruffled rim.**	BO, IO*	1979		X
	CA	1967		X
	CH, IO*	1981		X
	MI	1960		X
	TO	1959		X
8"h.	MI, TO	1959		X
9"h. #3483. Swung neck and rim.	MI, TO	1959		X
	RSC*	1982		X
10"h.				
#3431. Cracker, applied handle.	RSC*	1982		X
#3434. Basket, straight-sided, ruffled rim, applied reeded, looped handle.	RSC*	1982		X
Water set. #3407. ***				
Pitcher, scalloped top, 48 oz., 6–10 oz. goblets.	TO	1988		X

*Exclusively produced for the Levay Distributing Company of Edwardsville, Illinois.
**Introduced in 1967 as part of Fenton's "Olde Virginia Glass" line as Desert Tree. Prior to 1970, pieces were marked only with a paper label. In 1970 and subsequent years, the "OVG" mark was added to each item line.
***Exclusively produced as the "Collector's Extravaganza—Vaseline Opal Rarities" 1988 limited-edition offering for the Levay Distributing Company.

tinued all items in topaz opalescent, except the No.3428 footed nut dish, the No.3435 handled bonbon, and the No.3445 goblet. Milk-white items remained in production until July 1961, but, except for the 8-inch-high bud vase, all milk-white items had been discontinued by January 1963. Although Fenton used all features of the

Fig. 67. New Fenton No.3428 topaz opalescent Cactus footed nut dish (made from a goblet). Fenton Art Glass Co. Circa 1959.

Fig. 68. New Cactus seven-piece vaseline opalescent water set. Produced by the Fenton Art Glass Co. for Levay Distributing Co. Circa 1988.

Cactus pattern, only five forms are antique.

In 1967, Fenton reintroduced Cactus, renaming the pattern Desert Tree. Items were produced as part its "Olde Virginia Glass," a line intended for sale to large wholesale and mail-order houses. Like earlier pieces of Cactus, Desert Tree was offered in a number of contemporary colors. However, the only forms that are true reproductions are the bonbon, the cracker jar, the creamer, the salt and pepper shakers, and the sugar bowl.

In the late 1970s and early 1980s, Fenton produced various Cactus items in chocolate, aqua carnival, blue opalescent, and red sunset carnival exclusively for the Levay Distributing Company of Edwardsville, Illinois. Unlike items in the pattern produced under the Fenton name, those made for Levay are different in color and form. Characteristically, Levay used a single mold from which any number of new shapes could be produced by pulling or compressing the molten glass or by applying a handle. An example of this is shown in Fig. 65. As you can see from the illustration, a handled basket vase was made by crimping the rim of a vase and applying a handle. Strictly speaking, Levay is-

sues are not reproductions as they do not conform to any known original in shape or color.

Although Fenton items are of good-quality nonflint glass, a number of subtle discrepancies exist. Unlike original pieces, which are crisply molded and pressed in high relief, the design on new items is often blurred. This is best seen on the vertical bars of the patterns that carry the herringbone motif. On new pieces, the base and the top of each bar are noticeably blurred (Fig. 66), while on originals, this bar is well defined and pressed. Additionally, this bar extends to the bottom of the base on the old and abruptly stops above the ribbing of the base on the new. Another discrepancy is in the treatment of rims. The rims on original items are distinctly beaded, a feature not present on copies (Fig. 67). Moreover, genuine items have beading around the cactus that is higher, rounder, and more evenly spaced than on new items, on which the beading is oval, flat, and poorly spaced.

Early pieces in Fenton's Cactus are not marked. Prior to 1967, those items produced as part of the "Olde Virginia Glass" line carried only a paper label. Beginning in 1970, Fenton began to mark permanently all of its glass. While items in the "Olde Virginia" line were permanently embossed with the "OVG" trademark until the line was discontinued, those produced for Fenton

CHART 15 CACTUS. Summit Art Glass Company, Akron, Ohio.
CMN: Cactus
Mark: Unmarked, embossed "V," or paper label.
Color Code: AMB Amberina, BG Blue-green, COB Cobalt, E Evergreen, EG Emerald Green, GC Green
Custard, MG Morning Glory, MW Milk White, RUB Rubina, V Vaseline, W Watermelon

ITEM	COLOR(S)	YEAR	ORIG	NEW
Salt Shaker. #566. 2¾"h.	AMB, COB, E, MG, RUB, V	1985	X	
Toothpick holder. #565. 2½h.	AMB, BG, COB, E, EG,	1985	X	
	GC, MG, RUB, V, W	1985	X	
Tumbler. #567. Water, 4½"h.	MW, RUB, V	1985	X	

Each Summit item was supposedly produced from the original Indiana Tumbler & Goblet Co. mold. Note: A similar three-inch-high salt
and pepper shaker was offered by Sturbridge Yankee Workshop, Westbrook, Maine, in cobalt blue.

CHART 16 CACTUS. Other Reproductions Prior to 1975.
Maker: Unknown.
Mark: Unmarked.
Color Code: CS Caramel Slag.

ITEM	COLOR(S)	YEAR	ORIG	NEW
Creamer.	CS	1975	X	
Salt shaker.	CS	1975	X	
Sugar shaker.	CS	1975		X
Toothpick holder.	CS	1975	X	
Tumbler, water, flat.	CS	1975	X	

and Levay were permanently marked with the familiar Fenton logo.

As recently as 1985, the Summit Art Glass Company of Rootstown, Ohio, reproduced the three Cactus items enumerated in Chart 15. Supposedly made from original Indiana Tumbler & Goblet Company molds, each appears in an assortment of contemporary colors. A more deceiving item in the pattern, the toothpick holder, was produced by St. Clair Glass of Elwood, Indiana, in clear, chocolate, and golden agate (amber with opalescence). Unlike the Summit reproduction toothpick holder, those by St. Clair in chocolate are convincing and difficult to distinguish from the original. However, new chocolate toothpick holders tend to be lighter in color, and the beading around the cactus is unevenly spaced.

Hint: Reproduction items in Cactus have beads that are unevenly spaced.

CALIFORNIA

The United States Glass Company of Pittsburgh, Pennsylvania, christened this pattern No.15059, or California, to promote pressed-glass patterns named after states. Also known as Beaded Grape, Beaded Grape and Vine, and Grape and Vine, the pattern was first issued about 1899 in clear and emerald green nonflint glass (plain or with gilt trim). An extensive table service that included all table pieces as well as ten different sizes of covered bowls, open bowls, and compotes was offered in either color choice (see Fig. 69).

This design consists of large sprays of grapes, leaves, and branches against a plain background. Each design element is finely detailed and stands in high relief. Characteristic of the design is the square shape

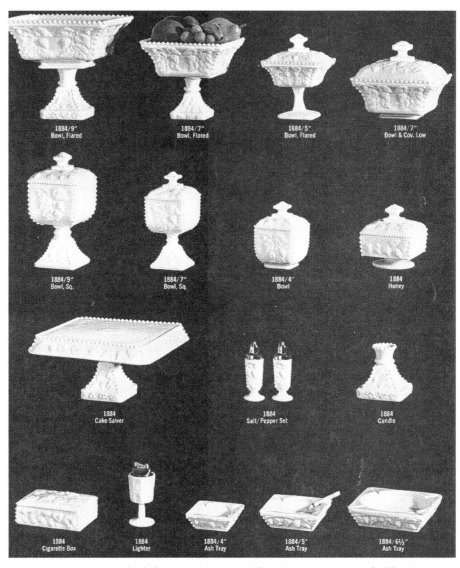

Fig. 69. Circa 1967 Westmoreland Glass Co. catalog reprint illustrating an assortment of California.

and the beaded rim. An exception is the round tankard pitcher with applied handle.

The first items reproduced in California from new molds were the goblet and large square plate in clear and emerald green (Fig. 70). Unmarked as to manufacturer, they date after the end of World War II. In general, reproductions are heavy, the design is less detailed than originals, and the glass is distinctly wavy. New goblets, in particular, are easy to detect. The stem of the

upper grape cluster is shorter than the one on original goblets, and the lowest leaf of the design turns under the base of the bowl.

Color is the easiest way to detect reproductions. Old colored items are always a deep, rich emerald green. Reproductions lack this vibrant depth of color and, depending upon the glass, vary from a pale green to an aqua.

Major contemporary production of California came about through the efforts of the

CHART 17   CALIFORNIA. Plum Glass Company, Pittsburgh, Pennsylvania.
CMN: Line No.1884 or Beaded Grape.
Mark: Embossed "PG" within a keystone and "WG."
Color Code: B Blue, BF Blue Frosted, BL Black, BLDG Black with Decorated Gold, C Clear, CO Cobalt, MW Milk White, MWD Milk White Decorated, P Pink.

ITEM	COLOR(S)	YEAR	ORIG	NEW
Ashtray, square, 5".	BLDG	1991		X
	MWD	1988		X
Box, chocolate, flat, rectangular, 4" × 5¾".	BLDG	1991		X
	MW	1987		X
	MWD	1988		X
Candlestick, low, 4"h.	B, BL, C, CO, MW, P	1989		X
	MWD	1988		X
Compote, flared, square.				
Covered, 7"h.	B, BL, C, CO, MW, P	1987	X	
	MWD	1988	X	
Open, 9"h.	MW	1987	X	
Creamer.				
Individual, small.	MW	1987		X
	MWD	1988		X
Table-size, large, round, footed.	MWD	1988		X
Cup and saucer set.	MW	1987		X
	MWD	1988		X
Plate, round.				
6"d., Bread and butter.	MW	1989		X
10"d., Dinner.	MW	1989		X
Salt shaker, footed.	MW	1987		X
	MWD	1988		X
Sugar bowl, open.				
Individual, handled, small.	MW	1987		X
	MWD	1988		X
Table-size, round.	MWD	1988		X
Vase, footed.	B, BF, BL, C, CO, MWD	1988		X
	MW	1987		X

Westmoreland Glass Company of Grapeville, Pennsylvania. Known as pattern No.1884, or Beaded Grape, Westmoreland began to reproduce it as late as January 1950. Throughout succeeding years, it produced an astonishing number of contemporary and original items in milk-white glass and a limited number of items in color. Milk-white items are often decorated with 22-karat-gold grapes and green leaves. All items are enumerated in Chart 18.

Created as giftware, new Westmoreland milk-white pieces are dead white rather than translucent and lack the depth and quality of original milk-white glass. Colored pieces are harsh, artificial, and strictly contemporary.

In general, reproductions are heavy and poorly detailed. When marked, they are impressed with the familiar "WG" insignia.

As late as 1969, the Anchor-Hocking Glass Company of Lancaster, Ohio, reproduced three items in California. Illustrated in its 1969 catalog are: No.W604, the 11-inch-diameter, high-standard cake stand; No.W617, the 10-inch-diameter, 12-sided scalloped open bowl; and No.W619, the 7½-inch-high, square, covered footed compote. As you can see from Fig. 71, the bowl and compote are not original to the pattern. All three pieces are heavy, poorly detailed, and made from a medium-grade nonflint glass. Each item was, moreover, available only in

CHART 18   CALIFORNIA. Westmoreland Glass Company, Grapeville, Pennsylvania.
CMN: No.1884 or Beaded Grape.
Mark: Unmarked, embossed "WG," or paper label.
Color Code: A Amber, AM Amethyst, B Blue, BB Brandywine Blue, C Clear, G Green, GS Golden Sunset, H Honey, IB Ice Blue, LG Laurel Green, MW Milk White, MWD Milk White Decorated, MWG Milk White with Gold.

ITEM	COLOR(S)	YEAR	ORIG	NEW
Ashtray.				
4"sq.	MW	1955		X
	MWD	1967		X
5"sq.	MW	1967		X
6½"sq.	MW	1967		X
Bowl, flared.				
Flat.				
Covered.				
4"sq.	MW	1950s	X	
7"sq.	MW	1967	X	
Open.				
7"sq.	MW	1962	X	
9"sq.	MW	1950s	X	
Footed.				
Covered.				
5"sq.	MW, MWD	1967	X	
7"sq.	MW	1983	X	
Open.				
5"sq.	MW	1950s	X	
7"sq.	MW	1967	X	
9"sq.	MW	1950s	X	
Box, cigarette or chocolate, flat, rectangular, 4" × 5¾".	MW	1955		X
Cake stand, high standard, 11"sq.	MW	1967	X	
Candlestick, low, 4"h.	MW	1967		X
Compote, square, high standard.				
Covered.				
5"h.	MW, MWD, MWG	1962	X	
7"h.	A, AM, B, C, G	1960s	X	
	MW	1954	X	
	MWD, MWG	1962	X	
9"h.	MW	1955	X	
Open, flared bowl.				
7"h.	MW	1961	X	
9"h.	MW	1983	X	
12"sq.	MW	1961	X	
Creamer, pressed handle.				
Small.	MW	1950s		X
Table size, 4"h.	BB, GS, LG	1964	X	
	MW	1954	X	
	MWD	1950s	X	
Cup and saucer.	MW	1950s		X
Decanter, matching stopper.	MW	1983	X	
Fruit cocktail, 3½"d., round.	MW	1950s		X
Goblet, 8 oz.	A, AM, B,	1960s	X	
	C, G	1950s	X	
	MW	1950	X	
Honey dish, covered, footed, 5"sq.	H, IB	1976	X	
	MW, MWD, MWG	1962	X	

ITEM	COLOR(S)	YEAR	ORIG	NEW
Lighter, cigarette.	MW	1967		X
Mayonnaise, footed, 4½"d.	MW	1950s		X
Plate.				
Round.				
6"d., Bread and butter.	MW	1950s		X
7"d., Salad.	MW	1950s		X
8½"d., Luncheon.	A, AM, B, C, G	1960s		X
	MW	1951		X
10½"d., Dinner.	MW	1951		X
11"d., Sandwich.	MW	1950s		X
12½"d., Serving.	MW	1950s		X
15"d., Torte.	MW	1950s		X
Square.				
6"sq., Bread and butter.	MW	1950s	X	
7"sq., Salad.	MW	1950s	X	
8½"sq., Luncheon.	A, AM, B, C, G	1960s	X	
	MW	1951	X	
10½"sq., Dinner.	MW	1951	X	
11"sq., Sandwich.	MW	1950s		X
12½"sq., Serving.	MW	1950s		X
15"sq., Torte.	MW	1950s		X
Parfait, footed.	MW	1950s		X
Sauce dish, flat, 4"sq.	A, AM, B, C, G, MW	1950s	X	
Salt shaker, footed.	MW	1983		X
Sherbert, low-footed, bell-shaped.	MW	1950s		X
Sugar bowl.				
Covered, 4"h.*	BB, GS, LG	1964	X	
	MW	1954	X	
	MWD, MWG	1967	X	
Open, small.	MW	1950s		X
Tumbler, flat.				
Iced tea, 10 oz.	MW	1950s		X
Juice, 5 oz.	MW	1950s		X
Water, 8 oz.	A, AM, B, C, G, MW	1960s	X	
Vase, footed.				
6"h., crimped.	MW	1967		X
9"h.				
Bell-shaped.	MW	1950s		X
Crimped.	MW	1967		X
Wine.	A, AM, B, C, G, MW	1960s	X	

*Distributed by the Levay Distributing Company, Edwardsville, Illinois, in 1983.

milk white—a color never used originally. In addition, items are not permanently marked, although you may occasionally find these reproductions with a paper label.

In 1987, the Plum Glass Company of Pittsburgh, Pennsylvania, issued a number of items in California produced from molds purchased after the closing of the Westmoreland factory (see Chart 17). Known as Plum's Beaded Grape pattern, each reproduction was offered in black (plain or decorated), blue (plain or frosted), clear, cobalt blue, milk white (plain or decorated), and pink. Although each item is permanently embossed with a "PG" within a keystone (signifying Plum Glass), pieces may also bear the "WG" logo of the Westmoreland Glass Company. It is not known what other

Fig. 70. Early reproduction emerald green California goblet. Circa 1950. Unmarked.

Fig. 71. Reproduction milk-white California. Anchor-Hocking Glass Co. Circa 1969. Unmarked.

molds Plum may have purchased in this pattern.

Hint: Any color other than clear or emerald green is new.

Fig. 72. Canadian look-alike milk-white lamp base, often mistaken for a celery vase. Circa early 1970s. Unmarked.

CANADIAN

Although the maker of Canadian is not known, this well-known pattern was originally made in an extended table setting made from clear nonflint glass. Characteristic of glass of the 1870s, the design consists of vertical panels, arched at the top, depicting rural scenes. Ivy and berry sprays against a lightly stippled background complete the basic design.

Canadian is a safe pattern to collect. The only item that may confuse a dealer or collector is a smooth-rimmed, 6¾-inch-high, white camphor lamp base that stands on a low pedestaled base. Illustrated in Fig. 72, this piece is often mistaken for a celery vase. As you can see from the illustration,

the reproduction lamp base is convincing. Arched panels and ivy and berry sprays stand against a stippled background similar to Canadian. However, upon close examination, you will notice an oriental influence in the design. The trees in the design are decisively of an oriental nature and the buildings are pagodas. Although the lamp base is unmarked, both the look and feel point to foreign manufacture. Commonly encountered in the early 1980s, this reproduction possibly dates well into the early 1970s.

Hint: A lamp base was never made originally in the Canadian pattern.
Reproduced items: Lamp base.

CARDINAL

Attributed to the Ohio Flint Glass Company of Lancaster, Ohio, Cardinal is one of the many bird patterns popular during the mid-1870s. Also known as Cardinal Bird, and Blue Jay, this pattern was originally produced in a bright, clear nonflint glass. Typical of the period, its design consists of well-defined birds in varying positions embossed upon a clear background (Fig. 73). Unfortunately, this lovely pattern was produced only in a limited table setting.

The only items reproduced in Cardinal, to date, are the creamer and goblet. The L.G. Wright Glass Company of New Martinsville, West Virginia, issued the No.76-1 goblet in 1975 and the No.77-13 creamer in 1984. Produced from new molds, each is in clear nonflint glass. Both reproductions are poor copies of the originals. Unlike the crisp, sculptured look of each old piece, the pattern on both the new creamer and the goblet is blurred. The birds are grotesque and misshapen. This deformity is most noticeable in the bird's beak, which is short and naturally proportioned in the original and elongated in the reproduction. Unlike the finely molded feathering on originals, reproductions are poorly detailed. Both reproductions are too heavy and the glass is grayed.

In the mid-1970s, the Summit Art Glass Company of Mogadore/Rootstown, Ohio, reproduced a similar Cardinal goblet in blue, clear, and green. Like those produced by L.G. Wright, Summit goblets were also is-

Fig. 73. Original clear Cardinal goblet. Maker unknown. Circa mid-1870s.

sued from new molds and share the same discrepancies.

Summit and L.G. Wright reproductions in Cardinal are not permanently marked.

Hint: Reproduction items have birds with elongated beaks and poorly detailed feathering.
Reproduced items: Creamer, goblet.

CHERRY

The Cherry pattern illustrated in Fig. 74 is typical of the many popular fruit patterns of the 1870s. Designed and patented by William M. Kirchner on April 5, 1870, the pattern was produced in a good-quality clear and milk-white nonflint glass by Bakewell, Pears and Company of Pittsburgh, Pennsylvania. Like many early patterns, it was originally issued in a limited table service.

The first reproduction in the Cherry pattern was the goblet. Produced in clear and milk-white glass, this goblet made from a new mold appeared about 1935. Since then, the champagne, also made from a new mold, entered the market in clear and contemporary colors. In all instances, the differences between the old and new are the same. Original items are adorned with natural-looking sprays of large, clear cherries and leaves against a clear background. Mellow in appearance, the design is well executed and natural looking; both leaf and cherry are well detailed. Cherry reproductions display a new look to the glass and, unlike original items, feel slick. The design is too sharp and, at times, the cherries are blurred and look like clear blotches on the glass.

Reproductions in Cherry are not marked.

Fig. 74. Original clear Cherry goblet. Bakewell, Pears & Co. Circa 1870.

Hint: Cherry reproductions in clear have a distinct blue cast to the glass.

Reproduced items: Champagne, goblet.

CHERRY LATTICE

Cherry Lattice is one of the more popular variations of the Cherry patterns. This attractive design consists of large, highly molded clusters of leaves and cherries on a clear, crisscrossed background that resembles a lattice (see Fig. 75). First introduced by the Northwood Glass Company in the 1890s, Cherry Lattice was originally offered in a limited table service from a medium-quality clear nonflint glass that was often decorated in pink and gold.

In 1976, Mosser Glass, Inc., of Cambridge, Ohio, offered a new covered butter dish in

Fig. 75. Original Cherry Lattice creamer. Northwood Glass Co. Circa 1890s.

Cherry Lattice. Known as item No.132, this new butter is round and flat with a flanged rim. Produced from a new mold, it is lightly decorated with ruby stain and gilt that rubs off easily. Unlike the originals, which are lightweight with a well-pressed and balanced design, reproductions are heavy, poorly pressed, and unevenly designed. Moreover, the new butter has a distinct bluish cast, unlike originals, which are crystal clear. Examples of this new butter dish have been seen marked on the outside of the lid near the knob handle with an underlined "W" in a circle.

As late as 1990, this butter dish has been seen in a poor-grade nonflint glass in amberina, cobalt blue, and pink. It is unsigned and made from a new mold, which is different from either the original or Mosser's. This reproduction butter dish is very poorly pressed, and the glass has an oily sheen. In fact, the glass is so greasy that the "Made in Taiwan" label will not adhere.

Hint: Reproduction items are heavier than original items and made from poor-quality glass.

Reproduced items: Butter dish.

CHERRY THUMBPRINT

Cherry Thumbprint is a popular pattern of the fruit group. This relatively late design was originally produced about 1904 by the Northwood Glass Company (all locations). The Westmoreland Glass Company of Grapeville, Pennsylvania, also issued it about 1907. Complete table services were created by both companies in clear and clear with color-stained nonflint glass.

Also known as Cherry and Cable, Cherry with Thumbprint(s), and Paneled Cherry, Cherry Thumbprint is a typical Northwood pattern. The design consists of large pairs of cherries and leaves suspended from a cable. Each pair is pressed into a clear vertical panel. The red-stained cherries are not patterned, while the leaves are veined and slightly stippled, producing a pleasing effect against the clear background. Large thumbprints at the base of each panel complete the design.

Fig. 76. Reproduction milk-white Cherry Thumbprint covered cookie jar. Westmoreland Glass Co. Circa 1967.

5½" Honey and Cover, Footed, "Cherry" Pattern. Hand painted cherries and leaves on cover. Also made in plain milk glass.

Fig. 77. Reproduction No.109 Cherry Thumbprint decorated milk-white covered honey dish. Westmoreland Glass Co. Circa 1967.

Between 1967 and 1983, the Westmoreland Glass Company of Grapeville, Pennsylvania, issued five items in this design: the low-standard covered compote, the flat, covered, double-handled cookie jar (Fig. 76), the individual creamer, the covered honey dish (Fig. 77), and the individual double-handled sugar bowl (Fig. 78). Known as Westmoreland's No.109 or Plantation pattern, each item was produced from a new mold in milk-white glass and was often enamel decorated in the Roses & Bows design. In addition, the creamer, the honey, and the sugar bowl were issued in decorated vaseline. Only the low-standard covered compote, the individual creamer, and the open sugar have contemporary forms. The remaining two items emulate known originals.

Of special interest is the covered cookie jar. Although this item was also produced in milk white and decorated vaseline, it was available only in mint green in 1979 and 1980. This green color was developed by master chemist Dwight V. Johnson, who adjusted an earlier formula that he created in 1970 for Westmoreland's antique green.

Westmoreland did not reproduce items in any known original colors.

Westmoreland reproductions are heavy and thick and the glass has a slight bluish cast when viewed under a strong light. The cable is not strongly defined on reproductions, while the veining on the cherry leaves is exaggerated and the stippling is sparse. Although all items are embossed with Westmoreland's familiar "WG" logo, you may occasionally find items marked with an original paper label.

As late as 1991, Mosser Glass, Inc., of Cambridge, Ohio, issued the Cherry Thumb-

CHART 19   CHERRY THUMBPRINT. Mosser Glass, Incorporated, Cambridge, Ohio.
CMN: Cherry Thumbprint.
Mark: Embossed "M," "M" within a circle, or unmarked.
Color Code: AC Amethyst Carnival, CD Clear Decorated (Pink cherries and Gold cable and leaves).

ITEM	COLOR(S)	YEAR	ORIG	NEW
Butter dish, flat, round, covered.				
Miniature.	AC, CD	1991		X
Table size.	CD	1991	X	
Celery vase, flat, handled.				
Miniature.	CD	1991		X
Table size.	CD	1991	X	
Cookie jar, double-handled, flat, covered.				
Miniature.	CD	1991		X
Table size.	CD	1991	X	
Creamer, pressed handle, flat.				
Miniature.	CD	1991		X
Table-size.	CD	1991	X	
Cup. #208D. Punch, miniature, 1⅞"d.	CD	1990		X
Goblet, miniature.	CD	1991		X
Pitcher, water, pressed handle.				
Miniature.	CD	1991		X
Table-size.	CD	1991	X	
Punch bowl. #206D. Miniature, 7⅝".	CD	1990		X
Spoonholder, handled, flat.				
Miniature.	CD	1991		X
Table-size.	CD	1991	X	
Sugar bowl, covered, flat, handled.				
Miniature.	CD	1991		X
Table-size.	CD	1991	X	
Tumbler, water, flat.	CD	1991	X	

CHART 20   CHERRY THUMBPRINT. Westmoreland Glass Company, Grapeville, Pennsylvania.
CMN: Westmoreland's No.109, Cherry Thumbprint, Plantation.
Mark: Embossed "WG" or paper label.
Color Code: MG Mint Green, MW Milk White, MWD Milk White Decorated (Roses & Bows), VD Vaseline Decorated.

ITEM	COLOR(S)	YEAR	ORIG	NEW
Compote, covered, low standard.	MW	1967		X
Cookie jar, covered, flat, double-handled.	MG	1979	X	
	MW	1967	X	
	VD	unknown	X	
Creamer, individual.	MW	unknown		X
	VD	unknown		X
Honey dish, covered, footed, square.	MW	1983	X	
	MWD	unknown	X	
Sugar Bowl, individual, double-handled.	MW	unknown		X
	VD	unknown		X

print miniatures enumerated in Chart 19. Although Mosser made the covered butter in amethyst, it produced all the other miniatures in clear glass lightly decorated with red stain and gold trim. These pieces are not original to the pattern, were produced from new molds, and (when signed) are permanently marked with an "M" or an "M" in a circle.

Mosser also reissued at least eight full-sized items in this pattern. Each of these items was produced from the original Westmoreland mold in clear nonflint glass and decorated in the same style as the miniatures. Interestingly, each full-sized item we examined retained a faint image of the Westmoreland trademark, which had been incompletely removed from the mold.

Mosser items are heavier than the originals and the pattern is not as crisply impressed. The coloring is applied by the cold-paint method and can scratch or chip easily. The gold is also painted onto the glass (not fired) and can be removed easily. Compared to the brilliant clear glass of original items, reproductions have a distinct grayish cast, look glossy, and feel oily or slick.

Collectors have reported seeing an unmarked covered cracker jar in opalescent blue, opalescent green, and pink slag glass with an iridized finish. We believe Mosser Glass also produced these items.

In 1991, a covered butter dish in Cherry Thumbprint was offered by various reproduction wholesalers in amberina, cobalt blue, and pink. This new butter should fool no one as it is quite crude when compared to the originals. The pattern is barely visible, the glass is extremely heavy, and the colors are harsh. Reproductions are made from an inferior-grade nonflint glass, which is very slick and oily. Although this butter dish is not permanently marked, it was originally issued with a small gold sticker

Fig. 78. Reproduction decorated milk-white Cherry Thumbprint individual creamer and open sugar bowl. Westmoreland Glass Co. Circa 1967.

printed "MADE IN TAIWAN." Unfortunately, because of the slickness of the new glass, this sticker does not adhere well and is often missing.

Hint: Original Cherry Thumbprint pieces are permanently embossed with Northwood's underlined "N" in a circle trademark.

CHRYSANTHEMUM SPRIG

Chrysanthemum Sprig is a lovely and highly collectible pattern greatly regarded among collectors of custard glass. About 1898, the Northwood Glass Company produced the original extended table service in yellow and blue custard glass. In both colors, large chrysanthemum flowers and leaves are beautifully gilded with gold. Additionally, yellow custard items are decorated with pale pink and green enamel. Applied to the raised portions of the design, these decorations have a tendency to wear thin through years of continued use.

The only known reproduction in Chrysanthemum Sprig is the toothpick holder. Known as item No.555, it is 2¾ inches high and allegedly produced from the original Northwood mold by the Summit Art Glass Company of Akron, Ohio, in 1985. This piece can be found in the contemporary colors of blue green, coral, mulberry, and rubina, and the original color of custard.

Prior to 1975, the St. Clair Glass Company of Elwood, Indiana, issued a similar copy of the toothpick holder. Produced from new molds, this piece is strictly a contemporary copy readily found in the nonoriginal colors of carnival and iridized glass.

Unlike original toothpick holders, which flare at the top, reproductions are straight-sided (Fig. 79). The only colors that might confuse beginning collectors are blue and yellow custard. Unlike the deep, rich color of the original yellow custard toothpick hold-

Fig. 79. Reproduction No.555 Chrysanthemum Sprig decorated custard toothpick holder. Summit Art Glass Co. Circa 1985. Unmarked.

ers, reproductions range from a pale yellow to a light ivory. The color of new blue custard is even more conspicuous and is entirely too deep and harsh. The decoration on original items is neatly done in pastel shades of pink and green. In contrast, reproductions are poorly decorated in deep, harsh colors.

In general, reproduction toothpick holders in Chrysanthemum Sprig are heavier than the originals, colors other than custard are strictly contemporary, and decorations are deep and harsh.

Hint: Reproduction toothpick holders are heavier than originals.
Reproduced items: Toothpick holder.

CLIO

As the Daisy and Button pattern gained in popularity throughout the late nineteenth and early twentieth centuries, a seemingly endless number of variations flooded the

market. About 1885, Challinor, Taylor & Company produced its own variation of the well-known pattern. Originally known as Clio, Challinor's design utilizes Daisy and Button–filled vertical panels separated by clear triangular-shaped prisms (Fig. 80).

Fig. 80. Reprint of the Challinor, Taylor & Co. (or Factory "C") catalog of the United States Glass Co. illustrating an assortment of Clio, circa 1891. (Only the butter dish has been reproduced.)

Clear bands of almond-shaped thumbprints appear around the rim and above the base of each item. Originally produced in a limited table service in a good-quality nonflint glass, items may still be found in amber, blue, clear, green, and canary yellow.

Only one reproduction is known in Clio, the No.133 covered butter dish illustrated in Fig. 81. Produced by Mosser Glass, Inc., of Cambridge, Ohio, in 1976, this dish is readily found in all original colors, plus amethyst. As you can see from the illustration, this new covered butter is a good reproduction. Each element of the old pattern is convincingly executed to produce an item that has caused considerable confusion among collectors.

Common to a majority of reproductions produced from new molds, the new Clio covered butter dish is heavier than the old one. Unlike the rich, mellow color of the originals, the colors of the new butter are deep, harsh, and artificial looking. Clear items are slick and brilliant.

Although the new Clio covered butter dish is not permanently marked, you can easily detect the reproduction when you consider color and weight.

Hint: Reproduction butter dishes are heavier than originals.

Reproduced items: Butter dish.

Fig. 81. Reproduction No.133 Clio blue and canary covered butter dishes. Mosser Glass, Inc. Circa 1976. Unmarked.

COLORADO

Colorado is part of the states series of pattern glass produced by the United States Glass Company of Pittsburgh, Pennsylvania (see Fig. 82). Originally known as No.15057 and issued about 1899 to as late as 1920, this pattern was produced in an extended table service in blue (called Dewey Blue), clear, and green (either plain or copper-wheel engraved). Occasionally, you may find an odd item in black, clear with ruby stain, or vaseline, but these are considered rare.

Unlike Lacy Medallion, which is flat, pieces in Colorado are three-footed. Aside from the medallion ornaments that adorn the feet, and rims that may be either beaded or smooth and hand tooled to resemble large ruffles. Colorado is a plain pattern.

To date, Colorado is a safe pattern to collect because only the version without feet has been reproduced (see Lacy Medallion).

Hint: There are no known reproduction items in Colorado.

Fig. 82. Excerpt from United States Glass Co. catalog illustrating the No.15057 or Colorado pattern, circa 1899.

COLUMBIAN COIN

When production of the U.S. Coin pattern was abruptly curtailed due to a supposed violation of a federal law, the United States Glass Company of Pittsburgh, Pennsylvania, quickly reworked the molds to capitalize on the pattern's immense popularity. It replaced the six representations of U.S. coins with Spanish ones to create the line known as Columbian Coin.

Often referred to as Columbus Coin,

Spanish Coin, and World's Fair, this pattern was originally known as line No.15005 ½ by the United States Glass Company, which produced the design from 1893 at its Nickel Plate or Factory "N" Plant. Made from a fine-quality nonflint glass, representations of a Crown & Shield, Eagle & Shield, two of Christopher Columbus, and two of Americus Vespucius adorn the same forms and shapes found on the U.S. Coin pattern. Identical to U.S. Coin, items in Columbian Coin were originally issued in an extended

Fig. 83. Original Columbian Coin goblet with frosted coins. United States Glass Co. Circa 1893.

table service in clear, clear in combination with frosting, clear in combination with amber or ruby stain, and clear with gold or platinum stain (Fig. 83).

Three items cause considerable confusion among collectors and dealers of the Columbian Coin pattern. As late as 1958, Alice Hulett Metz, in her book *Early American Pattern Glass* (vol. I), listed new goblets, toothpick holders, and water tumblers. These were supposedly produced abroad from new molds in clear and clear with frosting and imported by a large wholesale distributor. However, without positive catalog identification, this is impossible to confirm. We believe these reproductions were made by the Fostoria Glass Company of Moundsville, West Virginia, as its No.1372 or Coin Glass Pattern, which was introduced in 1958. A prudent approach to suspect items is to make a careful comparison of detail, quality, and weight.

Hint: Columbian Coin reproductions are unconfirmed; carefully examine suspect items.

Reproduced items: Goblet, toothpick holder, tumbler.

CORD AND TASSEL

Cord and Tassel is one of the many drape patterns in pressed glass. It was designed and patented by Andrew H. Baggs (general manager of the LaBelle Glass Company of Bridgeport, Ohio) on July 23, 1872 (design patent No.6002). This lovely pattern was first issued by LaBelle in 1872 from a good-quality clear nonflint glass in a medium-sized table service.

The design is highly embossed and consists of a clear horizontal cord looped around the midsection of each item. Hanging within the uppermost arch of each loop is a large tassel. Above and below this motif is another band of cord (Fig. 84). Typical of the period, handles are applied.

Allegedly, new, unmarked goblets and wines were produced in clear nonflint glass around 1986. However, without positive catalog identification, it is impossible to confirm that these items are reproductions. A

Fig. 84. Original Cord and Tassel clear wine. LaBelle Glass Co. Circa 1872.

prudent approach to purchasing items is to compare carefully detail, quality, and weight.

Hint: Cord and Tassel reproductions are unconfirmed; fully examine suspect items.
Reproduced items: Goblet, wine.

COTTAGE

The Cottage pattern was first produced in the 1870s by the firm of Adams & Company of Pittsburgh, Pennsylvania. A delightful design consisting of a large band of alternating clear and fine-cut filled medallions against a clear background, Cottage is also known as Dinner Bell and Fine Cut Band (Fig. 85). Handles on creamers and pitchers are in the shape of two outstretched arms holding a clear vertical bar. Highly popular in its time, the pattern was originally produced in a large and extended table service in a medium-quality nonflint glass. Although you can collect a complete table set in clear, you will find only odd items in amber, blue, and green.

Fig. 86 shows the 5⅜-inch-high goblet, one of two known reproductions. The other

is the wine. Each was produced, unmarked, from a new mold in the original colors of amber, blue, and clear. Both items are good reproductions; however, there are a number of discrepancies. Unlike the original colors, which are soft and mellow, new goblets and wines have a strikingly deep color. This discrepancy is especially true for those items in amber; they look almost orange. The glass glistens with a silvery sheen and is noticeably heavier than original items. Perhaps the easiest method of detecting reproduction goblets and wines is to observe the stem. On original items, it is thick with a large, well-patterned ball-knob; on reproductions, it is thin with a smaller, ill-patterned ball-knob.

Hint: Reproduction stemware has short thick stems and the colors are harsh.
Reproduced items: Goblet, wine.

Fig. 85. Original Cottage clear goblet. Adams & Co. Circa 1870s.

Fig. 86. Reproduction blue Cottage goblet. Unmarked. (Notice how the knob stem on this reproduction differs from the original.)

CROESUS

The original McKee & Brothers Glass Works catalog (circa 1901) illustrates a large assortment of the pattern originally named Croesus. This pattern was first introduced by the Riverside Glass Works of Wellsburg, West Virginia, in 1897 as pattern No.484. When the National Glass Company moved these molds to its McKee plant in Jeannette, Pennsylvania, in 1901, production continued.

Croesus is a somewhat fanciful pattern in which three "C-scrolls" form the basic design. Above and below each combination of scrolls are fan-shaped ornaments, while crosshatching separates one "C-scroll" grouping from another. Many available forms, including the four-piece table set, daintily stand on three splayed feet. Originally produced in amethyst, clear, and emerald green, complete table services were available either plain or with gold decoration.

The first reproductions in Croesus were the four-piece table set and the toothpick holder. They appeared prior to 1974 in the original colors of amethyst, clear, and emerald green and were poorly decorated with gold paint. They are unmarked, and their existence remained unknown for a number of years. Today, we know that they were made from a new mold by the Guernsey Glass Company of Cambridge, Ohio, for Smith Glass of Corning, Arkansas.

A second four-piece table set, also unmarked, is most likely an import of the Kamei Glass Company, Ltd., of Osaka, Japan, and is known in clear and the original colors of amethyst and green.

In 1977, the Summit Art Glass Company of Akron, Ohio, issued Croesus tumblers from a new mold in the contemporary color of sapphire blue with gold decor. Illustrated in Fig. 87 and known as Summit's No.541 tumbler, the tumbler is 3¾ inches high. Later, the same mold was used to produce tumblers in contemporary amber and in a variation of the original green (both without gold trim).

Reproductions in Croesus share a number of common discrepancies. As a general rule, new items are thick and heavy. This thickness, which often appears as excess glass, is most obvious around the rim of the butter base and the lid of the sugar bowl. Reproduction colors are deep, harsh, and artificial, while those items produced in clear are glossy and often feel slick.

However, the most obvious flaw on each new item is the design. Unlike original items, the overall design on reproductions is excessively thin. And, because new forms are also small and squat, the design is compressed. Moreover, the ends of each "C-scroll" sharply coil inward, creating a tightly closed loop, which is not present on new items. And unlike the old, new items are poorly decorated with a bright gold paint that is often applied to appear worn.

Although the toothpick holder and four-piece table set are not marked, Summit tumblers are permanently embossed with a "V" inside a circle and originally carried a gold and black label in the shape of a hand and printed "Hand Pressed in U.S.A.—Summit Art Glass" in capital letters.

Hint: Reproductions have a poor-quality gold paint that rubs off easily.

Reproduced items: Butter dish, creamer, spoonholder, sugar bowl, toothpick holder, tumbler.

Fig. 87. Reproduction Croesus No.541 sapphire blue tumbler with gold trim. Summit Art Glass Co. Circa 1977. Embossed "V" within a circle.

CRYSTAL WEDDING

The history of the Crystal Wedding pattern has long been established by early glass historians. Adams & Company of Pittsburgh, Pennsylvania, first made this pattern about 1890. Then, when Adams became a member of the United States Glass Company of Pittsburgh after 1891, production continued. Originally named Crystal Wedding, it is also known as Collins and Crystal Anniversary (Fig. 88).

This pattern was produced in a large and extended table service from a good-quality nonflint glass in clear, clear with machine frosting, and clear with amber or ruby stain. Complete table sets in each color treatment were offered with or without copper-wheel engraving.

Crystal Wedding is a heavy pattern. Covered compotes in particular are quite weighty, as are larger items such as the high-standard banana and cake stands. Due to the thickness of the glass, items sparkle with a lovely radiance and clarity.

The first copies of Crystal Wedding appeared during the late 1930s or early 1940s. Unmarked goblets and various sizes of covered compotes in clear glass flooded the market. Unlike the crystal-clear originals, early reproductions are greener and heavier than old pieces. Shortly after the first clear copies were issued, clear with ruby-stained goblets and covered compotes were made.

Unlike originals, which are a deep ruby red, the reproductions are stained a light cranberry.

As early as 1943, a number of contemporary glass manufacturers, including Duncan, Glasscrafts & Ceramics, Jeannette, L.E. Smith, and Westmoreland Glass, produced their own versions of the Crystal Wedding high-standard covered compote. Today, you can find these compotes in a variety of sizes produced from new molds in numerous contemporary colors and decorative treatments, as illustrated in Fig. 89.

Beginning in 1943, the Westmoreland Glass Company of Grapeville, Pennsylvania, produced the Crystal Wedding high-standard covered compote (known as No.1874 or Westmoreland's Wedding Bowl) in three sizes: 8, 10, and 12¼ inches high. A low-footed candleholder was also made as late as 1967. Items were offered in amber, Bermuda blue, clear, clear with ruby stain, milk white, milk-white decorated (known as Dresden Roses, Roses and Bows, and Grape Clusters), milk white with gold, and olive

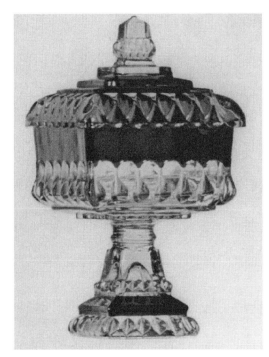

Fig. 88. Adams & Co. circa 1891 catalog reprint illustrating a number of items in Crystal Wedding—plain, banded, frosted, or engraved.

Fig. 89. Reproduction No.1874 Crystal Wedding clear with ruby-stain high-standard covered compote. Westmoreland Glass Co. Circa 1973. Embossed "WG."

green. Decorated milk-white items were often signed by the artist and offered in annual limited editions of one thousand pieces. Westmoreland reproductions may be signed with a paper label or embossed with a "WG."

Prior to 1953, Glasscrafts & Ceramics, Inc., of Yonkers, New York (wholesale distributors formerly known as Czecho-Slovak Glass Products Company), offered the No.5505 Crystal Wedding bowl. This unsigned bowl is a 7½-inch-high by 4-inch-square covered compote and was available in clear with ruby stain.

The Duncan Glass Company (a division of the United States Glass Company of Tiffin, Ohio) also produced Crystal Wedding (known as line No.712 or Wedding Bowl) covered compotes in several sizes before it closed in 1955. Today, you can still find 6½-, 10-, and 12-inch-high compotes in milk-white glass, reportedly made from original molds owned by the United States Glass Company. Although you may find these with an original blue and silver paper label, Duncan compotes are not permanently marked.

In 1956, the Jeannette Glass Company of Jeannette, Pennsylvania, reproduced the Crystal Wedding high-standard covered compote in 6½-inch and 8-inch sizes. Each was offered in blue, clear, clear with gold, green, and shell pink (an opaque color, highly collectible today). As late as 1968, covered compotes were still being offered by Jeannette as part of its "Crystal Classics" collection. Reproductions by Jeannette are not permanently marked.

Another reproduction of the Crystal Wedding covered compote (Fig. 90) is illustrated in the 1961 catalog of the L.E. Smith Glass Company of Mount Pleasant, Pennsylvania. Known as Smith's No.5000—Wedding Jar, it is 4 inches square by 8 inches high and is available in either plain or decorated milk white. Typical of most Crystal Wedding reproductions, items by Smith are not permanently signed.

In general, reproductions of Crystal Wedding share a number of discrepancies. With the possible exception of those produced by the Duncan Glass Company, all covered compotes were made from new molds. This

Fig. 90. New milk-white Crystal Wedding high-standard covered compote. L.E. Smith Glass Co. Circa 1961. Unmarked.

is readily seen in the treatment of finials, which are rounded on original pieces; above the almond-pointed thumbprints and below the crown, there is a distinct scalloped band. On reproductions, the finials are square and the scalloped band protrudes above an angular crown. Below the finial, the steps on original compotes are sharp with square corners. On new compotes, these steps are smooth and round, as are the corners. On original compotes, the scallops of the cover are round and slightly flared; on reproductions, they are flat and triangular.

On original compotes, the lower band of almond-shaped thumbprints is deeply pressed, rounded, and well defined. On reproductions, this band is lightly pressed, and the rounded thumbprints fade into the bowl. Unlike standards on original compotes, which are joined by a glass wafer, reproductions are made in one piece. Standards on reproductions are large, thick, and square, unlike the distinct bell shape of the old. The easiest way to determine quickly whether a piece is old or new is to examine the first step above the base. On original items, this step is scalloped; on reproductions, it is square.

Like new covered compotes, reproduction goblets emulate the antique form. They are good copies and are quite convincing. This faithful reproduction has caused considerable confusion among collectors and dealers. However, these new goblets are straight-sided, heavier, and smaller than originals. As on new compotes, the thumbprints on reproduction goblets are faint and tend to fade into the background. Although new goblets are unmarked, they are most likely a product of the L.G. Wright Glass Company of New Martinsville, West Virginia.

Unlike reproduction compotes and goblets, which imitate antique forms, Crystal Wedding candlesticks are strictly contemporary. They were made by adding a candle socket to the standard of the 10-inch compote and may still be found in the same colors as new Westmoreland compotes.

As late as 1991, new 14½-inch-high Crystal Wedding banquet lamps entered the market. New lamps feel greasy and are heavier and thicker than originals. Unlike the crystal-clear color of original lamps, new lamps are distinctly yellow and the font is diamond-latticed and gray-cast. Unlike the sharp and uneven lip of original fonts, the lips on the reproduction have been ground and polished smooth. Collars are attached by glue on reproductions and sit about ⅛ inch off the glass, while on originals they are always plastered and reside on top of the glass. These new lamps can be found with burnt wicks and new burners that have been antiqued. Reproduction lamps are not permanently marked.

Reproductions are heavier, less detailed, and squat. New items in clear glass tend to have a greenish tint. Those in clear with ruby stain are also greenish, with the stain ranging from pale cranberry to light purple rather than deep ruby red. Any contemporary color is new.

Recently, suspect items have been seen in clear glass with a satin frosting. Unlike the frosting on original items, which is always machine-ground, harsh, and coarse, this finish is too soft and smooth. Most likely they were made from original clear pieces that have been recently frosted to increase their value.

Hint: On original compotes, the bottom step above the base is always scalloped.

Reproduced items: Candleholder, compote, goblet, lamp.

CUPID AND PSYCHE

Since antiquity, mythology has played a role in the daily lives of humankind. Reflected in our art, literature, and music, mythology provides us with inspiration and substance. Without exception, nineteenth-century American manufacturers of pressed-glass tableware seized upon the allure and excitement of myth and legend. Exemplified in such patterns as Ceres, Classic, Cupid and Venus, and Minerva, ancient legends were once more immortalized in the enduring medium of pressed glass.

Also known as Psyche and Cupid, this pattern is gracefully designed to reflect the characters of its name. Cupid (the Roman god of Love) holds a mirror in front of the seated princess, Psyche, as she combs her hair (Fig. 91). To date, no one knows who

Fig. 91. Closeup of the original Cupid and Psyche pattern.

produced this most interesting design. It was originally issued in a limited table service from a low-grade nonflint glass with the design, as Ruth Webb Lee observed in *Early American Pressed Glass,* being "in such low relief as to appear etched on the surface" of each object.

Only one item might cause confusion among collectors and dealers of the Cupid and Psyche pattern. This is the 7½-inch milk-white plate, reissued by the Westmoreland Glass Company of Grapeville, Pennsylvania. These plates are not part of the original pressed-glass table pattern. However, their design is so similar to that of the original table pattern that novice collectors may mistake these for rarities in the pattern.

In 1938, Ruth Webb Lee first alerted collectors of the reissue of these plates from the original mold by the Westmoreland Glass Company. Unlike older plates, which are usually decorated, new plates are plain. Although Westmoreland began permanently marking reproductions, not all new plates are signed. When signed, however, they are permanently marked with the Westmoreland "WG" logo.

Hint: Cupid and Psyche plates were never made in milk white.
Reproduced items: Plate.

CUT LOG

Controversy has always surrounded the original manufacture of the Cut Log pattern. Erroneously attributed by early research to the Greensburg Glass Company of Greensburg, Pennsylvania, we now know the pattern was first produced by Bryce, Higbee & Company of Pittsburgh, Pennsylvania.

The original name of this pattern is Ethol. Often mistaken for Pioneer's No. 15 and Westmoreland's Cat's Eye and Block, Cut Log is an exciting pattern. The main elements of design are notched vertical bars resembling logs. This pattern was originally produced from a good-quality clear nonflint glass in a large and extended table service that included more than fifteen different sizes of covered and open high- and low-standard compotes.

Cut Log is a safe pattern to collect. However, for many years controversy and mystery have surrounded a high-standard open compote, thought to be the only reproduction in this pattern. Because this compote is unsigned, glass historians and authors have relentlessly perpetuated this fallacy.

Illustrated in the 1956 and 1958 catalogs of the Jeannette Glass Company of Jeannette, Pennsylvania, is Jeannette's No.3479 9-inch footed fruit bowl. As you can see from the illustration in Fig. 92, this new look-alike compote is completely different

Fig. 92. Jeannette Glass Co. 1958 catalog reprint of the Cut Log high-standard open compote. Unmarked.

from the original Cut Log pattern. Unlike original items, on which the bars of the design are notched and vertical, new items have a combination of vertical and horizontal bars. Moreover, the vertical bars are notched, while the horizontal bars are plain.

Look-alike compotes in Cut Log are easily found in aqua, clear, milk white, and shell pink and in the combination colors of blue-to-green, orange-to-green, red-to-orange, and yellow-to-green.

Hint: On original Cut Log pieces, the pattern is vertical, never horizontal.
Reproduced items: Compote.

DAISY AND BUTTON

Daisy and Button is one of the most popular pressed-glass patterns ever made. This design was in continuous production for more than three decades by nearly every major American glass manufacturer of pressed-glass tableware throughout the late eighteenth and early nineteenth centuries. Among its many manufacturers, Bryce Brothers, Doyle & Company (line No.300), and Hobbs, Brockunier & Company (line No.101) each reissued this pattern after 1891 as members of the United States Glass Company combine of Pittsburgh, Pennsylvania.

Because of its mass appeal and length of popularity, Daisy and Button was produced by the original manufacturers in an endless variety of tableware and novelties (Figs. 93 and 94). They offered more than 35 variations of the pattern, each displaying differences in the shape of finials, handles, stems,

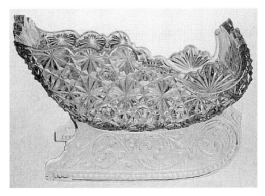

Fig. 93. Original sleigh-shaped vaseline Daisy and Button master berry bowl.

and bases. Original colors ranged from varying shades of amber, apple green, blue, clear, and vaseline to amberina.

Typical of Victorian pressed glass, original items retain a number of notable characteristics. Colors are always soft and mellow, never artificial in appearance. Only when

---

CHART 21 DAISY AND BUTTON. Boyd's Crystal Art Glass, Cambridge, Ohio.
CMN: Daisy and Button.
Mark: "B" in a diamond embossed.
Color Code: BC Blue Chiffon, BV Blue Variant, CB Cathedral Blue, CH Chocolate, CS Candy Swirl, D Delphinium, DA Dawn, DS Dogwood Slag, F Flame, FB Frosty Blue, FG Furr Green, FGS Furr Green Slag, GB Gateway Blue, H Heather, IB Ice Blue, IG Ice Green, I Impatient, JS John Surprise, MM Magic Marble, OI Olde Ivory, P Persimmon, PIN Pineapple, PV Purple Variant, R Redwood, RUB Rubina, WB Willow Blue, ZBS Zach Boyd Slag.

ITEM	COLOR(S)	YEAR	ORIG	NEW
Shoe.				
Boot, high.	CS, P, PIN	1978	X	
Bow slipper.	CH, D, DS, FG, IG, JS	1978	X	
	MM, OI, P, R, RUB, WB	1978	X	
	ZBS	1978	X	
Cat.	CB, CH, D, FGS, IB, IMP	1978	X	
	OI, P, R, RUB, WB	1978	X	
Toothpick holder.				
Hat, brimmed rim.	BV, DA, F, I, P, PV, RUB	1978	X	
Three-legged.	D, FB, GB, H, IB, IG	1978	X	
	RUB	1978	X	
Wine.	BC, H, P	1978	X	

CHART 22 DAISY AND BUTTON. Clevenger Brothers Glass Works, Clayton, New Jersey.
CMN: Daisy and Button.
Mark: Unmarked.
Color Code: A Amber, AM Amethyst, B Blue, C Clear, EG Emerald Green, RBY Ruby.

ITEM	COLOR(S)	YEAR	ORIG	NEW
Bottle. #32. Blown, 5"h.	A, AM, B, C, EG, RBY	1971		X

CHART 23 DAISY AND BUTTON. Crystal Art Glass, Cambridge, Ohio.
CMN: Daisy and Button.
Mark: Unmarked, embossed "D" in a heart, or paper label.
Color Code: A Amber, AG Apple Green, AL Amber Light, ACS Amber Custard Slag, AD Amber Dark, AM Amethyst, AMB Amberina, AMD Amethyst Dark, AML Amethyst Light, AQ Aqua, AUT Autumn, BB Bluebell, BBO Bluebell Opalescent, BBS Baby Blue Slag, BG Blue Green, BGS Baby Green Slag, BJS Blue Jay Slag, BLBS Blue & Brown Slag, BM Bloody Mary, BMS Blue Marble Slag, BS Bittersweet, BSS Bittersweet Slag, BWS Blue & White Slag, C Crystal, CA Carnival Amethyst, CAN Canary, CB Carnival Cobalt, CCL Chocolate Creme Light, CDC Carnival Dark Cobalt, CG Concord Grape, CH Champagne, COB Cobalt, CP Cambridge Pink, CR Caramel, CRD Caramel Dark, CRL Caramel Light, CSD Custard Slag Dark, CSL Custard Slag Light, CT Crown Tuscan, CUS Custard, CUSD Custard Dark, CUSL Custard Light, CUSS Custard Slag, DG Daffodil with Green, DI Dicromatic, EB End of Blizzard, ED Elizabeth's Delight, EG Emerald Green, ELI Elizabeth's Lime Ice, F Fawn, FG Forrest Green, FJ Frosty Jade, G Green, GLD Gold, GGS Gray Green Slag, GS Green Slag, HA Honey Amber, HB Heatherbloom, HE Heliotrope, HG Holly Green, I Ivorene, IV Ivory, IS Ivory Slag, J Jade, JA Jabe's Amber, LC Lemon Custard, LOS Lavender Opalescent Slag, MB Milk Blue, MBO Milk Blue Opalescent, MBS Milk Blue Slag, MG Mint Green, MGO Mint Green Opalescent, MW Milk White, NG Nile Green, O Olive, OCS Opal Custard Slag, OL Old Lavender, OP Opalescent, OPS Opalescent Slag, OW Opal White, P Persimmon, PB Peach Blo, PBL Pigeon Blood, PC Peach Clear, PD Persimmon Dark, PG Pine Green, PNK Pink, R Red, RBY Ruby, RM Rose Marie, RS Ruby Sapphire, RUB Rubina (Early), S Sapphire, SH Smoky Heather, SS Sunset, T Taffeta, TE Teal, TOM Tomato, TOP Topaz, V Vaseline, WB Willow Blue, WBL Wonder Blue, WG Willow Green, WGS Willow Green Slag.

ITEM	COLOR(S)	YEAR	ORIG	NEW
Boot.	AD, AL, AM, AMB, BB	1952	X	
	COB, C, CH, CT, CUSD	1952	X	
	CUSL, CUSS, EG, FG	1952	X	
	MB, MW, OP, OW, P, PB	1952	X	
	PG, PNK, R, RBY, RM	1952	X	
	S, SS, T, V, WG	1952	X	
Hat, with brimmed rim.	A, AD, AG, AM, AMB, AQ	1947	X	
	CA, COB, C, CT, CUS	1947	X	
	CSD, CSL, ELI, FG, FJ	1947	X	
	G, MB, MW, NG, OP, P, PB	1947	X	
	R, RM, RUB, RS, T, TOP	1947	X	
	V	1947	X	
Shoe or slipper.				
Bow.	A, AD, AG, AMB, AMD	1947	X	
	AML, BB, BBO, BG, BJS	1947	X	
	BMS, BS, BSS, BWS, C	1947	X	
	CB, CCL, CH, COB, CRD	1947	X	
	CRL, CSD, CSL, CT, CUS	1947	X	
	DG, EB, EG, F, FG, G	1947	X	
	GLD, HE, LOS, MB, MBO	1947	X	
	MBS, MGO, MW, O, OCS	1947	X	
	OL, OP, P, PB, PBL, PC	1947	X	
	PG, PNK, RM, RS, SH, SS	1947	X	
	T, TE, V, WG, WGS	1947	X	
Cat.	A, ACS, AD, AM, AMB, AQ	1947	X	
	AUT, BB, BBO, BBS, BG	1947	X	
	BLBS, BM, C, CAN, CG	1947	X	
	COB, CP, CRD, CRL, CSD	1947	X	
	CSL, CT, CUS, ED, EG	1947	X	
	ELI, FG, FJ, GS, GGS	1947	X	
	HA, HB, HE, HG, I, IS	1947	X	
	IV, J, JA, LC, MB, MG	1947	X	
	MGO, MW, OP, OPS, P, PB	1947	X	
	PBL, PD, PG, PNK, RM	1947	X	
	RS, SH, SS, T, TOM, V	1947	X	
	WB, WBL, WG, WGS	1947	X	
Toothpick holder, three-legged.	A, AG, AM, AMB, BB, BBS	1970	X	
	BS, C, CDC, COB, CP, CR	1970	X	
	CT, DI, ELI, F, FG, HE	1970	X	
	LC, MB, MW, MG, OP, PB	1970	X	
	PNK, S, TOM, V	1970	X	
Wine.	A, AM, C, CDC, CO, CT	1970	X	
	MB, OP, OW, S, SS, V	1970	X	

CHART 24 DAISY AND BUTTON. Fenton Art Glass Company, Williamstown, West Virginia.
CMN: Daisy and Button.
Mark: Unmarked, embossed Fenton logo or "OV," or paper label.
Color Code: A Amber, AM Amethyst, AR Antique Amber, BA Blue Satin, BG Opaque Blue, BJ Blue Jade, BP Blue Pastel, BR Burmese, CA Colonial Amber, CB Colonial Blue, CCG Cape Cod Green, CG Colonial Green, CN Carnival, CO Cameo Opalescent, CR Cranberry, CT Custard, CU Custard Satin, CY Clear, DK Dusty Rose, EO Minted Cream, FA Satin, FB Federal Blue, FO French Cream, GA Green Satin, GLD Gold, GP Green Pastel, JO Jonquil Yellow, LB Light Blue, LS Lime Sherbert, MI Milk White, OK Dusty Rose Transparent, OO Provincial Blue Opalescent, OR Orange, P Pink, PE Shell Pink, PH Sunset Peach Transparent, PW Periwinkle Blue Transparent, RA Rose Satin, RB Royal Blue, RP Rose Pastel, RU Ruby, TU Turquoise, UO Peaches N Cream, V Vaseline, WT Wisteria.

ITEM	COLOR(S)	YEAR	ORIG	NEW
Ashtray. #1976. Leaf shape, flat.	CA, CB, CG	1968		X
Basket.				
Hat, applied handle.				
#1930. 10½", ruffled rim.**	CA, CB, CG, OR, MI	1973		X
#1934. 4"h.	CY, MI	1953		X
#1935. 5"h.**	CA, CB, CG, OR	1973		X
	MI	1955		X
#1936. 6"h.**	CA, CB, CG, OR	1973		X
	CY, MI	1953		X
Low, footed, ruffled, 5"h.,				
#1953. Pressed handle.	CY, MI	1953		X
Oval, flat, twig handles.				
#1939.	CA, CB, CG, MI, OR	1965		X
	RU	1982		X
#1958. 8".**	CA, CB, CG, OR, MI	1973		X
Bell.				
#1966.	BA, CS, CU, LS	1981		X
	CN	1971		X
#1967.**	BG, CT	1976		X
	CA, CB, CG, MI, OR	1973		X
	CO	1980		X
	FB	1983		X
	RU	1982		X
#1976.	CY	1985		X
#3667.	CA, CB, CG, MI	1975		X
Boot.				
#1990. High heel.	BJ, JO	1968	X	
	CO	1971	X	
	LS	1973	X	
#1994. Childs.**	BP, GP, RP	1954	X	
	CA, CB, OR	1973	X	
	CG	1969	X	
	CN	1971	X	
	CY, MI	1953	X	
Bottle, perfume, matching patterned stopper. (from vanity set).	A, P	1937		X
Bowl, open.				
#1920. Square, 10½".	AR	1959*	X	
	MI	1953	X	
#1921. Oval.**	BG, CT	1976	X	
	CA, CB, CG, OR, MI	1973	X	
	CO, CY	—	X	
#1922. Footed.	MI	1954		X
#1924. Footed.	MI	1954		X
#1925. Round, flat, ruffled rim. 10½"d.**	CA, CB, CG, OR, MI	1973		X
	CO, CY	—		X
#1926. Footed.	MI	1954		X
#1927. Cupped 7"d.**	MI	1953		X
	TU	1956*		X
	CA, CB, CG, OR, MI	1973		X

ITEM	COLOR(S)	YEAR	ORIG	NEW
#1929. Oval, 9"l.**	CA, CB, CG, OR	1973	X	
	MI	1953	X	
	TU	1956*	X	
#3124. 11"d.	RS	1953*	X	
Box, covered, round, vanity.	A, P	1937		X
Candleholder.				
#1970. Single light.**	BG, CT	1976		X
	CA, CB, CG, OR	1973		X
	CO, CY	—		X
	MI	1953		X
#1974. two-light.	AR	1959*		X
	MI	1955		X
Creamer. #1903. Footed, butterfly handle.**	CA, CB, CG, OR	1969		X
	CY, MI	1953		X
	LB	1938		X
Cruet. #2063.	BA, RA	1953	X	
Cup and saucer. #1900. Butterfly handle.	LB	1938		X
Dish. #1937. Bonbon, 5½"h.	CY, MI	1953	X	
Hat.				
Brimmed, flat.				
#1991. No. 1. (Toothpick).	A, CB, CCG, CY, GLD	1937	X	
	LB, RB, V, WT	1937	X	
	MI	1953	X	
#1992. No. 2. (Spoonholder).**	CA, CB, CG, OR	1973	X	
	CN	1971	X	
	CT	—	X	
	CY, MI	1953	X	
#1993. No. 3. (Salt).	CY, MI	1953	X	
	LB	1938	X	
Ruffled rim.				
#1953. 3"h.	CY	1953		X
#1954. 4"h.	CY	1953		X
Lamp.				
Fairy.				
#2090. Electrified, boudoir.	BA, FA, GA, RA	1953		X
#2090. With candleholder.	BA, FA, GA, RA	1953		X
Hurricane.				
#2098.	BA, FA, GA, RA	1953		X
#3198.	RS	1953		X
Plate. 7½"d., round.	LB	1938	X	
Salt shaker. #1906.**	CA, CB, CG, OR, MI	1973	X	
Slipper, with cat's head.				
#1900.	A, CB, CCG, CY	1937	X	
	GLD, RB, V, WT	1937	X	
	RBY	1970	X	
#1995.**	BG, CT	1976	X	
	BR	—	X	
	CA, CB, CG, OR	1973	X	
	CN	1971	X	
	CO	—	X	
	CY	1953	X	
	DK	1988	X	
	EO, OO, UO	1986	X	
	FB	1983	X	
	MI	1954	X	
	PE	1988	X	

ITEM	COLOR(S)	YEAR	ORIG	NEW
Sugar bowl, table-size.				
Flat, tab-handled.				
#1930. Open.	CN	1982	X	
#1980. Covered.	BJ	1968	X	
	CA, CB, CG	1967	X	
	CY	1981	X	
	FB	1983	X	
	JO	1968	X	
Footed, butterfly handles.				
#1903. Open.**	CA, CB, CG, OR	1969		X
	CY, MI	1953		X
	LB	1937		X
Toothpick holder. #3795.	A, B, G, MI, OR	1975	X	
Tray, fan-shaped. #957.	A, AM, CB, CCG, CY	1937		X
	GLD, P, RB, V, WT	1937		X
Vase.				
#1050. 7"h.**	CA, CB, CG, OR, MI	1973		X
#1900. Fan, footed, 10"h.	CB, CCG, CY, GLD	1937		X
#1953. 3"h.	MI	1953		X
#1954. 4"h.	MI	1953		X
#1955. footed.	MI	1954		X
#1956. 6"h.	MI	1953		X
#1957. 7"h., footed.	BP, GP, RP	1954		X
	MI	1953		X
	TU	1955		X
#1959. 9"h., footed, fan.**	AR	1959*		X
	BP, GP, RP	1954		X
	CA, CB, CG, OR	1973		X
	MI	1953		X
	TU	1955		X
#3151. 11"h.	GS, RS	1953*		X
#3152. 8½"h.	GS, RS	1953*		X
#3153. 8½"h.	GS, RS	1953*		X
#3154. 4½"h.	GS, RS	1953*		X
#3156. 6"h.	GS, RS	1953*		X
#3157. 7½"h.	RS	1953*		X
#3159. 8"h.	GS, RS	1953*		X
#3160. 5"h.	CR	1953		X
#3252. 8"h.	CR	1954		X
#3253. 6"h.	CR	1954		X
#3255. 5"h.	CR	1954		X
Hand with cornucopia.	CB, CY, WT, V	1937	X	

*Year in which item was discontinued.
**These items in Daisy and Button were added to Fenton's "Olde Virginia Glass" line in 1969. Prior to 1970, each was marked with only a green and white paper label, which read "Olde Virginia Glass Handmade" with the figures of a colonial man and woman. From 1970 until 1979, when the line was discontinued, each item was permanently embossed "OV" (an "O" between the opening of a "V")

CHART 25 DAISY AND BUTTON. Imperial Glass Company, Bellaire, Ohio.
CMN: Daisy and Button.
Mark: Unmarked, embossed "IG," or paper label.
Color Code: C Clear, EG Emerald Green, MY Mustard Yellow, SP Siamese Pink.

ITEM	COLOR(S)	YEAR	ORIG	NEW
Basket, oval, flat, pressed handle. 8".	BM, EG, MY, SP	1959		X
Server.				
Broombox, wishbone-shape, covered.	C	1959		X
Whiskbroom-shape, 7½".	C	1959	X	
Vase, fan-shaped, footed.				
Smooth rim, 8"h.	C	1959		X

CHART 26   DAISY AND BUTTON. Indiana Glass Company, Dunkirk, Indiana.
CMN: Daisy and Button.
Mark: Unmarked.
Color Code: C Clear, GA Golden Amber, MB Matt Black, MBL Matt Blue, MG Milk Glass, MP Matt Pink,
OL Olive, TA Translucent Amber, TB Translucent Blue, TR Translucent Red.

ITEM	COLOR(S)	YEAR	ORIG	NEW
Snack set, cup and triangular plate.	C, GA, OL	1965		X
Top Hat, toothpick. 3¼"h, 2¾" deep.	C, MG, MBL, MG	1965	X	
	MP, TA, TB, TR	1965	X	

CHART 27   DAISY AND BUTTON. Kanawha Glass Company, Kanawha, West Virginia.
CMN: Daisy and Button.
Mark: Unmarked or paper label.
Color Code: A Amber, AZ Azure, C Clear, ED End of Day, MW Milk White, VG Vintage Green.

ITEM	COLOR(S)	YEAR	ORIG	NEW
Slipper, 5½". #810.	AM, AZ, VG	1976	X	
	C, ED, MW	1974	X	

CHART 28   DAISY AND BUTTON. John E. Kemple Glass Works, Kenova, West Virginia.
CMN: Daisy and Button.
Mark: Unmarked, embossed "K," or paper label.
Color Code: B Blue

ITEM	COLOR(S)	YEAR	ORIG	NEW
Slipper, kitten.	B	1967	X	

CHART 29   DAISY AND BUTTON. Mosser Glass, Inc., Cambridge, Ohio.
CMN: Daisy and Button.
Mark: Unmarked or paper label.
Color Code: A Amber, AM Amethyst, B Blue, C Clear, G Green.

ITEM	COLOR(S)	YEAR	ORIG	NEW
Bell. #145	A, AM, B, C, G	1976		X
Candleholder, #144. Top-hat shape.	A, AM, B, C, G	1976		X

CHART 30   DAISY AND BUTTON. Pilgrim Glass Corp., Ceredo, West Virginia.
CMN: Daisy and Button.
Mark: Unmarked.
Color Code: BM Blue Milk, V Vaseline.

ITEM	COLOR(S)	YEAR	ORIG	NEW
Hat. #454. Brimmed rim.	BM, V	1969	X	
Slipper.				
#450. Cat.	BM, V	1969	X	
#455. Bow.	BM, V	1969	X	

CHART 31   DAISY AND BUTTON. L.E. Smith Glass Company, Mount Pleasant, Pennsylvania.
CMN: Daisy and Button.
Mark: Unmarked or paper label.
Color Code: C Clear, BO Blue Opalescent, CO Cranberry Opalescent, MGO Mint Green Opalescent, MW Milk White.

ITEM	COLOR(S)	YEAR	ORIG	NEW
Ashtray, 6"d.	C	1975		X
Bowl, open.				
Collared, 6"d., round, crimped rim.	C	1975		X
Flat.				
Crimped rim, 6"d.	BO, CO, MGO	1975		X
6-sided, 5½"d.	C	1975		X
Four-legged, oval, 6½"l.	C	1975		X
Butter dish, covered, 8½"l., quarter-pound.	C	1975		X
Candy box, covered.				
Collared base, 6"h.	C	1975	X	
Footed, 7½"h.	BO, CO, MGO	1975		X
Low standard, 7"h.	C	1975		X
Canister, covered, flat. 4 sizes—1, 2, 3½, & 5 pound.	C	1975		X
Hat, salt dip, 2⅜" deep, 2½"h.	C	1975	X	
	MW	1961	X	
Kettle, 3-legged.				
Wire handle, toothpick.	C, MW	1961	X	
Ashtray, 2¾"d., 2⅛"h.	MW	1961		X
Lamp, oil. 12"h.				
Clear or matching designed shade.	C	1963	X	
Salt shaker. 4"h.	C	1975	X	
Slipper.	C	1975	X	
Toothpick holder.	C	1975	X	
Votive light.	C	1975		X

CHART 32   DAISY AND BUTTON. Summit Art Glass Company, Rootstown, Ohio.
CMN: Daisy and Button.
Mark: Unmarked or paper label.
Color Code: COB Cobalt Blue

ITEM	COLOR(S)	YEAR	ORIG	NEW
Butter dish, helmet shape. (limited edition of 500)	COB	1985	X	

CHART 33   DAISY AND BUTTON. Viking Glass Company, New Martinsville, West Virginia.
CMN: Daisy and Button.
Mark: Unmarked or paper label.
Color Code: C Clear, LI Lilac, PK Pink.

ITEM	COLOR(S)	YEAR	ORIG	NEW
Glimmer. #7421. Tall, flat.	C, LI, PK	1983		X
Plate, round, smooth rim.				
#8271. 9"d.	C	1982	X	
#8272. 10"d.	C	1982	X	

CHART 34   DAISY AND BUTTON. L.G. Wright Glass Company, New Martinsville, West Virginia.
CMN: Daisy and Button.
Mark: Unmarked.
Color Code: A Amber, AM Amethyst, AS Amber Satin, AMB Amberina, B Blue, BM Blue Milk, BS Blue
Satin, C Clear, COB Cobalt Blue, CUS Custard, G Green, GS Green Satin, P Pink, PS Pink Satin, PRP Purple,
RBY Ruby, V Vaseline, VO Vaseline Opalescent, VS Vaseline Satin.

ITEM	COLOR(S)	YEAR	ORIG	NEW
Ashtray, flat.				
Fan shape.				
#22-2. 4″ × 5″.	A, AM, B, G	1968		X
Square, cut corners.				
#22-3. 6″.	A, AM, AMB, B, C, G, P	1968		X
	RBY, V	1968		X
Basket. #22-4. Flat, applied handle, straight-sided, fan-shaped rim.				
5″w., 7¼″h.	A, AM, B, G	1968		X
	C	1972		X
	GS	1971		X
	V	1969		X
Bell.	RBY	1976		X
Bowl.				
Oval, 4-toed.				
#22-7. 10″d., 5″h.	A, AM, AMB, B, G, P	1968		X
	V	1969		X
#22-8. 5″d., 2½″h.	A, AM, AMB, B, G, P	1968		X
	AS, VS	1971		X
	C	1977		X
	R	1975		X
	V, VO	1969		X
Round.				
Covered, "Bell"-shaped lid.				
#22-70. 6½″d., 8½″h.	A, B, C	1968		X
	G, V	1969		X
	RBY	1975		X
Open, scalloped rim. Low circular foot.				
#22-5. 6″d., 3¼″h.	A, AM, AMB, B, G	1968		X
	P	1974		X
Shell-shaped, footed.				
#22-10. Large.	A, AM, AMB, B, G	1968		X
#22-72. Small.	A, AMB, C	1968		X
Star-shaped. #22-11.	A, AM, AMB, B, G	1968		X
	P, V	1969		X
Butter dish, covered, flat.				
Flanged base, inverted bell lid. #22-70. 6½″d., 8½″h.	A, B, C	1968		X
	G, V	1969		X
	RBY	1975		X
Oval. #22-12. Circular finial. 8½″l., 4½″h., serrated.	A, B, P	1968	X	
Candleholder. #22-14. 4-toed. 5″d.	A, AM, B, G, P, V	1968		X
	VO	1969		X
Canoe. #22-16. Flat, pointed ends. 11½″l. × 3½″w.	A, AM, AMB, B	1968	X	
Castor or pickle jar. #22-36. Metal lid, straight-sided, 7″h., 3″d.	A, AMB, B	1968	X	
	C, COB, G, V	1969	X	
	AM, BS	1974	X	
	VS	1971	X	
Compote, covered.				
#22-17. Low standard, 4″d., 6½″h.	A, AM, AMB, B, G, P	1968	X	
	AS, GS	1971	X	
	C	1969	X	
	COB	1974	X	
#22-20. Domed, patterned base. 6″d., 7¼″h.	A, AM, AMB, B, G, P	1968	X	

ITEM	COLOR(S)	YEAR	ORIG	NEW
Console set, 3-piece, 4-legged, large bowl and two smaller bowls.	A, AM, AMB, B, G, P	1969		X
Creamer. #22-23. Square-shaped, flat handle, 3"sq., 3½"h.	A, B, P, V	1968		X
	VO	1969		X
Cruet. #22-25. Bulbous, flat base, pyramid stopper, 6 oz., 6½"h.	A, AM, B	1968	X	
	C	1969	X	
Flower bowl and block, 4"d., low circular foot, patterned lid.	A, AM, AMB, B, C, G	1969		X
Goblet. #22-29. Plain flat stem. 6¼"h., 8 oz.	A, B	1968	X	
	P	1969	X	
	AS, V	1971	X	
Lamp, electric.	C	1978		X
Nappy. #22-35. Flat, square handle, triangular, 6½" × ¾"h.	A, B, P	1968	X	
Pitcher, water.	C	1976	X	
Plate, round, scalloped rim.				
#22-39. 10"d.	A, B, P, V	1968	X	
	VO	1969	X	
	VS	1971	X	
#22-41. 8"d.	A, B, P	1968	X	
Rose bowl. #22-44. Bulbous, ruffled rim, low circular foot, 4"d., 3¼"h.	A, AM, AMB, B, G	1968	X	
	AS, BS	1971	X	
	COB	1974	X	
Salt dip, flat, individual.				
#22-45. Round, straight-sided.	A, AM, B, G, RBY	1968	X	
#22-46. Triangular.	A, AM, B, G, P, RBY	1968	X	
	PRP	1969	X	
Salt shaker, flat, 2½"h. #22-47. straight-sided.	A, AM, B, G	1968	X	
	AMB	1969	X	
Sauce dish.				
Flat.				
#22-50. Square, 4".	V	1968	X	
	VO	1969	X	
#22-51. Star-shaped, 5"d., 1"h.	A, AM, AMB, B, C, G	1968	X	
Footed, oval, 5"d., 4-toed.	C	1977		X
	V	1971		X
Sherbert, footed, ball stem. #22-52. 3¾"sq.	A, B, P	1968		X
Sleigh.				
#22-54. Berry bowl, 7½"l., 5"h. with or without candleholder.	A, B, C, P, RBY	1968		X
	PRP	1969		X
#22-55. Small, 5"h., 7½"d., with candle insert.	A, B, C, P	1968		X
	G	1969		X
	RBY	1974		X
#22-56. Master berry bowl. 11½"l., 6¼"w.	A, B, C, P	1968	X	
	G	1974	X	
	PRP	1969	X	
Slipper, kitten.				
#22-58. Medium.	A, AM, B, G, P, RBY	1968	X	
	BM, CUS	1969	X	
#22-59. Small.	A, AM, B, G, P, RBY	1968	X	
	AMB, BM, CUS	1969	X	

ITEM	COLOR(S)	YEAR	ORIG	NEW
Spoonholder. #22-60. Scalloped rim, flat, 3"d., 4¾"h.	A, AMB, B	1968	X	
	C, V	1971	X	
Sugar bowl, #22-24. Square handles, open, 3"sq., 3½"h.	A, B, P, V	1968		X
	VO	1969		X
Toothpick holder.				
#22-62. Fan-shaped, 4"h.	V	1968		X
	VO	1969		X
#22-63. Round, straight-sided, 3-legged, 2½"h.	A, AM, AMB, B, G, P, V	1968	X	
	VO	1969	X	
#22-64. Triangular.	A, AM, AMB, B, G, RBY	1968	X	
Gypsy kettle, wire handle.	A, C, V	1974	X	
Wine, 4 oz.	A, AM, B, C, G, P, RBY, V	1969	X	

CHART 35 DAISY AND BUTTON. Metropolitan Museum of Art, New York, New York.
Maker: Unknown.
CMN: Daisy and Button.
Mark: Embossed "MMA."
Color Code: CAN Canary

ITEM	COLOR(S)	YEAR	ORIG	NEW
Pickle tray.				
#F1432. Yacht shape, 4½"l.	CAN	1977	X	

improperly mixed do original colors appear cloudy or muddy. Molds, developed to the height of perfection, produced items that are thin-bodied and thus light. Most important, craftsmanship produced a pattern that may be considered sharp and crisp.

Today, Daisy and Button enjoys a popularity that rivals its original production. An astounding number of tableware and novelty items from the early 1930s has entered the market. These reproductions are enumerated in Charts 21 through 35. Foremost

Fig. 94. Reproduction No.22–56 Daisy and Button sleigh-shaped master berry bowl. L.G. Wright Glass Co. Circa 1982. Unmarked.

Fig. 95. Reproduction Daisy and Button tab-handled covered sugar bowl. Fenton Art Glass Co. Circa 1968. (This is a direct copy of the original by Hobbs, Brockunier & Co.)

Fig. 96. Reproduction Daisy and Button No.4624 covered candy box. L.E. Smith Glass Co. Circa 1975. Signed with a paper label.

Fig. 97. Reproduction Daisy and Button bell. Moser Glass, Inc. Circa 1976. Unmarked.

Fig. 98. Reproduction 12-inch-high Daisy and Button oil lamp. L.E. Smith Glass Co. Circa 1975. Unmarked.

in the pattern's production is the L.G. Wright Glass Company of New Martinsville, West Virginia, although variations of the pattern have been issued by nearly every contemporary glass factory, including

Clevenger Brothers, Crystal Art Glass (under both the Boyds and the Degenharts), Fenton (Fig. 95), Imperial, Indiana, Kanawha, Kemple, Mosser, Pilgrim, Smith (Fig. 96), Summit, and Viking.

Unlike Lion, Three Face, and Westward Ho, patterns issued as genuine reproductions, a vast majority of Daisy and Button items have been introduced to meet the demands of contemporary life-styles. New colors, such as amethyst, azure, pink, and translucent red, and forms unknown to our Victorian ancestors, such as ashtrays, bells, snack trays, and votive lights, have all been developed to spark consumer interest (Figs. 97 and 98).

When you compare modern Daisy and Button items with originals, you will see a number of revealing differences between them. New items are thick and heavy, colors are harsh and artificial, and a majority of forms are modern. When you examine new items, you will also notice a distinct difference in the quality of the glass. Unlike the clear, smooth finish of originals, the surface of reproductions is crinkled and wavy. This defect, existing on both the patterned and unpatterned surface of new items, can easily be detected when you examine the reproductions under bright light. New items also feel slick or oily. Because Daisy and

Button has been copiously produced throughout the twentieth century, new items also differ in the treatment of bases, finials, handles, and stems.

Perhaps the easiest way to detect reproductions is to acquaint yourself with the original colors and forms. You will find a number of excellent reference books listed in the Bibliography.

Hint: Original items are well pressed and sharp.

DAISY AND BUTTON WITH NARCISSUS

Daisy and Button with Narcissus is an interesting variation of the Daisy and Button family. A later pattern produced from about 1910 until the mid-1920s, it was originally issued in a medium-sized table service by the Indiana Glass Company of Dunkirk, Indiana, as pattern No.124. Issued in a medium-quality nonflint glass in clear and clear with cranberry staining, Daisy and Button with Narcissus has also been referred to as Daisy and Button with Clear Lily.

Although a member of the Daisy and Button group, Daisy and Button with Narcissus has as its main design element large, clear lilylike flowers and foliage against a Daisy and Button background.

To date, the only items reproduced in Daisy and Button with Narcissus are the wine glass and a variety of sizes of flat oval bowls and vases (Fig. 99). These items have been produced from new molds and are most readily found in amber, dark blue, clear, green, and yellow. Unlike originals, reproductions are thick-walled and heavy. The pattern is often blurred and muddy in appearance. Like most reproductions, the design is poorly executed, lacking the refined detail of the old pieces.

Reproductions in Daisy and Button with Narcissus are not signed. However, from the look of the glass, they appear to be a product of the late 1930s.

Fig. 99. Reproduction Daisy and Button with Narcissus clear wine. Unmarked.

Hint: Reproductions are heavy and colors are harsh and muddy in appearance.

Reproduced items: Oval bowls, vases, wine.

DAISY AND BUTTON WITH THUMBPRINT PANEL

The Daisy and Button pattern was so popular in America throughout the last quarter of the nineteenth century that a majority of glass houses that manufactured pressed-glass tableware issued a variation of the pattern. The firm of Adams & Company of Pittsburgh, Pennsylvania, issued the pattern known today by collectors and dealers as Daisy and Button with Thumbprint Panel. Originally produced by Adams in 1886 as its No.86 line, the pattern continued to be produced after 1891 under the United States Glass Company (Fig. 100). This pattern is also known as Daisy and Button with Amber Stripes, Daisy and Button with Thumbprint, and Daisy and Button Thumbprint.

Daisy and Button with Thumbprint Panel was originally produced from a good-quality nonflint glass in clear, amber, blue, and vaseline (Fig. 101). It was also made in clear combined with amber, blue, and pink stain. Clear with ruby stain, solid green, or any other color is rare. A complete table service was originally offered in each color.

As late as 1968, the L.G. Wright Glass Company of New Martinsville, West Virginia, began producing a number of items in Daisy and Button with Thumbprint Panel in

Fig. 101. Original clear with blue stain Daisy and Button with Thumbprint Panels goblet. Adams & Co. Circa 1891.

Fig. 102. Reproduction Daisy and Button with Thumbprint Panels goblet. L.G. Wright Glass Co. Circa 1969. Unmarked. (Unlike originals, the decoration on new goblets is painted and can be easily removed.)

Fig. 100. United States Glass Co. circa 1891 catalog illustrating an assortment of Daisy and Button with Thumbprint Panels.

CHART 36 DAISY AND BUTTON WITH THUMBPRINT. L.G. Wright Glass Company, New Martinsville, West Virginia.

CMN: Daisy and Button with Thumbprint.
Mark: Unmarked.
Color Code: A Amber, AM Amethyst, AMB Amberina, AS Amber Stain, B Blue, C Clear, CPP Clear with Painted Panels, G Green, MW Milk White, P Pink, RBY Ruby, V Vaseline.

ITEM	COLOR(S)	YEAR	ORIG	NEW
Goblet. #22-30. Double-knob stem, 6"h., 8 oz.	A, AM, AMB, B, C, G, P	1968	X	
	AS	1969	X	
	CPP	1976	X	
	RBY, V	1968	X	
Lamp. Electric.				
#591. Brass base, D&B font, 19"h., 12"d. shade with metal band.	A	1969		X
#592. Brass base, D&B font, 19"h., tulip shade.	A, G	1969		X
#594. Gothic base, D&B font, metal connector, 24"h. 12" Tapered D&B half-shade, metal band.	MW	1969		X
#597. Brass base, D&B font, 19"h, ball shade.	G	1969		X
Pitcher. #22-37D. Water.	B	1974	X	
	CPP	1976	X	
Wine, #22-69, 4 oz., 4¾"h.	A, AM, AMB, B, G, P, RBY	1968	X	
	CPP	1976	X	
	V	1968	X	

both original and contemporary colors and forms (see Chart 36 and Fig. 102). Unfortunately, it is not known if Wright used original molds. However, it is relatively easy to distinguish the original items from reproductions. Although reproduced in all original colors, items in amethyst, amberina, ruby, or any other contemporary color are new. Unlike original solid-colored items, Wright colors are too deep or harsh and look artificial. Clear with color-stained items are poorly decorated; the color is painted rather than fired onto the surface of the glass. Like most reproductions, new items are heavy and often feel oily or slick. The most obvious difference between old and reproduced items is that old items are crisply molded with the design standing in high relief, while reproductions are blurred and feel smooth.

L.G. Wright reproductions of Daisy and Button with Thumbprint Panel are not permanently marked.

Hint: Reproduction items are heavier and the design is smooth.

DAISY AND CUBE

As figural and naturalistic patterns waned in popularity throughout the last quarter of the nineteenth century, renewed interest in cut glass began to be reflected in pressed-glass tableware and novelty items. Numerous new designs based on the age-old method of hand cutting glass gained in popularity in the form of geometric motifs. The Daisy and Cube pattern is a classic example of this new design.

Also known as Evangeline, Stars and Bars, and Stars and Bars with Leaf, Daisy and Cube consists of alternating bands of clear vertical bars and rectangular daisy-cut motifs. These bands are separated by a large clear band of vertical bars. Finials are square and carry the same design.

Originally produced in an extended table service in amber, blue, clear, and canary yellow by the Bellaire Goblet Company of Bellaire, Ohio, as the No.600 line, the line also included a four-piece novelty child's table set.

In the late 1930s and early 1940s, the first reproductions appeared in Daisy and Cube. The miniature oil lamp in amberina, amber, blue, clear, and canary yellow (Fig. 103) entered the market at this time. This lamp was followed by the goblet (in marble and milk white), which was apparently made from the same mold as the lamp. Some time later, the wine in the original colors of amber, blue, clear, and vaseline became available.

In 1968, the L.G. Wright Glass Company of New Martinsville, West Virginia, produced a number of items in Daisy and Cube. These items are listed in Chart 37. Wright characteristically used a number of original colors, including amber, blue, and clear as well as the contemporary colors of amberina, green, and ruby red (Fig. 105).

Fig. 104 shows an interesting Wright treatment of the pattern. Known as the Black Forest or Deer Hunt design, the design was etched onto the bowls of the high-standard open compote and goblet which were available in amber, blue, clear, green, and ruby red.

In general, due to their thickness, reproductions in Daisy and Cube are heavier than originals. Colors are harsh and artificial rather than soft and mellow. When new

Fig. 103. Grouping of No.77-45 Daisy and Cube 10-inch-high oil lamps. L.G. Wright Glass Co. Circa 1968. Unmarked.

Fig. 104. Reproduction No.77-22 Daisy and Cube clear goblet with "Black Forest" etching. L.G. Wright Glass Co. Circa 1989. Unmarked.

Fig. 105. Reproduction green Daisy and Cube No.77-21-10 goblet with white enamel decoration. L.G. Wright Glass Co. Circa 1971. Unmarked.

CHART 37   DAISY AND CUBE. L.G. Wright Glass Company, New Martinsville, West Virginia.
CMN: Daisy and Cube.
Mark: Unmarked.
Color Code: A Amber, AMB Amberina, B Blue, C Clear, G Green, RBY Ruby.

ITEM	COLOR(S)	YEAR	ORIG	NEW
Compote, open, high standard.				
Scalloped rim, 6"d., 4¾"h.				
#72-1.	A, G, RBY	1969		X
Smooth rim, 6"d., 4¾"h.				
#77-1. Not etched.	A, G, RBY	1968	X	
#77-2. "Black Forest" etching.	A, B, G	1968	X	
Goblet, 7 oz., 6"h.				
#77-21. Not etched.	A, AMB, B, C, G, RBY	1968	X	
#77-22. "Black Forest" etching.	A, B, C, G, RBY	1968	X	
Lamp. #77-45. Night or courting, 10"h.	A, AMB, B, G	1968	X	
Sugar bowl. #77-12. Open.	A	1984		X
Wine. #77-81. 2½ oz., 4½"h.	A, AMB, G, RBY	1968	X	

pieces are rubbed with the tip of the finger, they feel smooth or blunt.

Wright reproductions are not marked.

Hint: Reproductions are heavier and the design is smoother than the the originals.

DAKOTA

Dakota is a member of the states series of pattern glass. Also known as Baby Thumbprint, Etched Band and Baby Thumbprint, and Thumbprint Band, this design was first produced about 1885 by Ripley & Company of Pittsburgh, Pennsylvania. When Ripley merged with the United States Glass Company after 1891 and became Factory "F," it continued manufacturing the pattern.

Dakota has a relatively simple design composed of a clear band of circular thumbprints against a plain background. This band is usually found around the base of each item. Exceptions are the cruet and the salt shaker, which have two bands: the first around the rim and the second around the base. Covers also carry a single band of thumbprints, while finials and stems are sectioned balls of clear glass. This design (similar to a tic-tac-toe board) is also impressed upon the base of each item. Handles are applied.

Dakota was originally produced in a large and extended table service from a good-quality clear and clear with ruby-stained nonflint glass in two distinct forms: (1) a hotel set characterized by ruffled edges and flat bases, and (2) a household set characterized by plain edges and pedestaled, circular bases. Both versions were produced in complete table sets, which were either plain or copper-wheel engraved. Some known engravings are: No.76 (Fern and Berry), No.79 (Fish), No.80 (Fern, Butterfly, and Bird), and No.157 (Oak Leaf). Additional engravings include Bird and Flowers, Bird and Insect, Buzzard, Crane Catching Fish, Fern without Berry, Ivy and Berry, Peacock, Spider and Insect in Web, Stag, Swan, and Vintage Grape. More interesting items include the large cake cover, the flat cake basket with pewter handle, and the cruet set with original patterned stoppers. Cobalt blue or any other color is rare.

To date, only the 11-inch-high tankard water pitcher has been reproduced. As you can see from Fig. 106, this new pitcher is quite convincing. It is the same height as

Fig. 106. Reproduction clear Dakota tankard water pitcher decorated with light cranberry stain. Embossed with an "R" within a shield.

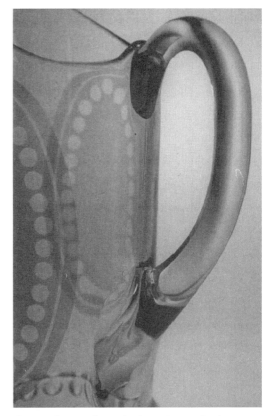

Fig. 107. Closeup of reproduction Dakota tankard water pitcher handle, which is pressed to appear applied.

the original and has a 4½-inch-diameter base. This reproduction is marked and was produced from a new mold in a good-quality clear nonflint glass. Often it has a large oval medallion stained in light cranberry on the sides, while the foot may be clear or stained.

Unlike original tankard pitchers, reproductions have pressed handles (Fig. 107). Although both bases carry the same waffle design, on new pitchers this design is larger and embossed with a capital "R" within a shield (Fig. 108), similar to the mark found on Beaded Grape Medallion reproductions (see Beaded Grape Medallion).

New tankards are also exceptionally thick and heavy and, unlike originals, have three distinct mold lines that run vertically from the base to the rim. One line runs directly through the center of the handle, while the remaining two appear one-third of the way back from the sweep of the lip.

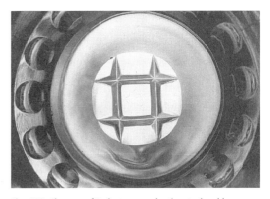

Fig. 108. Closeup of Dakota reproduction tankard base, which is embossed with an "R" within a shield in the center of the waffle design.

Hint: Reproduction tankard pitchers are embossed with an "R" within a shield.

Reproduced items: Tankard water pitcher.

DEER AND PINE TREE

Deer and Pine Tree is a popular pattern in the animal series of pressed glass. It is also known as McKee's Banded Diamond and Deer and Doe. McKee Brothers of Pittsburgh, Pennsylvania, first made this pattern about 1886 from clear nonflint glass in a small table service. Although collectors may find odd pieces in amber, apple green, blue, and canary yellow, complete table sets were not made in color.

Whoever named this pattern could not have been more descriptive. A lifelike deer and doe stand in high relief among foliage and tall pine trees (Fig. 109). Although the design is crisp and detailed, the quality of the glass tends to be mediocre.

Deer and Pine Tree is a safe pattern to collect. To date, only the goblet has been reproduced. New, unmarked goblets appeared as early as 1938 in clear nonflint glass. These are heavier than originals and are decisively yellow when viewed under a strong light. Another copy of the goblet, issued by the L.G. Wright Glass Company of New Martinsville, West Virginia, is illustrated in Fig. 110. Known as item No.77-103 in the Wright 1967 Catalog Supplement,

Fig. 110. Reproduction Deer and Pine Tree No.77-103 clear goblet. L.G. Wright Glass Co. Circa 1971. Unmarked. (Note the lack of detail, especially in the foliage beneath the deer's feet.)

this goblet is also of clear nonflint glass and appears yellow.

Both reproductions were produced from new molds and are quite convincing. Upon close observation, however, you will notice a number of subtle discrepancies. On original goblets, a vine clings to the pine tree. This vine is absent on the new. Unlike reproductions, the design on original goblets contains much more grass and shrubbery, and the trees are larger and more finely detailed than on the new. However, the most obvious difference between original and reproduction goblets is the doe's ear. On old goblets the doe's ear is easily seen, but it is missing on the reproductions.

Reproduction Deer and Pine Tree goblets are not marked.

Hint: Reproduction goblets lack fine detailing of the hairs on the deer's body.

Reproduced items: Goblet.

Fig. 109. Original clear Deer and Pine Tree goblet. McKee Brothers. Circa 1886.

DELAWARE

In its effort to name pressed-glass patterns after states, the United States Glass Company of Pittsburgh, Pennsylvania, christened this design No.15065, or Delaware. Also known as Four Petal Flower or New Century, it was originally produced about 1899 from a good-grade nonflint glass in an extended table service. Original colors are clear, clear with a rose stain, custard (plain or decorated with cold-painted blue, green, or pink), emerald green, and milk white (decorated the same as custard items). Each of these colors may also be trimmed with gold.

As you can see from the Pitkin & Brooks reprint in Fig. 111, Delaware's design consists of sprays of elongated leaves, four-petaled and bell-shaped flowers, buds, and stems—all highly embossed upon a finely stippled background. Handles are pressed, finials are raised, and covers have three-dimensional leaves spreading across their tops. The most interesting items, the covered pomade and puff box, have jeweled covers.

To date, only three items have been re-produced from new molds in Delaware. Covered butter dishes, creamers, and covered sugar bowls in cobalt blue, green, and pink were imported as late as 1991. They are unmarked and originally carried a small paper label printed "Made in Taiwan."

Unlike original items, reproductions are noticeably thick and heavy and the glass is slick or oily. In contrast to the smooth, unevenly stippled surface of originals, reproductions are evenly pitted. Moreover, reproduction finials are elongated and exaggerated. They are in low relief, small, and lack any fine detail. On original pieces, the leaves that form the finials are sharp, well defined, veined, and beautifully serrated. On reproductions they are thick, cumbersome, have no veins, and are bluntly serrated.

Reproductions are not permanently marked but can sometimes be found with a paper label.

Hint: Unlike the smooth stippled surface of originals, the surface of reproductions is pitted.

Reproduced items: Butter dish, creamer, sugar bowl.

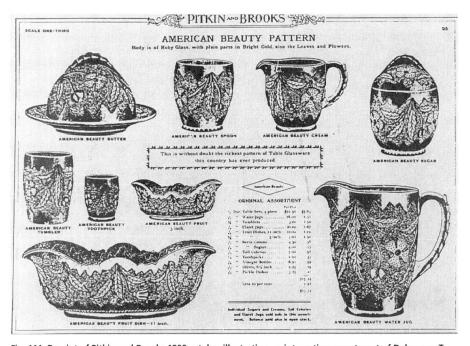

Fig. 111. Reprint of Pitkin and Brooks 1900 catalog illustrating an interesting assortment of Delaware. To date, only the butter dish, creamer, and spoonholder have been reproduced.

DEW AND RAINDROP

Dew and Raindrop is an interesting pattern of the later period of pressed glass. Also known as Dew with Raindrop and Dewdrop and Rain, this pattern was originally produced by a number of glass houses from a lesser-quality nonflint glass than many Victorian patterns. About 1901, the Kokomo Glass Company of Kokomo, Indiana, first issued Dew and Raindrop as its No.50 line. Production was continued in 1914 by the Federal Glass Company of Columbus, Ohio, as its line No.50. The pattern was originally produced in a limited table service from clear nonflint glass. Rare items may be found in clear with gold and clear with amber or ruby stain.

As its name implies, this pattern consists of a single row of large clear, connected ovals against a fine hobnail background (Fig. 112). Stems are of two varieties: (1) plain and (2) covered with tiny dewdrops.

The first reproduction in Dew and Raindrop was the clear wine, which appeared in the early 1930s. Next came solid amber, blue, and clear with light ruby stain cordials, clear sherbert cups, clear goblets, and blue and clear wines. Although unmarked, these items may have been reissued from original molds by the Federal Glass Company.

New items are heavier than the old ones. Unlike originals, which are clear with finely molded dewdrops in high relief, reproductions are gray or muddy and have smooth, low dewdrops. To date, only stemware, without the tiny dewdrops on the stem, has been reproduced.

Fig. 112. Dew and Raindrop original clear wine with amber stain. Kokomo Glass Co. Circa 1901.

Reproductions in Dew and Raindrop are not signed.

Hint: Reproductions have smooth hobnails in low relief.
Reproduced items: Cordial, custard cup, goblet, wine.

DEWBERRY

Dewberry is one of the many late designs typical of early twentieth-century manufacture. This pattern was originally produced about 1905 as line No.375 from a good-quality nonflint glass by the Co-operative Flint Glass Company of Beaver Falls, Pennsylvania. Also known as Blackberry Variant, Kemple's Blackberry, Pointed Blackberry, and Wild Loganberry,

the pattern was originally offered in clear, clear with ruby stain, and milk white. More widely collected in clear with ruby stain than in clear or milk white, Dewberry was first issued in a small table service, which included the standard four-piece table set, the celery vase, and the water pitcher.

The Dewberry design consists of well-molded clusters of large berries on long stems and leaves set against a smooth back-

Fig. 113. Reprint of the Phoenix Glass Co. circa 1937 catalog illustrating a selection of Dewberry.

ground. Handles are pressed and finials are mushroom-shaped.

In 1937, The Phoenix Glass Company of Monaca, Pennsylvania, acquired the original molds for Dewberry, Ivy-in-Snow, Jeweled Moon and Star, and Lacy Dewdrop patterns as a means of satisfying a debt from the bankrupt Co-Operative Flint Glass Company. At this time, all four patterns were reissued from the original molds as Phoenix's "Early American Glass" line (Fig. 113). For the first time, Dewberry was produced in milk white with either a caramel or pearlluster finish (see Blackberry). By 1942, however, Phoenix had discontinued all tableware production and these and other molds were either scraped or sold.

H.M. Tuska of New York City (a distributor of glassware) acquired the molds for all four of these patterns from the Phoenix Glass Company. From these molds, an undetermined number of new items were produced for Tuska by the Westmoreland Glass Company of Grapeville, Pennsylvania, including a teal spoonholder typical of West-

moreland. However, after a number of years of unsuccessfully working these patterns through private pot-work. Tuska sold these molds to the John E. Kemple Glass Works of East Palestine, Ohio. At Kemple, Dewberry was primarily produced in milk white. Upon the closing of the Kemple Glass Works with the death of John Kemple in 1970, the Wheaton Historical Society of Millville, New Jersey, purchased several hundred of the Kemple molds, including Lacy Dewdrop. To date, we have been unable to confirm whether the Dewberry molds were purchased by Wheaton.

The only Dewberry reproductions that may cause concern among collectors and dealers are those made in milk white. Although produced from original molds, they are of a better-quality glass than many other milk-white reproductions. Additionally, Phoenix reproductions (see Chart 39) are always lustered (a technique never used originally); those made by Kemple (see Chart 38) are of a dead white with little, if any, translucence; and Westmoreland repro-

CHART 38   DEWBERRY. John E. Kemple Glass Works, Kenova, West Virginia.
CMN: Blackberry.
Mark: Unmarked, embossed "K," or paper label.
Color Code: MW Milk White.

ITEM	COLOR(S)	YEAR	ORIG	NEW
Bowl, open, round, flat.				
#208. 9"d.	MW	1946	X	
#209. 8"d.	MW	1946	X	
#210. 7"d.	MW	1946	X	
#211. 6"d.	MW	1946	X	
#212. 5"d.	MW	1946	X	
#213. 4"d.	MW	1946	X	
Candlestick, 3½"h.	MW	1946		X
Compote, high standard.				
Covered.				
#202. 5".	MW	1946	X	
Open, high standard.				
#201. 8".	MW	1946	X	
#200. 7".	MW	1946	X	
Creamer. #205. 5"h.	MW	1946	X	
Goblet. #204. 8 oz.	MW	1946	X	
Pitcher. #203. Water, 36 oz.	MW	1946	X	
Plate. #207. Leaf-shaped, 8"l.	MW	1946		X
Sugar bowl. #206. Covered.	MW	1946	X	
Vase.				
#215-1. Cupped rim, 6"h.	MW	1946		X
#215-2. Pinched rim, 6"h.	MW	1946		X
#215-3. Flared rim, 6"h.	MW	1946		X
#215-4. Double, 6"h.	MW	1946		X

CHART 39   DEWBERRY. Phoenix Glass Company, Monaca, Pennsylvania.
CMN: Blackberry.
Mark: Unmarked or paper label.
Color Code: CL Caramel Lustre, PL Pearl Lustre.

ITEM	COLOR(S)	YEAR	ORIG	NEW
Bowl, open, round, flat.				
#925. 4"d.	CL, PL	1937	X	
#926. 6"d.	CL, PL	1937	X	
#927. 8"d.	CL, PL	1937	X	
Compote, high standard.				
Covered. #924. 5"d., 8½"h.	CL, PL	1937	X	
Open. #923. 5"d.	CL, PL	1937	X	
Creamer. #919. 4¾"h.	CL, PL	1937	X	
Goblet. #921. 7 oz.	CL, PL	1937	X	
Pitcher. #922. Water, 36 oz.	CL, PL	1937	X	
Plate. #918. Leaf-shaped, 8"l.	CL, PL	1937	X	
Sugar bowl. #920. Covered, 6½"h.	CL, PL	1937	X	

ductions were made in colors not original to the pattern. When you examine a piece of Dewberry, remember that color is the key factor in determining age.

Phoenix items were never permanently marked. However, occasionally you may find pieces with a paper label. Kemple reproduction items can sometimes be found with a paper label or with an embossed "K."

Hint: Dewberry items have not been reproduced in clear or clear with ruby stain.

DEWDROP

Originally issued from a good-quality clear nonflint glass, little is known of the origin of Dewdrop. By the appearance of available forms, this pattern seems to be a contemporary of Dewdrop and Star, the only difference being that Dewdrop does not have a star center (see Dewdrop and Star).

Contrary to popular belief, Dewdrop is a safe pattern to collect. Although Doris and Peter Unitt list a reproduction goblet in *American and Canadian Goblets, Volume 2*, it is not Dewdrop, but one that was produced by the Imperial Glass Corporation of Bellaire, Ohio (illustrated in its 1966 catalog as "Stamm House Dewdrop Opalescent" glassware). This collection of glass consisted of the Actress, Hobnail, and Hobnail with Fan patterns and was shown in vaseline opalescent glass. Although each item in this collection is marked with the Imperial "IG" logo, there is no resemblance between this pattern and Dewdrop.

If you remember that the original Dewdrop line did not include goblets, you will

Fig. 114. Reproduction Dewdrop goblet. Imperial Glass Corp. Circa 1966. Embossed "IG."

never mistakenly purchase a reproduction in this pattern (Fig. 114).

Hint: A true goblet in Dewdrop was never made.
Reproduced items: Goblet.

DEWDROP AND STAR

Dewdrop and Star is one of the earliest and most popular variations of the Dewdrop family. This pattern was originally designed and patented by Jenkins Jones (design patent Nos.10,296 and 10,297) and was produced by Campbell, Jones & Company of Pittsburgh, Pennsylvania, about 1877 from a good-quality clear nonflint glass. Although goblets and bread plates are known in amber, blue, and canary yellow, any color is rare.

The overall design of this pattern is composed of small pointed hobnails that cover each item. The centers of most pieces are further adorned with a large star made of similar hobnails. An exception is the center of the bread plate, which is a sheaf of wheat.

The first reproduction in Dewdrop and Star, the footed master salt, appeared as early as 1934 (Fig. 115). These salts were produced from a new mold and may be found in the contemporary colors of amethyst, apple green, and salmon pink. Shortly thereafter, baskets were made by applying a solid glass handle to the footed

CHART 40   DEWDROP AND STAR. Crystal Art Glass, Cambridge, Ohio.
CMN: Star and Dew Drop.
Mark: Unmarked or embossed "D" in a heart.
Color Code: A, Amber, AC Amethyst Carnival, AD Amber Dark, AM Amethyst, AMB Amberina, AQ Aqua, BB Bluebell, BP Burnt Persimmon, BWS Blue & White Slag, C Clear, CO Cobalt, CT Crown Tuscan, CU Custard, ELI Elizabeth's Lime Ice, EG Emerald Green, FG Forest Green, HB Heatherbloom, HNB Henry's Blue, IV Ivory, GLD Gold, J Jade, LC Lemon Custard, LMS Lavender Marble Slag, LO Lemon Opal, MB Milk Blue, MW Milk White, OP Opalescent, P Pink, PB Peach Blo, PR Persimmon, R Ruby, RM Rose Marie, SAP Sapphire, SN Snow White, T Teal, TO Tomato, TPZ Topaz, V Vaseline.

ITEM	COLOR(S)	YEAR	ORIG	NEW
Salt, individual, footed. 3³/₁₆"d., 1³/₈"h.	All colors.	1952	X	

master salt. These baskets are also found in a range of contemporary colors. The 7¼-inch-round plate and the round, footed sauce dish in clear and colors appeared next. Early reproductions are not signed, nor are they illustrated in any known contemporary catalog.

In 1952, the Crystal Art Glass of Cambridge, Ohio, first introduced new master salts in Dewdrop and Star in the contemporary colors enumerated in Chart 40. These new salts were produced from a new mold allegedly created by the Cambridge Glass Company of Cambridge, Ohio, for John Degenhart. New salts are unmarked before 1972, when each was embossed with a "D" in a heart trademark.

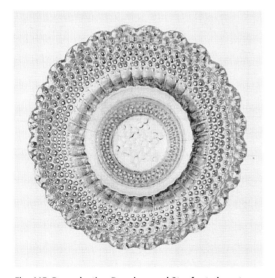

Fig. 115. Reproduction Dewdrop and Star footed master salt. Crystal Art Glass Co. Circa 1952. Unmarked.

In 1969, the Pilgrim Glass Corporation of Ceredo, West Virginia, issued a similar reproduction of the Dewdrop and Star master salt. Known as Star and Dew Drop, it may be found in blue milk glass and vaseline.

After October 1978, Boyd's Crystal Art Glass of Cambridge, Ohio, issued the Dewdrop and Star master salt. This salt was produced from the same mold owned by Crystal Art Glass when this firm was under the ownership of the Degenharts. Boyd's pieces can be found permanently embossed with the company's familiar trademark, "B" in a Diamond. You can find these new salts in the contemporary colors of buttercup, deep purple, ice blue, ice green, impatient, and redwood.

Rims, which are smooth on the original master salts, are scalloped with a ¼-inch indentation on reproductions. However, on plates, rims that are indented on originals slope smoothly toward the center on reproductions.

The easiest way to detect reproductions is by observing the size of the dewdrops. On original pieces, the dewdrops are small, creating a small overall design. This is most noticeable in the size of the star and the hobnail band around the base, both of which are smaller on originals than on reproductions. New pieces are thick-rimmed and heavier than the old.

Hint: Original pieces of Dewdrop and Star were made only in clear glass.

Reproduced items: Basket, plate, master salt, sauce dish.

DEWEY

The original name of this quaint old pattern is Flower Flange. The Indiana Tumbler and Goblet Company of Greentown, Indiana, which originally produced it about 1898, renamed it Dewey to commemorate Admiral Dewey's Spanish-American victories. Later, the Indiana Glass Company of Dunkirk, Indiana, manufactured Dewey until 1904.

Dewey was made from a good-quality nonflint glass in a moderate-sized table service. Although collectors may find items in amber, blue, chocolate, clear, emerald green, Nile green, opaque, vaseline, and a dull yellow-green, complete table sets are not available in all colors.

The only reproduction in Dewey, the large covered butter dish, is illustrated in Fig. 116. This new butter, known as the No.972 Box & Cover, was issued from a new mold by the Imperial Glass Corporation of Bellaire, Ohio, in a number of original and contemporary colors. As early as 1960, re-

productions appeared in milk white and were followed in 1962 by amber, blue, heather, and verde. By 1964, rubigold carnival had appeared and, in 1965, peacock carnival.

As you can see from the illustration, this new butter dish is an excellent copy of the old butter. However, unlike original butters, reproductions are heavier and larger, lids are dome-shaped, and the embossed vine appearing on the vertical bar separating each clear, oval medallion is straight. Whereas the skirting on old butters is sharply scalloped and proportionally indented, on new butters it is irregular and rounded. Like a majority of reproductions, colors are dark, harsh, and artificial.

Reproduction butter dishes are permanently marked on the base and cover with the "IG" trademark of the Imperial Glass Corporation.

Hint: Reproduction butter dishes are always permanently marked "IG."
Reproduced items: Butter dish.

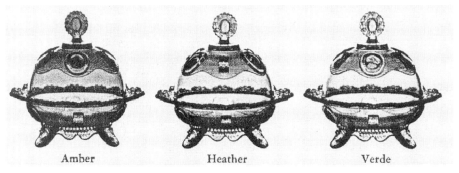

Fig. 116. Assortment of No.972 Dewey colored covered butter dishes. Imperial Glass Corp. Circa 1962. Embossed "IG."

DIAMOND CUT WITH LEAF

Diamond Cut with Leaf is an early American pressed-glass pattern of which little is known. Also referred to as Fine Cut and Leaf, it was originally made in a limited table service from a good-quality clear non-

flint glass. Although collectors may find odd items in amber and blue, any colored piece is rare. From the general characteristics of its design, this pattern seems to be a product of the mid-1880s.

A contemporary of the fine-cut era, the principal design of Diamond Cut with

Fig. 117. Original Diamond Cut with Leaf clear wine.

Leaf consists of large stippled leaves vertically embossed against a fine-cut background. Forms are squat and handles are pressed. The varying quality of the glass (most readily seen in goblets, plates, and wines) suggests more than one manufacturer.

To date, the only items reproduced in Diamond Cut with Leaf are the clear goblet and wine (Fig. 117). Unmarked, each item was produced from new molds as early as 1936. These new goblets and wines are lighter in weight and have a smaller foot than the originals. The design is also lightly pressed and less detailed than on old items. In general, reproductions look new and glisten with a sparkle that is not present in the old. Reproductions are not permanently marked.

Hint: Reproduction items are smaller and lighter than originals.

Reproduced items: Goblet, wine.

DIAMOND POINT

Diamond Point is a highly desirable pattern of the early flint era. It is a brilliant and sparkling design that was originally issued in flint or nonflint glass. This early glass, produced by a number of nineteenth-century glass houses, including the Boston and Sandwich Glass Company of Sandwich, Massachusetts, and the New England Glass Company of Cambridge, Massachusetts (which referred to it as Sharp Diamond), displays a fine belltone quality.

Also known as Diamond Point with Ribs, Grant, Grant Pineapple, Pineapple, Sawtooth, and Stepped Diamond Point, it was originally produced in a large and extended table service. The glass sparkles brilliantly due to the many small diamond points that create the pattern's basic design. Because it was produced over an extended period by a number of companies, an impressive number of forms are available, including more than fifteen open and covered high-stand-

Fig. 118. Reproduction emerald green Diamond Point goblet. Most likely a product of the Jeannette Glass Co. Circa 1930s. Unmarked. (Note the patterned knob stem.)

CHART 41   DIAMOND POINT. Cambridge Glass Company, Cambridge, Ohio.
CMN: Mt. Vernon.
Mark: Paper label or "C" in a triangle.
Color Code: A Amber, C Clear, CR Carmen Red, FG Forest Green, GK Gold Krystol, H Heatherbloom, LEG
Light Emerald Green, RB Royal Blue, T Topaz (vaseline), V Violet.

ITEM	COLOR(S)	YEAR	ORIG	NEW
Ashtray.				
#63. 3½"d.	A, C	1924		X
#68. 4"d.	A, C	1924		X
#71. Oval, 6" × 4½".	A, C	1924		X
Bonbon. #10. Footed. 7"d.	A, C	1924		X
Bottle.				
#18. Toilet, square, 7 oz.	A, C	1924		X
	CR	1931		X
#62. Bitters, 2½ oz.	A, C	1924	X	
#1340. Cologne, original stopper. 2½ oz.	A, C	1924		X
Bowl.				
Oval				
Flat.				
#79. Celery, 10½"l.	A, C	1924		X
#98. Celery, 11"l.	A, C	1924		X
#118. Crimped, 12"l.	A, C	1924		X
#135. 11"l.	A, C	1924		X
Footed.				
#136. 11"l.	A, C	1924		X
Round.				
Flat.				
#6. Fruit, 5¼"d.	A, C	1924	X	
#23. Finger.	A, C	1924		X
#31. Fruit, 4½"d.	A, C	1924	X	
#32. Cereal, 6"d.	A, C	1924	X	
#39. Handled, 10"d.	A, C	1924		X
#43. Deep, 10½"d.	A, C	1924	X	
#44. Flared, 12½"d.	A, C	1924		X
#45. Flanged, rolled edge,				
12½"d.	A, C	1924		X
#61. Shallow, cupped, 11½"d.	A, C	1924		X
#65. Pickle, 8"d.	A, C	1924	X	
#68. Belled, 11½"d.	A, C	1924		X
	FG	1931		X
#76. Preserve, 6"d.	A, C	1924	X	
#105. Sweetmeat, 4 part, handled, 8½"d.	A, C	1924		X
#106. Rose, 6½"d.	A, C	1924		X
#116. Shallow, crimped, 13"d.	A, C	1924		X
#117. Rolled edge, crimped, 12"d.	A, C	1924		X
#120. Salad, 10½"d.	A, C	1924	X	
#121. Flared, 12½"d.	A, C	1924		X
#126. Shallow, 11½"d.	A, C	1924		X
#128. Belled, 11½"d.	A, C	1924		X
#129. Flanged, rolled edge, 12"d.	A, C	1924		X
Box, covered.				
#15. Round, footed, 4½"d.	A, C	1924		X
#16. Round, 3"d.	A, C	1924		X
#17. Square, 4".	A, C	1924		X
	CR	1931		X
#69. Oval, cigarette, 6"l.	A, C	1924		X
Butter tub. #73. Covered.	A, C	1924		X
	FG	1931		X

ITEM	COLOR(S)	YEAR	ORIG	NEW
Cake stand. #150. Low-footed, 10½"d.	A, C	1924		X
Candelabrum. #38. 13½"h.	A, C	1924		X
	H	1931		X
Candlestick.				
#35. 8"h.	A, C	1924	X	
#110. two-light, 5"h.	A, C	1924		X
#130. 4"h.	A, C	1924		X
Candy dish. #9. Covered, footed.	A, C	1924		X
	CR	1931		X
Claret. #25. Square stem, 4½ oz.	A, C	1924		X
	RB	1931		X
Coaster.				
#60. Plain, 3"d.	A, C	1924		X
#70. Ribbed, 3"d.	A, C	1924		X
Cocktail, square stem.				
#26. 3½ oz.	A, C	1924		X
#41. Oyster, 4 oz.	A, C	1924		X
Cocktail icer. #85. 2-piece.	A, C	1924		X
Compote, footed, patterned stem.				
Oval.				
#100. Handled, 9"l.	A, C	1924		X
Round.				
#11. 7½"d.	A, C	1924		X
#33. 4½"d.	A, C	1924		X
#34. Twist stem, 6"d.	A, C	1924		X
	H	1931		X
#77. Handled, 5½"d.	A, C	1924		X
#81. 8"d.	A, C	1924		X
#96. Belled, 6½"d.	A, C	1924		X
#97. 6½"d.	A, C	1924		X
#99. 9½"d.	A, C	1924		X
Creamer.				
#4. Individual.	A, C	1924		X
#8. Footed, pressed handle.	A, C	1924		X
	H	1931		X
#86. Applied handle, 16 oz.	A, C, T	1924		X
Cup and saucer set. #7.	A, C	1924		X
	H	1931		X
Decanter, original stopper.				
#47. 11 oz.	A, C	1924	X	
#52. 40 oz.	A, C	1924	X	
	FG	1931	X	
Goblet. #1. Water, square stem, 10 oz.	A, C	1924		X
	CR	1931		X
Ice bucket. #92. Open.	A, C	1924		X
	CR	1931		X
Ivy ball or rose bowl. #12. Footed, 4½"d.	A, C	1924		X
	FG, H	1931		X
Lamp. #1607. Hurricane, 9"h.	A, C	1924		X
Marmalade or honey. #74. Covered.	A, C	1924		X
	RB	1931		X
Mayonnaise. #107. Divided.	A, C	1924		X

ITEM	COLOR(S)	YEAR	ORIG	NEW
Mug. #84. Stein, applied handle, 14 oz.	A, C, T	1924	X	
	FG, H, RB	1931	X	
	GK	1929	X	
Mustard. #28. Covered, 2½ oz.	A, C	1924		X
	CR, RB	1931		X
Pickle. #78. Handled, 6"l.	A, C	1924		X
Pitcher, applied handle.				
#13. 66 oz.	A, C	1924	X	
	CR, RB	1931	X	
#90. 50 oz.	A, C	1924	X	
#91. 86 oz.	A, C	1924	X	
	CR	1931	X	
#95. Ball shape, 80 oz.	A, C	1924		X
	H	1931		X
Plate.				
#4. Bread and butter, 6"d.	A, C	1924	X	
#5. Salad, 8½"d.	A, C	1924		X
	H	1931		X
#19. Bread and butter, 6⅜"d.	A, C	1924	X	
#23. Finger-bowl liner.	A, C	1924	X	
#37. Tab-handled, 11½"d.	A, C	1924		X
	H	1931		X
#40. Dinner, 10½"d.	A, C	1924		X
Relish.				
#80. 2-part, 12".	A, C	1924		X
#101. 2-part, handled, 8".	A, C	1924		X
#103. 3-part, handled, 8".	A, C	1924		X
	H	1931		X
#104. 5-part, 12".	A, C	1924		X
#106. 2-part, handled, 6".	A, C	1924		X
#200. 3-part, 11".	A, C	1924		X
Salt dip.				
#24. Individual.	A, C	1924	X	
#102. Oval, handled.	A, C, LEG	1924		X
	FG, RB	1931		X
Salt shaker.				
#28.	A, C	1924		X
#88. Short.	A, C	1924		X
#89. Tall.	A, C	1924		X
Sauce boat. #30-445. Handled.	A, C	1924		X
Sherbert, square stem.				
#2. Tall, 6½ oz.	A, C	1924		X
	V	1955		X
#42. Low, 4½ oz.	A, C	1924		X
Sugar.				
#4. Individual.	A, C	1924		X
#8. Footed.	A, C	1924		X
	H	1931		X
#86. Flat.	A, C	1924		X
Toothpick or cigarette holder. #66. Footed, with or without ashtray.	A, C	1924		X
	CR, RB	1931		X
Tray. #4. Small.	A, C	1924		X

ITEM	COLOR(S)	YEAR	ORIG	NEW
Tumbler.				
Flat.				
#51. Table, 10 oz.	A, C	1924	X	
#55. Whiskey, 2 oz.	A, C	1924	X	
#56. 5 oz.	A, C	1924	X	
#57. Old-fashioned, 7 oz.	A, C	1924	X	
#58. Tall, 10 oz.	A, C	1924		X
	FG	1931		X
#59. Tall, 14 oz.	A, C	1924		X
Footed, square stem.				
#3. Water, 10 oz.	A, C	1924		X
	CR	1931		X
#13. Barrel shape, 12 oz.	A, C	1924		X
#14. Barrel shape, 14 oz.	A, C	1924		X
#20. Iced tea, 12 oz.	A, C	1924		X
	CR, FG	1931		X
#21. 5 oz.	A, C	1924		X
#22. Juice, 3 oz.	A, C	1924		X
	CR, FG	1931		X
#87. Cordial, 1 oz.	A, C	1924		X
Vase.				
#42. 5"h.	A, C	1924		X
#46. Footed, 10"h.	A, C	1924		X
#50. Footed, 6"d.	A, C	1924		X
	H	1931		X
#54. Footed, 7"h.	A, C	1924		X
#58. 7"h.	A, C	1924		X
#107. Squat, 6½"h.	A, C	1924		X
#119. Crimped, 6"h.	A, C	1924		X
Wine. #27. Square base, 3 oz.	A, C	1924		X
	FG, RB	1931		X

ard compotes and an array of barware. Moreover, finials, standards, and stems vary greatly.

Reproductions that use the diamond-point motif have been produced since the early 1940s. They are in nonflint glass and contemporary shapes and colors, including blue or white milk, clear, cobalt blue, dark green, purple slag, and ruby.

The only item that may confuse beginning collectors is the goblet illustrated in Fig. 118. As on original goblets, the size of the diamond points decreases from the rim to the base. However, on reproductions, the points are noticeably more blunt than the sharp, crisp impression of the old. These new goblets also have a contemporary shape that does not emulate any known original. Additionally, reproductions feel waxy and have a distinct waviness that cov-

ers the entire pattern. Because they were made from a new mold, they are also extremely heavy. Reproductions are not permanently marked.

The Cambridge Glass Company of Cambridge, Ohio, first produced the Mt. Vernon pattern about 1920, enumerated in Chart 41. Mount Vernon was made in a good-quality nonflint glass. This pattern is similar to the older Diamond Point, but pieces have contemporary shapes. All the footed pieces have square bases. Finials are acorn-shaped with a diamond-point motif. Colors other than clear are strictly modern. Cambridge items, when marked, are permanently embossed with the company's familiar hallmark, "C" within a triangle.

Hint: The knob stems on reproduction goblets are covered with diamond points.

DIAMOND QUILTED

The original maker of Diamond Quilted has long been lost in the annals of glass history. You can find an extended table service of this attractive pattern in light and dark amber, light and dark amethyst, apple green, blue, clear, and vaseline. Judging from the characteristics of the design, this pattern appears to be a product of the mid-1880s.

Diamond Quilted is light and dainty. The inside of each item is decorated with rows of intertwined diamonds that create a pleasing optical effect, while the stems and bases of footed pieces are plain (Fig. 119). An interesting addition to the pattern is the effect caused by diagonal bands of clear and patterned bars that appear on the underside of flat pieces.

Contrary to popular belief, Diamond

Quilted is a safe pattern to collect. To date, only two reproductions have been authenticated—goblets and wines. New goblets in amber appeared as early as 1938. Unmarked, they most likely were produced by the L.G. Wright Glass Company of New Martinsville, West Virginia, which in 1968 issued the No.77-23 goblet shown in Fig. 120. New goblets stand 7 inches high and have an 8-ounce capacity. At the same time, Wright also issued the No.77-66 4½-inch-high wine with a 2½-ounce capacity. Each of these items was produced from a new mold in amber, amethyst, blue, canary yellow, clear, green, and ruby. The complete color history of Wright reproductions, however, is unknown because that company used various glass houses to produce the same article. For example, al-

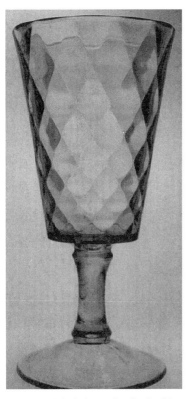

Fig. 119. Original Diamond Quilted goblet. Maker unknown. Circa mid-1880s.

Fig. 120. New No.77-23 Diamond Quilted goblet. L.G. Wright Glass Co. Circa 1968. Unmarked. (Note the long, thin stem.)

though it is known that the Fenton Art Glass Company of Williamstown, West Virginia, produced amethyst goblets for Wright, it is not know whether this color was exclusive to Fenton.

Reproductions in Diamond Quilted share the same basic discrepancies. New goblets and wines are heavy and thick, stems are noticeably long and thin, and colors are so deep that the diamonds and optical effect, clearly visible on originals, are nearly impossible to see.

Interestingly, in the late 1920s and early 1930s, the Imperial Glass Corporation of Bellaire, Ohio, produced the look-alike pattern known as Flat Diamond. This pattern was made in an extended table service in typical Depression-era shapes and colors.

These colors include amber, black, blue, clear, green, pink, and red. Because of the diamond optical motif of both patterns, collectors can easily mistake the Flat Diamond cake stand, champagne, cordial, plate, tumbler, and wine for Diamond Quilted. However, unlike Diamond Quilted, on which the design is pressed on the inside, the design on Flat Diamond is pressed on the outside, creating a diamond-cut effect.

Hint: Reproduction goblets and wines have longer and thinner stems, are heavier, and colors are harsher than the originals.

Reproduced items: Goblet, wine.

DIAMOND THUMBPRINT

Diamond Thumbprint is a brilliant, clear, heavy flint pattern of the 1840s. Attributed to the Boston and Sandwich Glass Company of Sandwich, Massachusetts, this pattern consists of large diamonds with thumbprints in their centers. When gently tapped, items will always ring with a fine belltone resonance due to the high lead content of the glass. Earliest pieces are crude and often pontil-scarred, whereas later items (those produced from 1850 and after) are more highly refined and have a polished pontil mark. The pattern was originally produced in an extended table service. Handles are beautifully applied and crimped, never pressed. Any item in color is rare.

Beginning in 1973, the Viking Glass Company of New Martinsville, West Virginia, began producing a number of new items in Diamond Thumbprint, enumerated in Chart 42, for the Sandwich Glass Museum of Sandwich, Massachusetts (Figs. 121 and 122). These new items were made from new molds in clear and contemporary colors and were extensively advertised as

Fig. 121. Reproduction Diamond Thumbprint No.7216 clear goblet. Viking Glass Co. for the Sandwich Glass Museum. Circa 1974. Embossed "SM."

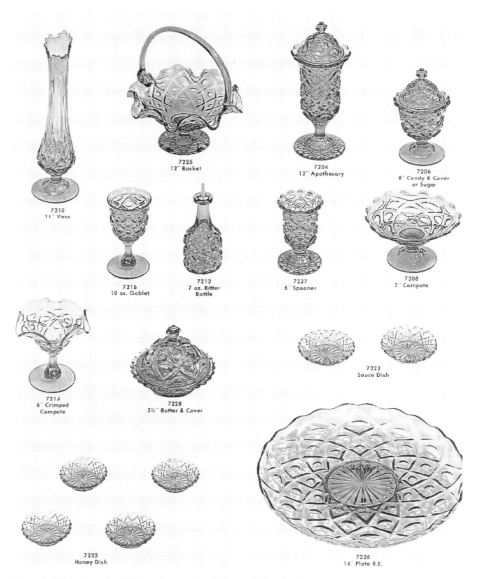

Fig. 122. Viking Glass Co. 1974 catalog reprint of Diamond Thumbprint.

authentic replicas. Each item, permanently embossed with the Sandwich Museum's "SM" insignia, was accompanied by a small information card printed "Creations patterned after Early American Pattern Glass—Handmade by Viking Glass Company." The inside of this card states: "Viking has reproduced a fine collection of authentic replicas of Sandwich glass, authorized by the Sandwich Historical Society, which have become so popular that a demand has grown for additional pieces.

For those who wish to enhance their collection of authentic Sandwich Glass replicas we have added certain pieces patterned after the original Diamond Thumbprint design. These pieces beautifully compliment the original Sandwich glass, and were crafted by Viking Glass craftsmen . . . to help you fulfill your growing desire for this unique (and gracious) pattern." Inside the four-fold booklet is a short history of the pattern, and on the back is the Viking trademark and address.

CHART 42 DIAMOND THUMBPRINT. Viking Glass Company, New Martinsville, West Virginia.
CMN: Diamond Thumbprint.
Mark: Embossed "SM" as an authentic Sandwich Museum Replica.
Color Code: A Amber, AM Amethyst, B Blue, C Clear, ER Epic Ruby, P Peach, R Ruby, SG Sterling Gray.

ITEM	COLOR(S)	YEAR	ORIG	NEW
Apothecary jar. #7204. Footed, covered, 12"h.	A, AM, ER	1973		X
	C	1972		X
Basket. #7225. Pattern on foot, clear applied handle, 12"h.	A, AM	1973		X
	C	1972		X
Bell, 5"h.	C, P, R, SG	1984		X
Bottle. #7212. Bitters, 7 oz.	A, AM	1973	X	
	C	1966	X	
Bowl, open, low footed. Patterned base.				
#7201. 10"d., Belled bowl.	A, AM, C	1973	X	
#7224. 10"d., Shallow bowl.	A, AM	1973	X	
	C	1972	X	
	P, R, SG	1984	X	
Butter dish. #7228. Covered, flat.	A, AM	1973	X	
	C	1966	X	
Cake plate. #7203. Flat, round, 12"d.	A, AM	1973		X
	C	1972		X
Candlestick. #7202. 6"h.	A, AM, ER	1973		X
	C	1972		X
	P, SG, R	1984		X
Celery vase. #7205. Footed, 10"h.	A, AM, ER	1973	X	
	C	1972	X	
Compote, open.				
High standard.				
#7214. Ruffled rim, 6"d.	A, AM	1973		X
	C	1972		X
	P, SG, R	1984		X
Low standard.				
#7208. Flared, 7"d.	A, AM	1973	X	
	C	1966	X	
Cordial. #7219. 1½ oz.	A, AM	1973	X	
	C	1972	X	
Creamer. #7207. Pedestaled, pressed handle, 12 oz.	A, AM	1973	X	
	C	1972	X	
Glimmer. #7209. (Candle holder).	AM	1972		X
	C	1974		X
	ER	1973		X
Goblet. #7216. 10 oz., 6½"h.	A, AM	1973	X	
	C	1966	X	
Honey dish. #7223. Flat, round.	A, AM	1973	X	
	C	1972	X	
Mug, applied handle.	C	1966	X	
Plate. #7226. 14"d.	A, AM, C, ER	1973		X
Relish dish. #7211. 7¼"l.	A, AM	1973	X	
	C	1972	X	
Salt shaker. #7215.	A, AM	1973		X
	C	1972		X
	P, R, SG	1984		X

ITEM	COLOR(S)	YEAR	ORIG	NEW
Sauce dish. #7222. Round, flat.	A, AM	1973	X	
	C	1966	X	
Sherbert. #7217. Footed, 6 oz.	A, AM	1973		X
	C	1972		X
Spoonholder. #7227. 6"h.	A, AM, C	1973	X	
	P, R, SG	1984	X	
Sugar bowl, covered, 8"h.				
#7206. Nonpatterned base.	A, AM, C, ER	1974	X	
#7206. Patterned base.	A, ER	1973	X	
	AM, B, C	1972	X	
	P, R, SG	1984	X	
Tumbler.				
#7220. Old-fashioned, 9 oz.	A, AM	1973	X	
	C	1972	X	
#7221. Juice, 5 oz.	A, AM	1973	X	
	C	1972	X	
Vase. #7210, swung, 11"h., nonpatterned foot.	A, AM	1973		X
	C	1972		X
Wine. #7218. 6 oz.	A, AM	1973	X	
	C	1972	X	

Fig. 123. Reproduction Diamond Thumbprint No.7205 10-inch-high amethyst celery vase. Made for the Sandwich Glass Museum by Viking Glass Co. Circa 1973. Embossed "SM."

Fig. 124. New Diamond Thumbprint No.7220 clear old-fashioned tumbler. Viking Glass Co. for the Sandwich Glass Museum. Circa 1974. Embossed "SM."

Fig. 125. New Diamond Thumbprint No.7207 amethyst creamer. Viking Glass Co. for the Sandwich Glass Museum. Circa 1973. (Unlike originals, the handles on reproductions are pressed.)

As you can see from Figs. 123, 124, and 125, Diamond Thumbprint reproductions are quite convincing. Produced from new molds, they have been fashioned after original forms and are notably heavy. The impression is crisp and well detailed, and the overall appearance exemplifies superior workmanship. However, unlike originals, handles on reproductions are pressed. The exception is the applied-handle mug. Colors such as amber, amethyst, blue, epic red, peach, ruby, and sterling gray are contemporary and deep, harsh, and artificial. The most obvious difference, however, is in the glass. Made from nonflint glass, reproductions are light and do not produce the customary belltone of flint. New items also lack the gloss and luster of the originals.

Hint: Reproduction items are always permanently marked with the "SM" insignia.

DIAMOND WITH PEG

Originally known as Jefferson's Star, this pattern was first issued by the Jefferson Glass Company of Follansbee, West Virginia, about 1915. Also known as Bon Secour, the design was produced in an extended table service from a good-quality glass in clear and clear with ruby stain, which was often souvenired. Items are sometimes marked "Krys-Tol." Handles are applied.

This pattern is another member of the cut-glass family of design and consists of a horizontal row of diamond-shaped ornaments. The top of each ornament is elongated and impressed with a stylized hobstar. Each ornament is further separated by a series of intersecting lines that produces a small diamond and a fan.

To date, only the water set has been reproduced. The 3¾-inch-high flared-rim tumbler illustrated in Fig. 126 and the pitcher were available as early as 1950. New pitchers and tumblers were made in clear and clear with purple stain. Most likely they

were made from original molds because the pattern design is the same. Unlike originals, however, reproductions are thick, heavy, and distinctly greenish. The glass is also exceptionally crinkled or wavy. Although new pitchers and tumblers have a clear "circle" embossed on the base, their maker is not known.

Fig. 126. Reproduction Diamond with Peg tumbler. Circa mid-1950s. Embossed clear circle.

The easiest way to detect new pitchers and tumblers is by noting the quality of the stain. Unlike the stain on original items, which is deep ruby and permanently fired onto the glass, the stain on new pitchers and tumblers ranges from a pale pink to a deep purple and can be removed easily.

Hint: New items have a distinctly green color and the stain can be removed easily.
Reproduced items: Pitcher, tumbler.

EGYPTIAN

Throughout the history of early American pattern glass, tableware manufacturers employed an endless variety of decorative designs in an effort to attract consumer interest. One such pattern is Egyptian. Also known as Parthenon, Egyptian is unique as an American pressed-glass design. As its name implies, camels, palm trees, pyramids, sphinxes, temples, and tents create images of ancient Egypt popularized by the Victorian Renaissance Revival.

Egyptian was originally produced in a medium-sized table service from a good-quality clear nonflint glass. Until recently, the history of this pattern remained unknown. However, through the diligent efforts of Jane Shadel Spillman, curator of American glass at the Corning Museum of Glass, Corning, New York, we now know that this pattern was originally produced by Adams & Company of Pittsburgh, Pennsylvania, in the mid-1880s.

Popular among collectors of historical pressed glass, the Mormon Temple bread tray commemorates the famed temple founded by Joseph Smith in Temple Square, Salt Lake City, Utah. This tray measures 13 inches long by 8½ inches wide and was originally made from a good-quality clear nonflint glass. Centered on this tray is a faithful representation of the Mormon Temple. Although only five of the temple's six spires are shown, they are beautifully molded. The temple itself is in excellent perspective and proportion. Embossed in Old English lettering above this scene is "Give Us This Day," while below reads "Our Daily Bread." The outer border is decorated with the berry motif typical of the Egyptian pattern.

Fig. 127. Reproduction Egyptian Mormon Temple clear bread tray. Embossed on the base "(C) 1983 LDS."

Unlike originals, new bread trays measure 13¼ inches long by 8¼ inches wide and are ill-proportioned, exaggerated, and poorly detailed. Additionally, reproductions are enhanced with trees, shrubbery, and walkways. Above the central temple scene is a clear inner border embossed "Holiness to," an open eye, and "The Lord." Embossed below this scene is "Salt Lake," a beehive, and "Temple."

The most significant difference between original and reproduction trays is their shape. Original bread trays are scalloped and do not have handles. As you can see in Fig. 127, new bread trays are handled, oval, slightly indented above and below the central scene, and lack the berry motif.

Reproduction bread trays are embossed on the rim of the base "(C) 1983 LDS" (signifies Latter Day Saints).

Hint: The reproduction bread tray measures 13¼ inches long by 8¼ inches wide.
Reproduced items: Bread tray.

ELLROSE

George Duncan & Sons of Pittsburgh, Pennsylvania, introduced the pattern commonly called Ellrose or Amberette in March 1886. This pattern was designed and patented by George W. Blair on May 25, 1886, and was produced in a large line of good-quality non-flint glass called Ellrose. Clear, clear with amber stain, clear with ruby stain, solid blue, and canary yellow were produced. The United States Glass Company continued making the pattern when Duncan became a member in 1891. Alternative names for Ellrose are: Amberette, Daisy and Button-Paneled Single Scallop, Daisy and Button-Single Panel, Paneled Daisy, and Paneled Daisy and Button.

Ellrose is a safe pattern to collect because only three items have been reproduced: the round covered bowl, the oval open bowl, and the goblet.

Figs. 128 and 129 illustrate the 6¾-inch-high reproduction goblet. Reproduced from a new mold in a brilliant clear glass that rings when gently tapped, the goblet is permanently embossed on the bottom of the base with the monogram "VPNT" within a large "S." Sears, Roebuck and Company joined with the actor Vincent Price to produce a line of glassware known as National Treasures. The monogram reflects the new partnership by combining the two logos: Sears (S) and Vincent Price National Treasures (VPNT).

Reproduction goblets are much taller, thicker, and heavier than the originals and ring when tapped (originals do not ring). Grinding off the monogram produces a highly polished base, which distinguishes an altered reproduction from an original.

The National Treasures line, produced throughout the late 1950s and early 1960s by the Imperial Glass Corporation of Bellaire, Ohio, included many classic antique pressed patterns. Each item was accompanied by a little booklet tag, on the front of which was printed "Vincent Price Presents National Treasures, Sears, Roebuck and Co." encircling an eagle. The bottom of the tag was printed with the words "Victorian Pressed Glass."

Fig. 128. New Ellrose clear flint goblet. Imperial Glass Corp. Circa early 1960s. Embossed "VPNT" within an "S."

Fig. 129. Closeup of "VPNT" with an "S" trademark embossed on the base of the reproduction Ellrose goblet.

Fig. 130. Excerpt from an original George Duncan & Sons catalog illustrating the Amberette or Ellrose covered bowl.

ferred to as item No.1987, it is round with a diameter of 8½ inches. At the same time, Fenton issued the No.1921 8½-inch true open oval bowl. Both bowls are exact copies of the original, including the characteristic collared base and the square-patterned finial on the cover (Fig. 130). However, the design is in low relief and feels smooth. Produced in a fine-quality clear nonflint glass from a new mold created by Fenton, both reproductions are permanently embossed with the Fenton logo.

To date, Ellrose has not been reproduced in the original color of clear with amber or ruby stain or in the solid colors of blue or canary yellow.

Hint: Reproduction items in Ellrose are permanently embossed with the Fenton logo or with "VPNT" within a large "S."
Reproduced items: Goblet, round covered bowl, oval open bowl.

In 1979, the Fenton Art Glass Company of Williamstown, West Virginia, produced the clear Ellrose large covered bowl. Re-

ENGLISH HOBNAIL

A common practice among Victorian manufacturers of pressed-glass tableware was to copy or imitate better-selling patterns. It is no surprise, then, that as the popularity of

Hobnail increased, variations rapidly followed.

Among these variations, the English Hobnail pattern was made about 1910 by the Westmoreland Glass Company of Grapeville, Pennsylvania. Originally called

CHART 43   ENGLISH HOBNAIL. Plum Glass Company, Pittsburgh, Pennsylvania.
CMN: No.555 or English Hobnail.
Mark: Embossed "PG" in a keystone or paper label.
Color Code: B Blue, BF Blue Frosted, BL Black, BLDG Black with Decorated Gold, C Clear, CO Cobalt, MW Milk White, PL Plum.

ITEM	COLOR(S)	YEAR	ORIG	NEW
Banana dish, folded sides, applied handle.	MW	1987		X
Basket, applied twisted handle.				
Small, flat, ruffled.	BLDG	1991		X
	CO	1989		X
	PL	1992		X
Tall, 6"h.	CO	1990		X
Bowl, ruffled rim.	B, BF, BL, C, CO, MW	1988	X	
Carafe, applied handle, footed.	MW	1987		X
Rose bowl, flat, cupped.	CO	1990	X	
Wine, patterned stem.	MW	1987		X

pattern No.555, it is also known as Millard's Diamond Point, Unitt's Sawtooth, and Westmoreland Diamond. The pattern was produced in an extended table service from a medium-quality clear nonflint glass. Amber or any other color is rare.

English Hobnail is an interesting pattern with an overall design of truncated pyramids, each topped with a cross. Handles are either applied or pressed, depending upon the item.

Interestingly, English Hobnail has been in continuous production by Westmoreland Glass and other contemporary glass compa-

nies since its earliest beginnings (Fig. 131). As the popularity of the pattern increased, contemporary forms were added (see Chart 44). Between 1920 and the closing of the Westmoreland plant in 1984, more than 137 open-stock items were offered in three distinct lines: No.555/1 (round forms with round feet), No.555/2 (square plates and square-footed stemware), and No.555/3 (barrel-shaped stemware with ball stems and round feet). These lines were reissued in a number of contemporary colors, including blue (plain or frosted), black (plain or gold-decorated), clear, cobalt, and milk white.

Fig. 131. New 15-piece clear English Hobnail punch-bowl set made from original molds. Westmoreland Glass Co. Circa 1967. Embossed "WG."

555
Goblet

555
Sherbet

555/3
Sherbet

555/3
Goblet

Fig. 132. Selection of new clear English Hobnail stemware. Westmoreland Glass Co. Circa 1967.

CHART 44   ENGLISH HOBNAIL. Westmoreland Glass Company, Grapeville, Pennsylvania.
CMN: English Hobnail, Westmoreland's No.555.
Mark: Unmarked, embossed "WG," or paper label.
Color Code: A Amber, B Blue C Clear, CB Cobalt Blue, CCR Clear with Cranberry Stain, J Jade-ite (Mint Green), MW Milk White, P Pink, R Red, TU Turquoise.

ITEM	COLOR(S)	YEAR	ORIG	NEW
Ashtray.				
3½"sq.	MW	1967		X
4½"sq.	A, B, C, CB, P, R, TU	**		X
	J	1979		X
	MW	1967		X
8"sq.	A, B, C, CB, P, R, TU	**		X
	J	1979		X
	MW	1967		X
Hat shape, low.	MW	1967		X
Basket, applied twisted handle.				
Oblong, 7"l.	MW	1975		X
Square edged.*	P	1983		X
Tall, 6"h.*	MW	1967		X
	P	1983		X
Bonbon, round, single-handled, flat, 6"d.	MW	1960		X
Bowl.				
Flat.				
Oval, relish.				
8"d.	A, B, C, P, R, TU	**	X	
9"d.	A, B, C, P, R, TU	**	X	
12"d.	A, B, C, P, R, TU	**	X	
Round.				
4½"d.	A, B, C, P, R, TU	**	X	
5"d.	A, B, C, P, R, TU	**	X	
6"d.	A, B, C, P, R, TU	**	X	
8"d.				
Plain rim.	A, B, C, P, R, TU	**	X	
Six-pointed rim.	MW	1967		X
10"d., flared rim.	MW	1967	X	
11"d.	A, B, C, CB, P, R, TU	**	X	
12"d.	A, B, C, CB, P, R, TU	**	X	
	MW	1975	X	
Cream soup, two-handled.	A, B, C, P, R, TU	**		X
Square.				
4½"d.	A, B, C, P, R, TU	**		X
5"d.	A, B, C, P, R, TU	**		X
Footed.				
Round, two-handled.				
6"d.	MW	1975		X
8"d.	A, B, C, CB, MW, P, R, TU	**		X
10"d.	MW	1967		X
Butter dish, ¼ lb.	MW	1967		X
Candlestick.				
3½"h.	A, B, C, P, R, TU	**		X
	MW	1967		X
8½"h.	A, B, C, P, R, TU	**		X
9"h.*	P, R	1983		X
Candy dish, covered.				
Cone-shape, footed.	A, B, C, P, R, TU	**		X
	CCR, MW	1967		X
Round, three-footed.	A, B, C, P, R, TU	**		X
	MW	1967		X

ITEM	COLOR(S)	YEAR	ORIG	NEW
Cigarette box.	A, B, C, CB, P, R, TU	**		X
Claret, 5 oz.	A, B, C, CB, P, R, TU	**		X
Cocktail, 3 oz.	A, B, C, CB, P, R, TU	**		X
Cologne bottle.	A, B, C, CB, P, R, TU	**		X
	MW	1975		X
Compote, high standard, 5"d., crimped rim.	MW	1967		X
Cordial, 1 oz.	A, B, C, CB, P, R, TU	**		X
Cruet.*	MW	1967	X	
	P	1983	X	
Creamer, pressed handle.				
Flat.	A, B, C, P, R, TU	**	X	
Footed.	A, B, C, P, R, TU	**		X
	MW	1967		X
Cup and saucer.				
Demitasse.	A, B, C, P, R, TU	**		X
Tea.	A, B, C, P, R, TU	**		X
Decanter, patterned stopper, 20 oz.	A, B, C, P, R, TU	**	X	
	MW	1975	X	
Eggcup, double.	A, B, C, P, R, TU	**	X	
Goblet, 6¼"., 8 oz.	A, B, C, CB, P, R, TU	**	X	
	MW	1955	X	
Grapefruit, 6½"d., flange rim.	A, B, C, P, TU	**		X
Honey or jelly, high standard.	MW	1967	X	
Ivy ball, low-footed.	MW	1967		X
Lamp, electric or oil.	A, B, C, CB, P, R, TU	**	X	
Lampshade, 17"d.	C	1920		X
Marmalade jar, covered.	A, B, C, P, R, TU	**		X
Pitcher.*				
Bulbous.				
23 oz.	A, B, C, P, R, TU	**		X
39 oz.	A, B, C, P, R, TU	**		X
60 oz.	A, B, C, P, R, TU	**		X
Straight-sided.				
64 oz.	A, B, C, P, R, TU	**	X	
Plate, flat.				
Round.				
5½"d., Bread and butter.	A, B, C, CB, P, R, TU	**	X	
6½"d., Sherbert.	A, B, C, CB, P, R, TU	**	X	
7¼"d., Pie.	A, B, C, P, R, TU	**	X	
8"d., Luncheon.	A, B, C, CB, P, R, TU	**	X	
10"d., Dinner.	A, B, C, P, R, TU	**	X	
Square.				
8"sq., Luncheon.	A, B, C, CB, P, R, TU	**		X
Punch bowl, footed.	C	1967		X
Salt, footed.				
Dip, with place-card holder, 2"h.	A, B, C, CB, P, R, TU	**		X
Shaker, round or square base.	A, B, C, CB, P, R, TU	**		X
	MW	1967		X
Sherbert, footed.	A, B, C, CB, P, R, TU	**		X

ITEM	COLOR(S)	YEAR	ORIG	NEW
Sugar, double-handled.				
Flat.	A, B, C, P, R, TU	**	X	
Footed.	A, B, C, P, R, TU	**		X
	MW	1967		X
Toothpick, top hat.	A, B, C, CB, CCR, P, R	**	X	
	MW	1967	X	
	TU	**	X	
Tumbler.				
Flat.				
Iced tea.				
4"h., 10 oz.	A, B, C, P, R, TU	**		X
5"h., 12 oz.	A, B, C, CB, P, R, TU	**		X
Juice, 3¾"h., 5 oz.	A, B, C, P, R, TU	**	X	
Water, 3¾"h., 9 oz.	A, B, C, P, R, TU	**	X	
Footed.				
Iced tea.				
9 oz.	A, B, C, P, R, TU	**		X
12½ oz.	A, B, C, P, R, TU	**		X
Water, 7 oz.	A, B, C, P, R, TU	**		X
Vase.				
Bud.*	P	1983		X
Fan-shaped.	MW	1975		X
Straight-sided, swung, 12"h.	A, B, C, P, R, TU	**		X
	MW	1967		X
Whiskey.				
1½ oz.	A, B, C, P, R, TU	**		X
3 oz.	A, B, C, P, R, TU	**		X
Wine, 2 oz.	A, B, C, CB, P, R, TU	**		X

*Made Exclusively for Levay Distributing Co., Edwardsville, Indiana.
**Original production date is unknown.

As late as 1983, Westmoreland produced 17 pieces of English Hobnail (including the covered candy dish, 9-inch-high candlestick, bud vase, and seven-piece water set) in ruby, pink, and other colors exclusively for the Levay Distributing Company of Edwardsville, Illinois. Most likely these pieces were marked with the Westmoreland hallmark.

When Westmoreland closed in 1984, these molds were sold. Russell and Joanne Vogelsang of the Summit Art Glass Company of Rootstown, Ohio, purchased the molds for the individual footed salt dip and the hat toothpick holder and then sold both items in amberina and milk-white glass. They subsequently offered the hat toothpick in amethyst (plain or iridized), cobalt, morning glory, and violet. Although Summit reproductions are not signed, most likely they were marked with a paper label.

The Plum Glass Company of Pittsburgh, Pennsylvania, purchased the Westmoreland molds for the seven forms enumerated in Chart 43. By 1987, Plum was producing the No.555, or English Hobnail, line. Made from the original molds in the contemporary colors of black, blue, blue frosted, clear, cobalt blue, milk white, and plum, each item is embossed permanently with a "PG" within a keystone. Interestingly, each Plum reproduction also carries Westmoreland's "WG" hallmark.

Although it is unknown who purchased the bulk of the Westmoreland molds, it is certain that they were taken overseas. Also unknown is whether Plum purchased any additional English Hobnail molds.

As you can see from Fig. 132, reproductions can be quite convincing. Because this pattern remained in continuous production, the most obvious way to detect new items is by examining the color and the quality of the glass. Aside from amber, any colored item is obviously new. Unlike original items in clear, which are light and crisply molded, reproductions are thick-walled and heavy,

the design is often blurred, and the glass appears crinkled or wavy.

Hint: Reproductions are thick and heavy and the design is blurred.

EXCELSIOR

Excelsior is a fussy pattern more reminiscent of French than American glass. Also known as Barrel Excelsior, Flare Top Excelsior, and Giant Excelsior, this pattern was originally produced by McKee Brothers of Pittsburgh, Pennsylvania, about 1859 from a clear, brilliant flint glass. Like many early flint designs, Excelsior was made in a limited table service that emphasized bar and utilitarian ware, as evidenced by the vast array of bottles, decanters, stemware, and tumblers produced.

Original items are heavy, well proportioned, and ring with a good belltone resonance. Handles are beautifully applied and crimped. This pattern also has the distinction of two sizes of candlesticks— forms rarely found in other early flint designs.

To date, only two items have been reproduced in Excelsior. New champagnes and goblets were introduced in 1988 by the Dalzell-Viking Glass Company of New Martinsville, West Virginia. Each item was

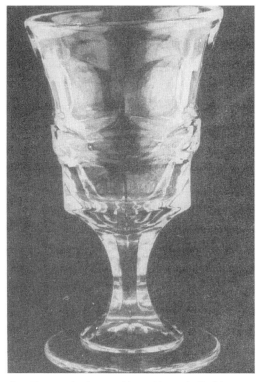

Fig. 133. Reproduction Excelsior goblet. Dalzell-Viking Glass Co. Circa 1988. (Note the shape of the goblet bowl.)

Fig. 134. Original Excelsior clear flint champagne. McKee Brothers. Circa 1860.

produced from a new mold in a brilliant, heavy glass of some flint quality. Created as Dalzell's premier line in the Oglebay Museum Collection of pressed glass, both items were initially offered in azure blue, clear, cobalt, pink, and ruby.

As you can see from Figs. 133 and 134, new champagnes and goblets should fool no one. Unlike original items, reproductions are square. Additionally, stems are thicker and heavier than original items,

while the bowls boldly flare outward at the rim.

Dalzell-Viking reproductions are not permanently marked: however, each item was originally issued with a transparent plastic label with the Dalzell-Viking name printed in black block letters.

Hint: Reproductions are completely different in shape from the originals.
Reproduced items: Champagne, goblet.

EYEWINKER

Eyewinker is a popular member of the geometric group of pattern glass. This pleasing design, also known as Cannon Ball, Crystal Ball, and Winking Eye, was first produced by Dalzell, Gilmore & Leighton of Findlay, Ohio, about 1889. The design is brilliant and heavy and was originally issued in a good-quality clear nonflint glass (Fig. 135). Today, collectors may still assemble a complete table service that includes more than 35 open and covered

compotes and three different sizes of oil lamps.

Between 1967 and 1984, the L.G. Wright Glass Company of New Martinsville, West Virginia, issued the 27 items enumerated in Chart 45. As you can see from this chart, only 13 items have contemporary shapes, while the remainder emulate known antique pieces. It is not known whether the reproductions with antique shapes were produced from original molds. However, by engaging the services of numerous glass houses, Wright enhanced the

CHART 45 EYEWINKER. L.G. Wright Glass Company, New Martinsville, West Virginia.
CMN: Eyewinker.
Mark: Unmarked.
Color Code: A Amber, AS Amber Satin, B Blue, BS Blue Satin, C Clear, DB Dark Blue, G Green, GS Green Satin, RBY Ruby, RS Ruby Satin, V Vaseline.

ITEM	COLOR(S)	YEAR	ORIG	NEW
Ashtray. #25-9. Round, 4½"d.	A, C, RBY	1968		X
	DB	1984		X
	G	1969		X
	V	1974		X
Bowl, open.				
#25-10. Low footed, 10"d.	A, C, RBY	1968	X	
#25-11. 4-toed. 5"d.	A, C	1968		X
Butter dish. #25-12. Covered, flat, flanged base, 7½"d.	A, C, G	1968	X	
	B, RBY, V	1974	X	
Celery vase, 3-toed, scalloped rim.				
#25-28. 6"h.	A, B, G, RBY	1968		X
	C	1976		X
	RS	1971		X
	V	1974		X
#25-30. 8"d.	A, B, G, RBY	1968		X

ITEM	COLOR(S)	YEAR	ORIG	NEW
Compote.				
Covered.				
High standard.				
#25-1. 6"d.	A, B, G, RBY	1968	X	
	C	1969	X	
	V	1974	X	
#25-14. 4"d.	A, B, G, RBY	1968	X	
	C	1976	X	
	RS	1971	X	
	V	1974	X	
Low standard.				
#25-15. 5"d.	A, G, RBY	1968	X	
	B, C, V	1974	X	
Open, smooth rim.				
High Standard.				
#25-2. Flared bowl, 7½"d.	A, B, C	1968	X	
	G, RBY, V	1970	X	
Low standard.				
#25-17. 6"d.	A, C, RBY	1968	X	
	G	1971	X	
Creamer. #25-18. Individual, pressed handle.	A, C, G, RBY	1968		X
	B, V	1974		X
Goblet. #25-3. 10 oz., 6"h.	A, B, C, G, RBY	1968		X
	V	1974		X
Honey dish. #25-20. Covered, round, flat, 5½"d.	A, G, RBY	1968	X	
	B, C, V	1974	X	
Lamp. #25-29. Fairy, 5½"h.	A, AS, B, BS, G, GS, RBY	1968		X
	RS	1968		X
Marmalade. #25-25. Covered.	A, B, G, RBY	1968		X
	C	1967		X
	V	1974		X
Pickle tray. #25-21. 9½"d.	A, G	1968	X	
Pitcher.				
#25-28. Milk, 1-qt.	A, B, C, G, RBY, V	1974	X	
#25-26. Water.	A, B, G, RBY	1968	X	
	C	1970	X	
Salt dip. #25-22. Flat, individual.	A, G, RBY	1968		X
	B, C, V	1969		X
Salt shaker. #25-24. Straight-sided.	A, B, C, G, RBY	1968	X	
Sauce dish. #25-5. Round, flat, 4"d.	A, B, C, RBY	1968	X	
	G, V	1974	X	
Sherbert. #25-4. 3½"d.	A, B, C, RBY	1968		X
	G, V	1974		X
Sugar bowl. #25-19. Covered, individual.	A, C, G, RBY	1968		X
	B, V	1974		X
Toothpick holder. #25-23. Flat.	A, G, RBY	1968		X
	B, V	1969		X
	C	1972		X
Tumbler. #25-27. Water.	A, B, G	1968	X	
	C	1970	X	
	RBY	1974	X	
Wine. #25-7. 4 oz., 4½"h.	A, B, G, RBY	1968		X
	C	1970		X

Fig. 135. Original Eyewinker goblet. Dalzell, Gilmore & Leighton Glass Co. Circa 1889.

Fig. 136. Reproduction Eyewinker No.25-15 low-standard covered compote. L.G. Wright Glass Co. Circa 1971. Unmarked.

overall look of the entire line by issuing these shapes in clear and an array of contemporary colors, including amber, blue, green (all plain or satin-finished), ruby, and vaseline.

Although any colored item is strictly contemporary, clear items may prove more troublesome for collectors to distinguish from the original pattern. As you can see from Figs. 136 and 137, reproductions are quite convincing because they are unmarked and appear in a number of original forms. However, you will have little trouble detecting a clear new item when you consider its weight and shade. New items are perceptively heavy, due to the excessive thickness of the glass. The lack of luster and poor impression also provide reproductions with a dull finish. Unlike the smooth quality of old items, the surface of new ones is wavy or crinkled. And reproduction glass items have a distinct yellowish-green cast.

During the mid-1980s, the Sturbridge Yankee Workshop of Sturbridge, Massa-

chussetts, offered another reproduction Eyewinker goblet. Advertised as Eye Winker, this goblet is in clear nonflint glass and was reportedly produced by the Imperial Glass Corporation of Bellaire, Ohio,

Fig. 137. Reproduction Eyewinker No.25-20 covered honey dish. L.G. Wright Glass Co. Circa 1974. Unmarked.

from the original Eyewinker goblet mold. But, because an original Dalzell, Gilmore & Leighton catalog that illustrates the true goblet (known today as Cannon Ball Variant) has recently surfaced, the validity of this report is highly suspect.

Reproduction items in Eyewinker are not permanently marked.

Hint: Reproduction items in Eyewinker are heavier and the glass has a yellowish-green cast.

FEATHER

Feather is another example of the late series of early American pattern glass. Originally known as Cambridge No. 669 and Doric, this pattern is also known as Cambridge Feather, Feather and Quill, Fine Cut and Feather, Indiana Feather, Prince's Feather, Swirl, and Swirls and Feathers (Fig. 138).

Feather was originally produced by the Beatty-Brady Glass Company of Dunkirk, Indiana (1903), the Cambridge Glass Company of Cambridge, Ohio (1902), and the McKee Glass Company of Pittsburgh, Pennsylvania (1896–1901). Due to the number of companies producing this pattern, items

may be either clear and glossy or dull and off-colored. Although complete table services were originally issued in both qualities of clear glass, clear with amber stain and emerald green items are rare. Only the water pitcher was produced in chocolate.

To date, only the 5¾-inch-high goblet illustrated in Fig. 139 has been reproduced. This goblet has been on the market since the early 1960s and is readily found in amber, blue, and clear. At first sight, it is quite convincing. Upon close examination, however, you'll readily notice a number of subtle discrepancies. Apparently produced from a new mold, these goblets are thicker and heavier than the originals, most noticeably around the rim of the bowl. Unlike the

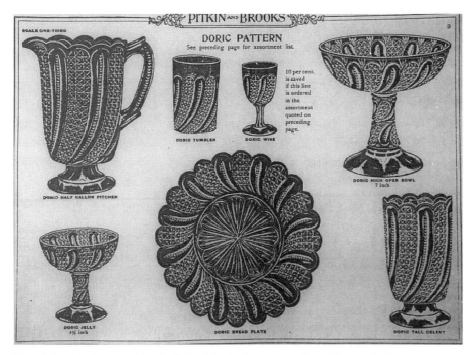

Fig. 138. Reprint of Pitkin and Brooks 1900 catalog illustrating a selection of Doric or Feather.

Fig. 139. New amber feather goblet. Unmarked.

old goblets, which have a straight, finely molded hexagonal stem, the stems of new goblets boldly flare outward at the base and appear knobby where they attach to the foot. Characteristically, the pattern on reproductions is smooth and you can often notice a distinct oily feeling. Also, the tails of the feather motif do not end in well-defined points as they do on the old goblets.

The most interesting discrepancy, however, is the inside shape of the bowl. When you insert your finger into the bowl of an old goblet, you can fit the tip of only one finger at the base. When you repeat this test on a new goblet, you'll notice that the base has triple the amount of space.

Reproduction goblets are not permanently marked.

Hint: Amber, blue, or any other contemporary colored goblet is new.

Reproduced items: Goblet.

FINE CUT AND BLOCK

Throughout the 1890s, the popularity of combination clear and stained pressed-glass tableware soared throughout America. This was the day of the independent decorating shop. Located in the major glass manufacturing centers, these shops created countless designs in clear glass stained with amber, blue, green, ruby, and other colors.

Fig. 140. Excerpt from a circa 1890 King, Son & Co. catalog illustrating the original Fine Cut and Block design, which has not been reproduced in clear with color stain.

Fig. 141. Reproduction clear No.9120 Fine Cut and Block open compote. Fenton Art Glass Co. Circa 1983–84. Embossed Fenton logo.

They also purchased blanks and old inventories and secured contract work from many of the leading glass houses.

Fine Cut and Block is well known for its collectibility in clear with color stain. Originally referred to as No. 25 by its manufacturer, King, Son & Company of Pittsburgh, Pennsylvania, this pattern was first issued about 1890 (Figs. 140 and 143). Original colors are clear, solid amber, blue, canary yellow, and clear stained with amber, blue, and pink. Large table services included novelty items such as the cologne bottle, the soap dish, and the spice slab, which may be found in each color.

Fine Cut and Block is attractive ware reminiscent of cut glass. The design is deeply pressed and covers a large portion of each item. When pieces are stained, it is the large blocks of the pattern that are colored.

As late as 1969, the Fenton Art Glass Company of Williamstown, West Virginia, issued a number of items in Fine Cut and Block. Illustrated in Figs. 141 and 142 and enumerated in Chart 46, these items were produced from new molds created at the Fenton factory and marketed as "Olde Virginia Glass." Unlike Fenton's regular product, this new line was created exclusively for large wholesale distributors and mail-order houses that might otherwise compete with the regular Fenton lines in the same sales areas.

Fenton's Fine Cut and Block pattern appears in a good-quality nonflint glass and is typical of all early American glass reproductions produced and sold under the Fenton trademark. The innovative use of contemporary colors combined with antique and modern forms identifies each item as Fenton.

Only three of the items enumerated in Chart 46 might cause confusion among collectors and dealers. They are the clear covered candy (similar to the original sugar bowl), the creamer, and the goblet. Unlike other forms that were made in contemporary shapes, these are fine examples of the originals, even though they are heavier.

Early items in the "Olde Virginia Glass"

Fig. 142. New No.9143 Fine Cut and Block clear goblet. Fenton Art Glass Co. Circa 1979. Embossed Fenton logo. (Unlike many Fenton creations, this is a direct copy of the original.)

Fig. 143. Excerpt from a circa 1890 King, Son & Co. catalog illustrating the original Fine Cut and Block creamer.

CHART 46 FINE CUT AND BLOCK. Fenton Art Glass Company, Williamstown, West Virginia.
CMN: Fine Cut and Block
Mark: Unmarked, Paper label, embossed "OV," or Fenton logo.
Color Code: AY Amethyst, BG Opaque Blue, CA Colonial Amber, CB Colonial Blue, CG Colonial Green, CN Carnival, CO Cameo Opalescent, CT Custard, CY Clear, DC Dark Carnival, DK Dusty Rose, FB Federal Blue, HG Heritage Green, KL Forget-Me-Not Blue, LO Sea Mist Green, MI Milk White, OR Orange, PW Periwinkle Blue, RT Country Peach, RU Ruby, YL Candleglow Yellow.

ITEM	COLOR(S)	YEAR	ORIG	NEW
Basket. #9137. Applied handle.*	BG, CT	1976		X
	CA, CB, CG, OR	1973		X
	CO	unknown		X
	CY	1978		X
	MI	1971		X
	RU	1982		X
Bonbon dish. #9121. Footed.*	CA, CB, CG, OR	unknown		X
	MI	1971		X
Bowl, open, footed.				
#9122. *	BG, CT	1976		X
	MI	1971		X
#9127. 7"d. Candle bowl.*	BG, CT	1976		X
	CO, CY	unknown		X
	MI	1971		X
#9172. Candle bowl, round, scalloped rim.*	CA, CB, CG, OR	1973		X
	CN, MI	1971		X
	CO, CT, CY	unknown		X
Candle bowl arrangements.				
#9140. "Spring."*	MI	1971		X
#9141. "Fall."*	MI	1971		X
#9142. "Christmas."*	MI	1971		X
Candy box. #9180. Covered, footed.*	BG, CT	1976	X	
	CA, CB, CG	1973	X	
	CN, MI	1971	X	
	CO	unknown	X	
	CY	1978	X	
	OR	1969	X	
Compote, open, ruffled rim.				
#9120. High standard.*	AY, FB, HG, KL, RT, YL	1983		X
	BG, CT	1976		X
	CA, CB, CG, OR	1973		X
	CN, MI	1971		X
	CO	unknown		X
	CY	1979		X
	DK	1984		X
#9157. Short, bulbous standard.	DK	1984		X
Creamer. #9103. Pressed handle, footed.*	BG, CT	1976	X	
	CA, CB, CG, OR	1973	X	
	CO	unknown	X	
	CY	1979	X	
	MI	1971	X	
Dish. #9151. Nut, open, flared rim.	CA, CB, CG, CO, CY, DC	unknown		X
	CN, MI	1971		X
	OR	unknown		X
Goblet. #9143.	CY	1979	X	
Lamp. #9102. Fairy, 2-piece.*	BG, CT	1976		X
	CA, CB, CG, OR	1973		X
	CO	unknown		X
	CY	1970		X
	MI	1971		X

ITEM	COLOR(S)	YEAR	ORIG	NEW
Ring holder. #9144.	AY, CY, KL, PW, RT	1982		X
	DK, HG, YL	1983		X
Salt shaker. #9106. Tall, footed.*	BG, CT	1976		X
	CA, CB, CG, OR	1973		X
	CO	unknown		X
	CY	1979		X
	MI	1971		X
Sugar bowl. #9103. Scalloped rim, open, bell-shaped foot, 4"h.	BG, CT	1976		X
	CA, CB, CG, OR	1973		X
	CY	1978		X
Vase.				
Flat.				
#9157. Bulbous, ruffled rim, 4½"h.	AY, FB, HG, KL, RT, YL	1983		X
	BG, CT	1976		X
	CY	1979		X
	DK	1984		X
	LO	1991		X
	MI	1971		X
	RU	1982		X
#9158. Swung. 7"h.*	BG, CT	1976		X
	CA, CB, CG, OR	1973		X
	CN, MI	1971		X
	CO	unknown		X
	CY	1979		X
#9159. Tall, ruffled rim.	CY	1979		X
Footed.				
#9120. Ruffled rim.	CY	1979		X
#9150. Bud, slender neck.	CN, FB, HG, MI, YL	1983		X
	CY, RU	1979		X
#9152. Bulbous base, swung.*	BG	1976		X
	CA, CB, CG, OR	1973		X
	MI	1971		X

*First introduced in 1969 by Fenton as part of its "Olde Virginia Glass" line.

line are not permanently marked. Rather, each carried a green and white paper label printed "Olde Virginia Glass Handmade" in block letters. A figure of a colonial man and woman completed the mark. From 1970 to 1979, when the entire line was suspended, each item was permanently embossed with an "O" within the opening of a "V," signifying Olde Virginia glass.

Hint: Original items are lighter and the design is sharper than reproductions.

FINE RIB

Fine Rib is one of the more simple, yet appealing, members of the ribbed family. Unlike other patterns in this group, it consists solely of vertical fine ribbing (Fig. 144). As evidenced by Cut Bellflower and other patterns, this fine rib motif was also used as a background for other designs. The pattern originally was named Reeded. The New England Glass Company of East Cambridge, Massachusetts, originally produced an extended table service of this quaint old pattern in a good-quality flint glass in the 1860s.

The glass is brilliant and resounds when

Fig. 144. Original Fine Rib clear flint goblet. New England Glass Co. Circa 1860s.

gently tapped. Handles are beautifully applied and finials are clear in conventional shapes. Although primarily produced in clear glass, you may find rare items in solid, opaque, and translucent white.

For a number of years, there has been considerable confusion among collectors and dealers of Fine Rib. As recently as 1950, reproduction goblets and wines have been cited. Most likely these reproductions are the depression glass goblets and wines known as Homespun (also called Fine Rib) that the Jeannette Glass Company of Jeannette, Pennsylvania, produced in clear and pink nonflint glass about 1939–40.

Hint: Reproduction Fine Rib goblets and wines are nonflint and shaped differently than originals.

Reproduced items: Goblet, wine.

FLAG

No other symbol brings to mind the American way of life as readily as the American flag. In decorative terms, it is found in virtually every medium of expression.

The rectangular Flag bread platter is well known among collectors of historical pressed glass. It is 8 inches wide by 11 inches long and may still be found in a good-quality clear nonflint glass. A full representation of the 1876 Union flag, consisting of thirteen stripes and a field of thirty-eight stars, fills its center. A clear, finely scalloped border completes the design (Fig. 145).

The No. PG/1654 reproduction Flag bread platter seen in Fig. 146 is illustrated in the 1976 bicentennial catalog of the A.A. Importing Company of St. Louis, Missouri. Like the original, it, too, is made of nonflint glass in the original clear and the contemporary ruby. However, the reproduction bread tray is 11 inches wide and 13 inches long. On original platters, there are seven

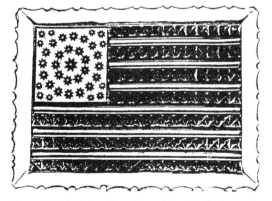

Fig. 145. Original clear Flag platter. (Note the six clear and seven patterned stripes.)

patterned bars on the flag, representing red stripes; on reproductions there are eight. Likewise, on the original there are six clear bars representing white stripes, and on the reproduction there are seven. Unlike the original bread platter's center, which completely fills the base, the reproduction's center is framed by a thin, clear

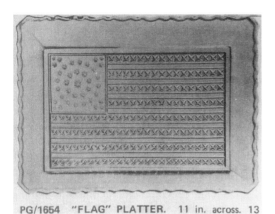

PG/1654 "FLAG" PLATTER. 11 in. across. 13

Fig. 146. Reproduction No.PG/1654 Flag clear platter offered by A.A. Importing Co., Inc. Circa 1976. Marked with a paper label.

border, which can be seen in the illustration.

The outer rim of old platters is sharply scalloped with four long, tapered corners. In comparison, scallops on the outer rim of the reproduction are smooth with short, blunt corners. Stripes are much wider on the original, and the design is more finely pressed.

Reproduction bread platters were produced from a new mold and imported into this country. Although not permanently marked, examples have been seen with the octagonal A.A. Importing Company gold label. This label is printed in black block letters with the words "A.A. Importing Co., Inc., St. Louis, MO. Made in Korea."

Hint: On reproduction Flag platters there are eight patterned bars and seven clear bars.

Reproduced items: Bread tray.

FLATTENED HOBNAIL

Flattened Hobnail, also known as Millard's Printed Hobnail, precedes the popularity of the Hobnail design. The original manufacturer of this pattern is not known, although this Victorian design appears to be a product of the 1880s. The pattern was originally produced from a medium-quality clear nonflint glass in a limited table service. Unlike true Hobnail, with its sharp, pointed hobs, Flattened Hobnail has a design that is rounder, smoother, and smaller (Fig. 147).

Flattened Hobnail is a safe pattern to collect. The only reproduced item is the water tumbler. Unmarked, these tumblers first appeared prior to 1969 in clear nonflint glass. They were made from a new mold and are considerably heavier than originals. When viewing these new tumblers in a strong light, you will notice an excessive amount of glass at the bottom and sides. Moreover, the pattern on reproductions is in low relief and the glass appears grayish.

Hint: Reproduction tumblers are heavier than originals and the design is in lower relief.

Reproduced items: Tumbler.

Fig. 147. Flattened Hobnail original goblet. Maker unknown.

FLEUR-DE-LIS AND DRAPE

The Fleur-de-Lis has always been a popular decorative design. In early American pattern glass, both early and late nineteenth-century tableware patterns make use of this motif. One such design has become known as Fleur-de-Lis and Drape.

Also known as Fleur-de-Lis and Tassel, this pattern was first made by Adams & Company of Pittsburgh, Pennsylvania, with production continued by the United States Glass Company, which referred to it as pattern No. 15009. The pattern was originally produced in clear and emerald green from a medium-grade nonflint glass, but you may find odd pieces in milk white (Fig. 148).

To date, only the wine has been reproduced. Introduced in 1967 by Crystal Art Glass of Cambridge, Ohio, this new wine was produced from a new mold and may be found in amethyst, blue, candy swirl, chocolate, delphinium, firefly, impatient, katydid, orange, opalescent orange, white, and willow blue. Known as Teardrop, this pattern was never worked by Crystal with any regularity. From 1972 to 1978, Crystal Art Glass reproductions were permanently embossed with a "D" within a heart (signifying Elizabeth Degenhart).

In 1978, Bernard Boyd acquired the mold to Fleur-de-Lis and Drape from Crystal. Although it is not known whether Boyd continued production to any extent, you may also find this wine in contemporary colors per-

Fig. 148. Excerpt from a circa 1910 United States Glass Co. catalog illustrating the original Fleur-de-Lis and Drape wine.

manently marked with a "B" within a diamond (Boyd's Crystal Art Glass of Cambridge, Ohio).

Collectors and dealers should have little difficulty in recognizing new Fleur-de-Lis with Drape wines. They are heavier and smaller than originals, and any color other than clear or emerald green is strictly contemporary.

Hint: Wines in colors other than clear or emerald green are new.
Reproduced items: Wine.

FLORAL OVAL

Floral Oval is a late pattern in early American pressed glass. This pattern was originally issued about 1910 as Banner by the John B. Higbee Glass Company of Pittsburgh, Pennsylvania, and was still being offered as late as 1916 by the New Martinsville Glass Company of New Martinsville, West Virginia.

Also known as Cane and Sprig, Pittsburgh Daisy, and Spray and Cane, Floral Oval is a fussy pattern composed of arched panels of

cane that alternate with panels of sprigs. This pattern was produced from a medium-quality clear nonflint glass.

Allegedly, large square plates were first reissued. However, it was not until 1938 that Ruth Webb Lee reported copies in this pattern, calling it Cane and Spray. These new plates were quite plentiful at that time and readily found in amber, clear, peach, and yellow. Although the plates Lee refers to were most likely produced by New Martinsville from the original mold, reissues are not permanently marked. However, reis-

Fig. 149. Catalog illustration of the original Floral Oval 7-inch-square plate.

Fig. 150. Reproduction Floral Oval No.99PH clear square plate. Viking Glass Co. Circa 1984. Unmarked.

sues are heavier than originals and have a slight greenish or yellowish cast to the glass.

In 1984, the Viking Glass Company of New Martinsville, West Virginia, issued a similar large, square plate in Floral Oval. Known as item No. 99, this plate was most likely produced from the original mold in clear and pink nonflint glass (Figs. 149 and 150). New plates are thicker and heavier than the originals and often appear gray when seen under a bright light.

In the same year, Viking also introduced the Floral Oval No. 7924 3¾-inch bell. Produced from a new mold in clear nonflint glass, this bell is strictly a contemporary form.

Unlike originals, which are permanently marked with the familiar Higbee trademark, New Martinsville and Viking reissues are unmarked.

Hint: New Floral and Oval plates are heavy and thick.

Reproduced items: Bell, plate.

FLORIDA

Florida is a member of the United States Glass Company's states series. Originally known as No. 15056 or Florida, it is often called Emerald Green Herringbone, Green Herringbone, Herringbone, Paneled Herringbone, and Prism and Herringbone. Produced by the United States Glass Company at Factory "B" or by Bryce Brothers of Pittsburgh, Pennsylvania, this pattern was first issued about 1898.

Florida was originally produced in an extended table service in clear and emerald green nonflint glass. It is a pleasing pattern of alternating plain and herringbone panels (Fig. 151). Although most items are pressed, cruets and syrups are blown and have lovely applied handles.

To date, the only authenticated reproductions in Florida are the 5¾-inch-high goblet (Fig. 152) and the large square plate. As early as 1948, both entered the market in the original colors of clear and emerald green. Since then, they have been made in amber, amethyst, blue, and ruby.

Although reproductions in Florida are unmarked, collectors should have little diffi-

Fig. 151. Original Florida goblet. United States Glass Co. Circa 1898.

Fig. 152. New amber Florida goblet. Circa mid-1950s. Unmarked.

culty in differentiating between old and new items. Produced from new molds, reproduction goblets and plates are smaller and heavier than the old ones. Additionally, the stem on new goblets is shorter and thicker than on old goblets. Both reproductions are distinctly wavy, a characteristic more easily seen in clear than in green. However, the most obvious difference between original and reproduction

pieces is in the color of the glass. Although contemporary colors are new, emerald green reproductions lack the deep, rich color of originals. New green goblets and plates are either a lighter or darker green and lack the warmth of old glass.

Hint: Reproductions are heavier and the pattern is smoother than the originals.
Reproduced items: Goblet, plate.

FLOWER BAND

Flower Band is a member of the group of early American pressed-glass patterns with flowers or fruit as its main decorative motif. Also known as Bird Finial and Frosted Flower Band, the pattern consists of a clear or frosted band of flowers against a plain background. Finials are two entwined love-

birds that are beautifully molded and detailed. The addition of oak leaves and acorns on the bases of most footed pieces adds to this pattern's overall charm. The history of Flower Band is not known, although early research has attributed manufacture to the 1870s.

On July 1, 1962, the Fenton Art Glass Company of Williamstown, West Virginia, is-

CHART 47   FLOWER BAND. Fenton Art Glass Company, Williamstown, West Virginia.
   CMN: Flower Band.
   Mark: Unmarked, embossed Fenton logo, or paper label.
   Color Code: CA Colonial Amber, CB Colonial Blue, CP Colonial Pink, CY Clear, KL Forget-Me-Not Blue, RT Country Peach.

Item	COLOR(S)	YEAR	ORIG	NEW
Ashtray. #6271.	CY, KL, RT	1982		X
Bowl. #6320. Open, flat, round, 9"d.	CY, KL, RT	1982		X
Candleholder. #6370.	CY, KL, RT	1982		X
Compote. #6380. Open, high standard.	CY, KL, RT	1982		X
Creamer. #6300. Pressed handle, footed.	CY, KL	1982	X	
Goblet. #6348. 9½ oz.	CA, CB, CP	1962	X	
	CY, KL	1982	X	
Salt shaker. #6301. Footed.	CY, KL	1982		X
Sherbert. #6321. (AKA: Nut Dish).	CY, KL, RT	1982		X
Sugar bowl. #6300. Open, footed.	CY, RT	1982		X

sued the new Flower Band goblet. This goblet was made from a new mold and was offered in Fenton's colonial colors of amber, blue, and pink. By 1982, the number of items in Flower Band had increased to nine

Fig. 153. New Flower Band goblet. Fenton Art Glass Co. Circa 1962. Unmarked.

and included the colors of crystal, Forget-Me-Not blue, and country peach. Enumerated in Chart 47, these items can still be found in contemporary and traditional colors and forms. Like Fenton's earlier goblet, each new form was also produced from a good-quality nonflint glass from new molds created at the Fenton factory.

Because Fenton used contemporary colors and shapes, these items are not true reproductions. The only item that might cause confusion among collectors and dealers is the clear goblet. As you can see in Fig. 153, this goblet is a good representation of the original and, like all Fenton

Fig. 154. New Flower Band clear No.6320 bowl and No.6380 open compote. Fenton Art Glass Co. Circa 1982. Embossed Fenton logo.

items, may be found in fine-quality nonflint glass. However, these new items are heavier and the pattern is less detailed than the originals (Fig. 154). In addition, you may find items with a paper label or, after 1970,

permanently embossed with the familiar Fenton logo.

Hint: Reproduction items in Flower Band are heavier than originals.

FLUTED SCROLLS

The original name of this charming pattern is Klondyke. The design was first introduced in 1897 by the Northwood Glass Company of Indiana, Pennsylvania, in a medium-sized table service in the opalescent colors of blue, canary yellow, and white. Although you may find odd pieces in carnival colors, crystal, custard, emerald green, and green opalescence, complete table sets were not made in these colors (Fig. 155).

This pattern was aptly described in the August 11, 1897, issue of *China, Glass and Lamps* as "well named, being of a very brilliant pattern and made in a beautiful Klondyke gold colored glass with pearl effects. It is also made in pearl blue, pearl flint and crystal. Treated artistically with raised enamel and gold decorations, it is very rich and surpasses anything ever produced from this well-known works. It is not an imitation cut pattern but is refreshingly new and original in shape and effect. The body rests on gracefully curved feet and is surmounted by a frill of great brilliancy. The whole is a beautiful shimmering effect of silky threads and prisms."

Fluted Scrolls is often mistaken for Northwood's Fluted Scrolls with Flower Band. However, unlike Fluted Scrolls, this latter pattern has the addition of a single band of embossed flowers that is often enamel-decorated.

Fig. 155. Fluted Scrolls master berry bowl by the Northwood Glass Co. as advertised in *China, Glass and Pottery Review* in 1898.

To date, only one item has been reproduced in Fluted Scrolls. This is the cobalt blue, four-toed master berry bowl produced by Boyd's Crystal Art Glass of Cambridge, Ohio. Though sometimes unmarked, these bowls were made from a new mold and are exceptionally thick and heavy. This thickness is more readily noticeable around the rim of the bowl and in the size of the feet. Although the bowl is a good copy of the original master berry bowl, you must remember that old bowls were never made in cobalt.

When signed, reproduction Fluted Scrolls master berry bowls have the "B" in a diamond trademark.

Hint: Reproduction berry bowls are heavy and thick.
Reproduced items: Bowl.

FOUR PETAL

Four Petal is one of the very early flint patterns of tableware. It is also known as Thumbprint Pillows and was originally made in a limited number of items from an

excellent quality of glass that resounds when gently tapped. Undoubtedly, this pattern was produced by more than one company, as there are three distinct styles of the covered sugar bowl. From the quality of the glass and the number of forms available,

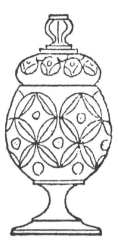

Fig. 156. Four Petal covered sugar bowl reproduced by the Fostoria Glass Co. for the Henry Ford Museum. Embossed "HFM."

Four Petal appears to be a product of the mid-1850s.

As the popularity of reproduction glassware increased in the early 1960s, the Henry Ford Museum in Dearborn, Michigan, granted the Fostoria Glass Company of Fostoria, Ohio, exclusive license to reproduce, on the museum's behalf, a number of pressed-glass patterns. Among them is the new Four Petal covered sugar bowl illustrated in Fig. 156. This new sugar, introduced on January 1, 1965, as Fostoria's No. 2778, was offered in clear and the contemporary colors of copper blue, olive green, and silver mist.

As you can see from the illustration, this new covered sugar is a good copy. Characteristic of all Henry Ford Museum reproductions, it is faithful to the original in shape and design and was made from a new mold in a good-quality lead oxide glass that resounds when gently tapped. Unlike the vast majority of reproductions, each of these new sugar bowls is permanently embossed with the museum's "HFM" insignia. In addition, a small paper tag with a brief history of the pattern was affixed to each new item with a gold HFM sticker.

Hint: Reproduction sugar bowls are permanently marked "HFM."

Reproduced items: Sugar bowl.

FROSTED CIRCLE

Frosted Circle is a highly collectible pattern that was originally produced in an extended table service from varying qualities of nonflint glass. Bryce Brothers of Pittsburgh, Pennsylvania, first issued this pattern about 1876 in clear and clear with frosted circles. Production was continued after 1891, when Bryce became a member of the United States Glass Company, which referred to this pattern as No. 15007, or Horn of Plenty. Although pieces in clear with ruby stain are known, any item in color is a rarity.

Frosted Circle is also known as Clear Circle when the circles are not frosted. It is an interesting design composed of large circles decorated with star-like centers. Each circle, in turn, is separated by a clear fan-shaped ornament.

The reproduction Frosted Circle goblet

Fig. 157. Frosted Circle clear reproduction goblet. Circa early 1940s. Unmarked.

made from a new mold is illustrated in Fig. 157. New goblets are unmarked and appeared as early as 1940 in clear and in clear and frosted glass. As you can see from the illustration, new goblets are quite convincing. However, while the original goblets are thin-walled and lightweight, reproductions are thick-footed and heavy. Reproductions also look glossy and appear greenish-yellow under strong light. Moreover, fine wavy lines (produced by poor pressing techniques) often appear at the rim of the bowl and the base of the foot.

The easiest way to detect new goblets is to examine the circles. On original goblets, they are round and in high relief; on reproductions, they are elongated and often look as if the surface of the sides have been ground to make them flatter.

Reproduction goblets are not permanently marked.

Hint: Reproductions are heavy and the circles in the design are oval-shaped.
Reproduced items: Goblet.

FROSTED LEAF

Similar in design to the well-known Magnet and Grape, Frosted Leaf is one of the many early flint patterns whose manufacture has long been lost in time. Attributed by early research to the Portland Glass Company of Portland, Maine, and the Boston and Sandwich Glass Company of Sandwich, Massachusetts, this pattern appears to date from the early 1860s.

Originally produced in a limited table service from a good-quality clear flint glass, Frosted Leaf is an attractive pattern consisting of machine-frosted leaves against a clear background. Below these leaves are clear vertical panels. Amethyst or any other color is a rarity.

In 1973, the Smithsonian Institution in Washington, D.C., granted the Imperial Glass Corporation of Bellaire, Ohio, exclusive license to reproduce the Frosted Leaf wine (Fig. 158). Produced from a new mold, this wine was known as Imperial's item No. 71250-1 and has a 4-ounce capacity. Like originals, new wines are made from a good-quality clear glass with a distinct lead content. However, unlike originals, which are coarsely ground to produce a frosted effect, new wines have a smooth and silky finish. When you compare the detailing of the leaves, you will notice that it is deeply cut into original wines and lightly cut into new ones.

Imperial reproductions are permanently

Fig. 158. Reproduction Frosted Leaf No.7125-1 clear and frosted nonflint wine. Produced by the Imperial Glass Corp. for the Smithsonian Institution. Circa 1973. Embossed "SI."

embossed with the Smithsonian Institution's "SI" insignia.

Hint: Reproduction wines are acid-finished, unlike originals, which are machine-ground.
Reproduced items: Wine.

FROSTED PHEASANT

Although the original manufacturer of this lovely design is unknown, Frosted Pheasant appears to be a product of the 1870s. The most popular item in this design is the oval, low-footed covered dish with frosted pheasant finial.

This bowl was originally produced with two covers: on the first, the bird looks toward the right; on the second, it looks toward the left. More interesting is the clear oval base, which was offered either unpatterned or decorated at the rim with a One-O-One border.

Frosted Pheasant was originally produced in clear glass with either a clear or frosted finial.

As late as 1950, reproductions of the Frosted Pheasant covered bowl by the Imperial Glass Corporation of Bellaire, Ohio, appeared in blue mist glass. Around 1976, Imperial Glass produced additional copies from the same contemporary mold. Named No. 5190 or the Dove Box, these copies were made in clear, clear and frosted, and milk-white glass.

As you can see from Fig. 159, Imperial reproduced only the bowl on which the pheasant's head is turned to the left and the base is unpatterned. Moreover, Imperial reproductions are 8½ inches. Since 1967, this reproduction has been permanently marked with the company's familiar "IG" hallmark.

Originals are more finely detailed and

Fig. 159. New 51906S Frosted Pheasant covered bowl. Imperial Glass Corp. Circa 1975. Embossed "IG."

molded than reproduction covered bowls. The original color is slightly gray and the frosting is lightly applied only to the pheasant and the very top of the cover. In contrast, reproductions are chalky white because the frosting is heavily applied to the entire cover, including the bowl. The glass has a distinct shine or glossiness that is never seen on original pieces.

Hint: Reproduction Frosted Pheasant bowls are sometimes marked with Imperial's "IG" logo.

Reproduced items: Oval covered bowl.

GALLOWAY

Throughout the late 1890s and early 1900s, numerous clear tableware patterns were stained in amber, blue, green, pink (often called maiden's blush), and ruby. To enhance the decorative effect, many of these designs were further trimmed with gold or platinum. One such pattern is known today by collectors and dealers as Galloway.

Galloway is also known as Mirror Plate, U.S. Mirror, Virginia, and Woodrow. The design was originally produced in 1904 by the United States Glass Company of Pittsburgh, Pennsylvania, as pattern No. 15086 at Factory "GP" (Glassport, Pennsylvania) and Factory "U" (Gas City, Indiana). Apparently, Galloway enjoyed a wide and lengthy popularity, as production continued from 1904 through 1919. Between 1900 and 1925, the Jefferson Glass Company of Toronto, Canada, also produced the design as its No. 15061 line (Fig. 160).

This pattern was originally offered in

Fig. 160. Butler Brothers 1907 catalog reprint of an interesting selection of Galloway.

Fig. 162. Original Galloway flared-rim punch cup. United States Glass Co. Circa 1904. (This shaped punch cup has not been reproduced.)

Fig. 161. Reproduction Galloway amber toothpick holder offered by Trans-World Trading Co. Unmarked.

varying qualities of nonflint glass in a large and varied table service that included more than one hundred different items. Complete settings were available in clear and clear with maiden's blush stain (with or without gold trim). Although items are known in clear with ruby stain, any color other than maiden's blush is rare.

To date, only four items have been reproduced in Galloway. Fig. 161 illustrates the 2½-inch-high toothpick holder. For many years, this toothpick holder has been of-

fered by Trans-World Trading Company of Robinson, Illinois, in clear and in the contemporary colors of amber, amethyst, blue, green, and orange. Produced from a new mold, this toothpick holder is most likely a product of Mosser Glass, Inc., of Cambridge, Ohio. Like most reproductions, it is thicker and heavier than the original. Those produced in clear glass are also off-colored and bubbly.

In 1955, the United States Glass Company of Tiffin, Ohio, reissued three additional items that made the Galloway punch-bowl set. This new punch set was referred to as the Old Mirror pattern and consisted of twelve punch cups, one six-quart punch bowl, and the 20-inch underplate. Although this set was most likely reissued from an original mold, new pieces differ in shape because they are not hand-finished. Unlike original punch cups, which are flared (Fig. 162), new cups are straight-sided. Reproduction punch bowls are also straight-sided with a flared rim, unlike the originals, which are bell-shaped. Reproductions are also glossy and heavy. At times, a distinct waviness may be seen in the glass, especially around rims and bases.

Reproductions in Galloway are not permanently marked.

Hint: Reproductions are heavy and tend to be straight-sided.
Reproduced items: Punch bowl, punch cup, toothpick holder, underplate.

GARFIELD MEMORIAL

Among the many items available in historical pressed glass commemorating great Americans is the Garfield Memorial plate, illustrated in Fig. 163. Elected in 1880, James Abram Garfield (1831–81) became the twentieth President of the United States. Shortly thereafter, he was assassinated by a fanatic. Garfield's portrait adorns the center of this 10-inch-diameter clear plate. Three-quarters of the way around his portrait is a laurel wreath on a stippled border. Embossed at the top of this border is "Memorial."

When and by whom the Garfield Memorial plate was first produced is not known. Apparently, it was created by the same factory that made the Grant Memorial plate because both plates are identical except for the center portrait.

Reportedly, the Summit Art Glass Company of Rootstown, Ohio, reproduced this plate in clear and in clear and frosted glass from a new mold. However, because we do not have a positive catalog identification, we cannot confirm this report. Therefore, we suggest that you carefully examine the

Fig. 163. Original Garfield Memorial plate. Circa 1881.

detail, quality, and weight of any Garfield Memorial plate.

Hint: Suspect items should be examined for detail, quality, and weight.
Reproduced items: Plate.

GATHERED KNOT

The toothpick holder has recently popularized the Gathered Knot pattern among collectors and dealers (Fig. 164). Originally produced by the Imperial Glass Company of Bellaire, Ohio, the design was referred to as line No. 3. Produced from a good-quality clear nonflint glass, Gathered Knot was first issued about 1903 in a limited table service.

The only known reproduction is the toothpick holder. For a number of years, new toothpick holders have been seen in amber, amethyst, blue, and clear. Undoubtedly, other contemporary colors may have been available.

Produced from a new mold, new toothpick holders are unmarked and are typically thicker and heavier than originals. Often the glass contains many bubbles and feels slick or oily. Also, unlike originals, the design is

Fig. 164. Gathered Knot toothpick holder. Imperial Glass Corp. Circa 1903.

blunt and not sharply cast and colors are artificial and harsh.

To date, it is unknown when, or by whom, this reproduction was first produced. From the look and feel of the glass, it appears to be a product of the mid-1970s.

Hint: Any color other than clear is a reproduction.

Reproduced items: Toothpick holder.

GIRL WITH FAN

Girl with Fan is one of the more popular goblets in the portrait series of pressed glass. This goblet was originally produced by the Bellaire Goblet Company of Findlay, Ohio, as early as 1888. This company excelled in the manufacture of bar and stemware and continued production after joining the United States Glass Company as Factory "M" in July 1891. Both Bellaire and the Columbia Glass Company of Findlay, Ohio (Factory "J" of United States Glass), ceased operations in December 1892 after a dispute with the Findlay Gas trustees. By mid-January 1893, the United States Glass Company had removed all equipment, including the mixing house, to the new factory under construction at Gas City, Indiana (Factory "U").

The basic design of the Girl with Fan goblet consists of a well-detailed profile of a young girl that is highly embossed against an open, eight-panel fan. The young girl has long, flowing curls and is wearing a brimmed summer hat and a blouse with a large bow. Her profile is outlined by a rope border. On each of the fan's eight panels is a vine with either berries or a flower that resembles a forget-me-not. This goblet may be found in a good-quality clear nonflint glass.

Reproductions of the Girl with Fan goblet made from a new mold first appeared in the late 1960s. On new goblets (Fig. 165), you will notice that the design is poorly detailed. On the original goblet (Fig. 166), the eight panels of the fan are clearly defined and well executed; on reproductions, they virtually disappear and only traces of the flowered design are evident. The large bow is smaller than the original and incorrectly positioned on the girl's blouse.

The girl's hair on original goblets forms an irregular outline and her curls are well defined in high relief. On reproductions, her

Fig. 165. Reproduction clear Girl with Fan goblet. Circa 1969. Unmarked. (Note the poor detailing and missing fan-motif.)

Fig. 166. Original clear Girl with Fan goblet. Bellaire Goblet Co. Circa 1888. (Note the fine details of the design.)

hair lays in a smooth arc at the back of her head and her blurred curls are in low relief. On originals, the cording of the rope borders is distinctly slanted and, under the portrait, well flared. On reproductions, these cords are not as slanted as originals and form a tighter arc.

One of the easiest ways to tell the difference between old and reproduction goblets is by comparing the stems. Original goblets have a ball with a band in the center of the stem. Reproduction goblets have straight stems and a smaller foot.

Reproduction goblets are not permanently marked. However, it is our opinion that they were produced by the L.G. Wright Glass Company of New Martinsville, West Virginia.

Hint: Reproduction goblets are straight-stemmed and lack fan detail.
Reproduced items: Goblet.

GOOD LUCK

Throughout the history of early American pressed-glass tableware, manufacturers vied for consumer interest by using a variety of decorative techniques. The Good Luck pattern, designed by Samuel G. Vogeley for the firm of Adams & Company of Pittsburgh, Pennsylvania, is a classic example of the designer's use of charm and wit (Fig. 167).

First issued about 1881, Good Luck, also known as Horseshoe, Prayer Mat, and Prayer Rug, was originally produced from a medium-quality clear nonflint glass in an extended table service. Perhaps the most charming design element is the use of horseshoes as finials and handles.

Good Luck is a safe pattern to collect. To date, only the smaller, oval bread platter with single horseshoe handles has been reproduced in clear nonflint glass. When, or by whom, this new platter was produced remains a mystery, although examples have been noted prior to 1975.

Reproduction platters are good copies of the original. Upon close examination, however, you can see subtle discrepancies between the platters. The design on originals is impressed crisply, whereas the design on

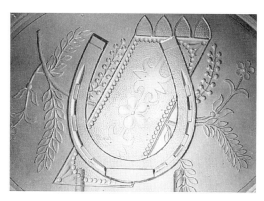

Fig. 167. Closeup of the original Good Luck design. This design on reproductions is distorted and poorly pressed.

new platters is weak and in low relief. Smaller than originals, reproduction bread plates are apparently from new molds. This is best seen in the size of the horseshoe handles, which are large and well designed on originals and short on reproductions.

The Good Luck reproduction bread platter is not permanently marked.

Hint: Reproduction Horseshoe platters are smaller than originals with noticeably smaller handles.
Reproduced items: Bread platter.

GOOSEBERRY

Gooseberry is a charming fruit pattern attributed to the Boston and Sandwich Glass Company of Sandwich, Massachusetts, and the Burlington Glass Works of Hamilton, Ontario. This pattern was originally produced in a limited table service from good-quality clear and milk-white nonflint glass. Judging from its general characteristics, Gooseberry appears to be a product of the early 1870s.

Typical of Victorian glass, Gooseberry is a well-designed pattern. As you can see from Fig. 168, large stippled gooseberries and

Fig. 168. Closeup of the original Gooseberry design.

quickly followed by a milk-white mug with pressed handle and a clear wine. All three items have been produced from new molds, but there are a number of apparent discrepancies. While the leaves and berries are pressed crisply onto original items, they are pressed weakly onto reproductions. The vibrant, lifelike design on originals becomes blurred and lifeless on reproductions.

Like many reproductions, new Gooseberry items are thick-walled and heavier than the old ones. Apparently, both the goblet and wine were reproduced by two different sources, for stems may vary, from fat and stubby to fat and long.

Gooseberry reproductions are not permanently marked to show point of origin or manufacturer.

Hint: The gooseberry design on reproductions is flat and blurred.

Reproduced items: Goblet, mug, wine.

leaves stand in relief against a clear background. Both berry and leaf are so natural as to be botanically correct.

Three items have been reproduced in Gooseberry. Prior to 1962, the goblet appeared in clear nonflint glass and was

GRANT

Commemorating Ulysses S. Grant (1822–85; baptized Hiram Ulysses), the plate known among collectors of historical glassware as the Grant Square Plate is com-

monly found in clear and, rarely, in amber. This plate, illustrated in Fig. 169, measures 9½ inches square by 1½ inches deep and proudly displays a large, well-sculpted bust of Grant in the center. Embossed

Fig. 169. Original clear Grant Memorial plate.

Fig. 170. Reproduction clear Grant plate offered by the A.A. Importing Co., Inc. Circa 1976. (Note that original plates are rectangular.)

above this portrait are the words "The Patriot and Soldier" and below it, "Gen. Ulysses S. Grant."

The A.A. Importing Company's 1976 bicentennial catalog illustrates the No. PG/1606 Grant Patriot and Soldier bread plate shown in Fig. 170. On both original and reproduction plates, General Grant's profile faces left. And, although the imprints read the same, the style of the letters differs. On the original plates, they are embossed in clear block letters; on reproductions, they are stippled and exceptionally large.

One obvious difference between the plates is that the General's buttons and

detailed, decorative shoulder patch, clearly visible on the original, are missing from the reproductions. Another major difference is the shape of the plates; originals are rectangular; reproductions are round (9⅛ inches in diameter) with a slightly scalloped rim.

Although the reproduction Grant plate originally carried a rectangular paper label reading "A.A. Importing Co., Inc., St. Louis, Missouri—Made in Korea," it is not permanently marked.

Hint: Reproduction bread plates are round; originals are rectangular.
Reproduced items: Bread plate.

GRAPE BAND

Grape Band is a member of the fruit series of pattern glass that was popular in the late 1860s and early 1870s. This pattern was designed and patented by John Bryce on October 19, 1869 (design patent No. 3716), and was issued in the same year by Bryce, Walker & Company of Pittsburgh, Pennsylvania. Also known as Ashburton with Grape Band, Early Grape Band, and Grape Vine-Under, this pattern was originally produced in a limited table service in a good-quality clear flint and, later, nonflint glass.

The design, illustrated in Fig. 171, consists of stippled leaves and grapes highly embossed on an otherwise clear background. Handles are beautifully applied and

crimped, finials are bunches of grapes, and the pattern is crisply molded and delicately detailed.

The only known reproduction is the goblet illustrated in Fig. 172. This new goblet made from a new mold is unmarked and can be quite convincing, as you can see from the illustration. It is the same size as the original goblet and readily found in clear nonflint glass. Based on the quality of

Fig. 171. Original Grape Band clear goblet. Bryce, Walker & Co. Circa 1869.

Fig. 172. Reproduction Grape Band clear goblet. Unmarked. (Note the difference between the tendrils on originals and reproductions.)

the glass, we believe this reproduction dates from the mid-1960s.

Upon close examination of this new goblet, you will quickly notice a number of discrepancies. Unlike the proportionally sized grapes on the original goblet, the size of the grapes on this reproduction varies. Also, the stem on the new goblet is thinner, less detailed, and often blurred (as are the stems of the leaf design).

The tendril that hangs between the leaf and berry cluster on original goblets is large. Overlapping itself to produce an oval loop, these tendrils extend to the left to create a "C" and then extend on to the fifth row of berries. Although the tendril on reproductions also overlaps itself, the loop it produces is circular and the tendril ends abruptly after creating a "C" to the left of the bowl. These tendrils do not extend downward as they do on original goblets.

Unlike the leaves on original goblets, which are pointed, the leaves on reproductions are rounded.

One of the most obvious differences between new and old goblets is the double band that appears above the central design. Although this band may vary on original goblets, it is always raised and can be felt easily. The corresponding band on reproduction goblets is indented instead of raised.

Reproduction goblets are not permanently marked.

Hint: The leaves on reproduction goblets are rounded, unlike the pointed leaves of originals.

Reproduced items: Goblet.

GRASSHOPPER

Grasshopper is an interesting figural design collectible in an extended table setting. Although the original manufacturer is not known, Grasshopper is a product of the late 1870s or early 1880s. This line, also known as Locust and Long Spear, was originally produced in a good-quality clear nonflint glass. While you may find odd items in amber, blue, and vaseline, any color is rare.

Whoever designed Grasshopper apparently enjoyed the charm and whimsical taste of the Victorian Era. This is a delightful pattern, originally made flat or footed, and offered in three distinct variations: (1) with insect, (2) without insect, and (3) with long spear. When present, insects are large and well molded. Below each insect are patches of what may be considered grass or shrubbery.

In 1968, the L.G. Wright Glass Company of New Martinsville, West Virginia, produced the goblet illustrated in Fig. 173. Known as Wright's No. 77-24 Grasshopper goblet, this look-alike is 6 inches high with an 8-ounce capacity. As you can see from the illustration, the new goblet is a good representation of the pattern. Produced from a new mold in a mediocre-quality nonflint

77-24
Grasshopper Goblet

Fig. 173. New clear Grasshopper No.77-24 goblet. L.G. Wright Glass Co. Circa 1968. (Goblets were never made originally in this pattern.) Unmarked.

glass, reproductions may be in amber, blue, and clear. Like many reproductions, new goblets are thick and heavy and have a distinctly yellow tinge to the glass. In addition, the grasshopper is molded crudely, with poor detailing on the face and body, and the wings are exaggerated. Because of the poor quality of glass, it is our belief that the Indiana Glass Company of Dunkirk, Indiana, produced these goblets for Wright.

Although the Grasshopper goblet may appear quite convincing to many collectors and dealers, it is not a true reproduction because an original goblet was never made. Typical of L.G. Wright creations, this goblet is not permanently marked.

Hint: Grasshopper goblets were never made originally.

Reproduced items: Goblet.

HEAVY GOTHIC

During the 1890s and early 1900s, stained tableware in America enjoyed a popularity that would never again be rivaled. As consumer interest flourished, independent decorating shops sprung up throughout the major glass centers, flooding the market with a variety of clear with combination color patterns. Amber, ruby, and a variety of other clear with color-stained glassware, often etched, souvenired, or cold-enamel-decorated, flooded the market.

One pattern that enjoyed widespread popularity has been known for years as Heavy Gothic or Whitton. It was first issued by the Columbia Glass Company of Findlay, Ohio, about 1890. When Columbia joined the United States Glass combine in 1891, Heavy Gothic was continued as the U.S. Glass Company's No. 15014 pattern. Originally, it was produced in a large and extended table service in both clear and in clear with ruby-stained nonflint glass. Odd items in green or any other color are rare.

Fig. 174. Reproduction Heavy Gothic clear goblet made for the Red-Cliff Distributing Co. by the Fenton Art Glass Co. Embossed mark.

Fig. 175. New Heavy Gothic bell made by the Fenton Art Glass Co. from the goblet mold owned by Red-Cliff Distributing Co. Circa 1983. Embossed Fenton logo.

The goblet is the first reproduction to appear in Heavy Gothic. Illustrated in Fig. 174, it is 6¼ inches high and may be amber, blue, or clear nonflint glass. These goblets are good copies of the originals. However, produced from new molds, they are larger and heavier than the old. And, unlike originals, reproductions are glossy in appearance.

Reproductions of the Heavy Gothic goblet are permanently embossed under the foot with a capital script "R" surrounded by "(C) RED-CLIFF C USA." This mark was used by the Red-Cliff Distributing Company of Chicago. Though unmarked as to manufacturer, because of the high quality of the glass, we believe this goblet was a product of the Fenton Art Glass Company of Williamstown, West Virginia.

In 1980, the Fenton Art Glass Company issued the Heavy Gothic bell (Fig. 175). Known as Fenton's Whitton pattern, this bell was produced in the opalescent colors of blue, cameo, French, and topaz. In 1983 it was available in carnival and, in 1986, in Burmese. Unlike most Fenton items, this new bell was produced from an original goblet mold, formerly owned by the Red-Cliff Distributing Company.

Like many known look-alike items in early American pattern glass, Fenton's Heavy Gothic bell is not a true reproduction as it does not conform to any known original.

Hint: Reproduction goblets are permanently embossed with the Red-Cliff name.

Reproduced items: Bell, goblet.

HEAVY PANELED GRAPE

Also known as Heavy Grape or Paneled Grape, the original name of this member of the grape family is Kokomo's No. 507. This pattern was designed by Auburn Long and was first issued about 1904 in an extended table service from a good-quality clear nonflint glass by the Kokomo Glass Manufacturing Company of Kokomo, Indiana. The D.C. Jenkins Glass Company of Kokomo contin-

Fig. 176. Reprint of Westmoreland Glass Co. 1955 catalog illustrating an assortment of milk-white Heavy Paneled Grape.

Fig. 177. Reproduction Heavy Paneled Grape clear goblet, most likely offered by the L.G. Wright Glass Co. Circa 1968. Unmarked.

ued manufacturing the pattern after a fire destroyed the Kokomo Glass Company in 1906.

The design consists of large clusters of grapes and stippled grape leaves highly embossed upon a background of clear vertical panels. Handles are pressed and resemble a finely molded branch. Finials are clear sectioned balls.

The most prolific reproducer of Heavy Paneled Grape was the Westmoreland Glass Company of Grapeville, Pennsylvania (see Chart 50). Westmoreland christened its line No. 1881 or Paneled Grape. J.H. Brainard created the Westmoreland molds for the goblet and iced-tea tumbler in 1948. The following year, he added the celery vase, the

creamer, and the covered sugar bowl. As late as 1952, 18 additional items were created in the Westmoreland mold shop. And in 1953, the punch-bowl set was introduced (Fig. 176).

Westmoreland produced Heavy Paneled Grape in clear, clear with ruby stain, and milk white (plain or enamel-decorated) from these new molds. Because the pattern was originally made in clear glass, any colored item is strictly contemporary. In addition, all items are heavy and thick, while clear items have a distinct yellowish cast and are glossy. This line remained in production from its introduction in 1948 until Westmoreland closed in 1985.

Because Westmoreland did not always

CHART 48 PANELED GRAPE. Fenton Art Glass Company, Williamstown, West Virginia.
CMN: Paneled Grape
Mark: Embossed logo.
Color Code: BO Stiegel Blue Opalescent.

ITEM	COLOR(S)	YEAR	ORIG	NEW
Basket. #4613. Applied handle, single crimp, miniature.	BO	1991		X
Butter dish. #4667.	BO	1991	X	
Creamer. #4614. Pressed handle.	BO	1991	X	
Pitcher, pressed handle.				
#4614. Child's (same as creamer).	BO	1991	X	
#4650. Water.	BO	1991	X	
Toothpick. #4616. Flat.	BO	1991		X
Tumbler.				
#4616. Child's (same as toothpick).	BO	1991		X
#4658. Water.	BO	1991	X	

CHART 49 PANELED GRAPE. Plum Glass Company, Pittsburgh, Pennsylvania.
CMN: Paneled Grape, Line No. 1881.
Mark: Embossed "PG" in a keystone and "WG."
Color Code: B Blue, BF Blue Frosted, BL Black, BLGD Black with Gold Decoration, C Clear, CO Cobalt, MW Milk White, SP Space Blue.

ITEM	COLOR(S)	YEAR	ORIG	NEW
Basket, small.				
Plain applied handle.	B, BF, BL, C, CO, MW	1988		X
Twist applied handle.	BLGD	1991		X
	SP	1989		X
Nappy, small, applied handle, heart shape.	B, BF, BL, C, CO, MW	1988		X
	BLGD	1991		X
Vase, swung, 15"h.	MW	1987		X

CHART 50   PANELED GRAPE. Westmoreland Glass Company, Grapeville, Pennsylvania.
CMN: Paneled Grape, Line No. 1881.
Mark: Unmarked, embossed "WG," or paper label.
Color Code: C Clear, CRS Clear with Ruby Stain, MW Milk White, MWD Milk White Decorated, MWG Milk White with Gold.

ITEM	COLOR(S)	YEAR	ORIG	NEW
Ashtray. Square.				
4".	C, MW	1955		X
5".	C, MW	1955		X
6½".	C, MW	1955		X
Banana stand, footed, 12"h.	C, MW	1950s		X
Basket.				
Oval.				
Applied handle, fireside, large, circular foot, folded sides.	CRS	1963		X
	MW	1983		X
Pressed handle, 6½"l.	CRS, MWD, MWG	1967		X
	MW	1960		X
Round.				
Low, crimped rim.				
Low applied handle.	MW	1983		X
Tall applied handle.	MW	1983		X
Tall, 8"h., applied handle, folded, ruffled rim.	CRS, MW, MWD, MWG	1967		X
Bonbon, handled, flat, round.	MW	1967		X
Bottle, toilet, 5 oz.	MW, MWD, MWG	1960		X
Bowl, open.				
Oval.				
Flat.				
10"l.	MW	1983		X
Scalloped rim, 11½"l.	MW	1960s		X
Footed.				
Lipped, 12"l.	MW	1967		X
Scalloped, 11"l.	C, MW	1950s		X
Round.				
Flat.				
Bell shaped, 9"d.	MW	1967		X
Cupped, 9"d.	MW, MWG	1967		X
Deep, salad, 10½"d.	C, MW	1955		X
Lipped.				
9"d.	CRS, MW	1967		X
12"d.	MW	1967		X
Shallow, 14"d.	C, MW	1960		X
Footed.				
Bell-shaped, 12½"d.	C, MW	1955		X
Crimped.	C, MW	1950s		X
Lipped, 9"d.	C, MW	1950s		X
Rippled.	MW	1960s		X
Shallow.	C, MW	1950s		X
Bread tray, oval.	C, MW	1950s		X
Butter dish, covered.				
Rectangular, ¼ lb.	C, MW	1952		X
Round.	MW	1967	X	
Cake stand.				
High standard, 11"d.	MW	1967	X	
Low standard, 10½"d.				
Plain rim.	MW	1967		X
Skirted rim.	C, MW	1950s		X
Canape set, 12½"d. tray, ladle, mayonnaise.	C, MW	1955		X

ITEM	COLOR(S)	YEAR	ORIG	NEW
Candlestick.				
Candelabra, three-light.	MW	1960s		X
Finger, nappy with holder, 6"d.	C, MW	1955		X
Quarter circle (4 to set, each quarter holds 3 candles).	C, MW	1950s		X
Skirted, 4"h.	CRS, MWD, MWG	1967		X
	C, MW	1955		X
Low-handled.	MW	1983		X
Candy dish, open, footed.				
Crimped.	C, MW	1950s		X
Lacy-edged.	C, MW	1950s		X
Canister set, 3-piece.	MW	1960s		X
Celery vase, 6½"h.	C, MW	1949	X	
Chocolate box, covered, round.	MW	1967		X
Cocktail, fruit, round, cupped.	MW	1967		X
Cordial, 2 oz.	C, MW	1950s		X
Compote, high standard.				
Covered.				
Round.				
7"d.	C, MW	1955	X	
	MWD	1967	X	
	MWG	1960	X	
9"d.	C, MW	1955	X	
Square, 9"sq.	MW	1967		X
Open.				
Round				
Crimped bowl.				
4½"d.	C, MW	1950s		X
6"d.	MW	1983		X
9"d.	CRS, MWD, MWG	1967		X
	C, MW	1955		X
Lipped rim, 9"d.	MW	1967		X
Rippled-piecrust rim, 9"d.	MW	1967		X
Shallow bowl, scalloped rim, 14"d.	C, MW	1955		X
Square, flared, 9"sq.	MW	1967		X
Cologne bottle, 5 oz.	MW, MWG	1960		X
Console bowl and base.	C, MW	1950s		X
Creamer.				
Individual.	C, MW	1952		X
	CRS, MWD	1967		X
Table size.	C, MW	1949	X	
	MWG	1967	X	
Cruet, 2 oz., flat, pressed handle, steeple stopper.	C, MW	1954		X
Cup and saucer.	C, MW	1951		X
Decanter, wine, steeple stopper.	MW	1967		X
Deviled-egg plate, round.	C, MW	1950s		X
Dish.				
Covered, candy, 3-footed.	CRS, MW, MWD, MWG	1967		X
Open.				
Bonbon, metal center handle.	MW	1983		X
Mint, crimped rim.	MW	1983		X
Dresser set, 2 cologne bottles, puff box, undertray.	C, MW, MWD	1955		X
	MWG	1960		X

ITEM	COLOR(S)	YEAR	ORIG	NEW
Epergne, one lily.				
Flat.				
9"d., Lipped.	MW	1955		X
12"d., Lipped.	MW	1955		X
14"d., Flared.	MW	1955		X
High standard, base 5"h.				
12"d., Lipped.	MW	1955		X
14"d., Flared.	MW	1955		X
Flower pot, round.				
Large.	MW	1950s		X
Medium.	MW	1950s		X
Small, flared top.	MW	1967		X
Goblet, 8 oz.	C, MW	1948	X	
	CRS	1967	X	
Gravy boat with undertray.	MW	1955		X
Ivy ball, stemmed.	MW	1967		X
Jar, covered, candy, footed.				
6½"h.	MW, MWD, MWG	1967		X
9"sq.	C, MW	1952		X
Jardiniere.				
5"h.	C, MW, MWG	1955		X
6½"h.	C, MW	1955		X
Jelly or puff box, covered, flat.	MW, MWG	1960		X
	MWD	1967		X
Marmalade jar, covered, ladle.	MW	1967		X
Mayonnaise, footed, deep, scalloped.	MW	1967		X
Napkin rings.	MW	1960s		X
Nappy, flat, round, smooth rim. 4½"d.	MW	1967	X	
Parfait.	C, MW	1952		X
Pickle dish, flat, oval.	C, MW	1952	X	
Pitcher, footed.				
1-pint, milk.	CRS	1963	X	
	MW	1967	X	
1-quart.	C, MW	1952	X	
	CRS	1967	X	
Planter.				
Oblong.	MW, MWD	1967		X
Rectangular, window box.	MW	1967		X
Square.	MW	1967		X
Plate.				
6"d., Bread and butter.	C, MW	1954		X
8½"d., Luncheon.	C, MW	1954		X
10½"d, Dinner.	C, MW	1954		X
14½"d., Torte, nonhandled.	C, MW	1955		X
14½"d., Serving, handled.	C, MW	1954		X
Punch set, 15-piece, ladle, 12 cups, 13"d. bowl and base.	C, MW	1953		X
Rose bowl, footed, 4"h.	C, MW	1955		X
Salt shaker.				
Blown, 4½"h.	C, MW	1954		X
Pressed, 4¼"h.	C, MW	1950s	X	

ITEM	COLOR(S)	YEAR	ORIG	NEW
Sauce.				
Flat.	C, MW	1952	X	
Footed, low.	C, MW	1954	X	
Sherbert.				
High-footed.	C, MW	1952		X
Low-footed.	C, MW	1952		X
Snack server, metal handle.				
Single-tier.	C, MW	1950s		X
Two-tier.	CRS, MW	1967		X
Soap dish, flat.	MW, MWD	1967		X
Spoonholder, footed.	MW	1967	X	
Sugar bowl, covered.				
Individual, handled.	C, CRS, MW, MWD	1967		X
Table size, footed.	C, MW	1949	X	
	CRS	1963	X	
	MWG	1967	X	
Toothpick, footed.	MW	1967	X	
Tray, oval.				
9"l.	C, MW	1955		X
13½"l.	C, MW, MWD	1955		X
Tumbler.				
Flat.				
Iced tea, 12 oz.	C, MW	1948	X	
	CRS	1963	X	
Juice, 5 oz.	C, MW	1950s		X
Old-fashioned cocktail.	C, MW	1952		X
Water, 8 oz.	C, MW	1952	X	
Footed.				
Iced tea, 12 oz.	MW	1970s		X
Vase.				
Blown, flat, 14"h.	C, MW	1955		X
Bud.				
9"h.	MW, MWD	1967		X
18"h.	MW	1967		X
Crimped, footed.				
6"h.	MW, MWD	1967		X
6½"h.	C, MW	1955		X
8½"h.	MW, MWG	1967		X
9"h.	CRS, MW, MWD	1967		X
9½"h.	C, MW, MWG	1955		X
11½"h.	C, MW	1955		X
Rose, footed.	MW, MWG	1967		X
Swung, flat, 15"h.	MW	1967		X
Wall pocket.				
6"h.	MW	1950s		X
8"h.	MW	1950s		X
Wine, 5 oz.	C, MW	1952	X	

mark its glass, you may find items unmarked, marked with only an original paper label, or permanently embossed with the company's familiar "WG" logo.

In 1950, the L.G. Wright Glass Company of New Martinsville, West Virginia, introduced the 22 items in Heavy Paneled Grape enumerated in Chart 51. They are unmarked and were produced in amber, amethyst, blue, clear (Fig. 177), green, milk

CHART 51 PANELED GRAPE. L.G. Wright Glass Co. New Martinsville, West Virginia.
CMN: Panel Grape
Mark: Unmarked.
Color Code: A Amber, AM Amethyst, B Blue, C Clear, CRS Clear with Ruby Stain, G Green, MW Milk White, P Pink, RBY Ruby, V Vaseline.

ITEM	COLOR(S)	YEAR	ORIG	NEW
Basket, oval, ruffled skirted base, pressed 2-piece handle.	CRS	1963		X
Bowl, 12"d.				
Console, open, flat.				
#55-1. Crimped rim.	RBY	1968		X
#55-1-1. Ruffled rim.	P	1977		X
	RBY	1968		X
#55-2. Lily, round.	P	1984		X
	RBY	1968		X
Compote, high standard.				
Covered.				
#55-3. 6"d., 10"h.	A, B, G, RBY	1968	X	
	C	1983	X	
#55-8. Jelly, 4"d., 6½"h.	A, AM, B, G, RBY	1968	X	
Open.				
#55-4. smooth rim.	C	1983	X	
Creamer, pressed handle.				
#55-2. Table-size.	C	1977	X	
#55-5. Breakfast.	A, AM, B, G, RBY	1968		X
Cup and saucer set. #55-17.	RBY	1974		X
Goblet, #55-7. 8 oz., 5¾"h.	A, AM, B, C, G, RBY, V	1968	X	
	MW	1950	X	
Pitcher, water, pressed handle. #55-9. 1-qt.	C, RBY	1968	X	
	CRS	1963	X	
Plate, round, flat, scalloped rim.				
#55-10. 15"d.	RBY	1968		X
	P	1977		X
#55-11. 10"d.	RBY	1968	X	
#55-12. 8"d.	RBY	1968	X	
Punch set, 15-piece, #55-14.	RBY	1968		X
Sherbert, round, footed. #55-18. 4"h., 3¾"d.	A, AM, B, G, RBY	1969		X
Sugar bowl.				
#55-5. Breakfast, open, handled.				
2½"d., 3½"h.	A, AM, B, G, RBY	1968		X
#55-21. Table-size, covered.	C, RBY	1977	X	
	CRS	1963	X	
Tumbler, iced tea, flat. Straight sided.	CRS	1963	X	
Wine, #55-20, 2 oz., 4"h.	A, AM, B, C, G, RBY	1968	X	

white, pink, ruby, vaseline, and clear with ruby stain. Because we know that, on rare occasions, Wright used molds from other glass makers, we believe Wright reissued these items from original Westmoreland molds on the condition that the company would not produce items in the Westmoreland colors. Because clear items were no

longer being offered by Westmoreland, only one item (the milk-white goblet) was produced concurrently by both businesses.

In 1953, Glasscrafts & Ceramics, Inc., of Yonkers, New York, offered the following four clear items in Heavy Paneled Grape: the creamer, the goblet, the spoonholder, and the covered sugar bowl. Most likely they were produced by the Westmoreland Glass Company and distributed by Glasscrafts. Like L. G. Wright reproductions, these items are unmarked.

In 1987 the Plum Glass Company of Pittsburgh, Pennsylvania, issued at least four additional items in Heavy Paneled Grape (see Chart 49). Produced from the original Westmoreland molds purchased by Plum, they are readily found in a number of contemporary colors and permanently embossed with a "PG" within a keystone (signifying Plum Glass). Interestingly, the "WG" hallmark of Westmoreland Glass also appears on these pieces.

In 1991 the Fenton Art Glass Company of Williamstown, West Virginia, issued several items of Heavy Paneled Grape in Stiegel blue opalescent (see Chart 48). Each item was made from an original Westmoreland Glass Company mold. All are permanently marked with Fenton's familiar logo. These items are in a color never made originally.

The easiest way to detect reproductions is by examining the detail of the pattern carefully. The leaves on originals are heavily stippled with strong veining, whereas on re-productions the leaves are poorly stippled and the veining is weak. The tendrils on originals are strongly defined on each item and almost touch the rim. On reproductions, these tendrils are so weak that they are either missing or barely visible. On originals, there are always at least two tendrils. On reproductions, there are no more than two.

The grape bunches on originals are molded beautifully and look natural. On new items, the bunches are deformed slightly and the individual grapes in the bunches are misshapen. The main branch or vine that connects the grapes to the top set of leaves on originals is strongly defined with fine lines to simulate bark. On reproductions, this branch is smooth and hardly visible. In general, the leaves, grapes, and vines are always strongly defined on originals, while they are weak and poorly detailed on reproductions (Fig. 178).

Typical of most heavily reproduced patterns, Heavy Paneled Grape remains relatively safe to collect because it originally was made only in clear glass. Still, you should study the original forms and designs because most reproductions were made

Fig. 178. An assortment of new milk-white Heavy Paneled Grape. Westmoreland Glass Co. Circa 1982. Embossed "WG."

Exquisite Crystal by Westmoreland

1881 | 1881 Goblet | 1881 Sherbet | 1881 Ice Tea | 1881 Old Fashion | 1881/1 Qt. Jug

Fig. 179. An assortment of new clear Heavy Paneled Grape. Westmoreland Glass Co. Circa 1967. Embossed "WG." (The goblet, pitcher, and tall tumbler are original forms.)

from the Westmoreland molds, which have since been transferred from one company to another (Fig. 179).

In general, all reproductions are heavier and thicker than the originals. And while the pattern detail of the originals is strongly defined and well proportioned, on reproductions it is weak and blurred. Also, reproductions are poorly shaped.

Hint: Heavy Paneled Grape originally was made only in clear glass.

HICKMAN

As the popularity of pressed glass in America waned in the late nineteenth century, and due to a depressed economy and slumping sales, manufacturers of pressed-glass tableware attempted, without success, to revive older patterns. As a result, designs based on the growing interest in cut glass once again captured the imagination of the mold maker.

Also known as Empire, Jubilee, and LaClede, the pattern commonly known as Hickman was issued by McKee Brothers of Pittsburgh, Pennsylvania, about 1897. One of many McKee patterns based on cut-glass designs, it was later continued by the Federal Glass Company as late as 1914. The pattern was originally produced in a large and extended table service in clear or emerald green; any other color is rare.

In the mid-1960s, a number of variations of the Hickman footed vase appeared. You can still find them in clear and contemporary colors. The 1966 catalog of the L.E. Smith Glass Company of Mount Pleasant, Pennsylvania, illustrated the No. 403, 12-inch-high clear fan-shaped vase shown in Fig. 180. A similar 10-inch-high vase, known as item No. 1966 in amberina, is illustrated in the 1967 catalog of the Viking Glass Company of New Martinsville, West Virginia.

As you can see from the illustration, the new vases are quite convincing. However, differences become most apparent when you study the shape of the rims. Although the rims of new vases are composed of four large scallops that are produced from the fan motif (as on originals), at least four contemporary variations exist. Milk-white examples are barrel-shaped and the scallops of the fan extend straight up and are well defined. Other examples in clear are either straight-sided or fan-shaped. In both instances, the fan motif is less defined and the scallops are rounded more than usual. These variations are characteristic of the L.E. Smith vases (Fig. 181). In the fourth variation, produced by the Viking Glass Company, the rim is distinctly flared. Here, the scallops arch outward from the body. Interestingly, all three clear reproductions

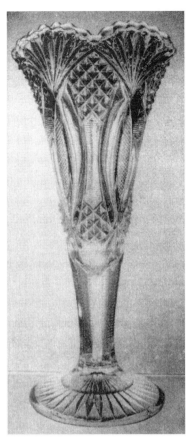

Fig. 180. New Hickman clear fan-shaped vase. L.E. Smith Glass Co. Circa 1966. Unmarked.

Fig. 181. Reproduction Hickman milk-white bud vase. L.E. Smith Glass Co. Circa 1971. Unmarked.

have rayed bases. Only the milk-white vase is unpatterned.

As a general rule of thumb, new Hickman vases are heavy with a smooth, blunt pattern. Any contemporary color signifies a reproduction. Reproduction vases are not permanently marked, although they may still retain their original paper label.

Hint: Hickman reproduction vases are heavier than originals.

Reproduced items: Vase.

HOBBS' BLOCK

One of many popular patterns of the firm of Hobbs, Brockunier & Company of Wheeling, West Virginia, is Hobbs' Block (Fig. 182). Produced by that company in a large table service about 1888, its original name is Hobbs' No. 330. Production of the pattern was continued after Hobbs became a member of the United States Glass Company in 1891.

Hobbs' Block, also known as Divided Squares, is an attractive pattern that was originally produced from a good-quality non-flint glass in clear, clear with amber stain, clear with acid finish, and clear with an acid finish and amber stain. Most pieces are oval, finials are faceted, and handles are applied

CHART 52   HOBBS' BLOCK. Fenton Art Glass Company, Williamstown, West Virginia.
CMN: Block and Star.
Mark: Unmarked or paper label.
Color Code: AR Amber, GD Goldenrod, GP Green Pastel, JB Jamestown Blue, LC Lilac, LG Light Green, MI Milk White, PC Peach Crest, RP Rose Pastel, SJ Silver Jamestown, TU Turquoise.

ITEM	COLOR(S)	YEAR	ORIG	NEW
Basket. #5637. Handled.	MI	1955		X
Bowl, open, flat.				
#5624. Square, 9".	MI	1955		X
#5625. Flared, 11"d.	MI	1955		X
#5626. Cupped, 10"d.	MI, TU	1955		X
#6929. 9"d.	MI	1957	X	
#7021. 11"d.	GP, MI	1955		X
Buffet set. #5602.	MI	1955		X
Cake plate, #6913. Footed.	MI	1957		X
Canasta set. #5808.	MI	1955		X
Candleholder.				
#5670. Handled.	MI, TU	1955		X
#5671. Square.	MI	1955		X
#5672. Flared.	MI	1955		X
#5673. Cupped.	MI, TU	1955		X
#6974.	MI	1957		X
#7073.	GP, MI	1955		X
Candy box.				
#6080.	MI, RP	1956		X
#6983. Footed.	MI	1957		X
#6985.	MI, TU	1955		X
Condiment set. #6909.	MI, TU	1955	X	
	GD	1956	X	
Console set.				
#5600. 3-piece.	MI, TU	1955		X
#5601. Square.	MI	1955		X
#5605. Flared.	MI, TU	1955		X
#5608. Cupped.	MI, TU	1955		X
#7003. 3-piece.	GP, MI	1955		X
Creamer. #5661.	MI, TU	1955	X	
Cruet.				
#6963.	MI	1957	X	
#7063.	GP, MI	1955	X	
Dessert.				
#5620. Square.	MI	1955		X
#5621. Flared.	MI	1955		X
#5622. Cupped.	MI, TU	1955	X	
Dish. #5635. Bonbon.	MI, TU	1955		X
Jam and jelly set. #5603.	MI, TU	1955		X
Jug, handled.				
#5667. 70 oz.	MI, TU	1955		X
#6066. 6"h.	MI, TU	1955		X
#6068. 6½"h.	LC, MI, TU	1955		X
Mayonnaise set.				
#5609.	MI, TU	1955		X
#7004.	GP, MI	1955		X
Mustard and spoon. #6989.	MI, TU	1955		X
	GD	1956		X

ITEM	COLOR(S)	YEAR	ORIG	NEW
Relish dish. #5623.	MI, TU	1955	X	
Salt shaker.				
#5606.	MI, RP, TU	1955	X	
#6606.	MI, RP	1955	X	
#7001.	GP, MI	1955	X	
Sugar bowl. #5627.	MI, TU	1955	X	
Tray. #6997. Sandwich.	MI	1957		X
Tumbler.				
#5647. 12 oz., 6"h.	MI, TU	1955		X
#5649. 9 oz.	MI, TU	1955	X	
#6550. 10 oz.	AR, LG, MI, TU	1955		X
Vanity. #7005. 3-piece.	GP, MI	1955		X
Vase.				
#5658. 8½"h.	MI	1955		X
#5659. 9"h.	MI	1955		X
#6056. 6"h.	PC	1955		X
	SJ	1957		X
#6058. 6½"h.	LC, PC	1955		X
	SJ	1957		X
#6059. 8½"h.	PC	1956		X
#7056. 6"h.	GP, MI, RP, TU	1955		X
	JB	1957		X

CHART 53   HOBBS' BLOCK. Other Reproductions Prior to 1975.
  Maker: Unknown.
  Mark: Unmarked.
  Color Code: C Clear.

ITEM	COLOR(S)	YEAR	ORIG	NEW
Bowl, open, round, flat, 10½"d., flared rim.	C	1975	X	
Celery vase, 5⅛"h.	C	1975	X	
Compote, open, high standard, jelly. 4⅝"h.	C	1975		X
Spoonholder, 4"h.	C	1975	X	
Tray, pickle, 10½"l.	C	1975	X	

beautifully. The squares of the pattern may be either starred or plain.

In 1955, the Fenton Art Glass Company of Williamstown, West Virginia, introduced the Block and Star pattern illustrated in Fig. 183. Primarily produced in milk white or turquoise, the pattern was issued by Fenton between 1955 and 1957 in a limited number of forms in several experimental colors. Known pieces are enumerated in Chart 52.

As you can see from the illustration, Fenton's Block and Star is a direct copy of the earlier Hobbs' pattern. However, only the design may cause confusion. Fenton successfully used a wide variety of contemporary shapes and colors that were unknown to our Victorian ancestors. Technically speaking, Fenton's Block and Star pattern is not a reproduction. Rather, it is a contemporary copy of an antique design and should be considered as such.

However, more disturbing copies of the old Hobbs' pattern entered the market prior to 1975. Enumerated in Chart 53, you may find each in clear nonflint glass. Unlike Fenton's use of the design, which reflects twen-

Fig. 182. Original frosted with amber stain Hobbs' Block goblet. Hobbs, Brockunier & Co. Circa 1888. (Note: this color treatment has yet to be reproduced.)

Fig. 183. New milk-white Hobbs' Block jug and tumbler. Fenton Art Glass Co. Circa 1955. Unmarked.

tieth-century America's growing interest in contemporary form and color, these clear reproductions can become quite confusing. At first sight, each appears to be an exact copy of an original. Upon closer examination, you can detect a number of basic discrepancies associated with glass produced from new molds. Clear reproductions are noticeably heavier than originals. Unlike the soft, mellow surface of glass aged by time and daily use, new items sparkle with a luster that is not present in the old. The most obvious difference, however, is in the sharpness of the design. Although crisply molded, the feel of original items is soft. In comparison, the design on new items is jagged, producing a harsh feeling.

To date, reproductions in clear with frosting and clear with amber stain are unknown. Reproduction items are not permanently marked.

Hint: Reproduction items are heavier and harsher than originals.

HOBBS' HOBNAIL

Like Daisy and Button, the Hobnail motif sustained its popularity over an extended period of time. There are so many variations of this design that you can easily assemble an interesting collection of each. The basic design consists of rows of hobnails that ordinarily decrease in size toward the base. An exception is the tumbler illustrated in Fig. 184.

Hobbs' Hobnail, one of the most popular variants of this motif, was first issued about 1885 by Hobbs, Brockunier & Company of Wheeling, West Virginia. Hobbs continued to produce this pattern after 1891, when it became Factory "H" of the United States Glass combine.

This pattern originally was made in an assortment of colors, which included amberina, clear, clear with amber stain, clear and frosted with amber stain, cranberry, rubina

Fig. 184. Original Hobbs' Hobnail frosted tumbler. Hobbs, Brockunier & Co. Circa 1885.

Fig. 185. Reproduction Hobbs' Hobnail cranberry opalescent barber bottle produced by the Fenton Art Glass Co. for L.G. Wright Glass Co. Circa 1930s. Unmarked.

(plain or frosted), rubina verde, sapphire blue, white, cased mauve, cased white, and opalescent clear, cranberry, and vaseline. Although an extended table service was offered, not all pieces were made in all colors.

The shape of the hobnail design is characteristic of the Hobbs' variation of this pattern. Unlike later variants, which have blunt, round, and short hobnails, the hobnails on Hobbs' version are long and pointed.

Although the hobnail motif has graced myriad reproductions, only eight items may prove troublesome. They are the barber bottle, the butter dish, the high-standard covered compote, the creamer, the cruet, the water pitcher, the salt shaker, and the tumbler.

The first Hobbs' Hobnail reproduction to appear is the barber bottle illustrated in Fig. 185. This bottle is unmarked and was introduced by the L.G. Wright Glass Company of New Martinsville, West Virginia. Produced for Wright in the late 1930s by the Fenton Art Glass Company of Williamstown, West Virginia, from an original Northwood mold, these new barber bottles are probably the most difficult reproductions to detect. However, when you examine a new bottle carefully, you will quickly notice that it is exceptionally heavy and

thick. Also, the neck is wider than the original and the hobs are placed too widely apart. Although reproduction bottles were produced in the original colors of opalescent cranberry and rubina (plain or satinized), both colors are pale and weak compared to the originals.

New, unmarked creamers, cruets, and water pitchers also appeared in rubina (clear or satinized) and opalescent blue, cranberry, and vaseline. The first reproductions were blown and so poorly made that the hobnails, or warts, as old glass makers refer to them, appear distorted. Like original items, the handles on early reproductions were applied and solid. Later, all three items reappeared with better-shaped hobnails. However, the design was now too perfectly round and too long while the glass remained thick and heavy—a condition most readily seen at the lip. As late as 1946, the same pieces reappeared again but with twisted handles, which are strictly contemporary.

At this same time, new water tumblers were also being made. These unmarked tumblers were excellent copies of the originals. However, they are characteristically heavy and thick and the hobnails at the base are too large and pointed. Also, when you examine the base of a new tumbler through a strong light, you will notice an excessive amount of glass. New tumblers are most commonly encountered in blue (plain or satinized), opalescent blue, cranberry, green, and vaseline.

As late as 1953, the Fenton Art Glass Company of Williamstown, West Virginia, issued two items in this pattern: the No. 3883 or Hobnail flat covered butter dish and the No. 3887 high-standard covered compote. Both items were produced from new molds in milk white. In 1958, the butter dish was also offered in cranberry opalescent and turquoise. The compote was offered only in turquoise. In 1959, the covered compote was available in opalescent green and plum.

During the late 1950s, salt shakers also entered the market. Typical of a majority of reproductions produced from new molds, these new shakers are unmarked. Compared to originals, they are heavy and thick. When you insert your index finger inside a reproduction shaker, you will notice an excessive amount of glass inside the base that permits your finger to enter only halfway. New salt shakers were made in solid amber, amberina, blue, clear, green, ruby, yellow (plain or satinized), and opalescent blue and vaseline.

In 1960, the Imperial Glass Corporation of Bellaire, Ohio, reproduced the No. 1950 or Hobnail flat covered sugar bowl in milk white. By 1977, the colors of nut brown and ultra blue were added to the line. Like other items copied in this pattern, Imperial reproductions were produced from new molds.

Hobbs' Hobnail reproductions appear in a good-quality nonflint glass and are excellent copies. Although no original Francesware color has been reissued, the reissue of antique forms in clear and original colors may cause confusion among beginning collectors. As a general rule, reproductions are larger and heavier than the old. On reproductions, the hobnails are blunt or flat and in low relief (compared to the long, sharp, tapered hobnails of originals). Milk white, nut brown, ruby, turquoise, and ultra blue are contemporary colors.

Early Fenton reproductions are not permanently marked; those by Imperial are embossed with the familiar "IG" logo.

Hint: Reproductions in Hobbs' Hobnail are heavier and thicker than originals.

Reproduced items: Barber bottle, butter dish, compote, creamer, cruet, pitcher, salt shaker, tumbler.

HOBNAIL WITH FAN TOP

Hobnail with Fan Top is a popular member of the Hobnail family. Produced in a limited table setting, it was first introduced by Doyle & Company of Pittsburgh, Pennsylvania, in the 1880s as its pattern line No. 150. When Doyle became a member of the United States Glass combine in 1891, it was reissued. Originally produced in a good-quality clear nonflint glass, this pattern was also offered in light and dark amber, blue, and canary.

As early as 1956, the Imperial Glass Cor-poration of Bellaire, Ohio, reproduced from new molds three milk-white items in the Hobnail with Fan Top: (1) the No. 640 round, flat, 4½-inch-diameter sauce dish, (2) the No. 641 8½-inch-diameter round, open, flat bowl, and (3) the No. 642 10-inch-diameter round, open, flat master berry bowl. Shortly thereafter, each was also available in the solid colors of amber, blue, and pink, and by 1966 in verde and vaseline opalescent (see Dewdrop). In 1962, the No. 641 bowl appeared in purple marble slag and in 1971 in antique blue, ambergio, and azalea. As late as 1982, the large clear, 10-

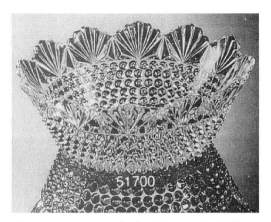

Fig. 186. Reproduction Hobnail with Fan Top No.51700 clear master berry bowl. Imperial Glass Corp. Circa 1982–83. Embossed "IG."

inch master berry bowl illustrated in Fig. 186 was still being listed in Imperial's catalog.

Reproductions in Hobnail with Fan Top

are quite convincing. The hobs are finely executed and each new item is the same size as the original. However, you can easily differentiate between the new and the old. Original items are light in weight, while reproductions, due to their thickness, are heavier. And, unlike the mellow, pale hue of Victorian colored glass, contemporary colors are dense and harsh, especially items in amber and blue. Perhaps the most obvious difference is the way the points of the fans create the rims. On original items, they are finely molded and sharp, and on reproductions they are smooth or blunt.

When signed, Imperial reproductions are permanently embossed with the company's familiar "IG" logo.

Hint: The fans of the design on reproductions are smooth and not as sharply defined as those on originals.

Reproduced items: Bowl, sauce dish.

HOBNAIL WITH THUMBPRINT BASE

A variant of the well-known Hobnail design is the pattern known for many years as Hobnail with Thumbprint Base. Made by Doyle & Company of Pittsburgh, Pennsylvania, which also produced the well-known Hobnail with Fan Top, this pattern's popularity reigned throughout the 1880s and was revived when Doyle became a part of the United States Glass Company in 1891 (Fig. 187).

Also known as Hobnail with Scalloped Top, Doyle originally issued this pattern in a small table service from a good-quality non-flint glass in amber, blue, and clear. The chief difference between this pattern and other variants of the Hobnail group lies in the band of thumbprints found on the collared base of each item (Fig. 188).

In 1974, the L.G. Wright Glass Company of New Martinsville, West Virginia, issued five items in Hobnail with Thumbprint Base. Originally known as Wright's Hobnail pattern, the No. 33-4 creamer with pressed

Fig. 187. Original Hobnail with Thumbprint Base blue covered sugar bowl. Doyle & Co. Circa 1880s.

handle, No. 33-5 spoonholder, No. 33-7 4-inch-diameter round finger bowl, and the No. 33-2 flat, 4-inch-high bulbous covered sugar bowl were produced in the original colors of amber or blue and the contemporary color of ruby. At the same time, the No. 33-10 salt shaker was issued in all three colors as well as clear and green.

Fig. 188. Closeup of an original Hobnail with Thumbprint Base mug illustrating the thumbprint motif around the base.

Whether Wright used original molds to produce Hobnail With Thumbprint Base is not known. Therefore, you must consider the color and quality of the glass when you examine a suspect item. Unlike the deep, warm tone of originals, the color of new items ranges from being too pale to being brash, deep, and artificial. This range is best seen in the shades of amber, blue, and green. While new items produced in blue appear pale and washed out (the same condition found on Wright's reproductions of Argonaut Shell in blue opalescence), remaining colors are harsh, muddy, and unlike any known original.

The quality of reproduction glass also varies from originals, which have deep, crisp impressions. Reproductions are heavy and thick and lightly pressed and, more often than not, smooth with a noticeably flat and blurred design. You can most often see this difference around rims and bases.

Although L.G. Wright reproductions are not permanently marked, the color and quality of the glass should alert dealers and collectors to their newness.

Hint: The pattern on reproductions is flat and often blurred.
Reproduced items: Creamer, finger bowl, salt shaker, spoonholder, sugar bowl.

HOLLY AMBER

Considering the enormous quantity of pressed tableware produced throughout the Victorian Era, only a handful of patterns collectible in complete table settings can be categorized as art glass. One such pattern is Holly Amber.

Holly Amber was originally produced about 1903 by the Indiana Tumbler and Goblet Company of Greentown, Indiana, which named the line No. 450. Jacob Rosenthal, who produced Indiana's famed chocolate glass, also created for this line the amber or agate color. The pattern was originally issued in a complete table service in clear and golden agate. Known examples in chocolate and holly blue are rare.

The name "Holly Amber" (or Golden Agate as it was originally called) is a misnomer. Holly amber (a blend of amber-white opalescent glass) refers to the color of the glass and not the design. This pattern, originally called Holly, was designed by Frank Jackson especially for use with the holly amber or golden agate color. The design consists of clear convex ribs that alternate with flat panels of long holly sprigs and berries. These panels are placed horizontally or vertically (depending upon the form) and are separated from each other by a narrow panel of tiny beading. Beading is also found around the bases and rims of such items as the cake stand, creamer, pickle tray, and true open compote.

The first reproductions in Holly were: the covered butter dish, the high-standard covered compote, the high-standard open jelly compote, the cruet, the 7½-inch-diameter plate, and the flat water tumbler. These unmarked reproductions were produced prior to 1975 from new molds in a number of contemporary colors.

As late as 1972, St. Clair Glass of Elwood, Indiana, reproduced the Holly Amber toothpick holder, illustrated in Fig. 189, from a

CHART 54 HOLLY AMBER. Summit Art Glass Company, Rootstown, Ohio.
CMN: Holly Band.
Mark: Unmarked or paper label.
Color Code: AMB Amberina, C Clear, CH Chocolate, COB Cobalt, EV Evergreen, ECHI Experimental Choco-
late Iridized, FF First Frost, GC Green Custard, MG Morning Glory, RAS Red Amber Slag, RUB Rubina, SBM
Sky Blue Milk.

ITEM	COLOR(S)	YEAR	ORIG	NEW
Butter dish. #591. Covered, 8"d.	C, CH	1985	X	
	RAS	1978	X	
Creamer. #561. 5½"h.	CH	1985	X	
	RAS	1978	X	
Mug. #560. 5"h.	RAS	1978	X	
	RUB	1985	X	
Sauce dish. #559. Round, flat.	CH	1985	X	
	RAS	1978	X	
Sugar bowl. #557. Covered, 6½"d.	CH, RUB	1985	X	
	RAS	1978	X	
Toothpick holder. #558. 2½"h.	AMB, C, CH, COB, EV	1985	X	
	ECHI, FF, MG, SBM	1985	X	
	GC	1984	X	
	RAS	1978	X	
Tumbler. #562. Water, 3¾"h.	CH	1985	X	
	RAS	1978	X	

new mold in chocolate, clear, green opaque, and the carnival colors amethyst, blue, and red. New toothpicks are unmarked and heavier and thicker than originals. You can readily see this difference in the excessive amount of glass around the base and rim. In 1978, St. Clair sold 50 molds, including those to the Holly Amber and Inverted Fan and Feather toothpick holders.

In 1978, the Summit Art Glass Company of Rootstown, Ohio, reproduced the seven forms enumerated in Chart 54. At this time, each item was produced in Summit's red

Fig. 189. Reproduction clear Holly Amber toothpick holder. Unmarked.

Fig. 190. Base of reproduction Holly Amber creamer illustrating the Summit Art Glass Co. paper label.

amber slag. Between 1978 and 1985, an additional eleven colors were added to this line, although not all pieces were available in all colors (Fig. 190).

Although the Summit toothpick holder was reportedly produced from the original Indiana Tumbler and Goblet Company mold, the remainder of this line was produced from new molds. You can see the differences best in the treatment of the design on reproductions. Compared to originals, the holly leaves on new items are too stippled, producing an unnatural look that becomes blurred toward the base. Additionally, while the stems on original items are thin and uniformly shaped, those on reproductions are overly thick. The beading on new items also varies, being either too large or too small. The most obvious difference, however, is the berry motif. On reproductions, a single berry alternates with each leaf on either side of the stem. On original items, the number of berries vary from one to bunches of two or three.

Because the size of new toothpick holders ranges from 2½ to 2⅜ inches high, it is entirely possible that other contemporary glass houses may have produced this item.

Hint: Reproduction items have a single holly berry alternating with each leaf and originals have from one to three berries.

Reproduced items: Butter dish, compote, creamer, cruet, mug, plate, sauce dish, sugar bowl, toothpick, tumbler.

HONEYCOMB

Like Daisy and Button, Hobnail, and a number of other patterns, there are a seemingly endless number of Honeycomb variations. These variations can be categorized into two primary types: "New York" and "Cincinnati" or "Vernon." In the first, only the lower portion of the item is patterned. In the second, the design covers the entire article.

Honeycomb was originally produced by

CHART 55 HONEYCOMB. Fenton Art Glass Company, Williamstown, West Virginia.
CMN: No.1611 or Georgian.
Mark: Unmarked or paper label.
Color Code: A Amber, BL Black, C Clear, G Green, MS Moonstone, P Pink, RB Royal Blue, RBY Ruby, TP Topaz.

ITEM	COLOR(S)	YEAR	ORIG	NEW
Claret, knob stem.	A, BL, C, G, P, RB, RBY	1930		X
	TP	1930		X
Cocktail.				
Knob stem.	A, BL, C, B, P, RB, RBY	1930		X
	TP	1930		X
Tall stem.	RB	1930		X
Cocktail shaker, 24 oz., with silver strainer top.	A, BL, C, G, P, RB, RBY	1930		X
	TP	1930		X
Cordial, footed, 1 oz.	A, BL, C, B, P, RB, RBY	1930		X
	TP	1930		X
Creamer, pressed handle.	A, BL, C, B, P, RB, RBY	1930		X
	TP	1930		X
Cup, footed, pressed handle.	A, BL, C, G, P, RB, RBY	1930		X
	TP	1930		X
Decanter. #1611. Bulbous, flat.	A, BL, C, G, P, RB, RBY	1930		X
	TP	1930		X
Finger bowl with underplate.	A, BL, C, G, P, RB, RBY	1930		X
	TP	1930		X

ITEM	COLOR(S)	YEAR	ORIG	NEW
Goblet.	A, BL, C, G, P, RB, RBY	1930		X
	TP	1930		X
Nut cup, footed, flared bowl.	A, BL, C, G, P, RB, RBY	1930		X
	TP	1930		X
Pitcher.				
½ Gallon, water, applied handle.	A, BL, C, G, P, RB, RBY	1930		X
	TP	1930		X
54 oz., 7"h., iced tea, with or without "ice" lip.	A, BL, C, G, P, RB, RBY	1930		X
	TP	1930		X
Plate.				
6"d., Bread and butter.	A, BL, C, G, P, RB, RBY	1930		X
	TP	1930		X
8"d., Salad.	A, BL, C, G, P, RB, RBY	1930		X
	TP	1930		X
10"d., Service.	A, BL, C, G, P, RB, RBY	1930		X
	TP	1930		X
11"d., Three-compartment.	A, BL, C, G, P, RB, RBY	1930		X
	TP	1930		X
Salt shaker, footed.	A, BL, C, G, P, RB, RBY	1930		X
	TP	1930		X
Sherbert.	A, BL, C, G, P, RB, RBY	1930		X
	TP	1930		X
Sugar bowl, open, double-handled.	A, BL, C, G, P, RB, RBY	1930		X
	TP	1930		X
Tumbler.				
Iced tea, 12 oz.	A, BL, C, G, P, RB, RBY	1930		X
	TP	1930		X
Juice, 5 oz.	A, BL, C, G, P, RB, RBY	1930		X
	TP	1930		X
Lemonade, 10 oz.	A, BL, C, G, P, RB, RBY	1930		X
	TP	1930		X
Water, 9 oz.				
Flat.	A, BL, C, G, P, RB, RBY	1930		X
	TP	1930		X
Footed.	A, BL, C, G, P, RB, RBY	1930		X
	MS	1933		X
	TP	1930		X
Whiskey, 2½ oz.	A, BL, C, G, P, RB, RBY	1930		X
	TP	1930		X

CHART 56   HONEYCOMB. Jeannette Glass Company, Jeannette, Pennsylvania.
   CMN: Hex Optic or Honeycomb.
   Mark: Unmarked or paper label.
   Color Code: C Carnival, G Green, P Pink.

ITEM	COLOR(S)	YEAR	ORIG	NEW
Bowl.				
Berry.				
4¼"d., Ruffled.	G, P	1928		X
7½"d.	G, P	1928		X
Mixing.				
7¼"d.	G, P	1928		X
8¼"d.	G, P	1928		X
9"d.	G, P	1928		X
10"d.	G, P	1928		X
Butter dish, rectangular, 1 lb.	G, P	1928		X
Creamer, flat, tab handle.	G, P	1928		X

ITEM	COLOR(S)	YEAR	ORIG	NEW
Cup and saucer.	G, P	1928		X
Ice bucket, metal handle.	G, P	1928		X
Pitcher.				
5"h., 32 oz., Flat.	G, P	1928		X
9"h., 48 oz., Footed.	C	1950		X
	G, P	1928		X
Plate.				
6"d., Sherbert.	G, P	1928		X
8"d., Luncheon.	G, P	1928		X
11"d., Platter	G, P	1928		X
Refrigerator dish, 4"sq.	G, P	1928		X
Salt shaker, flat.	G, P	1928		X
Sugar bowl, open, tab-handled.	G, P	1928		X
Sugar shaker.	G, P	1928		X
Sherbert, footed, 5 oz.	G, P	1928		X
Tumbler.				
Flat.				
2"h., 1 oz., Whiskey.	G, P	1928		X
3¾"h., 9 oz.	G, P	1928		X
Footed.				
4¾"h., 7 oz.	C	1950		X
	G, P	1928		X
5¾"h.	G, P	1928		X
7"h.	G, P	1928		X

CHART 57 HONEYCOMB. Viking Glass Company, New Martinsville, West Virginia.
CMN: Georgian.
Mark: Unmarked or paper label.
Color Code: A Amber, B Blue, BR Brown, G Green, RBY Ruby.

ITEM	COLOR(S)	YEAR	ORIG	NEW
Cocktail. #6910.	A, B, BR, G, RBY	1972		X
Creamer. #6922. Pressed handle.	A, B, BR, G, RBY	1972		X
Goblet.				
#6911. 11 oz.	A, B, BR, G, RBY	1972		X
#6912. 13 oz.	A, B, BR, G, RBY	1972		X
Pitcher, with ice lip.				
#6923. 32 oz.	A, B, BR, G, RBY	1972		X
#6908. 54 oz.	A, B, BR, G, RBY	1972		X
Plate. #6907. 8"d.	A, B, BR, G, RBY	1972		X
Salt shaker. #6920.	A, B, BR, G, RBY	1972		X
Sherbert. #6913. 6 oz.	A, B, BR, G, RBY	1972		X
Sugar bowl. #6922. Covered.	A, B, BR, G, RBY	1972		X
Toothpick. #6919.	A, B, BR, G, RBY	1972		X
Tumbler, flat, circular foot.				
#6902. 5 oz.	A, B, BR, G, RBY	1972		X
#6903. 9 oz.	A, B, BR, G, RBY	1972		X
#6904. 12 oz.	A, B, BR, G, RBY	1972		X
Wine. #6909.	A, B, BR, G, RBY	1972		X

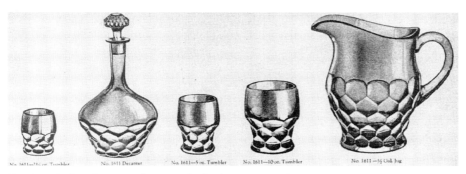

Fig. 191. Selection of Honeycomb or Georgian by the Fenton Art Glass Co. Circa 1930s. Unmarked.

myriad nineteenth-century glass houses, including Bellaire Goblet Company (No.40) of Findlay, Ohio; Cape Cod Glass Works (No.96) of Sandwich, Massachusetts; Central Glass Company (No.136) of Wheeling, West Virginia; Doyle & Company (No. 500) of Pittsburgh, Pennsylvania; J.B. Lyon & Company (New York and Cincinnati) of Pittsburgh; McKee Brothers (Cincinnati) of Pittsburgh; New England Glass Company (New York and Vernon) of Cambridge, Massachusetts; O'Hara Glass Company (No. 3) of Pittsburgh; and the United States Glass Company (New York and Cincinnati) of Pittsburgh.

Fig. 192. New Honeycomb or Georgian goblets, a popular adaptation. Viking Glass Co. Circa 1974.

This design was produced for many years in flint and nonflint glass. The pattern was issued in a large and extended table service in clear glass that was either plain or copper-wheel engraved. Early pieces are brilliant, heavy, and ring with a fine belltone resonance, while later pieces are nonflint, light, and do not resound.

Due to mass production, bases, finials, handles, and stems vary greatly. Although items came in amber, amethyst, apple green, blue, emerald green, opaque white, opaque green, pink, and fiery opalescent, any color in flint glass is rare. Colored nonflint pieces are of later manufacture and are considered scarce.

Since the 1920s, many contemporary glass houses have continued to use the honeycomb design in modern forms. (See Charts 55, 56, and 57). The Cambridge Glass Company of Cambridge, Ohio, produced Georgian pitchers and tumblers for a number of years. Meanwhile, both the Fen-

ton Art Glass Company of Williamstown, West Virginia, and the Viking Glass Company of New Martinsville, West Virginia, issued the pattern in an extended table service (Figs. 191 and 192). Another variation of Honeycomb, known as Hex Optic, was made by the Jeannette Glass Company of Jeannette, Pennsylvania.

Unlike other patterns that have been in continuous production, the treatment of the honeycomb design is completely different because the design has not been used on any known original form. Because of this use of contemporary shapes, new items should never be confused with the old. Reproductions in Honeycomb have distinctive shapes and colors and were made from a good-quality nonflint glass that is often fire-polished. New items are also heavier and thicker then earlier nonflint items.

Hint: Honeycomb was never produced in original shapes and items.

HORN OF PLENTY

Horn of Plenty is one of the most popular patterns in early American flint glass. This design was originally called Comet by McKee Brothers of Pittsburgh, Pennsylvania, which first issued it in the 1860s. Because enough fragments have been unearthed at the old site of the Boston and Sandwich Glass Company of Sandwich, Massachusetts, it is believed that pieces were also made at that factory.

Also known as Peacock Tail, this design was originally issued in a brilliant clear flint glass in a large and extended table service. The glass is crystal clear, heavy, and bell-toned, and handles are applied. Amber, amethyst, brilliant blue, canary yellow, clambroth, clear edged in color, milk white, or any other color in flint glass is rare.

The design consists of a large chain of alternating clear and decorated circles. The center of each clear circle is impressed with a bull's eye, while those circles that are decorated are filled with tiny diamond points. Below each circle hangs a cone-shaped ornament that swings toward the left. Those cones that hang beneath clear circles are decorated with tiny diamond points, while those that hang from decorated circles are decorated with a row of clear bull's eyes. The complete design creates the illusion of a cornucopia. Typical of the period, handles are beautifully applied. Finials are either acorn-shaped or flattened, although a covered butter dish has been documented with the finial in the shape of George Washington's head.

Until 1933, no major item of pressed-glass tableware had been reproduced. However, in late 1933 or early 1934, a major alarm was sounded throughout the world of pattern glass when it was learned that the clear Horn of Plenty tumbler, illustrated in Fig. 193, had been reproduced. Shortly thereafter, tumblers in amber also flooded the market. These unsigned tumblers were first imported from Czechoslovakia by a New York import house.

At first sight, early reproductions of the tumbler appear quite good. However, upon careful study, it is easy to detect numerous

Fig. 193. Reproduction Horn of Plenty tumbler in clear nonflint glass. Circa 1935. Unmarked.

discrepancies. Old tumblers are heavier than new ones, due to the presence of lead. For this reason, old tumblers will ring when gently tapped. New tumblers, lacking lead, do not ring and are naturally lighter in weight. The diamond point design on reproductions is also too sharp. The most obvious defect of new tumblers, however, is the fake pontil mark pressed into the base. Old pontil marks are always ground, never pressed.

The new forms that were produced from this new tumbler mold (in clear and color) are unlike anything made originally. By manipulating the rim of tumblers still in a molten state, hats with ruffled rims were easily created. And by pinching one side of the tumbler rim and applying a handle, tumbler-sized pitchers with pouring lips were produced.

More recently, The New England Post Boy, Williamstown, Massachusetts, offered the 8-ounce flat Horn of Plenty tumbler in clear nonflint glass.

By 1950, reproductions of the Horn of Plenty oil lamp had appeared in nonflint glass. These new lamps are $11\frac{1}{2}$ inches high and first appeared with a clear or dark blue font attached by a metal connector to a milk-white base. By April 1, 1960, the B&P Lamp Supply Company of McMinnville, Tennessee, offered the same oil lamp in amber, amethyst, blue, and green glass attached to milk-white bases.

New oil lamps are unmarked and were apparently produced from a new mold. Unlike originals, which are belltoned and heavy, new lamps are light and do not resonate when gently tapped. When you inspect a new lamp, you will also notice that the pattern is poorly impressed and feels blunt or smooth. This is especially true of the diamond points in the design.

Throughout the mid-1960s, new Horn of Plenty goblets also appeared. Like all reproductions in this pattern, new goblets are unmarked and were produced from new molds. Reproduction goblets are known in clear and colored nonflint glass and share the same discrepancies as other reproductions in this pattern.

Reproductions in Horn of Plenty are not permanently marked.

Hint: Original items in Horn of Plenty are made in flint glass.

Reproduced items: Goblet, hat, lamp, pitcher, tumbler.

ILLINOIS

Illinois is a member of the states series that has gained popularity through the years (Fig. 194). This pattern is also known as Clarissa or Star of the East. Originally produced in 1897 from a good-quality clear nonflint glass at Factory "G" (Gillinder & Sons) and Factory "P" (Doyle & Company) of the United States Glass Company of Pittsburgh, Pennsylvania, its original name is No. 15052 or Illinois. Today, you may still find rarities in emerald green or clear with ruby stain.

Illinois is another of the late patterns of the geometric group of pressed glass. Hobstar-like ornaments and fans constitute the bulk of the design. Most forms are square in shape and handles may be either applied or pressed. Like many other late patterns, it was produced in both a hotel and a table set.

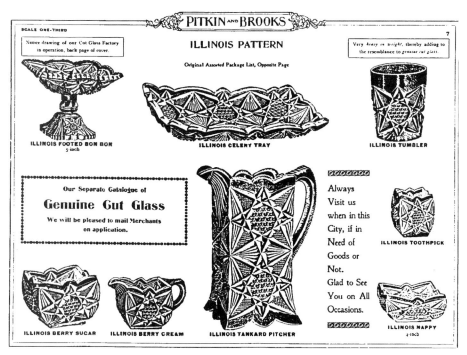

Fig. 194. Reprint of Pitkin and Brooks circa 1900 catalog illustrating an assortment of Illinois.

524L—5¼" SPOONHOLDER

Fig. 195. Reproduction No.524L Illinois white opalescent celery vase. L.E. Smith Glass Co. Circa 1981. Unmarked.

Fig. 195 illustrates the new celery vase. One of two known reproductions in the pattern, it is pictured in the L.E. Smith Glass

Company's 1981 catalog as item No. 5246. This new celery vase stands 5¼ inches high and is a dense white opalescent glass. As you can see from the illustration, it is a direct copy of the original. The second item reproduced was the covered butter dish. Examples of this new butter are known to exist prior to 1970 in clear and a number of light contemporary colors, including amber, blue, and pink.

Both the reproduction covered butter dish and celery vase are the products of new molds. The design on these reproductions is larger, less detailed, and more poorly impressed than on originals. Often, items in clear glass appear gray instead of crystal clear.

When signed, reproductions in Illinois originally carried a paper label.

Hint: Reproductions in Illinois are heavy and thick and the glass has a grayish cast.
Reproduced items: Butter dish, celery vase.

INVERTED FAN AND FEATHER

Throughout the history of colored glass in America, perhaps no single person influenced the production of both blown and pressed-glass tableware as much as Harry Northwood (1860–1919). Founder of the Northwood Glass Company, his legacy can still be seen and appreciated in the many forms of glassware that he left behind.

One of the aristocrats of pattern glass, Inverted Fan and Feather is also known as Beaded Medallion, Fan and Feather, Inverted Fan, and Ribbed Footed. Although an extended table service was originally produced by the Northwood Glass Company about 1904 in custard, emerald green, and pink slag and in the opalescent colors of blue and white, you may find odd items in canary yellow and carnival colors. Pieces are beautifully trimmed in gold gilt. And although items were not signed, occasionally a salt shaker may surface with the Northwood signature in reverse.

To date, Inverted Fan and Feather re-

mains a safe pattern to collect. Only a limited number of items has been reproduced in the original colors and forms. Starting in 1965, new toothpick holders appeared in amberina, custard, and pink slag and the carnival colors of cobalt blue, ice blue, marigold, and white. These toothpick holders were produced by the St. Clair Glass Works, Inc., originally of Elwood, Indiana. However, the custard and pink slag colors are quite unlike the old colors. New items in custard are pale and faded looking, while those in pink slag have a distinct purplish cast.

In 1978, the St. Clair Glass works sold about fifty molds (including Holly Amber and Inverted Fan and Feather) to the Summit Art Glass Company of Rootstown, Ohio. In 1985, Summit cataloged the four decorated custard pieces of Inverted Fan and Feather pictured in Fig. 196. All four of these items were produced from new molds. Although listed in the same catalog, the water tumbler was allegedly never put into production.

Characteristic of Summit reproductions,

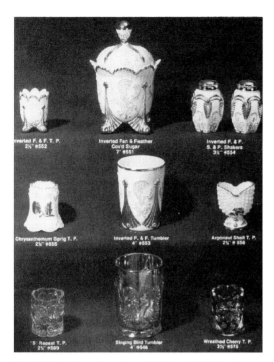

Fig. 196. Selection of new Inverted Fan and Feather in decorated custard glass. Summit Art Glass Co. Circa 1985. Unmarked.

Fig. 197. Reproduction Inverted Fan and Feather decorated custard salt and pepper shakers. Summit Art Glass Co. Circa 1985. Unmarked.

items came in a rainbow of contemporary colors. However, the only original color that Summit used is decorated custard. Unlike the deep, rich tone of original items, these reproductions vary between pale yellow and light ivory. When present, the enamel decoration on all colors is too dark and painted (rather than permanently fired) onto the glass. The same holds true of the use of gold paint to replace true gilding.

The Inverted Fan and Feather No. 554, 3¼-inch salt shaker was available in decorated custard in 1985 (Fig. 197). This reproduction should not cause you any alarm because it is an entirely different shape than the original shakers, which have ball feet. The reproductions are flat-footed.

The No. 551 6-inch-diameter covered sugar bowl also appeared at this time in decorated custard, green custard, lilac, and rubina (Fig. 198). This sugar bowl is 7 inches high and decorated in custard with pink and gold paint. The base comes to a definite point on originals, while on reproductions it is rounded. In addition, the rim

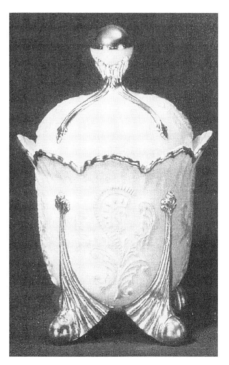

Fig. 198. Reproduction No.551 Inverted Fan and Feather decorated custard covered sugar bowl. Summit Art Glass Co. Circa 1985. Unmarked.

of this base is flared on original bowls but straight-sided on reproductions.

New toothpick holders by St. Clair and Summit share the same discrepancies. Reproductions are straight-sided and straight-rimmed, whereas on originals the body is slightly bulbous and the rim is flared. Compared to originals, the feather design on reproductions is tightly compacted. The bases are also different. Originals have a distinctively sharp point between the legs, whereas on reproductions they are rounded.

Reproduction No. 552 (Inverted Fan and Feather toothpick) by Summit was available in amberina, chocolate, chocolate iridescent, cobalt, coral, coral iridescent, carnation pink, custard, evergreen, first frost, green custard, light chocolate, nut brown, rubina, sapphire blue, and watermelon.

The last item reproduced by Summit is No. 553, the flat water tumbler. This piece is 4¾ inches tall and was available only in

decorated custard. Again, the decoration is pink and gold paint on an almost white custard. Original tumblers are tapered, while reproductions are straight-sided. The feather design is compressed on reproductions.

As a general rule, reproductions are poorly decorated with paints that are easily removed. Produced from new molds, they are heavier than originals, and pattern details are compressed.

Hint: Reproduction items are straight-sided and the colored decoration is easily worn.

Reproduced items: Salt shaker, sugar bowl, toothpick holder, tumbler.

INVERTED FERN

During the ribbed period of pressed glass, numerous patterns such as Bellflower, Fine Rib, Ribbed Grape, Ribbed Ivy, and Ribbed Palm captivated the designer's imagination. These designs were produced in varying qualities of lead glass from the early 1840s through the 1860s and were charac-

teristically developed around a single design element that was set in high relief against a finely ribbed background.

Inverted Fern is one of the many designs comprising this group of pressed glass. Shards have been found at the site of the old Boston and Sandwich Glass Company of

Fig. 200. Reproduction Inverted Fern clear goblet. Maker unknown. Circa 1970s. Embossed "Made in France."

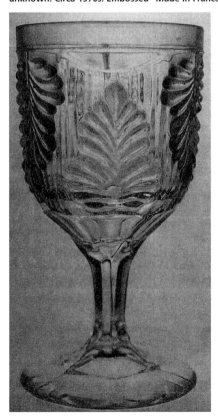

Fig. 199. Original Inverted Fern clear goblet. Maker unknown. Circa 1860s.

Sandwich, Massachusetts, but it is not known who originally produced this pattern. From its basic design, it appears to be a product of the 1860s.

This is a fine old flint pattern. The design consists of clear fernlike ornaments that alternately hang and rise in high relief against a finely ribbed background (Fig. 199). Handles are beautifully applied and crimped and finials are ribbed acorns. Although pieces contain lead, the glass is appreciably lighter in weight than many other flint patterns and does not resonate well.

The only known reproduction in Inverted Fern is the goblet (Fig. 200). Produced from new molds, reproductions first appeared throughout the early 1970s in a good-quality clear flint glass and are permanently embossed "Made in France" under the base. Although the design is deeply impressed, the pattern is not as crisply detailed as the original goblets. New goblets are also glossy and heavy and the glass simply looks new.

Hint: Reproduction goblets are permanently marked "Made in France."

Reproduced items: Goblet.

INVERTED STRAWBERRY

Inverted Strawberry is a late member of the fruit series of pattern glass. Also known as Late Strawberry Variant, the original name of this design is Cambridge No. 2870 or Strawberry. The Cambridge Glass Company of Cambridge, Ohio, first made this pattern from a good-quality clear nonflint glass in an extended table service about 1912. Later, it issued the design in the carnival colors of blue, green, marigold, and purple. Occasionally, you may also find an odd tumbler in clear with ruby stain.

As its name implies, the design consists of large strawberries, leaves, and vines pressed into a clear background. The glass is heavy and often has a very slight grayish

Fig. 201. New Inverted Strawberry bell by the Fenton Art Glass Co., another example of Fenton's use of antique designs with contemporary forms. Circa 1983–84. Embossed Fenton logo.

Fig. 202. Reproduction Inverted Strawberry toothpick holder in amberina. Kanawha Glass Co. Circa 1974. Unmarked.

CHART 58   INVERTED STRAWBERRY. Fenton Art Glass Company, Williamstown, West Virginia.
CMN: Strawberry.
Mark: Embossed Fenton logo.
Color Code: AO Aqua Opal Carnival, AY Amethyst, CK Chocolate, CY Clear, DK Dusty Rose, HG Heritage Green, KK Blue Royale, KL Forget-Me-Not Blue, OC Cameo Opalescent, OO Provincial Blue Opalescent, RT Country Peach, UO Peaches N Cream, VE Velvet Crystal, YL Candleglow Yellow.

ITEM	COLOR(S)	YEAR	ORIG	NEW
Basket, applied handle.				
#9433. 7"h., Low circular foot. ruffled rim.	AY, CY, KL, RT	1982		X
	DK	1984		X
	HG, YL	1983		X
#9437. Small, footed, ruffled rim.	CY	1982		X
	DK	1984		X
	KL, RT	1983		X
	VE	1980		X
Bell. #9465.	AY, CY, KL, RT	1982		X
	HG, YL	1983		X
	VE	1980		X
Bowl. #9427. 7"d.	VE	1980	X	
Compote. #9428. Open, high standard, fluted rim.	VE	1980		X
Creamer. #9503. Pressed handle, footed.	CY	1982	X	
Dish. #9531. Nut, low-footed, ruffled rim.	CY	1982		X
Fairy light. #9470.	DK, KK, OC, OO,	1988		X
	VE	1980		X
Jam jar. #9505. Covered. notched lid.	AY, HG, KL, RT, YL	1983		X
	CY	1982		X
	DK	1984		X
Relish dish. #9518. Flat, divided, oblong.	CY	1982	X	
Salt shaker. #9502. Tall, footed.	CY	1982		X
Sugar bowl. #9503. Footed, covered.	CY	1982	X	
Toothpick holder. #8295.	CK	1982		X
Vase.				
#9454. Bud, footed, swung.	AY, HG, YL	1983		X
	CY, KL, RT	1982		X
	DK	1984		X
	VE	1980		X
Jack-in-the-pulpit, footed.*	AO	1981		X

*Produced in a limited edition of 200 for Levay Distributing Company of Edwardsville, Indiana.

cast. When signed, items are embossed "Near Cut."

From 1980 through 1984, the Fenton Art Glass Company of Williamstown, West Virginia, produced the 15 items enumerated in Chart 58. As you can see from this chart, six items emulate known antique shapes, while the remainder have contemporary shapes (Fig. 201).

Known as Fenton's Strawberry, each item was produced from a new mold. Although a number of forms were issued in clear non-flint glass, those in color are typically Fenton. The strawberry motif was deliberately produced smaller on Fenton items compared to the Cambridge originals. Each item appears in a good-quality glass and is permanently marked with the firm's familiar hallmark.

In 1974, Kanawha Glass of Kanawha, West Virginia, issued the Inverted Strawberry toothpick holder illustrated in Fig. 202. Known as Kanawha's No. 911, this new toothpick holder is 2½ inches high and was produced from a new mold in clear and, undoubtedly, other colors. Although unmarked, it is often found with the original paper label still intact. In like manner, the Guernsey Glass Company of Cambridge, Ohio, issued the following look-alike items from new molds in amethyst, carnival colors, clear, and emerald green (plain or with gilt trim): the cruet, water pitcher, plate, toothpick holder, and water tumbler.

Inverted Strawberry reproductions are heavier and thicker than originals. Colors other than clear, clear with ruby stain, and emerald green are strictly contemporary. New items have an excessive amount of glass, which is most noticeable on the covered butter dish, the creamer, the water pitcher, and the tumbler. When you view these items under a strong light, you will notice this excess at the base of each item.

The glass is also glossy and, depending on the manufacturer, sometimes will feel oily.

Unlike the crisp impression found on original items, the design on reproductions is weak. This flaw is exemplified in the seeds on the strawberries, which are defined beautifully on originals and either misshapen or completely missing on reproductions. The veining on the vines and leaves is also heavily defined on original items and blurred or missing on the reproduction.

Hint: Inverted Strawberry reproductions are heavier and thicker than originals.
Reproduced items: Basket, bell, bowl, compote, creamer, cruet, fairy light, jam jar, nappy, pitcher, plate, relish, salt shaker, sugar bowl, toothpick, tumbler, vase.

IVY IN SNOW

Ivy in Snow is one of the more popular members of the stippled ivy patterns. This lovely pattern consists of three clear sprays of ivy leaves and buds in high relief against a soft, finely stippled background (Fig. 203). Also known as Forest Ware, Ivy in Snow with

Fig. 203. Closeup of clear original Ivy in Snow tumbler showing traces of ruby and green stain.

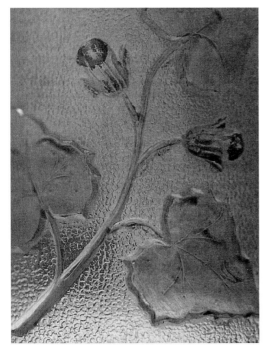

Red Leaves, and Ivy in the Snow, this design was originally produced about 1894 by the Co-Operative Flint Glass Company of Beaver Falls, Pennsylvania, as its Forrest pattern.

Ivy in Snow was originally produced in an extended table service from a medium-quality clear and clear with ruby-stained non-flint glass. Although the pattern was also made in amber and clear with amber and green stain, any color other than clear is rare.

In 1937, the Phoenix Glass Company of Monaca, Pennsylvania, acquired ownership of the original molds for Ivy in Snow and three other patterns (Dewberry, Jeweled Moon and Star, and Lacy Dewdrop) to satisfy a debt from the bankrupt Co-Operative Flint Glass Company. At this time, all four patterns were reissued from the original molds as Phoenix's "Early American Glass" line (Fig. 204).

Called Ivy and Snow by Phoenix, this line included complete sets in clear glass that were marked with only a paper label (see Chart 60). And, for the first time, the four-piece table set (butter dish, creamer, spoonholder, and sugar bowl) and the celery vase appeared in milk white (Figs. 205 and 206).

Fig. 204. Excerpt from the circa 1936 Phoenix Glass Co. catalog illustrating the Ivy in Snow No.6992 covered honey dish.

Fig. 205. Excerpt from the circa 1936 Phoenix Glass Co. catalog illustrating the Ivy in Snow No.6972 covered sugar bowl.

Fig. 206. Excerpt from the circa 1936 Phoenix Glass Co. catalog illustrating the Ivy in Snow No.6973 creamer.

By July 1943, Phoenix had discontinued all tableware production and either scrapped or sold these and other molds. A letter dated December 14, 1943, from A. H. Brown of the Phoenix Glass Company to J.

Stanley Brothers reported: "We . . . are sorry to advise that this [Early American Line] has been withdrawn for the duration. The last stock we had of this was closed out to the Czecho-Slovak Glass Products Company of 45 West 34th Street, New York City." At this time, H.M. Tuska of New York City (a distributor of glassware) acquired the molds to all four patterns from the Phoenix Glass Company. Tuska licensed numerous contemporary glass houses, including Westmoreland, to use these molds to produce an undetermined number of new items.

Like earlier reissues, these pieces were not permanently marked but may have carried paper labels. However, after a number of years of working these patterns unsuccessfully, Tuska sold the molds to the John E. Kemple Glass Works of East Palestine, Ohio, and, later, of Kenova, West Virginia.

At Kemple, Ivy in Snow (known as Ivy-in-Snow) was exclusively produced in milk white (see Fig. 207 and Chart 59). Wherever the design permitted, a "K" (signifying

Fig. 207. Reproduction No.124 Ivy in Snow milk-white pitcher. John E. Kemple Glass Works. Circa 1940s. Unmarked.

CHART 59 IVY IN SNOW. Kemple Glass Works, East Palestine, OH / Kenova, WV.
  CMN: Ivy-in-Snow.
  Mark: Unmarked, embossed "K," or paper label.
  Color Code: MW Milk White.

ITEM	COLOR(S)	YEAR	ORIG	NEW
Bowl.				
Covered, round.				
#107. 6"d.	MW	1940s	X	
#108. 7"d.	MW	1940s	X	
#109. 8"d.	MW	1940s	X	
Open.				
Oval.				
#100. 7"l.	MW	1940s	X	
#101. 8"l.	MW	1940s	X	
#102. 9"l.	MW	1940s	X	
Round.				
#103. 6"d.	MW	1940s	X	
#104. 8"d.	MW	1940s	X	
#105. 4"d.	MW	1940s	X	
#126. 7"d.	MW	1940s	X	
Candlestick.				
#140. 7"h., Top of base is stippled with matching ivy pattern encircling the base.	MW	1940s		X
#140. 4½"h.	MW	1948		X
Celery vase. #117. Pedestaled, scalloped rim, 8"h.	MW	1940s	X	
Claret. #123. 3 oz.	MW	1940s	X	
Compote. #128. Open, high standard. jelly, 6"h.	MW	1940s	X	
Creamer. #116. 4"h.	MW	1940s	X	
Cup.				
#114. 3"h.	MW	1940s		X
#118. Custard, 4"h., handled.	MW	1940s	X	
Goblet. #121. 8 oz.	MW	1940s	X	
Pickle dish. #112. Oval, 8"l.	MW	1940s	X	
Pitcher. #124. 36 oz.	MW	1940s	X	
Plate, round.				
#110. 7"d.	MW	1940s	X	
#111. 10"d.	MW	1940s	X	
Saucer. #113. 5"d.	MW	1940s		X
Sherbert. #106. Footed, 5"d.	MW	1940s		X
Sugar bowl. #115. Covered, 6"h.	MW	1940s	X	
Tumbler.				
#119. Water, 4"h.	MW	1940s	X	
#120. Iced tea, 6"h.	MW	1940s	X	
Vase.				
#117-1. Cupped rim, 8"h.	MW	1940s		X
#117-2. Pinched rim, 8"h.	MW	1940s		X
#117-3. Flared rim, 8"h.	MW	1940s		X
#117-4. Swung rim, 8"h.	MW	1940s		X
#127-1. Cupped rim, 6"h.	MW	1940s		X
#127-2. Pinched rim, 6"h.	MW	1940s		X
#127-3. Flared rim, 6"h.	MW	1940s		X
#127-4. Swung rim, 6"h.	MW	1940s		X
Wine. #122. 5 oz.	MW	1940s	X	

CHART 60   IVY IN SNOW. Phoenix Glass Company, Monaca, Pennsylvania.
CMN: Ivy and Snow
Mark: Unmarked or paper label.
Color Code: C Clear.

ITEM	COLOR(S)	YEAR	ORIG	NEW
Bowl, flat.				
Oval.				
#001. 7"l.	C	1940	X	
#002. 8"l.	C	1940	X	
#003. 9"l.	C	1940	X	
Round.				
#004. 6"d.	C	1940	X	
#005. 7¾"d.	C	1940	X	
#008. 4½"d.	C	1940	X	
Butter dish. #006. Covered, flat, 5¾"d.	C	1940	X	
Celery vase. #017. Pedestaled, 7¾"h.	C	1940	X	
Claret. #019. 3 oz.	C	1940	X	
Compote. #007. High standard, 8"d., covered.	C	1940	X	
Creamer. #015. 4"h.	C	1940	X	
Cup and saucer set. #011/012.	C	1940	X	
Custard cup. #013. 4¼"d.	C	1940	X	
Goblet. #021. 8 oz.	C	1940	X	
Pitcher.				
#023. Milk, 5½"h.	C	1940	X	
#024. Water, 9¼"h.	C	1940	X	
Plate, round.				
#009. 7"d.	C	1940	X	
#010. 10"d.	C	1940	X	
Sauce dish. #022. Round, flat.	C	1940	X	
Sugar bowl. #014. Covered, 6"h.	C	1940	X	
Tray. #016. Oval, 8¼"l.	C	1940	X	
Tumbler. #018. Water, 3½"h.	C	1940	X	
Wine. #020. 5½ oz.	C	1940	X	

Kemple) was placed on the bottom of each item. In addition, either yellow and gold or white paper stickers were used on all items. The yellow and gold sticker was printed "Hand Made—John E. Kemple Glass Works" and either "East Palestine, OH." or "Kenova, WV," depending on the location of the plant at the time. The white sticker denoted the pattern name, the town in which the mold was made, and the year the mold was made.

Upon the closing of the Kemple Glass Works with the death of John Kemple in 1970, the Wheaton Historical Society of Millville, New Jersey, purchased several hundred of the Kemple molds, including many novelty items. To date, we have been unable to confirm whether the Ivy in Snow pattern molds were among them.

According to Ruth Webb Lee in her book *Antique Fakes and Reproductions,* "It is claimed some of the Ivy in Snow pieces, if not all of them, are made from original molds. If so, the molds must have undergone some recutting or else became badly worn over the years, because it is possible to tell the old from the new glass by the appearance of the surface" (p. 118).

When you compare the original Ivy in Snow items to reproductions, you can clearly see an immediate dissimilarity between their surfaces. Unlike the crisp, well-molded look of old items, the pattern on new pieces is blurred, dull, and worn. Moreover, on new items, the stippling is exceedingly thin. These dissimilarities concur with Ruth Webb Lee's belief that some of the original molds may have been badly worn and thus recut.

Although this particular pattern was not originally produced in milk white, reproductions in this color are poor imitations of other original milk-white pieces. None achieves the density of white possessed by the old. Copies, moreover, are good but sometimes have a ricey appearance and, in the clear, the stippling is thinner than in the old.

Hint: Reproduction items have thin, even stippling and the ivy leaves are in low relief.

JERSEY SWIRL

This pattern is also known as Swirl, Swirl and Diamonds, and Windsor Swirl. It was originally produced by the Windsor Glass Company of Pittsburgh, Pennsylvania, about 1886 from a good-quality nonflint glass in an extended table service. Original colors are amber, blue, clear, and yellow.

The design consists of a band of swirls, a thinner band of design similar to hobnail, and another band of swirls. Depending on the form, this combination may vary (as in the covered butter dish), and some items may have the addition of a daisy-cut design around the rim and base.

From 1968 through 1974, the L.G. Wright Glass Company of New Martinsville, West Virginia, reproduced the seven items listed in Chart 61. Only two of these items

CHART 61   JERSEY SWIRL. L.G. Wright Glass Company, New Martinsville, West Virginia.
CMN: Jersey Swirl.
Mark: Unmarked.
Color Code: A Amber, AM Amethyst, AMB Amberina, B Blue, BO Blue Opalescent, C Clear, CY Canary Yellow, G Green, GS Green Satin, RBY Ruby, VO Vaseline Opalescent.

ITEM	COLOR(S)	YEAR	ORIG	NEW
Ashtray. #22-2. Fan shape, 4″ × 5″.	A, B, C, G, RBY	1969		X
Bowl. #35-1. Covered, low footed, 4″d., 5″h.	A, B	1968	X	
	AM, CY, RBY, VO	1974	X	
	C, G	1969	X	
Compote. #35-4. Open, high standard. Scalloped rim, 6½″d., 5¼″h.	A, B, C, G, RBY	1968	X	
	AMB, CY, VO	1974	X	
Goblet. #35-5. 11 oz., 6″h.	A, B, C, G, RBY	1968	X	
	AM, CY, GS, VO	1971	X	
Salt dip. #35-8. Individual, footed.	A, AM, B, G, RBY	1968		X
	AMB, C, CY	1969		X
	BO	1974		X
Sauce dish. #35-10. Round, footed, 5″d., 2½″h.	A, B	1968	X	
	AM, C, CY, G, RBY, VO	1974	X	
Wine. #35-11. 3½ oz., 4″h.	A, B, G, RBY	1968	X	
	AM	1969	X	
	C	1970	X	
	CY, VO	1971	X	

Fig. 208. Reproduction Jersey Swirl No.35-1 covered butter dish. L.G. Wright Glass Co. Circa 1971. Unmarked.

Fig. 209. Reproduction Jersey Swirl No.35-11 wine. L.G. Wright Glass Co. Circa 1971. Unmarked.

(the No.22-2 ashtray and the No.35-8 individual salt dip) are contemporary in form. The remainder correspond to known antique shapes. Each item (like those illustrated in Figs. 208 and 209) was produced from a new mold in all of the original colors, although each form was not produced in all colors at the same time. As you can see from the chart, these forms were also produced in the contemporary colors of solid amberina, amethyst and green (plain or satin), and opalescent blue and vaseline.

Unlike original items, reproductions are thick and heavy and the design is smooth and poorly molded. At times, the glass feels slick or oily and colors are harsh and artificial. Wright reproductions are not marked, and a number of these were produced by the Fenton Art Glass Company of Williamstown, West Virginia.

Unmarked round plates are also known in Jersey Swirl. Like other reproductions in this pattern, these plates were produced from a new mold and can be found in all original colors. New plates are also poorly pressed, excessively heavy, and do not have the fine, mellow color of original plates.

Jersey Swirl is a safe pattern to collect as long as you remember that reproductions are excessively heavy and thick. The diamonds that form the pattern are smooth compared to the sharp, well-defined points of originals.

Hint: Reproductions are heavy and thick and the pattern is poorly pressed.

JEWELED HEART

Jeweled Heart is an interesting pattern of the late period. The design consists of a row of clear stylized hearts pressed in high relief against a finely stippled background. The center of each heart is also stippled and contains a large, clear horizontal oval. Above and below this oval is a clear three-pronged fan. The entire design is outlined with a string of tiny beading.

This pattern was originally produced

CHART 62 **JEWELED HEART. Fenton Art Glass Company, Williamstown, West Virginia.**
CMN: Farmyard Collection.
Mark: Embossed "DSB."
Color Code: BC Black Carnival, HO Electric Blue Carnival, RN Red Carnival.

ITEM	COLOR(S)*	YEAR	ORIG	NEW
Basket. #8833. applied handle, 9"d.	BC(6), HO(1), RN(2)	1991		X
Cuspidor. #8821. 7".	BC(10)	1991		X
Plate. chop. #8819. 11"d.	BC(7), HO(3)	1991		X
Rose bowl. #8822. 6"d.	BC(8), HO(4)	1991		X
Whimsey bowl. #8821. 7"d.	BC(9), HO(5)	1991		X

*Issued in a limited edition of: (1) 116 copies, (2) 66 copies, (3) 92 copies, (4) 132 copies, (5) 138 copies, (6) 60 copies, (7) 47 copies, (8) 108 copies, (9) 72 copies, (10) 78 copies.

CHART 63 **JEWELED HEART. L.G. Wright Glass Company, New Martinsville, West Virginia.**
CMN: Sweetheart.
Mark: Unmarked.
Color Code: A Amber, AM Amethyst, B Blue, C Clear, G Green, P Pink, RBY Ruby.

ITEM	COLOR(S)	YEAR	ORIG	NEW
Creamer. #77-11. Pressed handle. table-size, 3¾"d., 6"h.	A, B, RBY	1968	X	
Goblet. #77-37. 8 oz., 6"h.	A, B, C, RBY	1968	X	
Lamp. #77-11. Fairy.	A, B, G, RBY	1976		X
Spoonholder. #77-11. 3¾"d.	A, B, RBY	1968	X	
Sugar bowl. #77-11. Covered, table-size, 3¾"d., 6"h.	A, B, RBY C	1968 1983	X X	
Toothpick holder. #77-64. 2½"h.	A, AM, B, C, P, RBY G	1968 1969	X X	
Wine. #77-82. 4½ oz., 4½"h.	A, RBY	1968	X	

about 1905 by the Dugan Glass Company of Indiana, Pennsylvania, from a good-quality nonflint glass. Although the design was not made in as many pieces as other late patterns, you can still assemble an interesting table service. Original colors are solid apple green, blue, and clear (plain or gold-trimmed), and opalescent blue and white.

Throughout the early 1960s, new blue and green opalescent creamers and covered sugar bowls flooded the market. They are unmarked and were apparently produced from new molds (as evidenced by the thickness of the glass). Compared to old items, the color of these reproductions is light and the opalescent effect barely covers the rims.

From 1968 through 1976, the L.G. Wright Glass Company of New Martinsville, West Virginia, reproduced the seven items enumerated in Chart 63. Known as Wright's Sweetheart line, reproductions (Fig. 210) appear in the original colors of blue and clear, and the contemporary colors of amber, amethyst, green, pink, and ruby (plain or gold-decorated).

Wright reproductions can be quite convincing. Although they are unmarked, you can detect new items through a number of obvious discrepancies. Produced from new molds, reproductions are thick-walled and heavy. Unlike the fine, smooth, and even stippling on old items, which is pressed in low relief, the stippling on reproductions is

Fig. 210. Reproduction green Jeweled Heart toothpick holder. L.G. Wright Glass Co. Circa 1971. Unmarked.

raised, coarse, and blotchy. The pattern is also larger on reproductions.

It is also prudent to consider the color of any suspect item, especially those reproduced in the original colors of blue and clear, on which the gold decoration has been applied to appear worn. In contrast, items in green are considerably darker, and those found in amber, amethyst, pink, and ruby are obviously contemporary.

In 1991, the Fenton Art Glass Company of Williamstown, West Virginia, adopted Jeweled Heart as an exterior pattern to the limited-edition Farmyard Collection enumerated in Chart 62. Produced from the "Mimi" mold and permanently marked "DSB," this series at present is being offered by Singleton Bailey of Loris, South Carolina.

Hint: Reproduction items are heavier and the stippling is too coarse and blotchy.

JEWELED MOON AND STAR

Jeweled Moon and Star is an interesting variation of the famed Moon and Star pattern. As you can see from Fig. 211, this variant consists of two horizontal rows of

Fig. 211. Catalog excerpt illustrating the original Jeweled Moon and Star No.6279 high-standard true open compote.

large, connected clear circles impressed in the center with a small rosette. Between them is another row of clear but undecorated circles. The stems of footed pieces are large knobs, often referred to as "pineapples" because of their fine diamond-point motif. Handles are beautifully applied.

Also known as Late Moon and Star, Moon and Star Variant, Moon and Star Variation, and Moon and Star with Waffled Stem, the pattern was originally produced about 1896 by the Co-Operative Flint Glass Company of Beaver Falls, Pennsylvania, which reportedly bought the molds from the Wilson Glass Company of Tarentum, Pennsylvania. Known as Co-Operative's Imperial line, the design was originally produced in an extended table service in clear and clear with acid finish (plain or stained with blue or yellow.)

In 1937, the Phoenix Glass Company of Monaca, Pennsylvania, acquired the original molds for Dewberry, Ivy in Snow, Jeweled Moon and Star, and Lacy Dewdrop to satisfy a debt from the bankrupt Co-Operative Flint Glass Company. At this time, all four

CHART 64   JEWELED MOON AND STAR. Kemple Glass Works. East Palestine, Ohio.
CMN: Moon and Star Variant.
Mark: Unmarked, embossed "K," or paper label.
Color Code: EG Emerald Green, MW Milk White.

ITEM	COLOR(S)	YEAR	ORIG	NEW
Banana bowl. #308. Low, long.	MW	1946	X	
Bowl.				
#300. Flat, 8"d.	MW	1946	X	
#310. Float, footed.	MW	1946		X
#311. Footed, crimped rim.	EG, MW	1946		X
Flat, cupped rim, 11"d.	MW	1946	X	
Cake plate.				
Flat.	MW	1946	X	
Footed.	MW	1946	X	
Candleholder, round.				
#307. Flat. 5"h.	EG, MW	1946		X
#312. Low, 3-legged.	MW	1946		X
Compote, open, high standard.	MW	1946	X	

CHART 65   JEWELED MOON AND STAR. Phoenix Glass Company, Monaca, Pennsylvania.
CMN: Moon and Star.
Mark: Unmarked or paper label.
Color Code: C Clear, CL Caramel Lustre, PL Pearl Lustre.

ITEM	COLOR(S)	YEAR	ORIG	NEW
Banana stand. #930. High standard, 12"w.	CL, PL	1937	X	
Bowl, open, low-footed.	C, CL, PL	1937	X	
Cake stand. #929. 11¼"d.	CL, PL	1937	X	
Celery vase, footed.	C	1937	X	
Compote, open, high standard.				
#917. Cupped, 8"d.	CL, PL	1937	X	
#928. Deep. 10½"d.	CL, PL	1937	X	
Goblet.	C, CL, PL	1937	X	
Wine.	C, CL, PL	1937	X	

patterns were reissued from the original molds as Phoenix's "Early American Glass" line. For the first time, Jeweled Moon and Star was produced in milk white with either a caramel or pearl luster finish (see Chart 65). By 1942, however, Phoenix had discontinued all tableware production and either scrapped or sold these and other molds.

H.M. Tuska of New York City (a distributor of glassware) acquired the molds for all four patterns from the Phoenix Glass Company. The Westmoreland Glass Company of Grapeville, Pennsylvania, produced an unde-termined number of new items for Tuska from these molds. However, after a number of years of working these patterns unsuccessfully through private pot-work, Tuska sold the molds to the John E. Kemple Glass Works of East Palestine, Ohio. Kemple produced Jeweled Moon and Star primarily in milk white.

Upon the closing of the Kemple Glass Works with the death of John Kemple in 1970, the Wheaton Historical Society of Millville, New Jersey, purchased several hundred of the Kemple molds, including

Lacy Dewdrop. To date, we have been unable to confirm whether the molds for Jeweled Moon and Star were among them.

The only reproductions in this pattern that may cause confusion among collectors and dealers are items produced by Phoenix in clear glass. In an uncommon reversal for twentieth-century glass making, Phoenix (using original molds) made these reproductions from a better-quality glass than the originals. These reproductions are, however, still heavier and thicker (Fig. 212).

In 1946 the Kemple Glass works issued various items in Jeweled Moon and Star, as enumerated in Chart 64. Kemple produced most items from original Co-Operative molds but made a few new additions of its own. Various bowls, the flat cake plate, and two candlesticks are among these new items. Kemple's major production was in milk white with a few pieces in emerald green. Typical of most reproductions, Kemple pieces are also heavier than originals.

In 1976, Wheaton reproduced a new item in Jeweled Moon and Star, illustrated in the company's 1976 catalog as item #198, the 8-inch Moon and Star compote. This compote is not original to the pattern, but rather is a low-footed, cupped bowl with a thumbprint base made from a new mold. The compote was available in clear and other colors.

Co-Operative never used the following colors in its original line: emerald green, milk white with or without luster finishes, or any other solid color.

Fig. 212. New Jeweled Moon and Star clear celery vase. Unmarked.

Phoenix items were never permanently marked; however, you may still occasionally find pieces with a paper label. Kemple reproduction items can sometimes be found with a paper label or with an embossed "K." You can still find Wheaton articles with original paper labels.

Hint: Reproduction items are heavier than originals and the glass is clear and brilliant.

KANSAS

The original name of this state pattern is No. 15072 or Kansas. It was produced about 1901 by the United States Glass Company of Pittsburgh, Pennsylvania. In 1903, the goblet, mug, and water pitcher were offered in an inferior grade of glass by the Kokomo Glass Manufacturing Company of Kokomo, Indiana.

As you can see from the catalog reprint in Fig. 213, this pattern consists of alternating clear and stippled panels arched at the top and bottom by C-scroll designs. Each stippled panel contains one large clear oval and, depending upon the size of the item, one or two clear round ornaments above and below each oval. A single column of tiny dewdrops separates each alternating panel.

Fig. 214. Reprint of the circa 1930s D.C. Jenkins catalog illustrating the No.40 Kansas mug, reissued from the original mold.

Fig. 213. Reprint of a United States Glass Co. catalog illustrating an assortment of Kansas.

Fig. 215. Original Kansas clear mug. United States Glass Co. Circa 1901. (This mug has not been reissued in this shape.)

Also known as Jewel with Dewdrop, this design was originally produced in an extended table service from a good-quality clear nonflint glass, which was offered plain, gold-trimmed, or stained in light cranberry.

As early as 1906, the D.C. Jenkins Glass Company of Kokomo, Indiana, issued the No.40 or Kansas goblet, hotel mug with pressed handle (Fig. 214), and water pitcher in clear nonflint glass. Each was made from an original mold. Both the goblet and the mug were offered with cardboard or tin lids and contained baking powder or dried mustard.

Unlike the brilliant, clear items made by U.S. Glass (Fig. 215), those by Jenkins were produced from a low grade of packer's glass, which is distinctly gray. Because of this, Jenkins's issues are excessively brittle, bubbly, and contain an

uncommon amount of annealing marks. Those pieces made by Jenkins should not be considered reproductions, because they were made at the same time as those of the U.S. Glass production.

Hint: Jenkins's production of Kansas is gray-cast and of a poor quality glass.

Reproduced items: Goblet, mug, water pitcher.

KING'S CROWN

Throughout the twentieth century, King's Crown has enjoyed lasting popularity. Like Daisy and Button, Moon and Star, and Sawtooth, this design has been in continuous production from its beginning.

Also known as Blue Thumbprint (when stained blue), Ruby Thumbprint (when stained red), and Ruby Thumbprint-Clear (when unstained), its original name is "X.L.C.R." or Excelsior. The design was first made about 1890 by Adams & Company of Pittsburgh, Pennsylvania. Production continued when Adams became Factory "A" of the U.S. Glass combine in 1891 (Fig. 216).

King's Crown was originally produced in a large and extended table service in a good-quality plain or stained nonflint glass. The glass is crystal clear, brilliant, and seems to sparkle. Although you may find items in solid green and clear with amethyst-, gold-, green-, and yellow-stained eyes, the pattern

Fig. 217. Original emerald green King's Crown goblet. Adams & Co. Circa 1890.

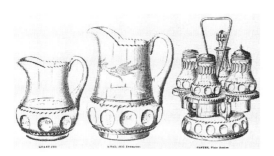

Fig. 216. Reprint of Adams & Co. or Factory "A" circa 1891 catalog illustrating an assortment of King's Crown.

CHART 66 KING'S CROWN. Glasscrafts & Ceramics, Inc., Yonkers, New York. (Formerly Czecho-Slovak Glass Prod. Company).
CMN: King's Crown.
Mark: Unmarked.
Color Code: CR Clear with Ruby Stain.

ITEM:	COLOR(S):	YEAR:	ORIG	NEW
Bowl. #447. Finger, flat. Smooth rim, 2"h., 4¼"d.	CR	1953	X	
Claret. #277. 4½"h.	CR	1953	X	
Cocktail. #677. 4¼"h.	CR	1953	X	
Goblet. #377. 5½"h.	CR	1953	X	
Plate. #777. Round, 8½"d.	CR	1953	X	
Sherbert. #577. 3¼"h.	CR	1953		X
Tumbler. #877. Water, flat, 5½"h.	CR	1953	X	
Wine. #177. 3½"h.	CR	1953	X	

CHART 67 KING'S CROWN. Imperial Glass Corporation, Bellaire, Ohio.
CMN: Line No.77 or Ruby Crown.
Mark: Unmarked or paper label.
Color Code: CC Clear with Cranberry Stain.

ITEM:	COLOR(S):	YEAR:	ORIG	NEW
Candlestick. #7291. 8½"h.	CC	1966		X
Cocktail, flared bowl, 4¼"h., 2½"d., 2½ oz.	CC	1966		X
Sherbert, 3¼"h., 3¾"d.	CC	1966		X

CHART 68 KING'S CROWN. Indiana Glass Company, Dunkirk, Indiana.
CMN: Line No.77 or King's Crown.
Mark: Unmarked or paper label.
Color Code: C Clear, CB Clear with Pastel Blue, CC Clear with Cranberry Stain, CG Clear with Gold, CP Clear with Platinum, CR Clear with Ruby Stain, GA Golden Amber, OG Olive Green.

ITEM	COLOR(S)	YEAR	ORIG	NEW
Bowl.				
Berry, 9"d., 4½"h.	C, CC	1964	X	
Fruit, open, footed, knob stem. 10¼"d.	CR	1966	X	
Cake stand, low standard. #2418. 4"h., 12"d.	CC, CR	1966		X
Candlestick.				
#0154.	OG	1966		X
#7290. 3"h., 3¾"d.	C, CR	1964		X
#7291. 8½"h., 4"d.	C, CR	1964		X
	CC	1966		X
Cocktail. #0146. 4"h., 2½"d.	CC	1964		X
	OG	1966		X
Compote.				
Covered, high standard.				
#0195. 6"d., 6"h.	OG	1966	X	
#0243. 5"d., 6"h.	C, CC, CG	1965	X	
	CR	1967	X	
#0245. 5"d., 5¼"h.	CP	1966	X	
#0246. 5"d, 6"h.	CP	1965	X	
#7293. 5"d.	C, CR	1964	X	
#7296. 8"d, 7½"h.	CC, CR	1966	X	
Open, high standard.				
#0242. 5"d., 5"h.	C, CG, CP	1965	X	
#0244. 7"d., 7"h.	C, CG, CP	1965	X	
#0245. 5"d., 5"h.	CP	1965	X	
#0247.	C, CC	1964	X	
	CP	1965	X	
#1676. 5"h., 5"d.	CC, CG, OG	1966	X	
#2424. 6½"h., 10¼"d.	CC	1966	X	
#7292. 5"h., 5"d.	C, CC, CR	1964	X	
#7287. 7"h., 7"d.	C	1966	X	
	CC, CR	1964	X	
Cordial, 3½"h, 2"d., 2 oz.	C	1969	X	
	CC, CR	1964	X	
	OG	1966	X	
Creamer. #7295. Table-size.	C	1964		X
	CC	1966		X
Cup. #0207. 2½"h., 3½"d.	C, CC, CR	1964	X	
	CG	1965	X	
	CP	1967	X	

ITEM	COLOR(S)	YEAR	ORIG	NEW
Cup and saucer set. #0208.	C, CC, CR	1964	X	
	CG	1965	X	
	CP	1967	X	
Goblet, 5¾"h., 3"d., 7½ oz.	C, CG, CC	1959	X	
	CG, CP	1965	X	
	OG	1966	X	
Nappy. #0148. 4"d., 2½"h.	OG	1966		X
Pitcher, water. #1417. 7½"h., 5½"d.	CC, CR	1966		X
Plate.				
8¼"d., Salad.	C, CC, CG	1965	X	
	CP	1967	X	
	OG	1966	X	
10¼"d.	C, CC, CG	1964		X
13½"d.	C, CC, CR	1964		X
Platter. #0226. 10½"d.	CR	1966		X
Relish dish. #2419. 13¼"d.	CC	1966		X
Salad set.				
3-Piece, master bowl, 2 spoons.	CC, CR	1964		X
4-Piece, 9"d. bowl, 2 spoons, 10¼"d. underplate.	CC, CR	1964		X
	CG	1965		X
	CP	1967		X
	OG	1966		X
Sauce dish. #0218. Round, flat. 4"d., 2¼"h.	C, CC, CR	1964	X	
Saucer. #0234. Round, 6"d.	C, CC, CR	1964	X	
	CG	1965	X	
	CP	1967	X	
Sherbert. #0236. 3½"h., 3¾"d.	C, CG	1965		X
	CC, CR	1964		X
	CP	1967		X
Snack set, 8-piece.	C, GA, OG	1965		X
	CC, CR	1964		X
Sugar bowl, open. #7295. 3"h., 3"d.	C, CC	1966		X
Tidbit tray.				
2-Tier, 10"h., 13"d.	CC	1966		X
3-Tier, 14"h.	CC	1966		X
Tumbler, iced tea, 5½"h.	C, OG	1966		X
	CC, CR, CP	1964		X
Wine.				
4½"h., 2½"d.	C, CC	1964	X	
4¾"h., 3½"d.	C, CC	1966	X	
4¾"h., 2½"d., #0145	CR, OG	1966	X	

CHART 69 KING'S CROWN. The D.C. Jenkins Glass Company, Kokomo, Indiana.
CMN: Line No.17.
Mark: Unmarked.
Color Code: Clear.

ITEM	COLOR(S)	YEAR	ORIG	NEW
Claret.	C	1930s	X	
Goblet.	C	1930s	X	
Wine.	C	1930s	X	

CHART 70 KING'S CROWN. Lancaster Colony Corporation, Lancaster, Ohio.
CMN: Colony's Ruby Crown, Colony's Color Crown.
Mark: Unmarked or paper label.
Color Code: CR Clear with Ruby Stain.

ITEM:	COLOR(S):	YEAR:	ORIG	NEW
Sherbert, footed, smooth rim.	CR	1974		X

CHART 71 KING'S CROWN. United States Glass Company, Tiffin, Ohio.
CMN: Line No.4016, Old Thumbprint.
Mark: Unmarked, embossed "USG" logo, or paper label.
Color Code: C Clear, CB Clear with Blue stain, CC Clear with Cranberry Stain, CR Clear with Ruby Stain (decorated with copper or gold).

ITEM:	COLOR(S):	YEAR:	ORIG	NEW
Ashtray, square, flat, 5¼"sq.	CB, CC, CR	1950s		X
Bowl, open, low circular foot.				
Center edge, Large brim-shaped rim, 3"h., 12½"d.	CB, CC, CR	1950s		X
Cone, deep, smooth rim.	CB, CC, CR	1950s		X
Crimped rim, 4½"h., 11½"d.	CB, CC, CR	1950s		X
Finger, smooth rim.	CB, CC, CR	1950s		X
Cake stand, low standard.				
12"d., 4¾"h.	C, CC, CR	1950s		X
12½"d., 4¾"h., no rim.	C	1950s		X
Candleholder, 2-light, 5½"h.	C, CC, CR	1950s		X
Candy box, flat, round, covered, 6"d	C, CC, CR	1960		X
Claret, 4 oz., flared bowl, flared.	C, CC, CR	1950s	X	
Cocktail, oyster, 4 oz.	C, CC, CR	1960		X
Compote, high standard.				
Covered, deep straight-sided bowl, 6"d., 10½"h.	C, CC, CR	1950s	X	
Open, smooth rim, round bowl, 7¼"h., 9¾"d.	C, CB, CR	1950s	X	
Creamer, bulbous, pressed handle.	C, CB, CC, CR	1960		X
Cup and saucer set, tea.	C, CB, CC, CR	1950s	X	
Goblet, 9 oz., straight bowl.	C, CC, CR	1960	X	
Juice, 4 oz., straight bowl. (Similar to wine).	C, CC, CR	1950s		X
Lazy Susan, 24"d., 8½"h., with ball-bearing spinner.	C, CC, CR	1950s		X
Mayonnaise set,				
3-Piece, 7⅜"d. round plate, 4"d. Round open bowl, ladle.	CB, CC, CR	1950s		X
4-Piece, same but with 2 ladles.	CB, CC, CR	1950s		X
Party server, 24"d., 8"h.	C, CC, CR	1950s		X
Plate, round.				
Dinner.				
5"d.	C, CC, CR	1960	X	
7⅜"d.	C, CC, CR	1960	X	
10"d.	C, CC, CR	1960		X
14"d.	C, CC, CR	1960		X
Flower floater, flat, shallow, Smooth rim, 12½"d.	C, CC, CR	1950s		X
Punch-bowl set, 12 cups, ladle.				
Flared 12-qt. bowl, round, flat, underplate 23"d.	C, CC, CR	1955	X	
Round 10-qt. bowl, flat, underplate 21½"d.	C, CC, CR	1955	X	
Relish, round, flat, 5-part, 14"d.	C, CC, CR	1950s		X

ITEM:	COLOR(S):	YEAR:	ORIG	NEW
Sugar bowl, low circular foot, open, double-handled, smooth rim,	C, CC, CR	1960		X
Sundae, smooth rim, footed, 5½ oz.	C, CC, CR	1960		X
Tumbler.				
Iced tea, bulbous base.				
11 oz., low circular foot, Tall straight bowl.	C, CC, CR	1960		X
12 oz., knob stem, footed.	C, CC, CR	1960		X
Juice, 4½ oz., flat.	C, CC, CR	1960		X
Water, low circular foot, Short straight-sided rim, Bulbous base.	C, CC, CR	1960		X
Wine, 2 oz., straight bowl.	C, CC, CR		X	

CHART 72   KING'S CROWN. L.G. Wright Glass Company, New Martinsville, West Virginia.
CMN: King Crown.
Mark: Unmarked.
Color Code: C Clear.

ITEM:	COLOR(S):	YEAR:	ORIG	NEW
Lamp, oil.				
#77-122. Daisy & Button font.	C	1979		X
#77-123. Beaded font.	C	1979		X

was primarily produced in clear and in clear with ruby stain. It was also often enameled, copper-wheel engraved, frosted, or gilded (Fig. 217).

Because this pattern was produced over an extended period, you can find original items with either applied or pressed handles.

Throughout the century, King's Crown has been reproduced by numerous contemporary glass companies, including Glasscrafts & Ceramics, enumerated in Chart 66; Imperial (Ruby Crown), enumerated in Chart 67; Indiana (No.77), enumerated in Chart 68; Jenkins (No.17), enumerated in Chart 69; Lancaster Colony

Fig. 218. Reproduction goblets and iced-tea tumbler in King's Crown. Indiana Glass Co. Unmarked.

sale

Ruby Crown stemware

at lowest price in 17 years!

formerly each 1.50 NOW **.69**

Now irresistibly low-priced . . . your favorite hand-pressed glassware by Tiffin in deep, glowing ruby-tone combined with crystal glass. Goblets, sherbets, wines, cocktails, footed juices, straight 5 oz, juices, 9 oz. water tumblers and 12 oz. highballs. Also available in Blue Crown in the same sizes and at the same sale prices. Matching 7⅜ in. salad plate or cereal bowl, each regularly 2.00 NOW **1.10**

Altman glassware, fourth floor

MUrrayhill 9-7000—FIFTH AVENUE AT 34TH STREET
AND AT WHITE PLAINS, MANHASSET AND SHORT HILLS

Fig. 219. Reprint of B. Altman & Co. ad from *Crockery and Glass Journal* for May 1959 illustrating King's Crown in clear with ruby stain.

Corporation (Color Crown), enumerated in Chart 70; U.S. Glass (No.4016), enumerated in Chart 71; and L.G. Wright Glass Company (King Crown), enumerated in Chart 72. However, the Indiana and the United States Glass companies were foremost in its production. Throughout the late 1950s and early 1960s, Indiana Glass produced more than 40 forms as its No.77 or King's Crown or Thumbprint design (Fig. 218). And U.S. Glass produced more than 65 different forms as its pattern No.4016 or Old Thumbprint pattern (Fig. 219). Today, after more than four decades, this pattern's antique and contemporary shapes and colors continue to captivate modern households.

Because of mass production, the bases, finials, handles, and stems of reproductions vary considerably. For example, unlike original items, Indiana Glass Company of Dunkirk, Indiana, produced items that have clear solid-ball finials, pressed and ear-shaped handles, and smooth rims.

In general, reproductions are thick, heavy, and distinctly wavy or crinkled. Unlike the crystal-clear glass of original items, new clear items may appear pale green or yellow. Any contemporary color is new.

Perhaps the easiest way to detect reproductions is by acquainting yourself with the original colors and shapes enumerated in the many references listed in the Bibliography.

Hint: King's Crown reproductions usually have a strong green or yellow cast.

KLONDIKE

One of the most highly collectible and expensive patterns in early American pressed glass today is the pattern known to collectors and dealers as Klondike. Produced by the firm of Dalzell, Gilmore, & Leighton of Findlay, Ohio, about 1898, its original name is simply Dalzell's No.75 and No.75D. These numbers refer specifically to the color treatment of the pattern: No.75 refers to clear

and stained pieces (known as Amberette), and No.75D refers to clear pieces without stain.

Klondike was originally produced in a good-quality nonflint glass in an extended table service. Complete table sets in clear, clear with acid finish, and clear with acid finish and amber stain may still be assembled in each color. This pattern may also have been produced in clear with acid finish and a rare lilac stain. Unlike the shapes of other

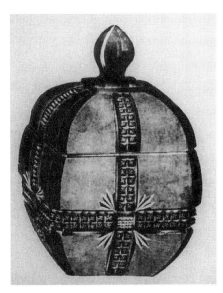

Fig. 220. Excerpt from January 12, 1898, *China, Glass and Lamps* ad illustrating the Klondike covered sugar bowl.

patterns of its time, forms in Klondike are square, with the exception of stemware and the tall beverage pitchers, which may be round or square.

KNOBBY BULL'S EYE

One of the late series of pressed-glass patterns, Knobby Bull's Eye typifies the early twentieth century's new attitude toward pressed glass. First issued as late as 1915 by the United States Glass Company of Pittsburgh, Pennsylvania, this line was originally known as No.15155 or the Cromwell line. Knobby Bull's Eye was produced in an extended table service from a good-quality nonflint glass. Complete table sets were issued in either clear or clear with decoration (Fig. 221).

As early as 1955, the United States Glass Company of Tiffin, Ohio, reissued the 15-piece punch-bowl set in Knobby Bull's Eye. Known as Moon and Star, this set consists of one 10½-quart flat bowl, one ladle, one 18-inch-round underplate, and twelve handled punch cups. New punch sets were made from a good-quality clear nonflint glass, most likely from the original molds.

To date, only one item has been reproduced in Klondike—the large open sugar bowl. It is not known when, or by whom, this new sugar was produced. It is unmarked and has been noted in the solid colors of amber and clear. From their make, new sugar bowls appear to be a product of the 1980s.

This new open sugar is a good copy. Like the old Klondike illustrated in Fig. 220, it is square in shape, utilizes all aspects of the original design, and is especially deceiving in clear glass. Upon close examination, however, reproductions in either color display a typical waviness in the glass. This waviness is most apparent on those portions of articles that are unpatterned. In addition, the design is smooth and undefined. Produced from a new mold, reproductions are also thicker and heavier than originals.

New Klondike open sugar bowls are not permanently signed.

Hint: Reproductions in clear have a distinct greenish-yellow tint to the glass.
Reproduced items: Sugar bowl.

In the November 1963 issue of *China, Glass and Tablewares,* the Red-Cliff Distributing Company of Chicago advertised new Knobby Bull's Eye goblets. Known as No.K-9045, new goblets have a 9-ounce capacity and can still be found in the contemporary colors of antique amber, Apple Valley green, Bedford blue, clear, Jamestown blue, milk white, Old Colony amber, and Shenandoah green. They were produced from 1963 through 1974 by the Fenton Art Glass Company of Williamstown, West Virginia, from a new Red-Cliff mold. At the same time, Red-Cliff also offered in the same colors the No.K-9028 scalloped nut dish made from the goblet mold. Both items are permanently embossed on the bases with a circular mark. "(C) RED-CLIFF C USA," which surrounds a large "R," written in script.

In 1977, Fenton introduced the first of two items produced in Knobby Bull's Eye. Known as Fenton's item No.9385, this cov-

Fig. 221. Reprint of a United States Glass Co. catalog illustrating an assortment of Knobby Bull's Eye.

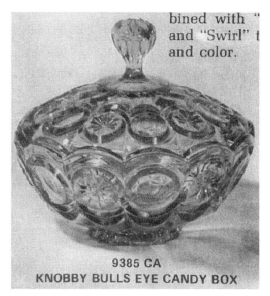

9385 CA
KNOBBY BULLS EYE CANDY BOX

Fig. 222. Reproduction Knobby Bull's Eye No.9385 covered bowl. Fenton Art Glass Co. Circa 1977. Embossed Fenton logo.

ered candy box is more similar to a covered bowl (Fig. 222). Round with a low, circular foot, the candy box can still be found in the

contemporary colors of colonial amber, colonial blue, colonial pink, springtime green, and wisteria. The finial on the cover is round and faceted.

The second item is the No.9061 Fenton bell, introduced in 1979 in the colonial colors of amber, blue, and pink. By 1980, bells were also being offered in the opalescent colors of blue, cameo, French, and topaz. Interestingly, unlike most Fenton creations produced from molds designed and created at the Fenton factory, these bells were produced from the original Knobby Bull's Eye goblet mold formerly owned by the Red-Cliff Company.

Typical of the Fenton Art Glass Company, both the covered candy box and bell are not true reproductions. Rather, they are adaptations of an antique pattern to contemporary forms and in contemporary colors.

Hint: Reproduction goblets are permanently embossed with the Red-Cliff logo.

Reproduced items: Bell, bowl, compote, goblet, punch bowl, punch cup, underplate.

LACY DAISY

Lacy Daisy is a member of the geometric group. Originally known as Daisy, this pattern, also called Crystal Jewel, was first issued by the United States Glass Company of Pittsburgh, Pennsylvania. It is a late design produced about 1918 in an extended table service from a mediocre-quality clear nonflint glass with limited color production in amber and light green.

The basic design of this pattern consists of rows of raised octagons that diminish in size toward the base. The top of each octagon is pressed with a hobstar and framed by two clear horizontal and vertical bands that intersect in such a way as to produce rows of triangles, which also diminish in size.

To date, three reproductions are known in Lacy Daisy. Illustrated in Fig. 223 is the 4¾-inch-diameter, single-handled, round nappy in an unusual shade of bluish-purple. Unmarked, it is not known when, or by whom, this item was produced. Undoubtedly, this nappy was produced from a new mold as the pattern is blurred and the glass is distinctly heavy, wavy, and slick.

The Westmoreland Glass Company of Grapeville, Pennsylvania, also reissued the 4-inch-diameter by 1⅝-inch-high flat sauce dish and the 2½-inch-diameter by 1-inch-high individual salt dip from the original United States Glass molds. Examples of both items are known in clear. The salt dip (No.909) has also been seen in milk white and teal green. When Westmoreland reproductions are signed, they are embossed with a "WG."

In 1985, the Summit Art Glass Company of Akron, Ohio, used the original molds it

Fig. 223. Reproduction Lacy Daisy handled nappy in an unusual purple-blue. Unmarked.

had purchased from the Westmoreland Glass Company to reissue the salt dip and the round, flat sauce dish. Summit reproduced these items in clear and teal green. It also combined them to create a child's seven-piece berry set. Examples of both the salt dip and the sauce dish have been seen with paper labels.

Because both the individual salt dip and the sauce dish have been reissued from original molds, there is little difference between new and old items. New items may have a distinct waviness in the glass that does not appear on originals. Therefore, a prudent approach to identifying suspect items is to compare their detail, quality, and weight carefully.

Hint: Any color other than amber, clear, and light green is modern.
Reproduced items: Nappy, salt dip, sauce dish.

LACY DEWDROP

Lacy Dewdrop was first issued about 1902 by the Co-Operative Flint Glass Company of Beaver Falls, Pennsylvania. Also known as Beaded Dewdrop, Beaded Jewel, Co-Op's No.1902, and Late Dewdrop, the design was produced in an extended table service from a medium-quality clear nonflint glass.

In 1937, the Phoenix Glass Company of Monaca, Pennsylvania, acquired ownership of the original molds for Lacy Dewdrop and three other patterns (Dewberry, Ivy in Snow, and Jeweled Moon and Star) to satisfy a debt from the bankrupt Co-Operative Flint Glass Company. At this time, all four patterns were reissued from the original molds as Phoenix's "Early American Glass" line.

Called Lace Dew Drop by Phoenix, this line included complete sets in milk white with either pearl or caramel luster or blue- or pink-stain finishes that were marked with only a paper label (see Chart 74).

By July 1943, Phoenix had discontinued all tableware production and either scrapped or sold these and other molds. A letter dated December 14, 1943, from A.H. Brown of the Phoenix Glass Company to J. Stanley Brothers reported: "We . . . are sorry to advise that this [Early American Line] has been withdrawn for the duration. The last stock we had of this was closed out to the Czecho-Slovak Glass Products Company of 45 West 34th Street, New York City." At this time, H.M. Tuska of New York City (a distributor of glassware) acquired the molds to all four patterns from the Phoenix Glass Company. Tuska licensed numerous contemporary glass houses, including Westmoreland, to use these molds to produce an undetermined number of new items.

Like earlier reissues, these pieces were not permanently marked but may have had paper labels. However, after a number of years of working these patterns unsuccessfully, Tuska sold the molds to the John E. Kemple Glass Works of East Palestine, Ohio, and, later, of Kenova, West Virginia.

At Kemple, Lacy Dewdrop (known as Old Lace and Dewdrop) was produced in amber, amberina, emerald green, and milk white (see Chart 73). Wherever the design permitted, a "K" (signifying Kemple) was placed on the bottom of each item. In addition, either yellow and gold or white paper stickers were used on all items. The yellow and gold sticker was printed "Hand Made— John E. Kemple Glass Works" and either "East Palestine, OH." or "Kenova, WV," depending on the location of the plant at the time. The white sticker denoted the pattern name, the town in which the mold was made, and the year the mold was made (Figs. 224 and 225).

When the Kemple Glass Works closed after the death of John Kemple in 1970, the Wheaton Historical Society of Millville, New Jersey, purchased several hundred of the Kemple molds, including many novelty items. To date, we have been able to confirm that Wheaton worked all the Lacy Dew-

Fig. 224. Reproduction milk-white Lacy Dewdrop goblet. John E. Kemple Glass Works. Circa 1950. Marked with a paper label.

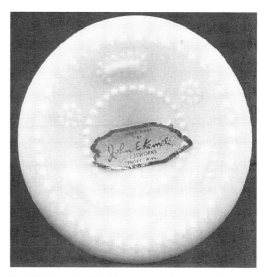

Fig. 225. Base of milk-white Lacy Dewdrop reproduction goblet showing the John E. Kemple Glass Works paper label.

CHART 73   LACY DEWDROP. John E. Kemple Glass Works, Kenova, West Virginia.
CMN: Old Lace and Dewdrop
Mark: Unmarked, embossed "K," or paper label.
Color Code: A Amber, AMB Amberina, EG Emerald Green, MW Milk White.

ITEM	COLOR(S)	YEAR	ORIG	NEW
Bowl, round, flat.				
Covered.				
#402. 6"d.	MW	1940s	X	
#403. 8"d.	MW	1940s	X	
#411. 4"d., Mint.	MW	1940s	X	
Open.				
#404. 6"d.	MW	1940s	X	
#405. 8"d.	MW	1940s	X	
#412. 10"d.	MW	1940s	X	
Butter dish. #402. Covered.	MW	1940s	X	
Candlestick. #420.				
Short.	A, EG	1967		X
	MW	1949		X
Tall, 7"h.	MW	1940s		X
Compote. #415. High standard, covered.	MW	1940s	X	
Creamer. #401.	MW	1940s	X	
Cup, punch.	A, AMB, EG	1967		X
	MW	1950s		X
Goblet. #408. 8 oz.	A, AMB, EG	1967	X	
	MW	1940s	X	
Hat.	MW	1950s		X
Pitcher. #409. Water, 36 oz.	A, EG	1967	X	
	MW	1967	X	
Sauce dish, #406. Round, flat, 4"d.	MW	1940s	X	
Spoonholder. #410.	MW	1940s	X	
Sugar bowl. #400. Covered.	MW	1940s	X	
Tumbler. #407. Water, 4"h.	A, EG	1967	X	
	MW	1940s	X	

CHART 74   LACY DEWDROP. The Phoenix Glass Company, Monaca, Pennsylvania.
CMN: Lace Dew Drop
Mark: Unmarked, paper label.
Color Code: BS Milk White with Blue Stain, CL Milk White with Caramel Lustre, PL Milk White with Pearl
Lustre, PS Milk White with Pink Stain.

ITEM	COLOR(S)	YEAR	ORIG	NEW
Banana stand, high standard.				
#832. 11"l.	BS, CL, PL, PS	1937	X	
#834. 7½"l.	BS, CL, PL, PS	1937	X	
Bowl, flat.				
Covered.				
#811. 8"d.	BS, CL, PL, PS	1937	X	
#815. 4½"d.	BS, CL, PL, PS	1937	X	
Open.				
#803. 6"d.	BS, CL, PL, PS	1937	X	
#804. 8"d.	BS, CL, PL, PS	1937	X	
#835. 10"d.	BS, CL, PL, PS	1937	X	

ITEM	COLOR(S)	YEAR	ORIG	NEW
Butter dish. #807. 6"d.	BS, CL, PL, PS	1937	X	
Cake stand, high standard.				
#831. 11"d.	BS, CL, PL, PS	1937	X	
#833. 7½"d.	BS, CL, PL, PS	1937	X	
Candlestick. #816. 7"h.	BS, CL, PL, PS	1937	X	
Compote, high standard.				
Covered.				
#805. 6"d., 9"h.	BS, CL, PL, PS	1937	X	
#812. 8"d., 12"h.	BS, CL, PL, PS	1937	X	
Open				
#806. 6"d.	BS, CL, PL, PS	1937	X	
#813. 8"d.	BS, CL, PL, PS	1937	X	
Creamer. #802.	BS, CL, PL, PS	1937	X	
Goblet. #808. 7 oz.	BS, CL, PL, PS	1937	X	
Pitcher. #810. Milk, 8"h.	BS, CL, PL, PS	1937	X	
Sauce dish. #814. 4½"d.	BS, CL, PL, PS	1937	X	
Sugar bowl. #801. Covered, 6"h.	BS, CL, PL, PS	1937	X	
Tumbler. #809.	BS, CL, PL, PS	1937	X	

CHART 75 LACY DEWDROP. Wheaton Craft, Millville, New Jersey.
    CMN: Lace and Dewdrop.
    Mark: Unmarked, embossed "K" or "KW," or paper label.
    Color Code: A Amber, C Clear.

ITEM	COLOR(S)	YEAR	ORIG	NEW
Bowl, round, flat.				
Covered.				
#284. 8"d.	A, C	1976	X	
#286. 4"d., Mint.	A, C	1976	X	
Open. #282. 10"d.	A, C	1976	X	
Butter dish. #280. Covered.	A, C	1976	X	
Candlestick. #290. Short.	A, C	1976		X
Compote. #296. High standard, covered.	A, C	1976	X	
Creamer. #294. 4½"h.	A, C	1976	X	
Cup. #254. Punch.	A, C	1976		X
Goblet. #272. 7 oz.	A, C	1976	X	
Pitcher. #276. Milk.	A, C	1976	X	
Plate.				
#250. 10"d.	A, C	1976		X
#252. 8"d.	A, C	1976		X
Sauce dish, #288. Round, flat, 4"d.	A, C	1976	X	
Saucer. #256.	A, C	1976		X
Sherbert. #258.	A, C	1976		X
Sugar bowl. #292. Covered, 6"h.	A, C	1976	X	
Tumbler. #268. Water, 6 oz.	A, C	1976	X	

Fig. 226. Reproduction Lacy Dewdrop milk-white covered butter dish. John E. Kemple Glass Works. Circa 1967.

Fig. 227. New Lacy Dewdrop milk-white water pitcher. John E. Kemple Glass Works. Circa 1967.

drop molds it purchased from Kemple that are enumerated in Chart 75. Wheaton produced these items in amber or clear glass, and the items can sometimes be found with a "W" or a "KW" embossed mark.

When you compare the original Lacy Dewdrop items to reproductions, you can clearly see an immediate dissimilarity between their surfaces. Unlike the crisp, well-molded look of old items, the pattern on new pieces is blurred, dull, and worn.

Although this pattern was not produced originally in milk white, the reproductions in this color are poor imitations of the milk-white glass found on other antique pieces. None achieves the density of white possessed by other old patterns because, unlike originals, these reproductions display an unmistakable ricey appearance (Figs. 226 and 227). In addition, clear reproductions have a distinct grayish cast.

Hint: Lacy Dewdrop was produced originally only in clear glass.

LACY MEDALLION

The original name of this highly confusing pattern is Jewel. This design was first issued about 1905 by the United States Glass Company of Pittsburgh, Pennsylvania, in a good-quality clear and emerald green nonflint glass. U.S. Glass also offered a limited production in clear with ruby stain and cobalt blue. Pieces were issued plain or with a lush gilt trim that was fired onto the surface of the glass.

Because Lacy Medallion is identical to another United States Glass design (No. 15057 or Colorado, which, except for the water tumbler, is always footed), we believe that Colorado and Lacy Medallion are one and the same. This belief is corroborated by the fact that Colorado was originally assigned a line number, while Lacy Medallion was not. Most likely, in 1905 U.S. Glass issued a limited number of forms in Lacy Medallion as souvenir ware while keeping Colorado as its full line of tableware.

This design consists of a large, round jewel that is surrounded by fine beading and set within a three-sided shield that is feathered at the edges. Because pieces in Lacy Medallion have flat bases, this design appears on the body of each item. Interest-

Fig. 228. Assortment of new Lacy Medallion toothpick holders. Summit Art Glass Co. Circa 1977. Unmarked.

ingly, the same design appears only on the footed portion of Colorado items.

In 1967, the Crystal Art Glass Company of Cambridge, Ohio, offered the new, unmarked wine as its "Lacy" or "Jewel" line. Produced from a new mold and offered in clear, cobalt blue, and ruby glass, each was trimmed in a luscious gold paint (rather than gilt).

In 1977, the Summit Art Glass Company of Mogadore, Ohio, offered the new, unmarked 2½-inch-high toothpick holder as No.536 Colorado (Fig. 228). Later, the No.550 Colorado 2½-inch-high individual creamer was added. Each item was produced from a new mold and offered in amber, clear, green, and sapphire blue, and each was trimmed in a luscious gold paint (rather than gilt).

As you can see from Fig. 229, new items in Lacy Medallion are quite convincing. However, they are thick, heavy, and almost always souvenired. While the beading on original items is evenly spaced and equal in size, the beading on new items is not. The lush, rich gold on originals is fired onto the surface of the glass, while reproductions are painted in gold trim, which can be removed easily.

Fig. 229. Reproduction Lacy Medallion toothpick. Summit Art Glass Co. Circa 1977. Unmarked.

Summit offered the individual creamer and the toothpick holder as a miniature creamer and open sugar set.

Hint: Lacy Medallion reproductions are thick-walled and heavy and the gold trim chips easily.

Reproduced items: Creamer, toothpick holder, wine.

LATE BUCKLE

The Late Buckle pattern, similar to the earlier Buckle design, consists of a row of large connected vertical ovals. Each oval is enhanced by a Daisy-in-Square motif that contains a much smaller and thinner clear oval center.

Late Buckle was originally produced by Bryce Brothers of Pittsburgh, Pennsylvania, about 1880. When Bryce became a member of the United States Glass Company in

Fig. 230. Original Late Buckle clear goblet by Bryce Brothers. Circa 1880.

1891, production continued. Made in an extended table service, the pattern was originally issued from a good-quality clear nonflint glass. Amber or any other color is rare (Fig. 230).

Late Buckle is a safe pattern to collect. To date, only the goblet has been reproduced. First appearing prior to 1975, these goblets are made from a good-quality clear nonflint glass. They are unmarked and were produced from a new mold, as evidenced by the following discrepancies: in comparison to originals, reproductions are smaller, the stem is shorter and thicker, and the design is lightly pressed and exceptionally smooth.

New goblets are not permanently marked.

Hint: Reproduction goblets are small and heavy and have thicker stems than originals.

Reproduced items: Goblet.

LATE JACOB'S LADDER

As the popularity of a particular pattern increased, it became a common practice among Victorian manufactures of pressed tableware to issue similar designs. Often they issued direct copies, with only the slightest change added to escape prosecution for patent infringement. More often than not, a majority of pressed-glass patterns were not patented, which inadvertently permitted the rampant copying of the better-selling designs.

Late Jacob's Ladder is one of these designs. It is similar to the well-known Jacob's Ladder pattern and was first issued in 1898 by the United States Glass Company of Pittsburgh, Pennsylvania, at Factory "B" (Bryce Brothers). Late Jacob's Ladder was produced in an extended table service from a medium-quality clear nonflint glass. Pieces have been found in amber, blue, and marigold carnival. However, any colored item is rare.

The Imperial Glass Corporation's 1956

catalog of vintage milk-glass illustrates the only two known reproductions in Late Jacob's Ladder. Known as Imperial's No.1950/740 open sugar and creamer set, each is in milk white. Unlike a vast majority of reproductions, those in Late Jacob's Ladder were made from the original molds (Fig. 231). These reproductions can be quite convincing, but they are heavy and the design is not as sharply pressed as on originals.

Reproduction items are not permanently marked, though you may occasionally find a

Fig. 231. Late Jacob's Ladder reproduction milk-white creamer and open sugar bowl. Imperial Glass Corp. Circa 1956. Unmarked.

piece with a paper label. Remembering that Late Jacob's Ladder was not originally produced in milk white will prevent you from purchasing new items for the old.

Hint: Late Jacob's Ladder was never made originally in milk white.
Reproduced items: Creamer, sugar bowl.

LIBERTY BELL

During the approaching centennial year of 1876, America's interest turned to its rich historical heritage. Championed in nearly all mediums of expression, historical motifs were abundant as manufacturers portrayed events and persons of the preceding century. Enticed by the lure of increased sales, manufacturers of pressed glass produced myriad tableware and novelty items depicting the centennial theme.

One such enterprising manufacturer was Adams & Company of Pittsburgh, Pennsylvania. The 1876 Centennial Exposition was held in Philadelphia, and Adams erected a working factory on the centennial grounds. There, Adams produced numerous souvenir items in the pattern Liberty Bell. Originally known as Centennial Ware, the pattern was produced in a good-quality clear nonflint glass in an extended table service. Odd items may be found in milk white, but they are rare.

Today, Liberty Bell remains a safe pattern to collect. Fig. 232 illustrates four reproductions produced from new molds in 1974 by the American Historical Replica Company of Grand Rapids, Michigan. Although each is an excellent representation of the original pattern, close examination quickly reveals a number of interesting discrepancies.

Unlike original goblets, which are 6¼ inches tall, reproductions are shorter and come in two sizes: the No.44229, or lady's goblet, which is 7 ounces, and the No.44228, or gentlemen's goblet, which is 10 ounces.

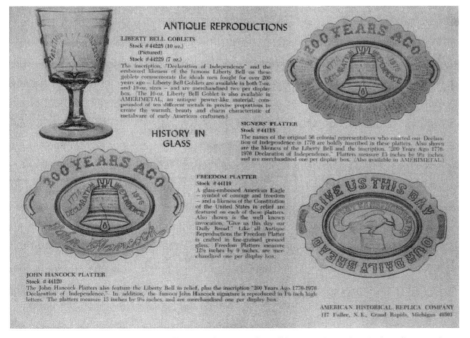

Fig. 232. Assortment of new Liberty Bell bread platters and a goblet. American Historical Replica Co. Circa 1975. Embossed "A.H.R.C."

Whereas original goblets are knob-stemmed, reproductions are hexagonal without a knob. However, the most obvious difference between old and new goblets lies in the inscription embossed on the bowl. Old goblets are embossed "Declaration of Independence 100 Years Ago 1776–1876." New goblets are embossed "Declaration of Independence 200 Years Ago 1776–1976."

In addition to the goblets, the American Replica Company also reproduced three bread platters (Fig. 233). The first is the No.44118 Signer's Plate. This platter is an exact copy of the original and is produced in a good-quality clear nonflint glass. Both old and new platters are 9½ by 13 inches and are embossed with all 56 signers of the Declaration of Independence. However, unlike originals, reproductions are embossed "Declaration of Independence 200 Years Ago 1776–1976."

The second reproduction bread platter is the No.44119 Freedom plate. This, too, is an exact copy of the original plate (better known as the Constitution Plate) and appears in a good-quality clear nonflint glass. Again, both the original and reproduction bread platters are 9 inches by 12½ inches and are embossed "Give Us This Day Our Daily Bread." Unlike other items in this series, Freedom plates are not dated 1976.

The third item reproduced in this series is the John Hancock plate. Although originals are known in clear and milk white, reproductions appear only in clear glass. Like other plates in this series, the new one is a good copy of the original. However, unlike the old, which measures 13½ inches by 9½ inches,

Fig. 233. American Historical Replica Co. circa 1975 sales brochure illustrating a number of new items in Liberty Bell.

reproductions are slightly smaller. While both plates are embossed with a representation of the Liberty Bell and the words "Declaration of Independence," reproductions are dated "200 Years Ago 1776–1976." Reproduction plates are also signed "John Hancock" in 1½-inch script letters that differ significantly from the original lettering.

All four items by American Historical Replica Company are permanently embossed "A.H.R.C. Grand Rapids, MI." Collectors should also note that all items except the Constitution or Freedom platter are dated "200 Years Ago 1776–1976."

Hint: All reproductions are permanently embossed "A.H.R.C. Grand Rapids, MI."
Reproduced items: Bread platter, goblet.

LINCOLN DRAPE

The pattern known as Lincoln Drape honors the death of our nation's sixteenth president, Abraham Lincoln (1809–65). Curiously, the basic design of clear drapery swagged between curtain tiebacks resembles bunting (lightweight, loosely woven fabric still used today during governmental occasions) and was produced with and without the addition of a tassel.

A product of the late 1860s, Lincoln

Drape was originally produced by the Boston and Sandwich Glass Company of Sandwich, Massachusetts. Issued from a good-quality clear flint glass in an extended table service, pieces are heavy and produce a fine belltone when gently tapped. Odd items may be found in milk white and sapphire blue, but any colored item is rare.

Lincoln Drape is a safe pattern to collect. Only one item, the miniature oil lamp with matching half-shade, may cause confusion. The 1947 No.75 catalog of the General

No. 12G1220
PERFUME
LAMP
REFILLS

Each......40¢
Per dozen..$4.00

Fig. 234. Clear Lincoln Drape miniature oil lamp. Circa 1947. Unmarked.

Merchandise Company of Milwaukee, Wisconsin (Fig. 234), illustrates this oil lamp. Frank and Ruth Smith, in their book on miniature oil lammps, state that this lamp could be purchased from the McCrory stores as early as 1938. Technically speaking, then, such lamps are not reproductions, as they are not original to the pattern.

Hint: Lincoln Drape is a safe pattern to collect because the miniature oil lamp is a new form.

Reproduced items: Miniature lamp.

LION

Lion is one of the most exciting patterns in the figural series of American pressed glass. For years, this pattern has been avidly sought by the most discriminating collectors. For this reason, many items, such as the cologne bottle, oblong master salt, milk pitcher, powder jar, and wine, have become exceedingly rare. Also known as Frosted Lion, Lion was originally produced by Gillinder & Sons of Philadelphia about 1877.

Lion was originally produced in an extended table service from a good-quality nonflint glass in clear with a lovely acid or satin finish. Pieces may be plain or copper-wheel engraved in a variety of decorative styles. Although all plain items are known, they are unusual and harder to find than those that are frosted.

As its name implies, this high-relief design consists of the king of the jungle stately reclining upon the bases and lower portions of articles. Typical of Victorian craftsmanship, the design is finely molded with a detail that appears chiseled rather than pressed. This is especially true of the lion's face, hair, and mane, which look almost lifelike.

Collectors and dealers often confuse Lion for Lion's Head, which is an entirely different design. On this pattern, bases are plain with a cable border, and finials are lion heads with or without thumbprints. In contrast, bases in Lion are collared and finials are in the shape of full-figured lions, which appear in two distinct styles: Lion and

Tree Trunk and Rampant Lion. Interchangeable items between both patterns are stemmed pieces, such as the celery vase, the goblet, and the wine.

Reproductions in Lion appeared as early as 1939. Goblets measuring between 6¾ inches and 6⅝ inches with rounded or slightly scalloped bases were made first (Fig. 235). They were followed by the 4-inch-round footed sauce dish and the celery vase. Unlike originals, early reproductions are either distinctively yellow or a dull, chalky white. By early 1940, the market had become flooded with new covered sugar bowls, medium-sized high-standard covered compotes, and spoonholders. These pieces were followed by the creamer, the covered butter dish, and the eggcup. Finally, the 8-inch-round high-standard covered compote with rampant lion finial and water pitcher appeared.

As a general rule of thumb, early reproductions share a number of similar discrepancies. Unlike originals, on which the pattern is well designed, finely molded, and in high relief, the design on reproductions is in low relief, lacking in detail, and often blurred and lifeless. Whereas the frosting on original items is grayish-white and uniform in its application, reproductions are chalky, entirely too white, and are coarse to the touch. Unlike the crystal-clear look of originals, reproductions often appear yellowed. Produced from new molds, reproductions are, moreover, noticeably heavier than originals.

In 1968, the L.G. Wright Glass Company

Fig. 235. Reproduction Lion clear and frosted goblet. Circa 1940. Unmarked.

Fig. 236. New Lion clear and frosted master salt introduced in 1977 by the Summit Art Glass Co. Impressed "V" within a circle mark and paper label.

Wright goblets are smaller than originals, have a slight scallop to the foot, and are distinctly yellow in color. Moreover, the lions on Wright goblets have the distinction of being pug-nosed.

Another item that has been causing considerable confusion among collectors is the new 1¾-inch-high by 2⅞-inch-diameter master salt illustrated in Fig. 236. It is unlike any known form in the Lion pattern. Introduced in 1977 by the Summit Art Glass Company of Akron, Ohio, these salts are found in clear and in clear with acid finish. To the unknowing, they may readily be purchased as original salts or children's miniatures. Although each salt originally carried a gold paper label in the shape of a hand imprinted "Hand Pressed in the U.S.A." in black block letters, the glass is only lightly

Fig. 237. Closeup of clear and frosted Lion reproduction master salt. Summit Art Glass Co. Circa 1977.

Fig. 238. Lion reproduction frosted paperweight. Viking Glass Co. Circa 1981–82. Unmarked.

of New Martinsville, West Virginia, reproduced the No.77-28 Lion goblet. Although the lion's mouth on new goblets does not sag like those on earlier reproductions,

CHART 76 LION. Other Reproductions Prior to 1969.
Maker: Unknown.
Mark: Unmarked.
Color Code: CF Clear Frosted.

ITEM	COLOR(S)	YEAR	ORIG	NEW
Butter dish, covered.	CF	1969	X	
Celery vase, pedestaled.	CF	1969	X	
Compote, oval, covered.	CF	1969	X	
Eggcup.	CF	1969	X	
Goblet.	CF	1969	X	
Pitcher, water, applied handle.	CF	1969	X	
Sauce dish, round, footed.	CF	1969	X	
Spoonholder.	CF	1969	X	
Sugar bowl, covered.	CF	1969	X	

impressed with a "V" within a circle (Fig. 237).

In 1981, the Viking Glass Company of New Martinsville, West Virginia, introduced an all-frosted reclining lion paperweight attached to a silver acrylic plinth. This paperweight is similar in design to the original but is so poorly designed and detailed that even the uninformed could not possibly mistake it for the old (Fig. 238).

To date, there are no known reproductions produced from original Lion molds. Aside from paper labels that may have been used, reproductions are not permanently marked as to maker or point of origin.

Typical of all reproductions, those in Lion are heavier than their original counterparts. The glass of new items is either yellow or gray and the frosting is chalky. Unlike original items, which have finely detailed hairs on the lion's body, well-propor-

tioned lion tails, and deeply chiseled, life-like lion faces, the lion on reproductions is smooth-bodied with almost no hair detail (especially on the creamer, spoonholder, sugar bowl, and water pitcher), the lion's tail is barely noticeable and sometimes is entirely missing at certain points, and the lion's face is poorly molded, creating a life-less expression. Moreover, bases of reproductions are not as heavily scalloped as the originals.

Known reproductions in Lion are enumerated in Chart 76. Most reproduction items in Lion are not permanently marked.

Hint: Reproductions in Lion are poorly detailed and the frosting is chalky white.
Reproduced items: Butter dish, celery vase, compote, eggcup, goblet, paperweight, salt, sauce dish, spoonholder, sugar bowl, water pitcher.

LION AND CABLE

A pattern in the figural series of American pressed glass is the Lion and Cable motif illustrated in Fig. 239. Also known as Proud Lion and Tiny Lion, this design was originally produced in the 1880s by the firm of Richards and Hartley of Tarentum, Pennsylvania, as line No.525. When Richards and

Hartley became Factory "E" of the United States Glass combine in 1891, production was continued.

Lion and Cable was originally produced in an extended table service from a good-quality nonflint glass in clear and in clear and frosted finish. Pieces are plain or copper-wheel engraved in a variety of decorative styles. As its name implies, Lion and

Fig. 239. Excerpt from an original United States Glass Co. catalog illustrating the Lion and Cable bread plate.

Fig. 240. New Lion and Cable No.77-49 clear and frosted bread plate. L.G. Wright Glass Co. Circa 1968. Unmarked.

Cable consists of a cable edge on the base of all pieces, with the exception of the goblet, where the cable edge appears at the bottom of the bowl. The finials on covered pieces and the handles of the celery, creamer, pitchers, spoonholder, and sugar bowl are molded in the shape of tiny reclining lions.

In 1968, the L.G. Wright Glass Company of New Martinsville, West Virginia, reproduced the Lion and Cable bread tray. Illustrated in Fig. 240, Wright's No.77-49 round, double-handled bread plate may still be found in clear and clear with frosted center. As you can see from the illustration, new bread plates are good copies of the original. Upon close observation, however, the discrepancies always associated with items produced from new molds become apparent. Original plates measure 12¼ inches in

diameter; reproductions measure 10½ inches. Unlike the smooth, well-proportioned cable border on original plates, the border on reproductions is more pronounced and sharper to the touch. On new plates, the figure of the lion is heavier than on the old; this is seen best in the lion's tail, which is thicker and less graceful on the new. On original plates, the border is finely stippled; the same border on reproductions is coarse. Although both are embossed "Give Us This Day Our Daily Bread," the lettering on reproductions is overly ornate and entirely unlike the old.

Hint: Reproduction bread plates are 10½ inches and originals are 12¼ inches.
Reproduced items: Bread tray.

LOG CABIN

Log Cabin is one of the more intriguing designs that depicts in pressed glass the great heritage of our nation. Unlike Westward Ho, which graphically illustrates America's pioneer past in scenes of the Old West, it is the shape of this pattern that makes it truly unique. For what could be more suitable to represent our common

roots than the humble beginnings of our forefathers?

Each item in this pattern is rectangular and shaped in the perfect likeness of a log cabin. Only the sauce dishes and covered butter dish lack windows and a door. When the door is present, it always has a latch or latch string. Although the standards of compotes are shaped like tree trunks, other items stand on four small log feet. In addition, the lids of covered pieces are fashioned in the form of a roof and have a chimney for a finial. An exception to this is the counter-display lid marked "Lutted's S.P. Cough Drops," which was produced for the cough-drop manufacturer James Lutted of Buffalo, New York.

Log Cabin is a pattern of the late 1870s and was originally issued in a medium-quality nonflint glass by the Central Glass Company of Wheeling, West Virginia, where it was known as line No.748. Due to its unusual shape, this design was produced in a very limited number of pieces. Although major production consisted of clear glass, rare pieces are known in amber, blue, and vaseline.

To date, four items have been reproduced in this pattern: the Lutted's flat, covered cough-drop displayer, the creamer, the spoonholder, and the covered sugar bowl. With the exception of the cough-drop displayer, the other three items were produced from a new mold in caramel, clear, and cobalt blue glass by the Mosser Glass Works of Cambridge, Ohio, about 1982.

New items may seem quite convincing. However, upon close examination, you can find a number of inconsistencies in the detail, shape, and weight of each item.

Unlike the crisp, deep impression of original pieces, reproductions are lightly molded, appear somewhat blurred, and reveal a definite waviness in the glass. There are also a number of appreciable differences in the pattern. The logs on genuine items are smaller, more natural in appearance, and more vividly detailed than on reproductions. In addition, the design on the front and back of original sugar lids is always composed of three horizontal boards, which are not on the new lids. However, the most obvious variation is in the treatment of the door. On old items, there is always a door latch, which was not included on reproductions (Fig. 241).

While it is possible to detect new items by pattern alone, shape provides us with still another method of uncovering reproductions. A good example of this can be seen in the structure of the creamer's handle and spout (Fig. 242). Unlike the straight

Fig. 241. Closeup of reproduction Log Cabin creamer by Mosser Glass. Inc. Unlike originals, new creamers do not have a door latch.

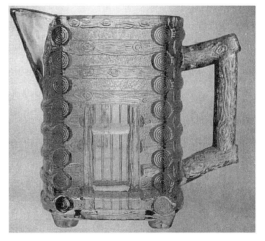

Fig. 242. Clear reproduction Log Cabin creamer. Mosser Glass. Inc. Circa 1982. Unmarked.

handles on new creamers, the tops and bottoms of original handles curve sharply inward. Spouts also differ in that originals are distinctly arched and reproductions are not. This can best be seen when viewed from the side. At this angle, old spouts somewhat resemble a slice of pie, while new spouts are triangular. Still another difference can be found in the shape of the rims. While they are flat on genuine items, the rims on reproductions are clearly round.

Little more can be said of the new spoonholder, which shares the same discrepencies as other reproductions in this pattern. Original spoonholders are $4^{11}/_{16}$ inches high and $3^{1}/_{8}$ inches wide.

The "Lutted's Cough Drops" covered-bowl counter display has also been reproduced from a new mold. This reproduction is $4^{3}/_{4}$ inches wide and $7^{1}/_{8}$ inches wide and appeared on the market as late as 1991 in clear, cobalt blue, and light pink. Like the Mosser items, this item also shows the same discrepancies. The latch on the door is missing, the chimney finial is rounded on the top instead of flat, and the brick detail is

poorly done. The logs are not as well defined as the originals: they lack bark detail and appear round and smooth. The new bowls are also heavier than the originals and are made from a poor-quality nonflint glass, and the lettering on the cover is slightly lopsided. Although new cough-drop displayers are not permanently marked, each originally bore a small gold label printed in black block letters "MADE IN TAIWAN."

Mosser reproductions are not permanently marked but can be found with a paper label.

Hint: Reproduction items do not have a latch on the cabin door.
Reproduced items: Lutted's covered bowl, creamer, spoonholder, sugar bowl.

LOOP AND DART WITH ROUND ORNAMENT

Fig. 243. Loop and Dart with Round Ornament spoonholder.

One of the more popular members of the Loop and Dart group of pattern glass is Loop and Dart with Round Ornament. This pattern was designed and patented by W.O. Davis (patent No.3494) on May 11, 1869, and originally produced by the Portland Glass Company of Portland, Maine, between 1869 and 1873.

Similar to Loop and Dart and Loop and Dart with Diamond Ornaments, this simple pattern consists of clear, short intersecting arches that produce open loops (Fig. 243). The loops alternate with clear, longer loops that extend toward the base to form open diamond-shaped ornaments. Both loop and dart motifs are pressed in high relief upon a finely stippled background. Above this design is a band of clear round ornaments. Produced from a good-quality nonflint glass, items are clear and brilliant, and handles are applied and beautifully crimped.

Although we cannot cite any reproductions in this pattern, Frank H. Swan in his book *Portland Glass* (1939) contends that

the round, flat sauce dish had been reissued. However, without positive catalog identification, this claim is impossible to confirm. A prudent approach to suspect items may be to make a careful comparison of detail, quality, and weight.

Hint: Loop and Dart reproductions are unconfirmed; examine suspect items carefully.
Reproduced items: Sauce dish.

LORD'S SUPPER BREAD PLATE

Religious themes are no stranger to American pattern glass. Pressed-glass manufacturers in the Victorian Era offered an impressive variety of religious articles as designers looked to the Bible for inspiration. You can still find these articles in decorative and utilitarian forms, and they remain prized examples of the mold maker's craft. One of the more popular items in this category is the Lord's Supper Bread Plate. Originally produced by the Model Flint Glass Company of Findlay, Ohio, in 1891 from a good-quality clear nonflint glass, production was continued after the firm moved to Albany, Indiana, in 1893.

Original Lord's Supper Bread Plates are 7 inches wide and 11 inches long and come in clear, clear with a frosted background, and clear with a background painted in gold, red, and other colors. The plate's center is a scene of Christ and the twelve apostles seated at supper. So fine is the molding that food, utensils, and the folds in each figure's garments are readily seen. Facial expressions are lifelike and the scene itself is in excellent proportion. Enclosing the entire scene is a generous clear border of stippled grapes and grape leaves in high relief. Interestingly, plates are known with either closed or open grapevine borders (Fig. 244).

The first reproductions of the Lord's Supper Bread Plate appeared between 1937 and 1944 in clear and clear with frosted centers. They were produced by the New

Martinsville Glass Company of New Martinsville, West Virginia, and appear without the elaborate border. Typical of early reproductions, clear plates are tinged in a peculiar yellow. On those that are clear with frosting, the frosting is harsh and blotchy. Early reproductions are unmarked.

In 1976, Mosser Glass, Inc., of Cambridge, Ohio, issued the No.147 miniature Lord's Supper Bread Plate shown in Fig. 245. Produced from a new mold, examples came in clear and the contemporary colors of amber, amethyst, blue, and green. As you can see from the illustration, it is quite easy to be fooled into thinking that this is a child's miniature bread plate. However, such a miniature was never originally produced.

By 1973, the Indiana Glass Company of Dunkirk, Indiana, was producing in red the large, table-sized bread plate known as the Last Supper. This was produced for Tiara Exclusives as an in-home party line developed by Indiana Glass. Issued from a new mold, plates in additional colors were added

Fig. 245. New Lord's Supper clear miniature bread tray. Mosser Glass, Inc. Circa 1976. Unmarked.

Fig. 246. Lord's Supper reproduction bread tray and chalice. Indiana Glass Co. Circa 1982. Unmarked.

Fig. 244. Reprint of Model Flint Glass Co. ad in *China, Glass and Lamps,* April 22, 1891, illustrating the original Lord's Supper bread tray with closed border.

in subsequent years: pink (1978), burnt honey (1981), and blue (1982). At about the time Indiana Glass produced this large tray, it was also making a smaller jewel tray to give away through Tiara Exclusives. Quite similar to that produced by Mosser Glass, neither form was ever produced originally.

The most interesting item produced by Indiana Glass in this pattern is a large chalice or goblet (Fig. 246). Although examples are known only in clear, it is likely that colors exist. Entirely new in form, they are of a generous size with a large flared foot and a faceted knob that appears on the stem just below the bowl. Spanning the bowl in low relief is the same scene that appears in the center of the bread plate.

The lack of workmanship found on originals is typical of all reproductions of the Lord's Supper Bread Plate. They are also heavy and poorly detailed. Plates with open grapevine borders have never been reproduced.

Hint: Original bread plates are 7 inches wide by 11 inches long.
Reproduced items: Bread plate, goblet.

LOUIS XV

After enjoying success with both the Alaska and the Klondike patterns a year earlier, the Northwood Glass Company of Indiana, Pennsylvania, introduced the Louis XV line in July 1898. Named after the King of France, this line was produced in an extended table service from a good-quality nonflint glass in custard and emerald green decorated with gold trim (Fig. 247).

The August 24, 1898, issue of *China, Glass and Lamps* aptly described Northwood's latest creation. "The Northwood Glass Co., Indiana, PA., always succeeds in giving the trade something different from the old conventional glass patterns. . . . There is a low relief figure, just a breath, being a combination of Hogarth's graceful lines of beauty, into which a spray of color is thrown. . . . The edges are gracefully scalloped, and tipped with bright gold. The tiny carved feet, in imitation of seashells, are in the style of the best English castor place laid on work, and are in gold decoration."

As late as 1959, the Imperial Glass Corporation of Bellaire, Ohio, used a new mold to reproduce the Louis XV covered sugar bowl in milk white. In the May 25, 1962, issue of *China, Glass and Tablewares,* Imperial advertised this covered sugar in frosted crystal (originally known as Doeskin), ruby, and marble slag. In 1964, it added rubigold and, by 1965, purple carnival.

Each new sugar bowl is permanently marked with Imperial's familiar "IG" logo. Produced in colors never made originally, this reproduction should confuse no one. It is heavy and poorly detailed, and the feath-

Be sure to see our new Fall Line

LOUIS XV.

Tableware in Ivory and Gold

The Northwood Co., Indiana, Pa.

NEW YORK	PHILADELPHIA	BALTIMORE
Frank M. Miller	Fitzpatrick & Pascoe	J. Beiswanger, Jr., & Co.
76 Park Place	930 Arch Street	Moore Building

EAST, George Mortimer   WEST, Carl Northwood

Fig. 247. Reprint of Northwood Glass Co. ad from *China, Glass and Pottery Review* for September 1898 illustrating Louis XV spoonholder.

ered scrolls of the design are not as sharply raised or well defined as the originals.

In 1956, the Jeannette Glass Company of Jeannette, Pennsylvania, offered the No.3425 oval four-toed master berry bowl and the double candleholder in shell pink. Later, these items were available in clear, milk white, and crystal with blue, green, or pink stain. Unmarked, they, too, were made from a new mold and are heavy and thick. The feathering on the pattern is flat and

dull when compared to the sharp, full feathers on originals. One of the easiest ways to determine originals from reproductions is to look for the heavy stippling on the sides of reproductions, which is absent on the original.

Hint: Louis XV originals were made only in custard and emerald green.
Reproduced items: Bowl, candleholder, sugar bowl.

MAGNET AND GRAPE WITH FROSTED LEAF

Magnet and Grape with Frosted Leaf is one of the patriarchs of early American pattern glass. This design has enjoyed a wide and lengthy popularity even though only a limited table service was produced. The glass dates from the 1850s and is a high-quality clear, brilliant flint that resounds when gently tapped. Although early writers have attributed this design to the Portland Glass Company of Portland, Maine, and the Boston and Sandwich Glass Company of Sandwich, Massachusetts, proof has yet to surface regarding its true manufacture.

The design consists of vertical panels that are arched at the top. Within each panel, large clusters of grapes and leaves alternate with a conventional shape that resembles a magnet composed of tiny diamond points. Each panel is separated by a thin vertical flute. Unlike later patterns, which are frosted with hydrofluoric acid, the frosting on Magnet and Grape with Frosted Leaf is machine-ground. In a rare variation of this design, an American shield replaces the Grape and Leaf.

New goblets appeared during the mid-1960s. They are unmarked and produced from a new mold in a clear nonflint glass. Although similar in design to the original, the pattern on these reproductions consists of a large cluster of grapes between two smaller grape leaves. When viewed under a strong light, new goblets display a

distinct green or yellow cast. You can also find these goblets in the contemporary colors of amber, amethyst, blue, ruby, and yellow.

In 1970, the Metropolitan Museum of Art in New York City appointed the Imperial Glass Corporation of Bellaire, Ohio, exclusive license to reproduce a number of items in Magnet and Grape for sale through the museum. The first reproduction was the 6½-inch-high goblet in clear and frosted glass illustrated in Fig. 248. In 1971, the clear and frosted 7-inch-high pedestaled creamer with applied handle and the 8¾-inch-high covered sugar bowl followed (Figs. 249 and

Fig. 248. Reproduction Magnet and Grape with Frosted Leaf goblet. Circa 1981. (Note how straight the base of the bowl is where the stem attaches.) Embossed "MMA."

Fig. 249. Reproduction Magnet and Grape with Frosted Leaf creamer. Imperial Glass Corp. for the Metropolitan Museum of Art. Circa 1971. Embossed "MMA."

Fig. 250. Reproduction Magnet and Grape with Frosted Leaf covered sugar bowl. Imperial Glass Corp. for the Metropolitan Museum of Art. Circa 1982–83. Embossed "MMA."

250). A year later, both items were introduced in sapphire blue. By 1979, clear and frosted eggcups and 3½-inch-high tumblers had been added to the line (Fig. 251). In 1984, 6¼-inch-high ale glasses (or open sugar bowls) were added.

According to advertisements in the museum's mail-order catalogs from 1970 through 1985, "So exact are copies, not only in size and weight but also in method and manufacturing technique, that each piece carries the museum's monogram on the bottom to keep them from being mistaken for originals." Moreover, the museum claimed that each reproduction was a direct copy of an original from within the museum's collection. Each item was permanently embossed with the museum's "MMA" hallmark, individually boxed, and accompanied by descriptive text.

In 1973, the Smithsonian Institution, in Washington, D.C., authorized the Imperial Glass Corporation to reproduce the 4-ounce wine in clear and frosted glass. These new wines were produced from a new mold in a good-quality clear and frosted nonflint glass and permanently embossed with the museum's "SI" hallmark.

Reproductions are good copies. Unlike those issued in sapphire blue (which is strictly a contemporary color), clear and

Fig. 251. Reproduction 3½-inch-high Magnet and Grape with Frosted Leaf tumbler introduced in 1979 by the Metropolitan Museum of Art. Embossed "MMA."

frosted examples can be quite convincing. However, reproductions are light and do not resonate as strongly as original items. When you encounter a reproduction, you will immediately notice that the frosting is entirely too satiny and soft. (The originals are rough and coarse.) You'll also notice that the design that cuts into the leaves is

too shallow and the overall look is glossy and new.

Hint: Magnet and Grape with Frosted Leaf reproductions are permanently embossed "MMA" or "SI."

Reproduced items: Ale glass, creamer, eggcup, goblet, sugar bowl, tumbler, wine.

MAGNET AND GRAPE WITH STIPPLED LEAF

Similar in design to Magnet and Grape with Frosted Leaf is the variation with the stippled leaf. Known as Magnet and Grape with Stippled Leaf, it is apparently a later pattern, for it is lightweight and has no belltone. Unlike its sister design, which is machine-ground to produce a coarse, white frosted appearance, this design has a lightly stippled leaf that resembles a pebbled surface.

Magnet and Grape with Stippled Leaf is a pattern of the 1870s and has been attributed by early glass writers to the Boston and Sandwich Glass Company of Sandwich, Massachusetts.

This pattern was originally produced in a small table service from a good-quality clear nonflint glass. Like Magnet and Grape with Frosted Leaf, the design consists of vertical panels that are arched at the top. Here, too, panels with large clusters of grapes and leaves alternate with panels with a conventional shape that resembles a magnet composed of tiny diamond points. Each panel is in turn separated by a thin vertical flute. However, unlike earlier patterns, which are machine-ground to produce a frosted effect, here the design is lightly stippled.

As late as 1960, the L.G. Wright Glass Company of New Martinsville, West Virginia, issued the No.37-1 champagne (Fig. 252) and the No.37-2 goblet. Both reproductions are unmarked and were produced from a new mold in solid amber, amethyst, and clear glass. A similar goblet with a large grape cluster and a bunch of leaves hanging from either side is also known in amber.

Fig. 252. Reproduction Magnet and Grape with Stippled Leaf amethyst champagne. Circa 1980s. Unmarked.

Compared to the originals, the design on reproductions is poorly executed. Grape leaves on reproductions are rounded (instead of pointed), and the veining of the leaves is thick and overly exaggerated. The grape cluster is elongated and overly embossed. On the magnet motif, the tiny diamond points are blunt and smooth (Fig. 253).

Reproductions are also heavier and thicker than originals. An excessive amount of glass at the base of the bowls produces a solid line that you can see in a strong light.

Fig. 253. Closeup of new amethyst Magnet and Grape with Stippled Leaf champagne.

In 1963, the Red-Cliff Distributing Company of Chicago advertised the new Magnet and Grape with Stippled Leaf No.G-9029 butterfly crimped compote, No.G-9129 garland-edged compote, No.G-9128 flared flip or tumbler, No.9345 straight-sided flip or tumbler, and No.G-9045 goblet. Known as Red-Cliff's Grape pattern, these pieces can still be found in the contemporary colors of antique amber, Apple Valley green, Bedford blue, clear, Jamestown blue, milk white, Old Colony amber, and Shenandoah green. They were produced from 1963 through 1974 by the Fenton Art Glass Company of Williamstown, West Virginia, from new Red-Cliff molds. These items are permanently embossed on the bases with a circular mark, "(C) RED-CLIFF C USA," which surrounds a large "R," written in script.

The Fenton Art Glass Company of Williamstown, West Virginia, also issued the Magnet and Grape with Stippled Leaf bell (No.9062), which it named Grape. Although the bell form is not original to the set, it is a direct copy of the original design. These bells were produced in the opalescent colors of blue, cameo, French, and topaz and are permanently marked with the familiar Fenton logo. Reproduction goblets and champagnes are not always permanently marked.

Hint: Reproductions have rounded leaves and grape bunches that are thicker than the originals.
Reproduced items: Bell, champagne, compote, goblet, tumbler.

MAIZE

Maize is one of the many novelty designs that appeared throughout the Victorian Era. Anyone familiar with the cornfields of the great Midwest in early fall will immediately recognize this pattern. The design resembles an open ear of corn with well-molded rows of kernels; trailing corn husks rise from the base (Fig. 254). Items were made in clear (plain or iridized) and custard or milk white (plain or decorated in blue, brown, green, and yellow). Although primarily blown, a number of pressed forms exist, including the salt shaker and condiment base. Handles are applied.

This pattern, originally referred to as Maize, was designed and patented by Joseph Locke on September 10, 1889, under the design patent No.19313. W.L. Libbey and Sons of Toledo, Ohio, first issued an extended table service in this pattern that same year (Fig. 255). It is also known as Maize Art Glass and New England Corn Glass.

From as late as 1968, the L.G. Wright Glass Company of New Martinsville, West Virginia, issued the eight Maize reproductions enumerated in Chart 77. These reproductions are unmarked and were produced from new molds in amber, light and dark blue, pink, and rose. Each color has an outer layer of clear glass and an inner layer of chalky-white glass. Only the No.40-3 sugar shaker and the No.40-4 water tumbler are original forms; the remainder of this group is contemporary. Because electric lamps in Maize are strictly contemporary, we have intentionally eliminated them from our listing.

CHART 77   MAIZE. L.G. Wright Glass Company, New Martinsville, West Virginia.
CMN: Maize.
Mark: Unmarked.
Color Code: AO Amber Overlay, BO Blue Overlay, DBO Dark Blue Overlay, PO Pink Overlay, RO Rose Overlay.

ITEM	COLOR(S)	YEAR	ORIG	NEW
Biscuit jar. #40-1. Covered, 6¾"d., 7¼"h.	AO, PO, RO	1968		X
	BO	1969		X
Castor or pickle jar. #40-8-5. Complete with silver-plate frame and tongs, 3"d., 12"h.	AO, DBO, PO	1968		X
Pitcher. #40-5. Water, bulbous, circular foot, ruffled rim, 78 oz. applied clear handle, 8½"h.	AO, PO	1968		X
Rose bowl. #40-2. Round, circular foot, 6¾"d., 7¼"h., with or without triangular pedestal.	AO, BO, DBO, PO, RO	1968		X
Sugar shaker. #40-3. 16 oz., 5⅜"h.	AO, PO	1968	X	
Tumbler. #40-4. Water, flat, straight-sided, 8 oz., 4½"h.	AO, PO	1968	X	
Vase.				
#40-6. Tapered, low-stemmed foot, tightly crimped rim, 7"h.	AO, PO	1968		X
#40-7. Bulbous base, ruffled rim, 9"h.	AO, PO	1968		X

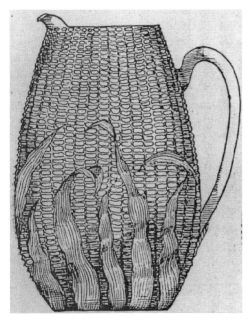

Fig. 254. Excerpt from a *Crockery and Glass Journal* ad illustrating the Maize water pitcher.

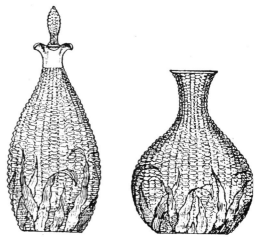

Fig. 255. Excerpt from a *Crockery and Glass Journal* ad illustrating the Maize carafe and water bottle. (Note the original stopper on the bottle.)

Wright reproductions are thick-walled and excessively heavy. This heaviness is caused by the inner and the outer glass lining (casing), and it becomes apparent as soon as you pick up a reproduction. This thickness is most readily seen around the rim of each item. Additionally, the leaves on reproductions are thick and ill-defined and the gold tracery found on original items is missing. When you compare original and reproduction items carefully, you will also notice that the shape and size of the corn kernels on old pieces is lifelike, while on new pieces they are overly exaggerated.

Hint: Maize reproductions are usually cased with a white inner lining.

MANHATTAN

The United States Glass Company's 1909 Domestic Catalog, in the Rakow Library's collection of original catalogs, fully illustrates the four-piece Manhattan table set. Originally named No.15078 or Manhattan, this pattern was first produced by the United States Glass Company of Pittsburgh about 1902 at the firm's Glassport, Pennsylvania, factory. Manhattan must have enjoyed lengthy production, for the pattern also appears in the firm's 1915 Mexican Export catalog.

Manhattan was originally produced from a good-quality nonflint glass. The company offered an extended table service in clear and in clear with green or rose stain (both gold-trimmed), including two sizes of cruets and a syrup pitcher. Although you may find odd pieces in clear with ruby stain, this or any other color is rare.

The design (as you can see from Figs. 256 and 257) consists of a horizontal row of beaded bull's eyes, vertical fluting that produces an icicle effect, and a band of hexagonal blocks. The positioning of each element may vary depending upon the item.

As early as 1942, the United States Glass Company of Tiffin, Ohio, issued the Manhattan flat basket with folded sides and applied handle. This new basket is unmarked and was produced from a medium-quality clear nonflint glass. In 1955, United States Glass also reissued the No.15078 or Bull's Eye 15-piece punch set. This set consists of an 11-quart one-piece round and flat punch bowl, 12 punch cups with pressed handles, one 23-inch-diameter round underplate, and a ladle. Both of these reproductions are unmarked and most likely were made from original molds.

In 1967, Bartlett-Collins Glass Company of Sapulpa, Oklahoma, issued the ten items enumerated in Chart 78. Known as Manhattan, each item is unmarked and was produced from a new mold in amber or clear nonflint glass. As you can see from this chart, only the footed sherbert has a contemporary form (Fig. 258).

As a general guideline, reproductions in Manhattan are heavy and thick, the glass is shiny and slick, the design is poorly developed (especially the dots around the bull's-eye motif), and the glass is often slightly yellowed. The glass also has

Fig. 256. Reprint of a United States Glass Company catalog illustrating the No.15078 or Manhattan pattern. At least ten of these items have been reproduced by the Bartlett-Collins Glass Co.

Fig. 257. Reprint of a United States Glass Company catalog illustrating the No.15078 or Manhattan pattern. At least ten of these items have been reproduced by the Bartlett-Collins Glass Co.

Fig. 258. Assortment of new Manhattan. Bartlett-Collins Glass Co. Circa 1967. Unmarked.

CHART 78   Bartlett-Collins Glass Company, Sapulpa, Oklahoma.
CMN: Manhattan.
Mark: Unmarked.
Color Code: A Amber, C Clear.

ITEM	COLOR(S)	YEAR	ORIG	NEW
Bowl, round, flat, 8½"d.	C	1967	X	
Creamer.	C	1967	X	
Goblet.	A	unknown	X	
	C	1967	X	
Plate.				
6"d.	C	1967	X	
11"d.	C	1967	X	
Sauce dish, round, flat, 4½"d.	C	1967	X	
Sherbert, footed.	C	1967		X
Sugar bowl, open.	C	1967	X	
Tumbler, iced tea.	C	1967	X	
Wine.	C	1967	X	

a distinctive waviness, which you can see when you hold the piece up to a strong light. In general, reproductions are poorly pressed and the design is blurred and missing the finer details found on originals.

Hint: Reproductions are heavy and the pattern's detail is poorly done.

Reproduced items: Basket, bowl, creamer, goblet, plate, punch bowl, punch cup, sauce, sherbert, sugar bowl, tumbler, undertray, wine.

MAPLE LEAF

One of the most charming patterns employing the leaf motif has become known as Maple Leaf (Fig. 259). According to Ruth Webb Lee, this pattern originally was called Leaf by Gillinder & Sons of Greensburgh, Pennsylvania, which produced the design in the 1880s in a large and extended table service from a good-quality nonflint glass. Although the design was produced in amber, apple green, blue, clear, clear and frosted, emerald green, and vaseline, not all pieces may be found in all colors.

Also known as Leaf or Maple Leaf on Trunk, the basic design consists of finely molded leaves that are more reminiscent of grape leaves than maple leaves. This would account for the shape of the finials and the handles of covered dishes. The finely molded finials are well-sculpted clusters of grapes and leaves, and the handles are grape clusters without leaves. Most shapes are ovoid and, except for stemware, have feet that are splayed and stippled.

The only known reproduction in Maple Leaf is the goblet illustrated in Fig. 260. New goblets appeared as early as 1938 in the original colors of amber, blue, clear (plain or frosted), and green and the contemporary color of amethyst. This goblet (known as Wright's No.77-29) appears in the same color combination in the 1971 master catalog of the L.G. Wright Glass Company of New Martinsville, West Virginia. These goblets are unmarked and were produced from a new mold, as evidenced by the following discrepancies: they are noticeably thick and heavy, stems are stubby and

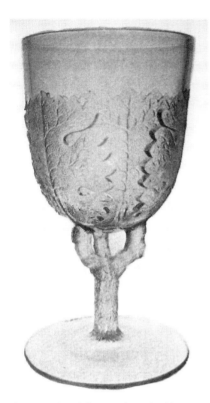

Fig. 259. Original clear Maple Leaf goblet.

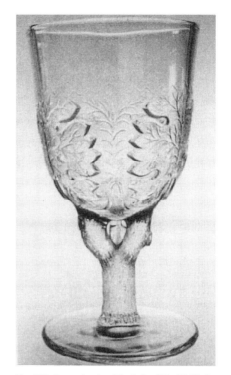

Fig. 260. Reproduction Maple Leaf No.77-29 clear goblet. L.G. Wright Glass Co. Circa 1971. (Note the thickness of the stem.)

exceptionally thick, colors are artificial, deep, and harsh, and the design is small and undetailed.

Hint: Reproduction goblets are heavy and the stem is extremely thick.
Reproduced items: Goblet.

MARDI GRAS

Originally known as Duncan No.42 or Empire, this pattern is also known as Paneled English Hobnail with Prisms or Siamese Necklace. George A. Duncan Sons & Company of Washington, Pennsylvania, originally produced this pattern in a large and extended table service about 1899. In 1900, the Duncan & Miller Glass Company of Pittsburgh continued its production.

Mardi Gras is an interesting pattern comprised of cut-glass elements. The quality of the glass is clear and brilliant, and handles are applied or pressed. Apparently two versions of the design were issued: (a) those with a plain rim, and (b) those with a ring and a thumbprint rim.

Although you may find complete table settings in clear and clear with ruby stain (plain or gold-trimmed), dark amber, sapphire blue, clear with amber stain, clear with frosting, and any other color is rare.

Like a majority of early American pattern glass, Mardi Gras is a safe pattern to collect because only a small number of items have been reissued. As early as 1943, the Duncan & Miller Glass Company reintroduced the two-piece two-gallon punch bowl and the 5-ounce punch cup in clear glass from original molds. In 1955, as a division of the United States Glass Company of Tiffin, Ohio, Duncan reissued two versions of the 16-piece punch set (Fig. 261). The first set consisted of a 13-inch-diameter, 8½-quart two-piece cupped punch bowl with twelve 5-ounce

Fig. 261. New 16-piece Mardi Gras clear punch-bowl set. Duncan & Miller Glass Co. Circa 1955. Unmarked.

punch cups, a ladle, and an underplate. The second set was identical, except the punch bowl is flared and 14½ inches in diameter. In 1955, Duncan Glass also reissued two 8-inch-high vases in milk white: the No.742-1 with flared rim and No.742-2 with straight sides (Fig. 262).

Both unmarked punch-bowl sets and the unmarked vases were produced from original U.S. Glass molds. Therefore, the best way to determine the originals from reissues is to examine the quality of the glass. Reissues are heavier and thicker than originals and the glass has a distinct glossy sheen. However, vases should not cause confusion because Mardi Gras was not originally made in milk white.

In 1973, the Indiana Glass Company of Dunkirk, Indiana, reissued two additional items in Mardi Gras: the clear 15-piece punch set and the straight-sided 8-inch-high bud vase in amber and vaseline (Fig. 263). These are unmarked and most likely were reissued from the original Duncan molds owned by the United States Glass Company.

Unlike the normal quality of glass produced by Indiana for its Tiara home line,

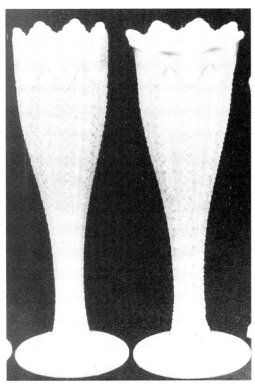

Fig. 262. Pair of reproduction milk-white bud vases in Mardi Gras. Duncan & Miller Glass Co. Circa 1955. Unmarked.

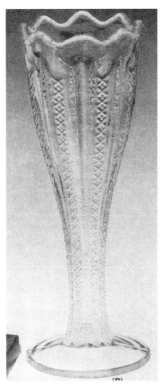

Fig. 263. Reproduction Mardi Gras bud vase. Indiana Glass Co. for Tiara Exclusives. Circa 1973. Unmarked.

reproductions in Mardi Gras are of a higher-quality nonflint glass. However, like other reproductions, they are heavier and thicker than the originals and the glass looks new.

Unmarked round luncheon plates are also known in glossy amber. Like other reproductions, these new plates are thick, heavy, and slick or oily.

Hint: Reproductions in Mardi Gras are heavier and thicker than originals.
Reproduced items: Plate, punch bowl, punch cup, underplate, vase.

MASCOTTE

Mascotte is a well-known member of the block group that has long enjoyed favorable interest with collectors and dealers. The well-balanced design of clear rows of blocks covers the lower half of each item. The number of blocks in the design varies according to the shape and size of each piece. Handles are applied. The unpatterned half of each item is either plain or engraved with a Fern and Berry etching known as No.75. Mascotte is also known as Dominion, Etched Fern and Waffle, and Minor Block.

Mascotte was originally produced by Ripley & Company of Pittsburgh, Pennsylvania, about 1884. Ripley continued to produce this pattern after becoming a member of the United States Glass combine in 1891. Ripley originally produced an extended table service from a good-quality clear nonflint glass. You may find pieces in amber, blue, and milk white, but any color is rare.

In 1956, Tiffin Glass (a division of the United States Glass Company) of Tiffin, Ohio, reproduced the series of clear cylinder, Egyptian, globe, and stack jars enumerated in Chart 79. The cylinder and the globe jars were originally known as Dakota. Produced from original United States Glass Company molds, new jars have become a problem for dealers and collectors because the glass is the same quality and weight as the originals (Fig. 264). Fortunately, you may still find jars that retain their original paper labels.

CHART 79 MASCOTTE. Tiffin Glass, Tiffin, Ohio.
CMN: Dakota.
Mark: Unmarked or paper label.
Color Code: C Clear.

ITEM	COLOR(S)	YEAR	ORIG	NEW
Jar.				
Cylinder, covered, straight-sided.				
Low circular foot.				
#20055/6. 23½"h.	C	1956	X	
#20054/5. 17⅞"h.	C	1956	X	
#20051/2. 12¹⁄₁₆"h.	C	1956	X	
#20050/1. 9¹¹⁄₁₆"h.	C	1956	X	
Egyptian, covered, flat.				
Bulbous high shoulder.				
#20036. ½-Pint.	C	1956	X	
#20046. 2-Pint.	C	1956	X	
#20044. 5-Pint.	C	1956	X	
#20448. 8-Pint.	C	1956	X	
Globe, covered, bulbous.				
Low-footed.				
#20047. 8-Pint.	C	1956	X	
#20045. 5-Pint.	C	1956	X	
#20043. 3-Pint.	C	1956	X	
Stack, flat, straight-sided.				
#5891. Covered				
4-Piece.	C	1956	X	
5-Piece.	C	1956	X	

#20045
5 pt.
packed 1 to carton.

#20047
8 pt.
packed 1 to carton.

Fig. 264. Pair of clear new Mascotte apothecary jars as illustrated in an undated, contemporary United States Glass Co. sales brochure.

A more effective method of detecting new items is to examine the glass. Newer glass has a distinctly glossy sheen that is un-

like the fine patina found on original items. Unfortunately, this method is not foolproof because reissues already display the wear of three decades.

In 1960, the L.E. Smith Glass Company of Mount Pleasant, Pennsylvania, issued the clear footed cylinder covered jar in three sizes. These jars are unmarked and most likely were produced from the original molds once owned by Tiffin. L.E. Smith and Tiffin produced pieces with a similar quality of pattern detail, but the glass quality is different. Smith items are heavier than originals and the glass has a definite yellowish cast. In comparison, Tiffin pieces are noticeably clear.

Both sets of reproduction jars have been seen with the original patent dates on the bottom. None of these reproductions, however, has been recorded with the Fern and Berry etching.

Hint: Mascotte has only been reproduced in storage jars.

MASSACHUSETTS

Massachusetts, one of the state patterns, is also known as Arched Diamond Points, Cane Variant, Geneva, and Stars and Diamonds. The original name of this design is No.15054 or Massachusetts. It was first produced between 1898 and 1909 from a good-quality nonflint glass by the United States Glass Company of Pittsburgh, Pennsylvania, at its Factory "K" (or King Glass factory). Although an extended table service was offered in clear, you may find rarities in emerald green, clear with ruby stain, and cobalt blue.

This pattern is typical of late Victorian imitation cut glass. The design, composed of an array of cut-glass elements, is fussy and heavy and covers the entire surface of each object. The glass is also clear and brilliant and handles are pressed.

Massachusetts is one of the many safe patterns to collect because, to date, only the covered butter dish illustrated in Fig.

265 has been reproduced. In 1984, the A.A. Importing Co., Inc., of St. Louis, Missouri (and Carson City, Nevada, and San Francisco, California), offered the new

PG/1692 "STAR AND DIAMONDS" GREEN BUTTER DISH. 8⅜ in.
Each . . . 7.00

Fig. 265. Reproduction Massachusetts green covered butter dish offered in 1984 by the A.A. Importing Co., Inc. Unmarked.

No.PG/1692 covered butter dish as its Star Diamonds pattern. This new butter is 8¾ inches in diameter, unmarked, and was produced from a new mold in clear and in the contemporary colors of green and pink and later in blue and ruby. A similar butter dish in amberina is also unmarked and apparently is produced from a new mold.

New covered butter dishes are poor representations of the originals. Unlike old butters, which are thin-walled, light, and crisply molded, reproductions are thick-walled, heavy, and poorly molded. Additionally, the design on these copies feels smooth and the glass is noticeably crinkled or wavy.

The easiest way to detect a new butter dish is by its color. Any butter in the contemporary colors of amberina, blue, green, pink, and ruby is obviously new.

Reproduction butter dishes are unmarked, but you may occasionally find them with a "MADE IN TAIWAN" gold label with black lettering.

Hint: Reproduction butter dishes are heavy and the glass is slick and oily.
Reproduced items: Butter dish.

MEDALLION

As competition between manufacturers of pressed-glass tableware increased during the third quarter of the nineteenth century, a strong interest in colorful nonflint patterns promised increased sales. Common colors in which numerous complete table services were offered include varying shades of solid amber, blue, canary yellow, and apple green.

Also known as Hearts and Spades or Spades, Medallion is a typical pattern of the colorful era of pressed glass. This pattern of the early 1890s was produced in a large table setting in amber, blue, clear, and vaseline nonflint glass. Handles are pressed.

Although it is not known when or by whom Medallion was originally produced, John and Elizabeth Welker suggest in *Pressed Glass in America* that the original manufacturer may be the United States Glass Company of Pittsburgh, Pennsylvania. It is a pleasing pattern consisting of a large clear rectangle in the center of which is a large conventional medallion-like ornament set against a clear background.

In the mid-1960s, the Medallion covered butter dish was reproduced in amber, clear, and green by the Imperial Glass Corporation of Bellaire, Ohio. Imperial produced this new butter from a new mold in which the design is reversed from side to side. The new design is not as crisp and is less defined and proportionately smaller than the old. Also, the colors are harsh and lack the mellow feeling of the old (Fig. 267). New items are always marked with Imperial's entwined "IG" hallmark.

Hint: Reproduction butter dishes are permanently embossed "IG."
Reproduced items: Butter dish.

Fig. 266. Closeup of the original Medallion pattern. This design is reversed on the reproduction covered butter dish offered by the Imperial Glass Corp.

Fig. 267. Reproduction Medallion butter base. Imperial Glass Corp. Circa 1960s. Embossed "IG."

MELLOR

Also known as Block and Circle, Mellor was designed and patented by Thomas W. Mellor on February 17, 1874 (design patent No.7186). In the same year, the pattern was produced by Gillinder & Sons of Philadelphia in an extended table service from a good-quality clear nonflint glass (Fig. 268).

The design consists of a row of large overlapping circles. Within each circle there is a small stylized square within a larger square. Above and below this row of circles is a band of ellipses. Typical of the period, handles are applied.

As late as 1961, the L.E. Smith Glass Company of Mount Pleasant, Pennsylvania, adapted the Mellor pattern to the seven forms enumerated in Chart 80. Only two of these forms (the goblet and the wine) have original shapes: the remainder are contemporary. Known as Smith's New Bristol pattern, each new form is unsigned and was produced from a new mold in the contemporary colors of amber, antique green, and colonial blue. Both the goblet and the low-footed vase were also offered in milk white. Sold as florist ware, they were most likely intended to hold small floral bouquets.

As you can see from Figs. 268 and 269, reproductions can be quite convincing. How-

Fig. 268. Original clear Mellor goblet. Gillinder & Sons. Circa 1874. Fig. 269. Reproduction milk-white Mellor goblet. L.E. Smith Glass Co. Circa 1961. Unmarked.

ever, because there are no known clear glass reproductions, Mellor is a safe pattern to collect. You need only remember that this pattern was originally made from clear glass and that any colored item is strictly contemporary.

Reproduction items in Mellor are not permanently marked, but you may find some pieces with a paper label.

Hint: Original Mellor items were never made in color.

CHART 80   MELLOR. L.E. Smith Glass Co., Mount Pleasant, Pennsylvania.
CMN: New Bristol.
Mark: Unmarked or paper label.
Color Code: A Amber, AG Antique Green, CB Colonial Blue, MW Milk White.

ITEM	COLOR(S)	YEAR	ORIG	NEW
Goblet, 6½"h., 3"d.	A, AG, CB, MW	1961	X	
Plate.	A, AG, CB	1961		X
Sherbert.	A, AG, CB	1961		X
Tumbler. Ice tea. Juice.	 A, AG, CB A, AG, CB	 1961 1961		 X X
Vase, low-footed, straight-sided. Scalloped rim, 11"h.	A, AG, CB, MW	1961		X
Wine.	A, AG, CB	1961	X	

MICHIGAN

Michigan, a member of the state series, is also known as Loop and Pillar or Paneled Jewel and was originally referred to as No.15077 by the United States Glass Company of Pittsburgh, Pennsylvania. It was introduced about 1902 in an extended table service from a good-quality nonflint glass in clear, clear with maiden's blush and gilt (known as sunrise), clear with yellow, blue, and green paint (plain or enameled), and clear with ruby stain.

In 1967, the Crystal Art Glass Company of Cambridge, Ohio, issued the new $2^{11}/_{16}$-inch-high by $1^3/_4$-inch-diameter toothpick holder (known as Beaded Oval) illustrated in Fig. 270. Under the direction of Elizabeth Degenhart, these toothpick holders were produced from a new mold created by the Island Mold and Machine Company of Wheeling, West Virginia. Early copies are not permanently marked but may carry the telltale signs of a hand-marked signature. From 1972 until the death of Elizabeth Degenhart in 1978, new toothpick holders were permanently signed with an embossed "D" within a heart.

Reproductions of the Crystal Art Glass toothpick holder were produced in a rainbow of contemporary colors. Thy include amber (dark), amber (light), amberina, amethyst (light), amethyst (dark), apple green, aqua, bittersweet, bittersweet slag, bloody Mary, bluebell, Cambridge pink, caramel, carnival cobalt, clear, concord grape, Crown Tuscan, custard, custard slag, emerald green, fawn, fog, forest green, heliotrope, holly green, ivory, lavender blue, maverick, milk blue, milk white, mint green, mulberry, old lavender, opalescent, peach blo, pearl gray, persimmon, pidgeon blood, pink, red, Rose Marie, royal violet, rubina, ruby, sapphire, smokey heather, taffeta, teal, toffee, tomato, and vaseline.

Upon the death of Elizabeth Degenhart, Bernard Boyd of Cambridge, Ohio, acquired the Crystal Art Glass Company and renamed it Boyd's Crystal Art Glass, Inc.

Fig. 270. Michigan reproduction light amber toothpick holder. Crystal Art Glass Co. Circa 1972. Embossed "D" within a heart.

Since that time, the mold to the Michigan toothpick holder was worked as the Beaded Oval pattern in the contemporary colors of butterscotch, candy swirl, chasm blue slag, cathedral blue, frosty blue/orange, Mardi Gras, redwood slag, and rubina. Also at this time, the trademark was changed to an embossed "B" within a diamond (signifying Boyd).

Reproduction toothpick holders are easy to detect. Because the pattern has not been reproduced in any original color treatment, all contemporary colors are new. Reproductions are also noticeably slick or oily, and the glass is often streaked or wavy. You will also notice that the new toothpick holders in clear are often grayed. In general, the pattern is often blurred and in lower relief than the old, and the glass is thick and heavy.

Hint: Michigan reproduction toothpicks are usually signed and come in contemporary colors that were not made originally.

Reproduced items: Toothpick holder.

MONKEY

Monkey is one of the most whimsical designs in early American pattern glass. This pattern consists of a series of seated monkeys, each holding the tail of the one in front with his hands and usually pressing against a palm tree with his feet. The design is crisp, well molded, and beautifully detailed. Finials are also in the shape of full-figured seated monkeys. Because the pattern was originally produced in a limited number of table items in clear (plain, cold-painted, or amber stained) and white opal, original pieces are rare and always in demand.

For years, Monkey has been attributed to George Duncan & Sons of Pittsburgh, Pennsylvania. However, Bredehoft, Fogg, and Maloney, in their book *Early Duncan Glassware* (1987), suggest that the pattern was more likely a product of the short-lived Valley Glass Company of Beaver Falls, Pennsylvania.

To date, only one item has been reproduced in Monkey, the 4¾-inch-high spoonholder illustrated in Fig. 271. Known as item No.PG/1635 by the A.A. Importing Company, Inc., of St. Louis, Missouri, which began importing copies into this country about 1975, new spoonholders are commonly found in clear and vaseline.

On new pieces, the finely chiseled detail is missing, especially the fur on the monkey. The fine detailing on the palm tree's trunk and leaves is also missing. In addition, the face of the monkey is more grotesque on new items, and there is little, if any, detailing of the monkey's toes, fingers, and feet. Perhaps due to poor pressing techniques, the entire design on new pieces is blurred. Overall, the glass is exceptionally heavy and thick on reproductions with a distinct waviness and a minutely pitted surface that is slick, smooth, and oily.

In 1977, A.A. Importing also imported the

Fig. 271. Reproduction Monkey vaseline spoonholder offered by A.A. Importing Co., Inc. Circa 1975. Unmarked.

Monkey on a Stump toothpick holder in amber, blue, clear, and milk white. Unfortunately, numerous contemporary writers have erroneously identified this toothpick holder as part of the original Monkey pattern. A toothpick holder was never originally made in Monkey.

Reproductions are not permanently marked, although each originally carried a small sticker printed "Made in Korea."

Hint: Reproduction spoonholders are larger than originals, look like open sugar bowls, and were never originally made in color.
Reproduced items: Spoonholder.

MOON AND STAR

Few designs have enjoyed as much interest and lasting popularity as Moon and Star. Originally known as Palace, the design was first issued about 1888 by Adams & Company of Pittsburgh, Pennsylvania. At this time, Adams offered an extended table service in a good-quality clear nonflint glass. When Adams became a member of the United States Glass combine in 1891, production of the pattern continued (Fig. 272).

Fig. 272. Reprint of Adams & Company or Factory "A" catalog of the United States Glass Co. illustrating Moon and Star. (Note the applied twisted handles which are not found on reproductions.)

Moon and Star is a fussy pattern. Forms are large and heavy and well suited to the design, which consists of two rows of connected circles. The upper row of circles can be undecorated, frosted, or ruby-stained, and the bottom row of circles (each containing a small star-like ornament) is always clear. Pieces with ruby stain were decorated by the Oriental Glass Company of Pittsburgh (Fig. 273).

To say that Moon and Star has been heavily reproduced is an understatement. For more than fifty years, reproductions have flooded the market, and today myriad forms

Fig. 273. Original clear Moon and Star water pitcher (Note applied handle not found on reproductions.)

exist in both original and contemporary shapes and colors. An example of the adaptation of this antique design to modern forms includes the amethyst carnival miniatures produced exclusively for the Levay Distributing Company of Edwardsville, Illinois, by the L.E. Smith Glass Company of Mount Pleasant, Pennsylvania. Another modern form is the hand-made and signed half-sized miniatures produced as late as 1988 by Weishar Enterprises of Wheeling, West Virginia (see Chart 82). However, as you can see in the following charts, the most prolific producers of the pattern are the L.E. Smith Glass Company and the L.G. Wright Glass Company of New Martinsville, West Virginia (see Chart 83).

Beginning in the late 1930s, the L.G. Wright Glass Company issued clear unmarked copies of the Moon and Star pattern in eggcups, goblets, sauce dishes, and miniature night lamps made from the eggcup mold. Items in color quickly followed and, by 1960, the pattern had been adapted to a multitude of contemporary shapes (Fig. 274).

We believe that Wright reproductions were made from new molds. When you examine these items, you will see immediately that they are exceptionally heavy—a condition caused by the thickness of the glass. You will also notice an unmistakable sheen (especially on clear items), which is not ap-

CHART 81   MOON AND STAR. L.E. Smith Glass Company, Mount Pleasant, Pennsylvania.
CMN: Moon and Star.
Mark: Unmarked or paper label.
Color Code: A Amber, AC Amethyst Carnival, AMB Amberina, B Blue, BO Blue Opalescent, BR Brown, C Clear, CO Cranberry Rose Opalescent, G Green, MGO Mint Green Opalescent, RBY Ruby.

ITEM:	COLOR(S):	YEAR	ORIG	NEW
Ashtray.				
#4240. 4½"d., Round. flat.	A, B, BR, C, G	1968		X
#4280. 8"d.	A, B, BR, C, G	1968		X
#4286. 4"d.	A	1975		X
#4287. 6"d.	A, B, BR, C, G	1982		X
#4288. 8"d.	A, B, BR, C, G	1982		X
Banana dish, folded sides.				
#5202. 9"l.	A, B, BR, C, G	1968		X
	AMB	1975		X
#6212. 12"l, collared base.	A, B, BR, C, G	1975		X
Basket.				
#5207. 9"h., collared base, folded sides, solid handle.	A, B, BR, C, G	1975		X
	AMB	1979		X
#6222. Double-twig handle, scalloped rim, collared base.	A, B, BR, C, G	1968		X
	AMB	1975		X
Bell. #6235. 6"h.	A, AMB, B, C, G	1979		X
	BO, BR, CO, MGO	1982		X
Bowl, round, collared base.				
Covered.				
#5204. 7½"d.	C	1975	X	
#6124. 10"d.	A, AMB, B, C, G	1979	X	
Open.				
#5201. Flared bowl, scalloped rim, 8"d.	A, B, BR, C, G	1968	X	
	BO, CO, MGO	1982	X	
#5204. 7½"d.	A, B, BR, C, G	1968		X
Box. #6223. Covered, oval, 7½"l.	C	1982		X
Butter dish, covered.				
Oval, tab handles.				
#6229. ¼ lb., 8½"l.	A, B, BR, C, G	1975		X
	AMB	1979		X
Round, flat, nonpatterned base, flanged, 7"d.				
#4209.	A, B, BR, C, G	1968		X
#4209A.*	AC	unknown		X
Cake stand.				
#5232. High standard, skirted rim.	A, B, BR, C, CO, G	1968	X	
	AMB	1979	X	
#4202. Low standard, no rim, 11"d.	A, B, BR, G	1982		X
	C	1968		X
Canister, covered.				
#6281. 1-lb.	A, B, C, G, RBY	1968		X
	AMB	1979		X
	BR	1982		X
#6282. 2-lb.	A, B, C, G, RBY	1968		X
	AMB	1979		X
	BR	1982		X
#6283. 3½-lb.	A, B, C, G, RBY	1968		X
	AMB	1979		X
	BR	1982		X
#6285. 5-lb.	A, B, C, G, RBY	1968		X
	AMB	1979		X
	BR	1982		X

ITEM:	COLOR(S):	YEAR	ORIG	NEW
Candlestick.				
Short, 4½"h.				
#4231.	MGO	1982		X
#5231.	B, C	1975		X
	BO, CO	1968		X
Tall.				
#5211. 9¼"h.	A, B, BR, C, G	1982		X
#5221. 6"h.	A, B, BR, C, G	1968		X
	AMB	1979		X
#5281. Footed, plain base.	A, B, BR, C, G	1968		X
Candy box. #6204. Covered.	A, B, BR, C, G	1968		X
Candy jar. #4204. Covered.	A, B, BR, C, G	1968		X
Cheese dish, covered, round.				
Flat.				
#4209. Nonpatterned base.	RBY	1975		X
#4284. Patterned base, clear dome lid, footed, 9½"d.	C	1982		X
Compote.				
High standard.				
Covered.				
#4204. 10"h.	A, B, BR, C, G	1982	X	
#5214. 7"h.	A, B, BR, C, G	1982	X	
#5283. 4½"h., Clear base.	A, B, BR, G	1982		X
	C	1975		X
#5284. 6½"h.	A, AMB, B, G	1979	X	
	BR, C	1982	X	
#5294. 8"h.	A, B, BR, C, G	1968	X	
#6204. 12"h.	C	1975	X	
Open.				
#3601. Crimped rim, 6"h.	A, B, BR, C, G	1968		X
#4201. Crimped rim.	A, B, BR, C, G	1968		X
	AMB	1979		X
#4206. Rolled edge.	A, B, BR, C, G	1968		X
#6201. Crimped edge.	A, B, BR, C, G	1968		X
#6202. Rolled edge.	A, B, BR, C, G	1968		X
#6203. Barrel shaped bowl, scalloped rim.	B, C	1975		X
Low standard.				
Covered.				
#6224. 6"h.	A, B, BR, C, G	1968	X	
	BO, CO, MGO	1982	X	
#6223. 7½"h.	A, B, BR, C, G	1982	X	
Open. #5291. Scalloped rim, flared bowl, 5"h.	AMB, B, C, CO, MGO	1975		X
	BO	1982		X
Cracker jar, covered, flat, 7¾"h.				
#4224.	A, AMB, B, C, G	1979		X
#4224A.*	AC	unknown		X
Creamer, pressed handle, scalloped.				
Individual.				
#4261. 3"h.	A, B, BR, C, G	1968		X
Table size.				
#4259. 6¼"h.	A, B, BR, C, G	1982		X
	AMB	1979		X
#4259A. 6½"h.*	AC	unknown		X
Cruet, flat, pressed handle.	A, AMB, B, C, G	1975		X
Eggcup. #4272. Footed, 3 oz.	C	1975	X	
Epergne. #5285.	A, B, BR, C, G	1968		X

ITEM:	COLOR(S):	YEAR	ORIG	NEW
Goblet.				
#3602. 11 oz.	A, B, BR, C, G	1968	X	
	AMB	1975	X	
#3602A. 11 oz.*	AC	unknown	X	
#4272A. Miniature, 3 oz.*	AC	unknown		X
Lamp.				
Candle.				
#5276. Matching half-shade.	A, AMB, B, C, G	1975		X
	BR	1982		X
#6227. 7½"h. Clear stem base.	A, B, BO, BR, C	1975		X
	CO, G, MGO	1975		X
Courting. #6225. Saucer base with patterned shade.	A, AMB, B, BO, BR	1975		X
	C, G, MGO	1975		X
	CO	1982		X
Electric, metal base with matching half-shade.				
#4232.	A, B, BR, C, G	1968		X
#4239. 16"h.	A	1968		X
Oil. #4231. Flat, bulbous base.	A, B, BR, C, G	1968		X
	AMB	1979		X
Nappy. #5216. Round, pressed handle, 5½"d.	A, AMB, B, C, G	1979		X
Pitcher.				
#4259A. Miniature, 6½"h.*	AC	unknown		X
#6228. 40 oz.	A, B, BR, C, G	1975		X
	AMB	1979		X
#6228A. 40 oz.*	AC	unknown		X
Plate, round, flat.				
#6240. Dinner, 8"d., smooth rim.	A, AMB, B, BR, C, G	1975		X
#6250. Egg, 13"d.	A, B, BR, C, G	1982		X
	AMB	1979		X
Relish. #4281. 3-Part, 8"l., flat.	A, B, BR, C, G	1968		X
	AMB	1975		X
Ring holder. #4200. 4"d.	A, B, BR, C, G	1982		X
Salt.				
Dip. #5210.	A, B, BR, C, G	1968		X
	AMB	1975		X
Shaker.				
#4251. Straight, 4"h.	A, B, BR, C, G	1968		X
	AMB	1979		X
#4254. Bulbous, 5"h.	A, B, BR, C, G	1982	X	
	AMB	1979	X	
Sauce dish, round, collared base. #6220. Scalloped rim, 4½"d.	A, B, BR, C, G	1968	X	
	BO, CO, MGO	1982	X	
Sherbert. #4292. 6 oz.	A, B, BR, C, G	1968		X
	AMB	1979		X
Smoke set. #4219. 4-piece.	A, B, BR, C, G	1968		X
Spoonholder, footed, 6"h.				
#4260.	A, AMB, B, C, G	1979	X	
#4260A.*	AC	unknown	X	
Sugar bowl.				
Individual, open, handled. #4261. 3"h., Scalloped rim.	A, B, BR, C, G	1968		X
Table size, covered, 7"h.				
#5214.	A, AMB, B, C, G	1975	X	
#5214A.*	AC	unknown	X	

ITEM:	COLOR(S):	YEAR	ORIG	NEW
Sugar shaker. #4225. Bulbous, 5"h.	A, B, BR, C, G	1982		X
Syrup pitcher. #4256. 5"h.	A, B, BR, C, G	1982		X
	AMB	1979		X
Tobacco jar. #4214. Flat, covered.	A, AMB, B, C, G	1979		X
Toothpick holder. #4211. 3⅛"h.	A, B, BR, C, G	1968		X
	AMB	1975		X
Tumbler.				
Flat.				
#4222. Water, 11 oz.	A, B, BR, C, G	1968	X	
	AMB	1979	X	
#4242. Old-fashioned				
9-oz.	A, B, BR, C, G	1982		X
11-oz.	A, B, BR, C, G	1982		X
	AMB	1979		X
#4252. Rocks, 9 oz.	A, AMB, B, C, G	1979		X
#6292. Juice, 5 oz.	AMB	1975		X
Footed.				
#6252. 10 oz.	A, AMB, B, C, G	1975		X
#6262. Iced tea, 13 oz.	A, B, BR, C, G	1975		X
	AMB	1979		X
#6272. 7 oz.	B	1975		X
Urn. #5271.	A, B, BR, C, G	1968		X
Vase.				
#6223. 9"h.	A, B, BR, C, G	1982		X
#6231. Bud, 6½"h.	BO, CO, MGO	1982		X
	C	1968		X
	AMB	1979		X
#6233. Pyramid-shaped.	A, AMB, B, C, G	1979		X
#6263. Circular foot, fluted rim, 7"h.	A, AMB, B, C, G	1975		X
Wine.				
#4262. 6 oz., barrel-shaped bowl.	A, B, BR, C, G	1975	X	
	AMB	1979	X	
#4272. 3 oz.	A, B, BR, C, G	1968	X	

*Exclusively produced in amethyst carnival as a limited edition for Levay Distributing Company.

CHART 82 MOON AND STAR. Weishar Enterprises, Wheeling, West Virginia.
CMN: Moon and Star.
Mark: Signed.
Color Code: C Clear, CC Clear Carnival, CO Cobalt, COC Cobalt Carnival, P Pink, PC Pink Carnival.

ITEM	COLOR(S)	YEAR	ORIG	NEW
Banana stand, miniature, footed, folded sides.	C, CC, CO, COC, P, PC	1991		X
Bowl, miniature, footed.				
Cupped.	C, CC, CO, COC, P, PC	1991		X
Flared.	C, CC, CO, COC, P, PC	1991		X
Candleholder, miniature, footed.				
Plate.	C, CC, CO, COC, P, PC	1991		X
Nappy, cupped.	C, CC, CO, COC, P, PC	1991		X
Pitcher, miniature, pressed handle.	C, CC, CO, COC, P, PC	1991		X
Plate, miniature, footed.	C, CC, CO, COC, P, PC	1991		X
Tumbler, miniature, water.	C, CC, CO, COC, P, PC	1991		X

All of these pieces were originally introduced in 1988. Colors: Unknown

CHART 83   MOON AND STAR. L. G. Wright Glass Company, New Martinsville, West Virginia.

CMN: Moon and Star.

Mark: Unmarked.

Color Code: A Amber, AM Amethyst, AMB Amberina, B Blue, BS Blue Satin, C Clear, G Green, GS Green Satin, MW Milk White, P Pink, PS Pink Satin, RBY Ruby, RS Ruby Satin, V Vaseline, VO Vaseline Opalescent, VS Vaseline Satin.

ITEM	COLOR(S)	YEAR	ORIG	NEW
Ashtray.				
#44-1. 8½"d.	A, AM, AMB, B, G, P, RBY	1968		X
	C	1977		X
#44-53. 5"d.	A, AMB, B, G, P, RBY	1968		X
	C	1977		X
Bowl, open.				
#44-43. Circular foot, 6"d., crimped rim, 2¾"h.	A, B, G, RBY	1969		X
#44-46. Console, low-footed, 8"d.	A, AMB, B	1968		X
Butter dish. #44-2. Covered, round, 5¾"d., 6"h.	A, B, C, P	1968	X	
	PS, VS	1971	X	
	RBY, V	1969	X	
Cake stand. #44-32. Low standard, 12"d.	A, AM, B, C, G, P, RBY	1968		X
	AMB	1969		X
Candlestick. #44-6. 6"h.	A, AMB, B	1968		X
Champagne. #44-38. Flared bowl.	A, AM, B, C, G, RBY	1974		X
Compote, high standard.				
Covered.				
#44-8. 4"d.	A, AM, B, C, G, P, RBY	1968	X	
	BS, GS, RS, VS	1971	X	
	V	1969	X	
#44-9. 6"d.	A, AM, B, C, G, P, RBY	1968	X	
	V	1969	X	
	VS	1971	X	
#44-10. 6"d.	A, AM, B, C, G, RBY	1968	X	
#44-11. 8"d.	A, B, C, G, P, RBY	1968	X	
#44-24. 3½"d., 6¾"h.	A, AM, B, C, G, RBY	1968	X	
#44-40. 4½"d.	A, B, G, P, RBY	1974	X	
#44-50. 4½"d., Knob stem.	A, B, G, P, RBY	1968		X
Open.				
#44-12. Ruffled rim, 8½"d.	A, AM, B, C, G, RBY	1968		X
#44-14. Flared rim, 8"d.	A, B, G, RBY	1968	X	
#44-15. Shallow bowl, scalloped rim, 10"d., 7"h.	A, AM, B, C, G, P, RBY	1968		X
	AMB	1969		X
Creamer. #44-16. Pressed handle.	A, B, C, P, RBY	1968		X
	V	1969		X
	PS, VS	1971		X
Decanter. #44-18. Bulbous, clear stopper.	A, AM, B, C, G, RBY	1968		X
Goblet. #44-22. 9 oz.	A, AM, B, C, G, P, RBY, V	1968	X	
	BS, PS	1971	X	
	VO	1969	X	
Lamp.				
#44. Miniature, footed, 10"h. with matching half-shade.	A, AM, B, MW, RBY	1968		X
#90. Table, 10"d. shade, 24"h.	A, B, G, RBY	1969		X
Nappy.				
#44-27. Triangular, handled, 8"l., 2"h.	A, B, C, G, P	1968		X
#44-43. Crimped rim, 6"d.	A, B, G, RBY	1968		X
Pitcher. #44-56, Water, 32 oz., pressed handle, 7½"h.	A, B, C, G, RBY	1968		X
	P	1969		X

ITEM	COLOR(S)	YEAR	ORIG	NEW
Relish.				
#44-29. Rectangular, 8"l.	A, AM, B, C, G	1968		X
#44-40. Oval, boat-shaped.	A, AM, B, G	1968	X	
	C	1974	X	
Rose bowl. #44-44.	A, G	1984		X
Salt.				
#44-30. Dip, round, flat.	A, AM, B, C, G, P, RBY	1968		X
	V	1969		X
	VS	1971		X
#44-31. Shaker.	A, AM, B, C, G, RBY	1968	X	
	V, VS	1971	X	
Sherbert. #44-36. Footed, flared, 3¾"d., 4¼"h.	A, AM, B, C, G, RBY	1968		X
Soap dish. #44-55. Flat, oval.	A, B, G	1968		X
	RBY	1969		X
Spoonholder. #44-37.	A, B, C, P, RBY	1968	X	
	V	1969	X	
	VS	1971	X	
Sugar bowl, covered.				
#44-38. Table-sized.	A, B, C, RBY	1968	X	
	P, V	1969	X	
	RS, VS	1971	X	
#44-52. Low-footed.	A, B, G, P, RBY	1968		X
	C, V	1974		X
	PS	1971		X
Sugar shaker. #44-54. Bulbous, 4½"h., 3½"d.	A, B, C, G, RBY	1968		X
Toothpick holder. #44-39. Flat.	A, AM, B, C, G, P, RBY	1968		X
	V	1969		X
Tumbler, footed.				
#44-23. Iced tea, 11 oz.	A, B, G, RBY	1968		X
	C, V	1974		X
#44-25. Juice, 5 oz.	A, B, G, RBY	1968		X
#44-41. Water, 7 oz.	A, B, G, RBY	1968	X	
	C	1969	X	
Wine. #44-42. 2 oz.	A, AM, B, C, G, P, RBY, V	1968	X	
	VO	1969	X	

parent on originals. Of course, any new shape or color would indicate contemporary manufacture.

Although the Fenton Art Glass Company of Williamstown, West Virginia, produced a large quantity of glass for Wright, it is difficult to determine the actual forms and colors because Wright did not permanently mark its reproductions.

During the 1940s, the L.E. Smith Glass Company of Mount Pleasant, Pennsylvania (see Chart 81), also engaged in the manufacture of early American pressed-glass reproductions. While early production most likely included the Moon and Star design, the pattern appears frequently in Smith's catalogs of the 1960s in clear and a rainbow of contemporary colors. Like other reproductions in the pattern, Smith copies are unmarked and were made from new molds, including those created by the Island Mold and Machine Company of Wheeling, West Virginia (Figs. 275 and 276).

Similar to Wright copies, Smith reproductions are heavy, thick, and distinctly glossy, especially those in clear glass. Although they are unmarked, each copy originally carried a small paper label.

While Smith and Wright reproductions emulate a number of known antique forms,

Fig. 274. New No.44-11 Moon and Star clear high-standard covered compote. L.G. Wright Glass Co. Circa 1971. Unmarked.

Fig. 276. Reproduction Moon and Star No.6229 covered oval butter dish. L.E. Smith Glass Co. Circa 1975. (The flat finial is typical of Smith Moon and Star reproductions.) Unmarked.

a unique treatment of the pattern can be found in those items produced by the Kanawha Glass Company of Kanawha, West Virginia. As late as 1974, Kanawha issued

the No.898 5-inch candleholder in end-of-day, the No.806 8-inch-high standard covered compote in clear, end-of-day, and milk white, the No.898 5-inch-high true open compote with ruffled rim in end-of-day, and the No.809 10-inch swung vase in end-of-day. By 1978, the No.806 compote was also being offered in azure blue, and in 1980 the No.809 vase was available in green.

The covered compote in Fig. 277 illustrates Kanawha's characteristic use of the spiral finial and stem. Obviously, Kanawha reproductions are the products of new molds.

Because of the astonishing number of reproductions in Moon and Star, it is prudent for dealers and collectors to consider the color, detail, shape, and weight of suspect items. Because this pattern was originally produced in clear and decorated clear glass, any item in color is strictly contemporary. Unlike the clear, bright glass of original items, clear reproductions have a distinctly yellowish or greenish cast. As a general rule of thumb, reproductions are heavy, thick, and glossy and often feel oily.

Although color plays an integral part in detecting reproductions, also consider detail and shape (Fig. 278). Unlike old items, which are crisply pressed, reproductions are often blurred, poorly pressed, and display a distinct waviness in the glass. A more interesting discrepancy is found in the shape of many reproductions. For example, handles of original Moon and Star pieces were always applied and twisted or plain.

Fig. 275. New Moon and Star No.6228 pitcher with pressed handle. L.E. Smith Glass Co. Circa 1975. (Original pitchers were never made in this shape.) Unmarked.

Fig. 277. New Moon and Star No.806 amber covered compote. Kanawha Glass Co. Circa 1965. (The spiral finial and stem are typical of Kanawha reproductions.) Unmarked.

6241
6 ¾″ Cruet

Fig. 279. Reproduction Moon and Star No.6241 cruet. L.E. Smith Glass Co. Circa 1975. (Unlike the applied handles on originals, handles on reproductions are pressed.) Unmarked.

Fig. 278. New No.5232 Moon and Star high-standard skirted cake stand. L.E. Smith Glass Co. Circa 1950s. Unmarked.

On reproductions, handles are always pressed and thus are shaped differently (Fig. 279).

Because Moon and Star has been reproduced from new molds, copies are noticeably heavy. When you encounter a new item, you will immediately notice how heavy it is in relation to its size.

Hint: Moon and Star was never made in solid colors other than clear.

MORNING GLORY

Morning Glory is one of the most difficult patterns to assemble in a complete table setting. Because of the limited length of production and the number of forms produced, original pieces are rare and expensive.

This pattern was first issued by the Boston and Sandwich Glass Company of Sandwich, Massachusetts, in the 1860s from a low-grade clear flint glass. Moreover, items

Fig. 280. Reproduction clear Morning Glory nonflint goblet. Circa mid-1950s. Unmarked.

resound with a minimal resonance and forms are dull and crudely fashioned.

The design consists of an abundance of highly embossed morning-glory flowers, leaves, and stems that are finely detailed and stippled against a clear background. The bases of footed pieces are decorated by four leaves, each of which extends from a long, thin vine that runs down the stem from the base of the bowl.

To date, two items have been reproduced in Morning Glory, the 6⅓-inch-high goblet (Fig. 280) and the wine. Both are unmarked and first appeared prior to 1958 in clear and color. We believe that both of these reproductions were produced by the L.G. Wright Glass Company of New Martinsville, West Virginia, because identical new goblets and wines appear in Wright's 1969 catalog.

Reproductions are quite convincing. The pattern on new items is placed lower on the bowl than on originals and is in lower relief than the pattern on originals. Unlike the fine-pointed leaves on original items, the leaves on reproductions are round and blunt. The vine's stem that runs down the standards of reproductions is much thicker than the one on the old. The stippling on original pieces is finer and more pronounced than on copies, and reproductions are too brilliant and too well made, while original items are crude.

Reproduction items are not permanently marked.

Hint: Reproduction items are made from a better-quality glass than originals.
Reproduced items: Goblet, wine.

NEW ENGLAND PINEAPPLE

New England Pineapple, also known as Loop and Jewel or Pineapple, was originally produced in an extended table service from a good-quality clear flint glass. It is a brilliant, heavy pattern that resounds with a fine bell-tone when gently tapped. It was originally made about 1860 by the Boston and Sandwich Glass Company of Sandwich, Massachusetts.

As Ruth Webb Lee noted, this design consists of "an ornament shaped not unlike a pineapple, with a small sawtooth center alternating with a long three-petaled flower similar to a tulip." The glass is clear and brilliant and handles are beautifully applied and crimped. Any colored item in flint glass would be rare.

Clear goblets and wines appeared as early as 1937. Each was produced from a new mold in clear nonflint glass without a manufacturer's mark.

Prior to 1950, the Fenton Art Glass Company of Williamstown, West Virginia, produced the goblet (Fig. 281), the sherbert, and the wine. Known as Fenton's Pineapple, these reproductions were produced from a good-quality clear nonflint glass. By 1962, Fenton was offering the goblet and the No.9129 high-standard open compote with ruffled rim in the colonial colors of amber, blue, and pink (Fig. 282). This goblet was ad-

Fig. 281. New England Pineapple clear reproduction non-flint goblet. Fenton Art Glass Co. Circa 1950. Unmarked.

Fig. 282. Reproduction New England Pineapple clear non-flint goblet and high-standard open compote (made from the same mold). Fenton Art Glass Co. Circa 1962. Unmarked.

vertised by Fenton in the July 1962 issue of *China, Glass and Tablewares*. Both the sherbert and the wine were discontinued in 1950, and by 1984 the goblet and compote were discontinued in all colors. The compote and sherbert are strictly contemporary in form.

In 1953, Glasscrafts and Ceramics, Inc. (formerly Czecho-Slovak Glass Products Co.), of Yonkers, New York, offered a No.5151 6-inch-high New England Pineapple goblet in clear nonflint glass.

In 1989, a new, lightweight goblet appeared in white opalescent glass that displays a good flint tonal quality. Underneath its base is a concentric-ring design.

Although New England Pineapple reproductions are not permanently marked, new items may be found with an original paper label. Reproductions are light and the fine belltone quality of this early flint pattern is missing. The pattern is also blunt or smooth compared to the sharp, deep impression of originals. Additionally, any contemporary color is new.

An interesting note to collectors is that new unmarked goblets can also be found in a high-quality Meissen-like porcelain with gold decoration.

Hint: New England Pineapple reproductions do not have the fine belltone of originals.

Reproduced items: Compote, goblet, sherbert, wine.

ONE-O-ONE

Also known as Beaded 101, One-Hundred-and-One, and 1-0-1, this lovely pattern dates from the 1870s. You can assemble an extended service in a good-quality clear nonflint glass. Although the original manufacturer of the pattern is not known, the goblet was made by the Bellaire Goblet Company of Findlay, Ohio. It is highly unlikely, however, that Bellaire produced One-O-One in a complete table service.

The design consists of a row of large clear, alternating ornaments reminiscent of the numbers "1" and "0." Each number is pressed in high relief and outlined with

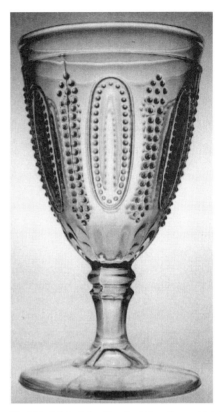

Fig. 283. Reproduction One-Hundred-One clear goblet. Unmarked. (Notice the double band above the design, which is not present on originals.)

Fig. 284. Original One-Hundred-One clear goblet. Bellaire Goblet Co. Circa 1870s.

small clear dewdrops. The glass is clear and brilliant. Handles may be applied or pressed.

Only one item has been reproduced in One-O-One: the new goblet illustrated in Fig. 283. New, unmarked goblets appeared in the mid-1970s in amber, blue, and clear nonflint glass, although other colors may have been used. As you can see from the illustration, reproduction goblets can be quite convincing. However, upon close examination, you will readily notice a number of interesting discrepancies. Both the numbers and the beading on reproductions are larger than those on the originals. And the lower-most bead of

the new goblet extends further down the bowl. Additionally, while the stem of the reproduction goblet is thick, the knob where the bowl and stem are attached is small. The most obvious difference, however, is that the double clear band that appears above the One-O-One design on reproductions is missing on originals (Fig. 284).

Reproduction One-O-One goblets are not permanently marked as to manufacturer.

Hint: Reproduction One-O-One goblets have a bead that is set lower on the "ones" than on original goblets.
Reproduced items: Goblet.

OPEN ROSE

The original name of this attractive floral design produced during the 1870s remains unknown. The original manufacturer is also unknown, but this pattern has for many

years been attributed to the Boston and Sandwich Glass Company of Sandwich, Massachusetts. An extended table service available in two varieties (normal and heavy impression) was originally issued from a good-quality clear nonflint glass.

Fig. 285. Reproduction Open Rose No.123 goblets. Mosser Glass, Inc. Circa early 1960s. Unmarked. (These are often mistaken for footed tumblers.)

Fig. 286. New Open Rose spoonholder. Mosser Glass, Inc. Circa early 1960s. Unmarked.

The design consists of a large floral cluster composed of a single clear rose amid clear leaves. Both of these elements are highly embossed on a plain background. Each rose is tightly sculpted and the foliage is natural and well detailed. In addition, handles are beautifully applied and crimped; finials are stylized acorns.

Open Rose is one of the many patterns you can safely collect. To date, only two items have been reproduced in this pattern. Throughout the early 1960s, Mosser Glass, Inc., of Cambridge, Ohio, issued new No.123 goblets and No.146 spoonholders (Figs. 285 and 286) from new molds in amber, amethyst, clear, cobalt blue, and deep green.

Unlike originals, these reproductions are exceptionally heavy. Although heavily embossed, the design is a mild representation of the original and lacks all of the fine detail. On old goblets and spoonholders, the roses and foliage are crisp and lifelike; on new items, they are poorly executed and often blurred. On reproductions, the leaves are smaller and raised higher above the surface than on the originals. In addition, reproductions feel slick and oily, and those in clear have a slightly bluish tint.

New goblets (which look more like a footed tumbler) were made from the same mold as the spoonholder. Both the spoonholder and the goblet are exceptionally thick. You will notice this attribute when you hold either piece up to a bright light and see the large mass of smooth glass at the bottom of the bowl.

Reproductions are not permanently marked.

Hint: Reproduction items are thicker and heavier than originals.

Reproduced items: Goblet, spoonholder.

OREGON

Also known as Beaded Loop(s) or Beaded Ovals, the original name of this state pattern is No.15073 or Oregon. The United States Glass Company of Pittsburgh, Pennsylvania, produced it in an extended table service from a good-quality clear nonflint glass about 1910 (Figs. 287 and 288). Al-

though you may find pieces in clear with ruby stain, any colored item is rare.

The design consists of a row of large clear vertical ovals. Each oval is separated by a panel of finecut arched at the top. The entire design is outlined by a string of clear, fine beading. Interestingly, Oregon has the distinction of possessing three differently shaped covered butter

Fig. 287. Reprint of a United States Glass Co. catalog illustrating an assortment of No.15073 or Oregon.

Fig. 288. Reprint of a United States Glass Co. catalog illustrating an assortment of No.15073 or Oregon.

975/Dec

Fig. 289. Reproduction Oregon No.975 clear with cranberry stain covered sugar bowl. Imperial Glass Corp. Circa 1962. Embossed "IG."

dishes: the English, the flanged-rim, and the plain.

In 1960, the Imperial Glass Corporation of Bellaire, Ohio, issued the milk-white Oregon covered sugar bowl. In 1962, the same mold was worked in blue, clear with cranberry stain (Fig. 289), frosted crystal (known as doeskin), and ruby glass. In 1964, the carnival colors of peacock and rubigold were added to the line, and by 1980 sugar bowls appeared in glossy and satin pink.

Apparently produced from a new mold, Imperial's Oregon covered sugar bowl is quite convincing. However, upon close examination, you will notice a number of discrepancies. Unlike the original, which is barrel-shaped and somewhat squat, the new sugar is distinctly straight-sided—a flaw noted in both the bowl and the lid. In general, this reproduction simply looks new, and any color other than clear is contemporary. This new sugar is glossy or brilliant, the pattern is blunt or flat, and the glass feels smooth or slick. The reproduction is also noticeably thick and heavy, unlike the original, which is thin-walled and lightweight.

Imperial reproductions are permanently embossed with the company's familiar "IG" hallmark.

Hint: Reproduction sugar bowls are permanently marked with Imperial's "IG" logo.

Reproduced items: Sugar bowl.

OSTRICH LOOKING AT THE MOON

As you can see from Fig. 290, Ostrich Looking at the Moon is one of the more novel designs produced during the Victorian Era. Unfortunately, this pattern does not appear illustrated in any known catalog, and its maker remains a mystery. From its general characteristics, the design appears to date from the 1870s.

Ostrich Looking at the Moon is aptly named. Proudly standing against a clear background is an ostrich or stork, as the bird in the design is sometimes called. This bird is whimsically posed looking upward at the moon through a lorgnette, which hangs from its neck by a ribbon. On the ground is a garden of flowers and foliage.

Fig. 290. Line drawing of the Ostrich Looking at the Moon design. (This pattern is always poorly pressed on original goblets.)

Fig. 291. Reproduction No.77-114 Ostrich Looking at the Moon clear goblet. L.G. Wright Glass Co. Circa 1974. Unmarked.

The goblet is illustrated in the L. G. Wright Glass Company 1974 catalog as item No.77-114 or Stork goblet (Fig. 291). For many years, this goblet has caused much confusion and caution among collectors and dealers. However, a few simple observations will quickly settle the matter between old and new goblets. Unlike most original designs, which are strong and crisp, original goblets are poorly impressed. More often than not, the design is faint and in low relief. In contrast, the impression of the new goblet is too perfect. On original goblets, the underbase of the foot is concave; on new goblets, the center of the base is raised with an impressed "O" barely visible. Moreover, the moons on new goblets are smaller and with noticeable stippling. Original goblets have larger moons with the stippling in the moon barely noticeable.

Produced from a good-quality clear nonflint glass, Wright reproductions are not permanently marked.

Hint: Reproduction goblets have smaller moons and the overall impression is stronger than on originals.

Reproduced items: Goblet.

OWL AND POSSUM

A highly desirable pattern of the figural series is Owl and Possum, illustrated in Fig. 292. Like its contemporary, Ostrich Looking at the Moon, Owl and Possum exemplifies the whimsical nature of the Victorian Era. Tree branches rise from a tree-trunk stem over the clear nonflint bowl of the goblet. An owl perches on one branch, while, on the opposite side of the bowl, a possum rests on the other. The design is detailed and molded in high relief. Although the original manufacturer and date of production are not known, this pattern appears to be a product of the 1880s.

Prior to 1958, new clear Owl and Possum goblets flooded the market. Because they are unmarked, it is not known when or by whom they were produced. Reproduction goblets can be quite deceiving. Apparently, these copies have been produced from new

Fig. 292. Original clear Owl and Possum goblet. (Unlike original goblets, which have a bent stem, the stem on reproductions is straight.)

molds; they are heavier than originals and the pattern lacks detail. This lack of detail is especially true of the owl and the possum, which are poorly pressed. Perhaps the easiest way to detect a reproduction is by observing both animals. The owl appears cross-eyed because the eyes are placed too close together. The possum's legs are placed too high above the branch so that it appears to be falling off the branch.

Hint: The animals on the reproduction goblets are poorly done.
Reproduced items: Goblet.

PALM BEACH

Palm Beach is a pattern that is better known in opalescent than in clear glass. This design was originally known as line No.15119 or Palm Beach and was first produced about 1909 by the United States Glass Company of Pittsburgh, Pennsylvania, at its Glassport, Indiana, factory (Fig. 293). Although Palm Beach was issued in an extended table service, all pieces were not available in all colors. Original colors are clear, clear decorated, and opalescent blue and canary. Items are also known in carnival colors.

This pattern is rather fussy. The basic design consists of unevenly shaped triangular

Fig. 294. Excerpt from a circa 1910 United States Glass Co. catalog illustrating an original Palm Beach celery vase.

Fig. 293. Excerpt from a circa 1910 United States Glass Co. catalog illustrating the original Palm Beach covered sugar bowl and spoonholder.

Fig. 295. Excerpt from a circa 1910 United States Glass Co. catalog illustrating the handle on an original Palm Beach water pitcher.

CHART 84 PALM BEACH. Duncan Glass (a division of the U.S. Glass Co.), Tiffin, Ohio.
CMN: No.719 or Duncan's Grape.
Mark: Unmarked or paper label.
Color Code: MW Milk White.

ITEM	COLOR(S)	YEAR	ORIG	NEW
Bowl, low circular foot, round.				
#719-1. Master berry, 7½"d.	MW	1955	X	
#719-2. 6½"d.	MW	1955	X	
#719-10. Ivy.	MW	1955	X	
Butter dish. #719-12. Covered, flat, round, flanged base, ½ lb.	MW	1955	X	
Creamer. #719-8. Bulbous, pressed handle, low circular foot, 7 oz.	MW	1955	X	
Dish, olive. #719-5. Flat, round, single handle, 4½"d.	MW	1955	X	
Pickle dish. #719-13. Flat, 7½"d.	MW	1955	X	
Pitcher, water. #719-6. Low circular foot, pressed handle, 52 oz.	MW	1955	X	
Sauce dish, round.				
#719-3. Low circular foot, 5½"d.	MW	1955	X	
#719-4. 4½"d.	MW	1955	X	
Sugar bowl. #719-9. Covered, 7 oz., double-handled.	MW	1955	X	
Tumbler. #719-7. Water, flat.	MW	1955	X	
Vase. #719-11. Low circular foot, 6"h.	MW	1955	X	

Fig. 296. Reproduction Palm Beach No.719-8 milk-white water pitcher. Duncan Glass. Circa 1955. Unmarked.

panels created by three large clear grape-vines. The top of each panel is arched, while the bottom comes to an irregular point produced by the intersection of adjoin-ing arches. Within each panel is a large clear cluster of grapes and leaves, and between each panel is a larger grape leaf (Fig. 294). Handles resemble grape branches, and finials are in the shape of a large cluster of grapes (Fig. 295).

Today, at least 13 pieces in Palm Beach enumerated in Chart 84 have been reproduced by Duncan Glass (a division of the United States Glass Company of Tiffin, Ohio). Known as Duncan's No.719 or Grape line, each item emulates known antique forms (Fig. 296).

Each reproduction is unmarked and was produced in milk-white glass, most likely from an original mold. Unlike original items, new pieces are noticeably thick and heavy and the design is blunt and smooth. Simply remembering that Palm Beach was never originally made in milk white will prevent you from purchasing new items for old.

Hint: Palm Beach was never originally made in milk white.

PANELED DAISY

As the 1890s began, pressed-glass production in America continued to decline. Faced with growing labor problems and a depression in 1893 that would close many glassware factories, numerous manufacturers opted to join glass combines to remain afloat. At this time, the United States Glass combine reissued many of the old patterns of member concerns.

One such pattern is Paneled Daisy. Christened Brazil by its creator, Bryce Brothers of Pittsburgh, Pennsylvania, this interesting floral design consists of long vertical flowers and leaves that alternate with thinner clear vertical panels (Fig. 297).

After Bryce joined the United States Glass combine in 1891, it continued making Paneled Daisy in a good-quality clear non-flint glass in more than 35 different forms (Fig. 298).

The first reproduction in Paneled Daisy, the clear goblet, appeared in the early 1960s and was quickly followed by the clear water tumbler. At the same time, a number of items in milk white entered the market. Although these reproductions are unmarked, we believe they were most likely produced from new molds by the John E. Kemple Glass Works of Kenova, West Virginia.

By 1969, the L. G. Wright Glass Company of New Martinsville, West Virginia, had is-

Fig. 298. Original Paneled Daisy goblet.

Fig. 297. Reprint of a circa 1891 United States Glass Co. catalog illustrating an assortment of Paneled Daisy (Brazil).

sued the No.77-31, or Paneled Daisy, 7-ounce, 6-inch-high goblet in clear and in the contemporary colors of amber, blue, pink, and ruby. By 1984, Wright also was offering the No.77-4 relish scoop in amber, amethyst, blue, and green.

The Wright reproductions were made from new molds and are noticeably heavy, thick, and oily or slick. (New goblets and tumblers, in particular, display an excessive thickness at the base.) While clear items have a distinctively grayish or yellowish cast, those in any color are not as detailed as original items. In addition, the leaves are rounded and less stippled and have an exaggerated central branch or vine.

Following Wright in 1970, the Fenton Art Glass Company of Williamstown, West Virginia, issued the No.9185 high-standard covered compote from a new mold in carnival colors. From 1973 through 1989, Fenton worked this mold in blue opalescent, blue satin, Burmese, clear, country peach, custard, dusty rose, forget-me-not blue, French opalescent, lime sherbert, orange carnival, periwinkle blue, shell pink, and teal marigold. In 1973, Fenton also issued the Paneled Daisy No.8294 toothpick holder or votive in carnival glass. This toothpick was available in blue opalescent in 1977, cameo opalescent in 1979, and ebony in 1983.

Only the No.9185 large covered compote by Fenton illustrated in Fig. 299 emulates an original form. (The footed toothpick holder was never made originally.) New covered compotes are heavier than originals and the glass is thicker. This difference is most noticeable when you hold the base up to a strong light. You will immediately notice an excessive amount of glass at the base of the bowl, which is not apparent on the old. Unlike Wright reproductions, those by Fenton have a strong pattern design.

Both Fenton reproductions are permanently signed with its familiar logo.

Fig. 299. New Paneled Daisy clear high-standard covered compote. Fenton Art Glass Co. Circa 1973. Embossed Fenton logo.

Hint: Paneled Daisy originally was made only in clear glass.

Reproduced items: Compote, goblet, relish dish, toothpick, tumbler.

PANELED DIAMOND POINT

The original maker of this interesting pattern was the Richards & Hartley Glass Company of Tarentum, Pennsylvania. Originally produced in a limited number of table pieces from an excellent-quality clear non-flint glass, the design was first made about 1885 and consists of alternating vertical panels of diamond points and clear thin bars. Original colors are solid amber, blue, canary yellow, and clear.

As late as 1974, the Fostoria Glass Company of Moundsville, West Virginia, was re-

CHART 85   PANELED DIAMOND POINT. Fostoria Glass Co., Moundsville, West Virginia.
CMN: Line No.2860.
Mark: Unmarked or paper label.
Color Code: C Clear, PS Purple Marble Slag.

ITEM	COLOR(S)	YEAR	ORIG	NEW
Goblet. #2860/2. 6½"h, 10½ oz.	C, PS	1974	X	
Plate. #2869/550. Round, 8"d.	C	1974		X
Sherbert. #2860/7. 4⅝"h., 7 oz.	C	1974		X
Tumbler. #2860/63. Low-footed. Iced tea, straight-sided. 6⁵⁄₁₆"h., 13 oz.	C	1974		X
Wine. #2860/26. 5½"h., 6½ oz.	C	1974	X	

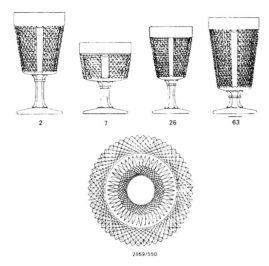

Fig. 300. Fostoria Glass Corp. catalog reprint illustrating a selection of Paneled Diamond Point in clear flint.

producing the five items enumerated in Chart 85 (Fig. 300). Known as Fostoria's No.2860, each item is unmarked and was produced from a new mold in clear flint glass. Only the goblet (Fig. 301) and wine are original in shape, while the remainder are contemporary.

Unlike original items, Fostoria reproductions are thick-walled and resound with a belltone resonance when gently tapped. Because of the lead content, they are also heavier and display a brilliance lacking in the old. Perhaps the most noticeable difference between original items and reproductions is the clear bar on reproductions,

Fig. 301. Reproduction Paneled Diamond Point purple slag goblet. Fostoria Glass Corp. Circa 1974. Unmarked.

which is notably thin. Although new items are unmarked, you may occasionally find items that bear the original Fostoria paper label.

Hint: Original Paneled Diamond Point items were not produced in flint.

PANELED THISTLE

Paneled Thistle is one of the late imitation cut glass designs that became popular in the early 1900s (Fig. 302). This pattern was originally called Delta and was first issued by the John B. Higbee Glass Company of Bridgeville, Pennsylvania, about 1908. The Higbee trademark, a small bumblebee with the letters "HIG" across its wings and body, was often pressed into the bottom of each item. Paneled Thistle was also produced by the Jefferson Glass Company of Toronto,

Ontario, Canada, from 1910 through 1920. Aside from the missing trademark, the Canadian version differs only in the addition of an extra thistle bud on the lower portion of the design.

Paneled Thistle was originally produced from a medium-quality clear nonflint glass in a large and extended table service. The design consists of vertical panels of stylized thistle buds and stems alternating with panels of conventional cut glass designs. In turn, each panel is separated by clear vertical prisms (Fig. 303).

CHART 86   PANELED THISTLE. L. G. Wright Glass Company, New Martinsville, West Virginia.
CMN: Thistle.
Mark: Unmarked or embossed elongated bee.
Color Code: A Amber, AM Amethyst, AMB Amberina, B Blue, C Clear, CS Clear Satin, G Green, IP Ice Pink, RUB Rubina, RBY Ruby.

ITEM	COLOR(S)	YEAR	ORIG	NEW
Basket, applied handle.				
#64-27. Flared sides, small.	C	1975		X
#64-34. Flared sides, large.	C	1977		X
Bowl.				
Covered.				
#64-25. Double-handled.	C	1974	X	
Open.				
Flat.				
Deep.				
#64-2. 7½"d.	C	1969	X	
Shallow.				
#64-1. 5½"d., flared.	C	1969	X	
#64-5. 7"d.	C	1974	X	
Footed.				
#64-36. Oval, 4-toed, 5"l.	C	1977	X	
Butter dish. #64-11. Covered, flat, flanged base.	C	1969	X	
	IP	1980	X	
Cake stand. #64-29. High standard, 10"d.	C	1976	X	
Candleholder. #64-35. Round. handled.	C	1977		X
Celery vase. #64-16. Double-handled.	C	1978	X	
Compote, round, high standard.				
Covered.				
#64-18. 6"d.	C	1969	X	
#64-42. 4"d.	C	1975	X	
Open, scalloped rim.				
#64-17. 6"d., Deep, flared.	C	1969	X	
Creamer, pressed handle.				
#64-8. Berry, low circular foot.	C	1969		X
#64-22. Table-size, 4-footed.	C	1974	X	
	IP	1980	X	
Cruet. #64-20. Bulbous, flat, pressed handle.	C	1969	X	
Cup. #64-43. Punch.	C	1975	X	
Dish. #64-28. Nut, flat, rectangular.	C	1975		X
Goblet. #64-3. 5⅜"h.	C	1969	X	
	CS	1970	X	
Honey dish. #64-10. Square, covered, 4-footed.	C	1969	X	
Lamp, fairy. #64-33.	C	1976		X
Nappy. #64-26. Flat, round, handled.	C	1974		X
Pitcher. #64-19. Water, pressed handle.	C	1969	X	
	IP	1980	X	
Plate.				
Round.				
#64-30. 7"d., Rolled sides.	C	1976	X	
#64-37. 10"d.	C	1978	X	
	IP	1984	X	
#64-39. 7½"d.	C	1979	X	
#64-40. 10"d.	C	1979	X	
Square. #64-4. 7½".	C	1969	X	

ITEM	COLOR(S)	YEAR	ORIG	NEW
Relish. #64-5. Flat, oval, 8"l.	C	1969	X	
Salt dip.				
#64-6. Individual, round.	A, AM, B, C, G	1969		X
	IP, RUB, RBY	1969		X
#77-53. Individual, 3-footed.	A, AM, AMB, B, C, G, P	1968		X
	RUB	1969		X
Salt shaker. #64-14. Bulbous, flat base.	C	1969	X	
Sauce dish, round, flat.				
#64-21. No handle.	C	1969	X	
#64-26. Handled.	C	1978	X	
Sherbert. #64-32. Round, footed.	C	1976	X	
Spoonholder. #64-23. Double-handled.	C	1974	X	
	IP	1980	X	
Sugar bowl.				
Covered.				
#64-9. Berry.	C	1969		X
#64-41. Table-size, handled.	C	1975	X	
Open. #64-23. 3-Handled.	C	1969	X	
	IP	1980	X	
Sugar shaker. #64-15. Flat, bulbous.	C	1969		X
Toothpick holder. #64-17.	C	1969		X
Tumbler. #64-24. Water.	C	1974	X	
	IP	1980	X	
Wine. #64-7.	C	1969	X	

Goblets were the first reproductions in Paneled Thistle. Reproduction goblets (Fig. 304) have flared rims; they are not straight-sided. Unmarked, new goblets appeared as early as 1940 and were quickly followed by the 7½-inch-square (Fig. 305) and the 10-inch-round plates and the footed individual salt dip. All four items were made from new molds in a mediocre-quality clear nonflint glass. Unlike originals, early reproductions are glossy and have a sparkle and brilliance that are not apparent in the old.

Today, more than 30 forms have been reproduced in Paneled Thistle. As you can

Fig. 302. Butler Brothers 1914 catalog reprint illustrating an assortment of Paneled Thistle as Thistle and Sunburst.

Fig. 303. Butler Brothers 1914 catalog reprint illustrating an assortment of Paneled Thistle as Thistle and Sunburst.

Fig. 304. New Paneled Thistle No.64-3 clear goblet. L.G. Wright Glass Co. Circa 1969. Unmarked.

Fig. 306. Closeup of the fake "Bee" mark found on the base of many L.G. Wright Glass Co. reproductions of Paneled Thistle.

Fig. 305. Reproduction Paneled Thistle No.64-4 clear square plate. L.G. Wright Glass Co. Circa 1969. Unmarked.

see from Chart 86, 10 have contemporary shapes. They are the basket, the low-footed berry creamer, the flat rectangular nut dish, the fairy lamp, the flat-handled nappy, the salt dip (two styles), the berry covered sugar bowl, the sugar shaker, and the toothpick holder. The remainder consist of forms that correspond to original shapes. Each item in this series was produced from a new mold by the L. G. Wright Glass Company of New Martinsville, West Virginia. Known as Wright's Thistle, this set was primarily produced in clear nonflint glass, although a limited number of pieces were issued in various contemporary colors.

Like earlier reproductions, new items by Wright are glossy and have a sparkle and brilliance that are not apparent in the old. In addition, reproductions are thick and heavy. Although they are not permanently marked, many new items are embossed

with a bee, suggestive of the old Higbee trademark. However, unlike the original mark, which is round, that used by Wright is noticeably elongated and lacks the "HIG" initials (Fig. 306).

Hint: Reproduction items have an elongated bee mark.

PARROT

An interesting member of the bird group has for many years been known as Parrot (Fig. 307). Also known as Owl in Fan, this whimsical design consists of three large unconnected circular medallions. Each medallion contains an owl or parrot and is flanked on either side by a stylized fern. A thin stippled band above both motifs completes the design.

It is not known when or by whom Parrot was produced. The design was originally issued in a medium-grade clear nonflint glass in only two items: the goblet and the wine. Curiously, the goblet was made in two versions: (1) plain Parrot, and (2) Parrot Plus, or Bird Chasing Insect, which consists of the addition of a single small bird chasing an insect on the right side of one of the medallions.

Copies of the Parrot goblet entered the market throughout the 1980s. New goblets are unmarked and were produced from a new mold. Although clear examples are frequently encountered, most likely additional colors also were used. Unlike original goblets, the fan on reproductions is misshapen and irregular, the bird has a pointed and more pronounced beak, and the design is poorly pressed.

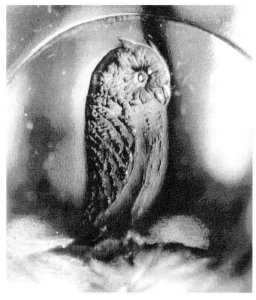

Fig. 307. Closeup of an original clear Parrot goblet. Unlike originals, the design on reproductions is blurred and poorly detailed.

Because reproductions are not permanently marked, it is not known where these goblets originated.

Hint: The parrot on reproductions has a pointed beak and the fans are lopsided.
Reproduced items: Goblet.

PENNSYLVANIA

Pennsylvania, or No.15048, as it was known by the United States Glass Company of Pittsburgh, Pennsylvania, was named in honor of the Keystone State. Also known as

Balder, Hand, and Kamoni, this pattern was originally produced in 1897 by the United States Glass Company at its Factory "O" (Central Glass Company, Wheeling, West Virginia) and Factory "GP" (Glassport, Pennsylvania).

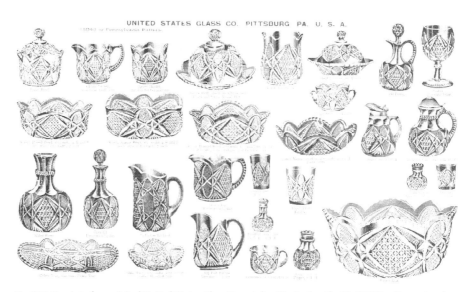

Fig. 308. Reprint of an original United States Glass Co. catalog illustrating the No.15048 or Pennsylvania pattern.

Pennsylvania was first issued in an extended table service from a good-quality clear nonflint glass (plain or gilt-trimmed). Although items were made in clear with ruby stain, or emerald green, these or any other colors are rare (Fig. 308).

This is a fancy, heavy pattern consisting of fans, crosshatching, vesicas, and other classic designs reminiscent of cut glass. Finials are ball-shaped and share the same pattern design.

During the mid-1980s, new, unmarked spoonholders, such as the one illustrated in Fig. 309, entered the market. They were made from a new mold and reportedly were imported from Taiwan. These spoonholders originally were distributed as pickle-caster inserts and can sometimes be found in a silver-plated frame.

Compared to originals, reproductions are heavy, smooth, and appear cloudy or muddy. They also have very poor pattern detail. For example, the waffle design in the oval panels is sharp on originals and very smooth with a pebbly surface on reproductions. This flaw is also true for the large diamond motif with a diamond cut design, which is sharp and well detailed on originals but is so poorly pressed on repro-

Fig. 309. Pennsylvania reproduction clear spoonholder. Circa mid-1980s. Unmarked.

ductions that it appears flat with bare patches.

Reproduction spoonholders are not permanently marked.

Hint: Reproduction spoonholders are poorly pressed and are heavier than originals.

Reproduced items: Spoonholder.

PLEAT AND PANEL

Pleat and Panel is an attractive pattern reminiscent of older stippled designs. This pattern (originally known as Derby) was introduced about 1882 by Bryce Brothers of Pittsburgh, Pennsylvania. When Bryce joined the United States Glass Company combine in 1891, it continued making the pattern. Shards have also been found at the site of the Burlington Glass Works in Hamilton, Ontario, suggesting that the design may also be of Canadian origin.

This pattern was originally produced in an extended table service from a good-quality clear nonflint glass. Although you may find odd pieces in amethyst, amber, blue, green, milk white, and vaseline, any color is rare. The design consists of heavily stippled panels separated by clear fluted bars. Forms are square and handles are pressed. Curiously, goblets were originally produced

Fig. 311. Reproduction Pleat and Panel clear square plate. Circa mid-1930s. Unmarked. (Unlike originals, the stippling on reproductions is too fine and even.)

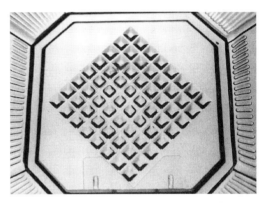

Fig. 312. Closeup of Pleat and Panel square plate. (Unlike originals, the waffle design on reproduction plates is smooth.)

Fig. 310. Original Pleat and Panel clear goblet. Bryce Brothers. Circa. 1882. (This version of the goblet has not been reproduced.)

in two versions: one version has bars that rise above the stippled design (Fig. 310) and the other has bars that are even with the stippled design. The former are thought to be American, while the latter are thought to be Canadian.

Reproduction goblets and 7-inch-square plates (Figs. 311 and 312) first appeared in the late 1930s. They are unmarked and were produced in clear glass from new molds. As a general rule, the stippling is fine and even (unlike the blotchy, uneven stippling on original items). New goblets and plates are also heavy and brilliant and feel oily or slick.

To date, only one goblet has been re-produced—the one with the bars extending above the stippled design. Compared to the original, the foot of this new goblet is smaller and not as highly cupped. Additionally, the stripes on the stem of this reproduction are wide, thick, and lop-sided.

Hint: Stippling on reproductions is even and fine; on originals it is blotchy.
Reproduced items: Goblet, plate.

PLUME

As innovative as the Victorian Era was, inspiration for tableware designs had often been borrowed from the past as many older designs were immortalized again in nonflint glass. A classic example is Plume.

Adam's Plume is a direct imitation of the earlier Sandwich plume motif and was first issued by Adams & Company of Pittsburgh, Pennsylvania, about 1874. At this time, the pattern was produced in an extended table service from a good-quality clear nonflint glass. When Adams became a member of the United States Glass Company in 1891, the pattern was reissued in clear and in clear with ruby stain (plain or copper-wheel engraved).

Plume is a highly attractive pattern. The glass is clear and brilliant and, although not flint, pieces are exceptionally heavy. The design consists of a large single plume horizontally arranged around the top and bottom of most items. An exception is the celery vase and pickle dish, on which the design is arranged in a vertical position. Of special interest to collectors is the bitters bottle and the lemonade set (tankard pitcher and

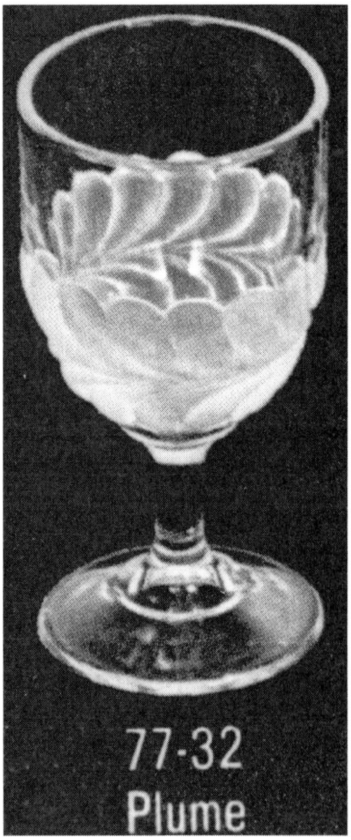

Fig. 313. New Plume No.77-32 clear and frosted goblet. L.G. Wright Glass Co. Circa 1968. Unmarked. (Original goblets were never made in this color.)

Fig. 314. Original Plume clear goblet. U.S. Glass Co. Circa 1891.

Fig. 315. New No.77-32 Plume clear goblet. L.G. Wright Glass Co. Circa 1968. Unmarked.

Plume is a safe pattern to collect. To date, only the barrel-shaped goblet made from a new mold has been reproduced (Fig. 313). New goblets in this shape have been on the market at least since the late 1950s. They are most likely the same as the No.77-32 clear and clear with satin finish goblets illustrated in the 1968 catalog of the L. G. Wright Glass Company of New Martinsville, West Virginia.

As you can see from Figs. 313 and 315, new goblets are quite convincing. Old and new goblets are similar in weight, quality, and detail. In addition, both goblets are approximately the same size. However, upon close examination, you will notice that, unlike original goblets, which have the plume design on the lower portion of the stem, this design is absent from the stems of new goblets. Aside from the obvious newness of clear and frosted reproductions, it is this omission that distinguishes old goblets from the new.

Reproductions are not permanently marked.

matching tumblers), which are blown rather than pressed. Here again, the plume design is arranged in a vertical position.

Hint: Reproduction goblets are missing the plume design at the base of the stem.
Reproduced items: Goblet.

POINTED JEWEL(S)

Pointed Jewel(s) was first introduced from a good-quality clear nonflint glass by the Columbia Glass Company of Findlay, Ohio, in 1888. Production was continued in 1892 in clear nonflint glass by the United States Glass Company of Pittsburgh, Pennsylvania, as evidenced by full-page ads in the January 1892 and the April 13 and 20, 1892, issues of *China, Glass and Lamps*. At United States Glass, the design was known only as line No.15006 and was produced at Factory "J" (Columbia Glass Company) and Factory "N" (the Nickel Plate Glass Company of Fostoria, Ohio). Alternative names for the pattern are Long Diamond, and Spear Point.

As late as 1960, the Imperial Glass Corporation of Bellaire, Ohio, reproduced the No.1950/981 individual creamer in milk-white glass. In addition, the mold was used for solid amber, heather, purple marble slag, and verde. Made from original molds, these reproduction creamers are heavier than originals (Fig. 316). The design is smoother on new creamers than on originals. The glass also has a glossy look typical of reproductions. However, if you remember that this pattern originally was made only in clear glass, you will have little difficulty in distinguishing originals from reproductions.

In recent years, collectors have noted heavier punch cups with slightly different rims than you might expect. We believe that these are old cups and the weight and rim differences are due to the use of a different plunger and cap ring.

Verde   Amber   Heather

Fig. 316. Assortment of new creamers in Pointed Jewel. Imperial Glass Corp. Circa. 1960. Unmarked.

Reproduction creamers can sometimes be found with a paper label, but items were not permanently marked.

Hint: Pointed Jewel individual creamers were never originally made in color.
Reproduced items: Creamer.

POLAR BEAR

Polar Bear is one of the most intriguing designs in pattern glass. This design consists of three Arctic scenes containing a large polar bear standing on all four paws, two seals, one larger than the other, and a large resting seal. The rim of the bowl is fashioned to resemble hanging icicles and the lower portion of the bowl portrays water, ice, and snow. Through the years, the pattern has appropriately been called Arctic, Frosted Polar Bear, Ice Berg, North Pole, and Polar Bear and Seal.

Originally issued in a limited number of table pieces, Polar Bear was made in a good-quality clear and frosted nonflint glass. The acid finish on this pattern is sometimes poorly done because the frosting appears blotchy.

When, or by whom, this pattern was produced is not known. Because the water tray bears the initials "C.G.Co.," many researchers attribute its manufacture to the Crystal Glass Company of Bridgeport, Ohio. However, other glassworks of the time shared these initials, and, without conclusive evidence, positive attribution to the Crystal Glass Company is inappropriate.

Fig. 317. Reproduction blue Polar Bear goblet. Summit Art Glass Co. Circa 1977. Embossed "V" in a circle.

To date, only colored goblets have been reproduced in Polar Bear. New 6-inch-high goblets appearing as late as 1977 were produced from a new mold by the Summit Art Glass Company of Rootstown, Ohio, as its No.539 goblet (Fig. 317). They are good copies. However, unlike the originals, which are clear and frosted, new goblets are either amber or blue and heavily stippled. In addition, the stem on reproductions is thinner than on originals. Whereas original goblets are either flared or barrel-shaped, the rim of reproductions is distinctly cupped. This goblet was produced for less than one year, as it was no longer available in the June 1978 Summit price list.

New goblets are signed with a paper label in black and gold and are sometimes impressed with a "V" within a circle.

Hint: Original Polar Bear goblets were never made in amber or blue.

Reproduced items: Goblet.

PORTLAND

Known as U.S. Glass pattern No.15121, Portland was originally produced about 1910 by the United States Glass Company of Pittsburgh, Pennsylvania, at Factory "F" (Ripley & Company, Pittsburgh), Factory "O" (Central Glass Company of Wheeling, West Virginia), and Factory "GP" (Glassport, Pennsylvania).

Produced in an extended table service from a good-quality nonflint glass, the design consists of flat, buttressed panels. Each panel is arched at one end and straight-sided at the other, creating a buttress or protrusion. The configuration of this design varies, depending on the shape and the size of each item. Handles are either applied or pressed (Figs. 318 and 319).

Although Portland is similar to the well-known Banded Portland, the chief difference between them is the thin band of

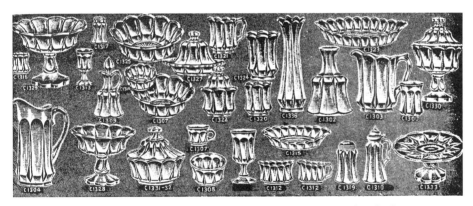

Fig. 318. Reprint of Butler Brothers 1914 catalog illustrating a large assortment of Portland.

Fig. 319. Excerpt from the circa 1910 United States Glass Co. catalog illustrating the original Portland breakfast creamer, Jersey creamer, and breakfast open sugar bowl.

diamond point that appears on Banded Portland but not on Portland.

As late as 1976, Wheaton-Craft Giftware of Millville, New Jersey, reproduced five items in Portland. They are: the No.300 individual creamer and flat, open sugar bowl set, the No.302 round, flat open nut dish with scalloped rim, the No.304 flat pickle tray, and the No.306 flat relish. Known as Wheaton-Craft's Cape May pattern, each piece is unmarked and produced from a new mold in clear nonflint glass.

Reproductions in Portland can be quite deceiving. The glass is brilliant and each shape conforms to a known original. However, reproductions are heavier, thicker, and smaller than originals. In addition, reproductions feel slick or oily and have a distinct crinkled or wavy appearance.

Hint: Reproductions are heavier and the glass is oily and slick when compared to originals.
Reproduced items: Creamer, nut dish, pickle tray, relish, sugar bowl.

PRESSED BLOCK

Pressed Block is a heavy, brilliant flint pattern of the 1850s. The design was possibly produced by Bakewell, Pears and Company of Pittsburgh, Pennsylvania. Because fragments have also been found at the site of the Boston and Sandwich Glass Company of Sandwich, Massachusetts, it is safe to assume that it may have produced some items.

This pattern is a member of the block family of pattern glass and was offered in a limited number of table forms. Finials are characteristic of the period and appear as stylized acorns (Fig. 320).

In 1964, the Fostoria Glass Company of Fostoria, Ohio, reproduced the high-standard true open compote for the Henry Ford Museum in Dearborn, Michigan. This compote was made from a new mold in an excellent-quality clear, copper blue, and olive green glass that exhibits a belltone resonance when gently tapped. These new compotes are exact replicas of the original compote in the Henry Ford collection. Because of this affinity to the original, each

Fig. 320. Line drawing of original Pressed Block high-standard covered compote.

compote was permanently embossed with the museum's "HFM" hallmark.

Hint: Reproduction compotes are permanently marked "HFM."
Reproduced items: Compote.

PRISCILLA

Priscilla is also known as Alexis, Late Moon and Star, Steele, and Sun and Star. This pattern was first introduced in January 1895 by Dalzell, Gilmore & Leighton of Findlay, Ohio, from a good-quality clear nonflint

glass in an extended table service. Clear with ruby stain or any other color is rare.

This design consists of vertical convex panels. Impressed within each panel is a clear serrated circle. Below each circle is a six-pointed star. Depending on the item, a star may also appear above each circle. Han-

CHART 87   PRISCILLA. Fenton Art Glass Company, Williamstown, West Virginia.

CMN: Line No.1890 or Priscilla.
Mark: Unmarked, embossed logo, or paper label.
Color Code: CY Clear, DK Dusty Rose, EG Emerald Green, LB Light Blue, SR Salem Blue.

ITEM	COLOR(S)	YEAR	ORIG	NEW
Basket. #9036. Low, flared rim, 12"h., handled.	CY	1950		X
	DK, SR	1990		X
Bowl, open flat, round.				
Cupped rim. 9"d.	CY	1950	X	
	EG	1951	X	
Flared rim. #9068. 10½"d.	CY	1950	X	
	SR	1990	X	
Cocktail.	CY	1950		X
Creamer, pressed handle.	CY	1950		X
Dish, Bonbon, 6"d. Ruffled rim, handled.	CY	1950		X
Goblet.	CY	1950	X	
Plate, flat, round.				
Rolled edge, 11"d.	CY	1950		X
Smooth rim.				
6"d.	CY	1950	X	
8"d.	CY	1950	X	
12½"d.	CY	1950		X
Sherbert, 4"h.	CY	1950		X
	LB	1951		X
Sugar bowl, open double handles.	CY	1950		X
Wine.	CY	1950	X	

CHART 88   PRISCILLA. L.G. Wright Glass Company, New Martinsville, West Virginia.

CMN: Priscilla.
Mark: Unmarked.
Color Code: A Amber, AM Amethyst, B Blue, C Clear, CRS Clear with Ruby Stain, G Green, RBY Ruby.

ITEM	COLOR(S)	YEAR	ORIG	NEW
Ashtray. #56-5. Flat, 7".	A, B, C, G, RBY	1968		X
Bowl, round, low circular foot.				
Covered.				
#56-15. 4"d., 4½"h.	A, B, C, G, RBY	1968	X	
Open.				
#56-6. Hand-crimped rim. 6½"d., 2¾"h.	A, B, C, G, RBY	1968	X	
#56-14. Scalloped rim. 4"d., 2¼"h.	A, B, C, G, RBY	1968	X	
Compote, high standard.				
Covered				
#56-1. 4"d., 7½"h.	A, B, C, G, RBY	1968	X	
	CRS	1970	X	
#56-11.	C	1983	X	
Open.				
#56-12. Flared bowl.	C	1983	X	
Goblet. #56-2. 8 oz., 6"h.	A, B, C, G, RBY	1968	X	
	CRS	1970	X	
Rose bowl. #56-8. Low circular foot, crimped rim, 4"d., 3¼"h.	A, B, C, G, RBY	1968		X
Sauce dish. #56-3. Flat, round, 5½"d., 1¼"h.	A, C, G	1968	X	
Wine. #56-10. 3 oz., 4"h.	A, B, C, G, RBY	1968	X	

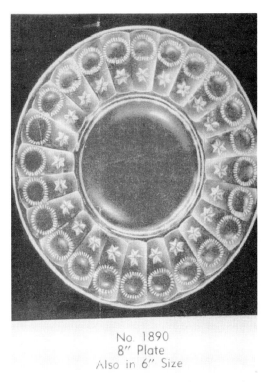

No. 1890
8" Plate
Also in 6" Size

Fig. 321. New Priscilla No.1890 clear reproduction round plate. Fenton Art Glass Co. Circa 1950. Unmarked.

dles may be applied or pressed and finials are clear balls.

In 1950, the Fenton Art Glass Company of Williamstown, West Virginia, introduced the 14 forms enumerated in Chart 87. Issued as Fenton's No.1890 pattern or Priscilla, each item was produced in a good-quality clear nonflint glass. A year later, only two items appeared in color: the emerald green 9-inch cupped open bowl and the light blue 4-inch-high sherbert. Apparently, this pattern was short-lived because it does not reappear in subsequent Fenton catalogs until 1990. That year, it was listed as the No.9036 basket (in dusty rose and Salem blue) and the No.9068 bowl (in clear and Salem blue).

As you can see from Chart 87, Fenton adopted this pattern in both antique and modern forms (Fig. 321). While six of these items emulate known antique forms, the remainder are strictly contemporary. Although any contemporary color is new,

Fig. 322. New Priscilla No.1890 clear reproduction goblet. Fenton Art Glass Co. Circa 1950. Unmarked.

56-2
8 oz. Goblet
A, B, C, G, R.

Fig. 323. Reproduction clear Priscilla No.56-2 goblet. L.G. Wright Glass Co. Circa 1968. Unmarked.

collectors and dealers may find clear pieces more troublesome.

Produced from new molds, reproductions are notably heavy. One of the most obvious differences between old and new goblets and wines is that the foot of an original is patterned with moons, while the foot of a reproduction is plain. You can clearly see this difference from the illustration in Fig. 322. Moreover, Fenton used a higher-quality glass than that used on the originals. As a collector or dealer, remember that whenever you encounter an item that is exceptionally heavy or in any color other than clear, that item is modern.

Between 1968 and 1983, the L.G. Wright Glass Company of New Martinsville, West Virginia, issued the 11 forms enumerated in Chart 88 (Fig. 323). Unlike Fenton creations, only two of Wright's items (the No.56-5 ashtray and the No.56-8 rose bowl) are modern: the remainder are direct copies of known antique shapes. Also,

unlike those items created by Fenton, Wright reproductions are not permanently marked.

Most reproductions have been flared, ruffled, or crimped at the rim of bowls and compotes. However, because this method of decoration is also commonplace in the original Priscilla pattern, we do not recommend that you use the rim's treatment as a guideline in spotting Priscilla reproductions. Examples of this decorative technique are well known in a number of patterns produced by Dalzell, Gilmore & Leighton, including Beaded Medallion, Columbia, Delos, Eyewinker, Retort, and Reverse Torpedo. Again, you must consider the weight and clarity of the glass. And, like Fenton's reproductions, any item in color is modern. Also, the goblets and wines issued by Wright have patterned bases, while those by Fenton do not.

Hint: Priscilla items in color are modern.

PRISM AND FLATTENED SAWTOOTH

Also known as Ribbed Pineapple, Prism and Flattened Sawtooth may have been first issued from a good-quality clear flint glass during the 1840s and 1850s by Curling, Robertson & Company of Pittsburgh, Pennsylvania. The pattern consists of a flattened sawtooth base under ribbing. The glass is exceptionally heavy and produces a fine belltone resonance when gently tapped. Handles are applied.

From 1968 through 1974, the L.G. Wright Glass Company of New Martinsville, West Virginia, reproduced the five items enumerated in Chart 89 (Fig. 324). This pattern was known as Wright's Sawtooth and was produced from new molds in clear and contemporary colors. Only the goblet and the wine are copies of original forms; the remaining forms are strictly contemporary.

Each new item is unmarked and was made from nonflint glass. Reproductions are quite good. However, unlike originals,

Fig. 324. Reproduction Prism and Flattened Sawtooth No.77-99 iced-tea tumbler (often mistaken for the original spoonholder). L.G. Wright Glass Co. Circa 1969. Unmarked.

CHART 89   RIBBED PINEAPPLE. L. G. Wright Glass Company, New Martinsville, West Virginia.
CMN: Sawtooth.
Mark: Unmarked.
Color Code: A Amber, AM Amethyst, B Blue, C Clear, DB Dark Blue, G Green, P Pink, PS Purple Slag, RBY Ruby, V Vaseline.

ITEM	COLOR(S)	YEAR	ORIG	NEW
Goblet. #77-35. Knob stem, 8 oz. 6¼"h.	A, AM, B, C, DB, G, P	1968	X	
	PS	unknown	X	
	RBY	1968	X	
Sherbert. #77-80. Knob stem, 3½"d., 4½"h.	A, C, G, P	1969		X
	RBY	1974		X
Toothpick holder. #77-100.	A, AM, B, G, RBY	1968		X
	C	1972		X
	P	1969		X
	V	1974		X
Tumbler. #77-99. Iced tea, 12 oz., low knob stem, 6¼"h.	A, P, RBY	1968		X
	C	1969		X
Wine. #77-77. Knob stem, 2 oz., 4½"h.	A, B, G, P, RBY	1968	X	
	AM, C	1969	X	

copies are lightweight and will not resonate. In addition, they are thick-walled and the design is noticeably flat and smooth.

Hint: Original Prism and Flattened Sawtooth items are made from flint glass and will resonate when gently tapped.

QUEEN

Queen is a variation of the famed Daisy and Button pattern. Also known as Daisy and Button with Pointed Panels, Daisy and Depressed Button, Paneled Daisy and Button, Pointed Panel Daisy and Button, and Sunk Daisy and Button, the original name of this pattern is McKee's No.2 or Queen. The design was originally produced by McKee Brothers of Pittsburgh, Pennsylvania, about 1885 from a good-quality clear nonflint glass in an extended table service. Original colors are amber, apple green, blue, clear, and yellow.

As you can see from Fig. 325, this pattern consists of a large band of daisy and button upon an otherwise undecorated background. Suspended from this band are three triangular spears filled with a daisy motif. Like a majority of patterns from the last quarter of the nineteenth century, handles are pressed.

Throughout the 1980s, Boyd's Crystal Art Glass Company of Cambridge, Ohio, reproduced the true open low-footed bowl, the

Fig. 325. Original clear Queen goblet. McKee Brothers. Circa 1885.

high-standard cake stand, and the high-standard open compote in clear and cobalt blue. Each reproduction is unmarked and was produced from a new mold. Unlike originals, new items are excessively thick and heavy, the glass is glossy and slick, colors are harsh and artificial, and the design is poorly pressed. Upon examining

any of these reproductions, you will immediately notice a distinct waviness in the glass.

Hint: Reproductions are unusually heavy and the glass is oily and slick.
Reproduced items: Bowl, cake stand, compote.

RED BLOCK

The history of Red Block is one of the most complicated to untangle. This design had been extensively produced throughout the 1880s by numerous manufacturers, including Bryce Brothers (No.175) of Pittsburgh, Pennsylvania; the Central Glass Company (Nos. 881 and 893) of Wheeling, West Virginia; Doyle & Company (No.250 or Eva) of Pittsburgh; George Duncan & Sons (No.328) of Pittsburgh; Fostoria Glass Company (No.150 or Captain Kidd) of Fostoria, Ohio; and Pioneer Glass Company (No.250) of Pittsburgh. Later, the United States Glass Company of Pittsburgh reissued the line when Bryce, Doyle, and Duncan became member companies.

Red Block was originally produced in an extended table service from varying qualities of nonflint glass and is called Clear Block when unstained. Although the pattern is more readily known in clear with ruby stain, you may find examples in clear stained with amber, blue, green, and yellow, although complete table services were not produced in these colors. Items may also be plain or copper-wheel engraved in a number of decorative designs. Because Red Block was so copiously produced, bases, finials, handles, stems, and the shape of forms vary considerably.

As you can see from Fig. 326, the basic design of Red Block consists of heavily pressed hexagonal blocks, the surfaces of which are flat and either stained or undecorated. These blocks also form the finials of covered pieces, such as the butter dish and the sugar bowl. Handles are also pressed and ear-shaped.

Contrary to popular belief, Red Block is a safe pattern to collect. To date, only two items have been reproduced. New wines

Fig. 326. Reproduction Red Block goblet. Circa 1950s. Unmarked. (Unlike originals, the stain on reproductions is pale.)

first appeared as early as 1938 and were quickly followed by goblets. Both are unmarked and were made from new molds in amber, amethyst, blue, clear, orange, yellow, and clear stained with blue, green, ruby, and yellow. In addition, solid colors may be plain or iridized.

In general, reproductions are heavier and thicker than originals, but the bases are thinner and the points between the blocks are slightly rounder. Reproductions in blue, green, and yellow are painted rather than stained and show no translucency. Clear with ruby stain reproductions are too light in color and tend to have holes or blotches along the rim where the stain ran. Reproduction items also tend to be slightly yellow instead of brilliantly clear like originals.

Reproductions in Red Block are not permanently marked.

Hint: Reproductions are heavier and thicker and the glass has a slight yellowish cast.

Reproduced items: Goblet, wine.

RIBBED PALM

This pattern has been called Ribbed Palm for so many years that its original name, Sprig, has all but been forgotten. A member of the early group of pressed glass that has a ribbed background as a central part of its motif, this pattern was designed and patented by Frederick McKee (design patent No.1748) on April 21, 1863, and produced in that year by McKee Brothers of Pittsburgh, Pennsylvania. Through the years, it has also been known as Acanthus, Leaf, and Oak Leaf. In excavations at the site of the Boston and Sandwich Glass Company of Sandwich, Massachusetts, enough shards have been unearthed to attribute early pro-

duction to that company. This dual manufacture explains the number of variations that exist.

Ribbed Palm consists of large stylized palm ornaments that are highly embossed against a ribbed background. Compared to the fine ribbing on Bellflower, this ribbing is wide and coarse. The glass is brilliant and heavy and produces a fine belltone resonance when gently tapped. Finials are acorn-shaped and handles are applied.

The first reproduction in Ribbed Palm is the goblet issued by the L.G. Wright Glass Company of New Martinsville, West Virginia, in 1969. Referred to as Wright's No.77-98 or Ribbed Palm goblet, it stands 6½ inches high and has a capacity of 8 ounces. Produced in the contemporary colors of amber, green, and ruby from new molds, new goblets are nonflint, noticeably lightweight, and lack the fine belltone of old flint.

In 1977, Old Sturbridge Village Museum of Sturbridge, Massachusetts, authorized the Imperial Glass Corporation of Bellaire, Ohio, to produce the No.6501 or Ribbed Palm goblet illustrated in Fig. 327 (E). Issued from a new mold, this goblet is 6¼ inches high and was also produced in clear nonflint glass. Unlike the original, which is heavy and belltoned, the Sturbridge goblet is lightweight and lacks any tonal quality. The design on this new goblet is shallow and the ribbing is finer than that of the old. New goblets are permanently marked with the "OSV" insignia (signifying Old Sturbridge Village Museum).

Unlike the goblets issued on behalf of the Sturbridge museum, goblets by Wright are not permanently marked.

Fig. 327. Catalog reprint illustrating the clear reproduction Ribbed Palm goblet made by Imperial Glass for Old Sturbridge Village Museum. Circa 1977. Embossed "OSV."

Hint: Reproduction goblets are neither belltoned nor heavy.

Reproduced items: Goblet.

RIBBON

Prior to the development of the decorative technique of frosting glass with hydrofluoric acid, many pressed-glass patterns such as Frosted Leaf or Magnet and Grape with Frosted Leaf were frosted by roughing the high surfaces of the design. This was accomplished either by holding the article against a coarse stone wheel or by sandblasting those portions of the design to be decorated. Gradually, both of these machine-ground techniques were abandoned in favor of the hydrofluoric acid technique, which produced a smoother, more refined surface.

Ribbon is one of the more popular patterns produced during the period of machine-ground frosting. It is also known as Frosted Ribbon, Rebecca at the Well, and Simple Frosted Ribbon. This pattern originally was produced by the firm of Bakewell, Pears & Company of Pittsburgh, Pennsylvania, about 1870. Bakewell made an extended table service in clear and frosted glass. The basic design consists of alternating vertical clear and frosted panels roughened by a wheel or sandblasting. Thus, its surface is coarse and rough.

The first item reproduced in Ribbon was the goblet. This unmarked goblet was made from a new mold as early as 1945. Most likely, it was a product of the L.G. Wright Glass Company of New Martinsville, West Virginia. In 1969, the Wright catalog illustrated a similar clear and frosted goblet as item No.77-104 (Fig. 328). Although issued in the original color of clear with frosted panels, these goblets are heavy, poorly frosted, and smoother than originals. These reproductions also have a distinct yellowish cast, which can be seen best when viewed under strong light.

In 1965, the Henry Ford Museum in Dearborn, Michigan, authorized the Fostoria Glass Company of Fostoria, Ohio, to reproduce four items in Ribbon. They are: the No.2767 6½-inch-diameter covered bowl on a low foot, the No.2777/377 9¾-inch-high Rebecca at the Well candlestick, the No.277/388 8-inch-high Rebecca at the Well compote, and the No.2780 oblong compote with scalloped rim and dolphin stem. Collec-

Fig. 328. New Ribbon No.77-104 clear and frosted goblet. L.G. Wright Glass Co. Circa 1969. Unmarked.

tors also report Rebecca at the Well candlesticks with solid glass inserts embedded in the sockets.

Aside from candlesticks, which are strictly contemporary, each of these items was made from a new mold and is a direct copy of an original item from the museum's collection. Typical of Henry Ford Museum reproductions, each item is hand-molded, hand-finished, and machine-ground to produce a frosted appearance.

All four reproductions were offered in at least four additional color treatments. In 1965, the low covered bowl and both compotes were available in the contemporary colors of copper blue and olive green. Each color was available plain or frosted. And, in 1967, the Rebecca at the Well candlestick was offered in the same four colors.

Although Fostoria reproductions have been advertised as faithful imitations of the originals, there are a number of differences between old and new pieces. Because each reproduction was made from a new mold, copies are thick and noticeably heavy. Unlike the crisply sculpted details on originals, those on reproductions are poorly designed and lack detail. In general, the serrated rim on the bowls of all reproductions has a flat, sharp edge, while the rim on original items is polished and round. Upon closer examination, you will also notice that the ribbon motif on reproductions is wider and coarser than on originals.

More specifically, the most obvious difference between old and new compotes is the detailing of the figures. While Fostoria reproductions use the original dolphin and Rebecca motif, the design is weak, poorly modeled, and lacking in detail. An excellent example of these flaws is the shape of the openings at the bend of the statue's elbows. On the Rebecca at the Well compote, these openings are well defined and follow the natural curve of the statue's arm. On reproductions, they are either round or completely missing, as seen in Fig. 329.

Because this pattern was originally produced in clear and frosted glass, any colored item is strictly contemporary.

Each Fostoria reproduction is permanently embossed with the letters "HFM" for the Henry Ford Museum. Each item was attractively boxed and accompanied by a small folded card (bearing the pattern name

Fig. 329. Reproduction Ribbon Rebecca-at-the-Well clear and frosted compote. Produced by the Fostoria Glass Co. for the Henry Ford Museum. Circa 1965. Embossed "HFM."

and descriptive text) attached by a gold HFM sticker.

Hint: Fostoria reproductions are permanently embossed "HFM."
Reproduced items: Bowl, candlestick, compote, goblet.

ROMAN ROSETTE

Roman Rosette is a simple pattern composed of large clear rosettes highly embossed against a lightly stippled background. Clear bands of fluting above and below this central motif complete the basic design. Finials are round, flat, and pressed with a similar rosette. Unlike the silvery appearance of other stippled designs, the stippling on Roman Rosette is delicate, soft, and more subdued.

This pattern was originally produced from a good-quality nonflint glass in 1891 by the United States Glass Company at its Bryce Brothers factory in Pittsburgh, Penn-

sylvania, where it was known as No.15030. Items are bright and brilliant and especially attractive when stained in ruby red. This light and airy design is well suited to the variety of forms in which it was made.

To date, only one item has been reproduced in Roman Rosette. New clear goblets produced from new molds entered the market as early as 1945. They are unmarked and can be quite convincing, as you can see from Figs. 330 and 331. However, upon close examination, you will note a number of interesting discrepancies. Unlike the soft, delicate stippling on originals, the stippling on new goblets is thin and even. In addition, the bowl of new goblets is elongated (unlike

Fig. 330. Reproduction clear Roman Rosette goblet. Circa 1945. Unmarked.

Fig. 331. Original clear Roman Rosette goblet. U.S. Glass Co. Circa 1891.

the round bowls of originals), and the fluting around the top and bottom is much wider. When you place an original and a new goblet side by side, you can see that the base of new goblets is thinner.

Reproduction goblets in Roman Rosette

are not permanently marked as to manufacturer.

Hint: Reproduction goblets have thin and even stippling.
Reproduced items: Goblet.

ROSE IN SNOW

Rose in Snow is one of the aristocrats of the floral group of pattern glass and often referred to as Rose. This design was originally produced by Bryce Brothers of Pittsburgh, Pennsylvania, as No.125 during the 1880s. Production was continued after 1891, when Bryce became a member of the United States Glass Company of Pittsburgh.

This lovely pattern consists of clear leaves and roses in high relief against a stippled background. While the handle of the creamer is always pressed, the large handled tumbler and the bulbous water pitcher each have an applied handle. In addition,

the four-piece table set and the low-footed covered compote were produced originally in two distinct styles (round and square). The remainder of forms are round. You can find this pattern readily in a good-quality clear nonflint glass, although complete table services were also produced in amber, blue, and canary yellow.

Rose in Snow is a safe pattern to collect. To date, only five forms have been reproduced. During the 1930s, new goblets and 9-inch-round plates first appeared, followed by pickle dishes and "In Fond Remembrance" mugs with pressed handles. In addition, the Summit Art Glass Company of Akron, Ohio, issued the No.601

Rose in Snow goblet about 1978. Unmarked, each was produced from a new
mold in the original colors of amber, blue,
canary yellow, and clear. Unlike the
coarse, pebbled stippling of original items,
however, the stippling on reproductions is
thin and blotchy, producing a silvery or
frosted surface. Moreover, the finely detailed leaves are missing completely on reproductions, and the size of items may
vary. This is especially true of goblets,
which are smaller than the old and lack
the two small leaves of the design (Figs.
332 and 333). In like manner, new plates
are thinner than the originals, and the size
of the handle is smaller.

By 1960, two additional reproductions entered the market. In the April 1, 1960, sales
brochure, the B&P Lamp Supply Company
of McMinnville, Tennessee, illustrated a
similar unsigned Rose in Snow goblet. Produced in amber, blue, clear, and vaseline,
this goblet was also produced from a new
mold and shares the same discrepancies as
other reproductions. Also at this time, the
Imperial Glass Corporation of Bellaire, Ohio,
issued the Rose in Snow covered sugar bowl
illustrated in Fig. 334. Known as Imperial's

Fig. 333. Closeup of original Rose in Snow goblet. Bryce Brothers. Circa 1880s. (Note that the right stem on original goblets has six leaves, while that on reproductions has only four.)

Fig. 332. Closeup of clear reproduction Rose in Snow goblet. Circa 1950. Unmarked. (Notice the poor detailing and missing leaves on the stem that bends from left to right.)

No.976, this covered sugar was advertised
in the December 1960 issue of *China,
Glass & Tablewares* in clear glass. Along
with this advertisement, the journal an-
nounced that pieces in color and milk white
would be produced at a later date. In the
May 25, 1962, issue, the colors of doeskin
and ruby were added. By 1966, milk white
was offered and, in 1968, sunset ruby carnival.

Often, you may find clear covered sugar
bowls that are permanently embossed on
the bottom of the base with the monogram
"VPNT" within a large "S." Sears, Roebuck
and Company joined with the actor Vincent
Price to produce a line of glassware known
as National Treasures. The monogram reflects the new partnership by combining the
two logos; Sears (S) and Vincent Price National Treasures (VPNT). This line, produced throughout the late 1950s and early
1960s by the Imperial Glass Corporation of
Bellaire, Ohio, included many classic antique pressed patterns. Each item was ac-

976
Jar and Cover

Fig. 334. Reproduction clear Rose in Snow No.976 square covered sugar bowl, often embossed "VPNT," signifying "Vincent Price National Treasures." Imperial Glass Corp. Circa 1960. (To date, only this square form has been reproduced.)

Fig. 335. Reproduction Rose in Snow blown bottle by Clevenger Brothers. Glass Works. Circa 1988. Signed.

companied by a little booklet tag, on whose front page was printed "Vincent Price Presents National Treasures, Sears, Roebuck and Co." encircling an eagle. The bottom of the tag was printed with the words "Victorian Pressed Glass."

An interesting adaptation of this design, the Rose in Snow bottle illustrated in Fig. 335 was produced by Clevenger Brothers of Clayton, New Jersey, in the mid-1980s. These bulbous bottles are 8 inches high

and 5½ inches in diameter and can be found in amber, amethyst, blue, and green. Unlike original pieces in this pattern, which are always pressed, bottles are mouth-blown. When signed, bottles are permanently embossed with the Clevenger hallmark.

Unless otherwise mentioned, most reproduction items are not permanently marked, though occasionally you may find pieces with a paper label.

Hint: Reproduction items are missing the two small leaves on the right stem.

Reproduced items: Bottle, goblet, mug, pickle dish, plate, sugar bowl.

ROSE SPRIG

Rose Sprig is a lovely design typical of the floral group of early American pattern glass. This pattern consists of large stippled sprigs of roses highly embossed upon

a plain background. It was designed and patented by Henry Franz on May 25, 1886 (mechanical patent #342743), and first issued by Jones, Cavitt & Company of Pittsburgh, Pennsylvania, in 1886. Complete table sets, produced from a good-quality nonflint glass, may still be found in amber, blue, clear, and vaseline.

Rose Sprig is an interesting pattern. Although most forms are round, plates are boat-shaped, oblong, and square. The most intriguing items seem to be the sleigh-shaped salt dips and berry bowls, which come in several sizes.

To date, only two items have been reproduced in Rose Sprig. Shown in Fig. 336, the No.77-105 goblet was issued by the L.G. Wright Glass Company of New Martinsville, West Virginia. These goblets were introduced as early as 1968. They are unmarked and were produced from a new mold in the original colors of amber, blue, canary yellow, and clear. Compared to originals, new goblets are heavy and the colors are harsh and artificial. In addition, the design is smaller and blurred. Old goblets are finely stippled and detailed; new goblets are not.

The second item reproduced in this pattern is the individual salt dip shaped like a sleigh. These salts were also made in amber, blue, canary yellow, and clear and have been in circulation since the early 1960s. Although they were produced from a new mold and are unmarked, new salts are embossed with the same "1888" patent date as the originals.

Both pieces share the same discrepancies. New items are heavier than originals, the glass is thicker, and the colors are harsher, the rose sprig design is not as finely stippled as the original, and the

Fig. 336. Reproduction Rose Sprig No.77-105 clear goblet. L.G. Wright Glass Co. Circa 1968. Unmarked.

rose is slightly larger. On the goblet, the tip of the leaf points to one o'clock, while, on the original, it is in the two o'clock position.

Reproductions are not permanently marked.

Hint: Rose Sprig reproductions are heavier and the colors are harsher than the originals.

Reproduced items: Goblet, salt dip.

SAWTOOTH

Sawtooth is a simple yet effective pattern. Originally known as Gillinder's Diamond and Mitre Diamond by the New England Glass Company, the design consists of sharp four-sided diamonds. It was originally produced by numerous concerns, including Bryce-Richards (1854) of Pittsburgh, Pennsylvania; Bryce-Walker (1865) of Pittsburgh; Bryce Brothers

(1880s) of Pittsburgh; Gillinder & Sons (1860s) of Philadelphia (only a tumbler); James B. Lyon & Company (1860s) of Pittsburgh; McKee & Brothers (1859–65) of Pittsburgh; the New England Glass Company (1865–85) of East Cambridge, Massachusetts; and the United States Glass Company of Pittsburgh. Production has also been attributed to the Boston and Sandwich Glass Company (1860s) of Sandwich, Massachusetts.

Due to its length of production, Sawtooth was originally produced in varying qualities of flint and, later, nonflint glass. Early pieces were produced from an excellent-quality flint glass, are heavy, and produce a fine belltone resonance when tapped. In addition, handles are applied and often crimped. Although flint items were originally produced in clear and milk white, deep sapphire blue, amber, amethyst, fiery opalescence, medium blue, opaque blue, canary yellow, translucent blue, translucent

Fig. 339. Reproduction milk-white Sawtooth No.556 covered high-standard compote. Westmoreland Glass Co. Circa 1956. Embossed "WG."

Verde

194—9" "Sawtooth" Vase

Fig. 337. Reproduction No.194 Sawtooth verde celery vase. Imperial Glass Corp. Circa early-1950s. Unmarked.

556 Dish

Fig. 338. Reproduction No.556 Sawtooth covered butter dish in antique green. Westmoreland Glass Co. Circa 1970. Embossed "WG."

556

Fig. 340. Reproduction No.556 Sawtooth true open high-standard compote. Westmoreland Glass Co. Circa 1972. Embossed "WG."

CHART 90 SAWTOOTH. Indiana Glass Company, Dunkirk, Indiana.
CMN: Diamond Point.
Mark: Unmarked or paper label.
Color Code: BS Blue Satin, C Clear, CCS Clear with Cranberry Stain.

ITEM	COLOR(S)	YEAR	ORIG	NEW
Ashtray, 5½"d.	C, CCS	1966		X
Bowl, open, low circular foot.				
Flared, 13¼"d., 3½"h.	C, CCS	1966		X
Scalloped rim, 11½"d., 4¼"h.	BS	unknown		X
	C, CCS	1967		X
Straight-sided, 9¾"d., 4¾"h.	BS	unknown		X
	C, CCS	1966		X
Cake stand, high standard, 10"d.	C	1966		X
Chalice, covered, 15¼"h., 6"d.	BS	unknown		X
	C, CCS	1966		X
Compote, high standard.				
Covered.	C, CCS	1966		X
Open.				
Plain rim.	C, CCS	1966		X
Scalloped rim.	C, CCS	1966		X
Goblet.	C, CCS	1968		X
Plate, 14½"d.	C, CCS	1967		X
Sauce dish, flat.				
Plain rim.	BS	unknown		X
	C, CCS	1966		X
Scalloped rim.	BS	unknown		X
	C, CCS	1967		X
Tumbler, iced tea.	C, CCS	1967		X

jade green or any other color in flint is rare. Later pieces commonly were produced in clear and colored nonflint glass; these pieces are lightweight and do not resonate. Because of the number of firms issuing this pattern, differences may be readily seen in the treatment of bases, finials, handles, and standards.

In 1947, the John E. Kemple Glass Works produced the No.40 or Sawtooth 8-inch-high candlestick. Allegedly produced from an original 1840s mold, this new candlestick was available in amber, amethyst, blue, blue opaque, end-of-day, green, and milk white. Although Kemple candlesticks were not permanently marked, you may still find them bearing the original paper label.

New candlesticks are lightweight due to the absence of lead. Only clear and milk white are original. Clear candlesticks have a bluish-gray cast to the glass, while those in milk white have a ricey appearance. The sawtooth design on originals is sharp and well defined; on reproductions, it is blunt and smooth.

As early as 1950, the Imperial Glass Corporation of Bellaire, Ohio, issued the 9¼-inch-high pedestaled celery vase with scalloped rim illustrated in Fig. 337. Known as Imperial's No.194 or Sawtooth design, this new celery is unmarked and was made from a new mold in 1950 in milk white; in 1962 in amber, blue, heather, and verde; in 1966 in clear; and in 1971 in clear with fired gold.

New celery vases by Imperial are lightweight compared to the original flint vases. While the sawtooth design is sharp and well defined on originals, reproductions have

CHART 91   SAWTOOTH. **Westmoreland Glass Company, Grapeville, Pennsylvania.**
CMN: No.566 or Sawtooth.
Mark: Unmarked, embossed "WG," or paper label.
Color Code: A Amber, AG Antique Green, BB Bermuda Blue, BWB Brandywine Blue, C Clear, DRR Deep Rich Ruby, GM Green Marble, GS Golden Sunset, LG Laurel Green, MW Milk White, OG Olive Green, PM Purple Marble, RBY Ruby.

ITEM	COLOR(S)	YEAR	ORIG	NEW
Banana stand, high standard.	DRR*	1983		X
Butter dish, covered, flat, 6½"d., 5"h.	AG	1970	X	
	GM, PM	1966	X	
	MW	1951	X	
Cake stand, low standard.	DRR*	1983		X
Compote, high standard.				
Covered.				
9½"h., 6½"d.	MW	1951	X	
10"h.	DRR*	1983	X	
13"h.	A, BB, OG	1967	X	
	AG	1970	X	
	BWB, GS, LG	1964	X	
	DRR*	1983	X	
	GS, MW	1961	X	
14"h.	C	1982	X	
	MW	1956	X	
15"h.	MW	1955	X	
Open.				
12"d., 9"h., flared bowl.	A, BB, OG	1967	X	
	GS	1961	X	
	MW	1983	X	

*Distributed by Levay Distributing Company, Edwardsville, Illinois.

blunt, rounded teeth. The glass has a glossy sheen not found in originals and is thicker at the bottom of the bowl.

In 1951, the Westmoreland Glass Company of Grapeville, Pennsylvania, issued the No.556 6½-inch-diameter round, flat covered butter dish illustrated in Fig. 338. Similar to the original covered butter dish, it was made from a new mold in antique green, milk white, and green and purple marble glass. At the same time, the milk-white 6½-inch diameter covered compote was made by attaching a standard or stem to the No.556 bowl (Figs. 339 and 340). From 1951 through 1983, at least seven items were made from new molds and added to the line (see Chart 91). As you can see from this chart, none of these items was produced in clear glass. At least four items (the high-standard banana stand, the low-standard cake stand, and the 10- and 13-inch high-standard covered compotes)

were produced in deep rich ruby as late as 1983 and distributed as preferred seconds by the Levay Distributing Company of Edwardsville, Illinois.

In 1966, the Indiana Glass Company of Dunkirk, Indiana, introduced a similar Sawtooth pattern, enumerated in Chart 90. Unmarked items in this pattern, known as Indiana's Diamond Point (Figs. 341 and 342), were made from new molds and offered in blue satin, clear, and clear with cranberry stain nonflint glass. Unlike originals, reproductions are poorly molded and the glass has a distinct yellowish cast. Although they are heavy like originals, reproductions will not resonate when tapped. The most obvious difference, however, may be found in the shapes of reproductions, which do not emulate known antique forms. Although copies are not permanently marked, you may often find items with paper labels.

Fig. 341. New No.3876 Sawtooth clear covered chalice. Indiana Glass Co. Circa 1982. Unmarked.

Fig. 342. Reproduction clear nonflint Sawtooth goblet. Indiana Glass Co. Circa 1982. Unmarked.

In general, reproductions are slick, the diamond point design is noticeably blunt, and the scallops at the rim are noticeably round and smooth.

Hint: Sawtooth reproductions are thicker than originals and the design is blunt and smooth.

SHELL AND TASSEL

Shell and Tassel is one of the aristocrats of early American pattern glass. Curiously, two versions of this pattern were produced originally—the square form and the round form. Square items are more fanciful than those in the round. The pattern consists of shell corners, stippled drapery, and tassels. Finials are stippled shells (Figs. 343 and 344.)

In contrast, round items are less fanciful, although the pattern is basically the same. Forms are round with square handles, the design is smaller, and much of the clear glass is unpatterned. Moreover, the finials are reclining dogs. Apparently, few round items were produced since the only pieces we have encountered are the four-piece table set, celery vase, water pitcher, and footed double-handled sauce dish.

Also known as Shell and Tassel-Round, Shell and Tassel-Square, and Shell and Spike, this design was patented by Augustus H. Heisey on July 26, 1881, under design patents No.12371 and No.12372. In the same year, Shell and Tassel Square was produced in an extended table service by the firm of George Duncan & Sons of Pittsburgh, Pennsylvania, from a good-quality clear nonflint glass. Although you may find odd pieces in the square in amber,

Fig. 343. George Duncan & Sons 1881 catalog excerpt illustrating the original Shell and Tassel bread plate.

Fig. 344. George Duncan & Sons 1881 catalog excerpt illustrating the two styles of Shell and Tassel water pitchers. (The round shape is on the left and the square is on the right.)

Fig. 345. Reproduction Shell and Tassel clear goblet. L.G. Wright Glass Co. Circa 1969–70. Unmarked.

blue, and canary yellow, any colored item is rare.

In the late 1930s, new clear goblets appeared in Shell and Tassel. They are unmarked and made from new molds. Compared to originals, reproductions are noticeably yellowed and heavy and have a distinct waviness in the glass around the rim and base. In 1969, the L.G. Wright Glass Company of New Martinsville, West Virginia, issued the 6½-inch-high goblet illustrated in Fig. 345. Known as Wright's No.77-106 Shell and Tassel goblet, it was also produced from a new mold. Like earlier copies, Wright goblets are unmarked and share the same discrepancies as earlier reproduction goblets.

At one time, Ruth Webb Lee suggested that you could detect a reproduction goblet by looking through the clear area in the center of the design between the shell ornaments for a waviness in the glass. However, because new goblets have been in production since Mrs. Lee's observation, this test is no longer always valid.

Reproductions are quite convincing. However, upon close examination, you will notice that new goblets are off-colored and look yellowed or grayed. Reproductions also have a distinct waviness in the glass, which you can detect around the base and clear portion of the bowl. This waviness often produces a crinkled effect on the surface of the glass. Because new goblets are thick-walled, they are also heavier than original goblets.

Reproduction Shell and Tassel goblets are not permanently marked.

Hint: Reproduction goblets tend to have a waviness to the glass, which is not noticeable in the old.

Reproduced items: Goblet.

S-REPEAT

S-Repeat is a simple yet pleasing design that consists of a horizontal row of large, clear stylized figures that resemble an "S." The glass is brilliant and clear and handles are pressed. This pattern was originally produced in a limited number of table pieces by the National Glass Company at its Northwood factory in Indiana, Pennsylvania. The Dugan Glass Company most likely continued production after 1903. Original colors are blue and white opalescent and solid amethyst, apple green, blue, and clear (plain or gold-decorated).

From as late as 1968, a number of items have been reproduced in S-Repeat in contemporary and original colors and forms. From 1968 through 1984, the L.G. Wright Glass Company of New Martinsville, West Virginia, issued the six items enumerated in Chart 90. Known as Wright's "S" pattern, each item is unmarked and was produced from a new mold. With the exception of the No.77-110 punch cup, each form also corresponds to an original (Figs. 346 and 347).

Between 1974 and 1978, Kanawha Glass Company of Kanawha, West Virginia, issued a second version of the S-Repeat toothpick holder (Fig. 348). Known as Kanawha's No.811 or Scroll pattern, this new toothpick holder stands 2½ inches high. Kanawha also produced its toothpick from a new

Fig. 346. Reproduction S-Repeat No.77-34 amethyst goblet. L.G. Wright Glass Co. Circa 1968. Unmarked.

mold in the original color of clear and the contemporary colors of amber, azure, and milk white. Kanawha reproductions are not permanently marked but originally carried a paper label.

In 1985, the Summit Art Glass Company

CHART 92   S-REPEAT. L.G. Wright Glass Company, New Martinsville, West Virginia.
CMN: "S" Pattern.
Mark: Unmarked.
Color Code: A Amber, AM Amethyst, B Blue, BM Blue Milk, COB Cobalt Blue, CUS Custard, G Green, RBY Ruby.

ITEM	COLOR(S)	YEAR	ORIG	NEW
Cruet, #77-12. Bulbous base, flat, ground clear stopper.	A, B, G, RBY	1968	X	
Cup, punch, #77-110.	CUS	1969		X
Goblet, #77-34. 8 oz., 6"h.	A, AM, G, RBY	1968	X	
	B	1984	X	
Toothpick holder.				
#77-12. Original shape.	B, G, RBY	1969	X	
#77-63.	A, AM, B, BM, COB, CUS	1969	X	
	G	1969	X	
Wine, #77-71. 4 oz., 4¼"h.	A, AM, G, RBY	1968	X	
	B	1984	X	

77-71
Wine
A, G, Am, R.

Fig. 347. New S-Repeat No.77-71 amethyst wine. L.G. Wright Glass Co. Circa 1968. Unmarked.

Fig. 348. Reproduction amber S-Repeat No.811 toothpick holder. Kanawha Glass Co. Circa 1975. Unmarked.

of Akron, Ohio, issued a third version of this toothpick holder, known as No.569. This new toothpick holder stands 2¾ inches high and was also produced from a new mold. Unlike Wright and Kanawha reproductions, new toothpick holders by Summit are not known in any original colors. Contemporary colors include amberina, blue-green, chocolate, coral iridized, cobalt blue, evergreen, first frost, morning glory, and rubina. Summit toothpick hold-

ers are not permanently marked but originally carried a paper label.

In general, reproductions are quite heavy and have an uneven thickness most noticeable around their rim. Compared to originals, the pattern on new items is small, often blurred, and poorly pressed. The glass is often crinkled or wavy and feels slick or oily. The easiest way to detect new items is by color. Unlike the rich, mellow flavor of original colors, the color of reproductions is artificial, harsh, and dissimilar to any known original. This is especially true of items reproduced in the original colors of apple green, blue, and amethyst.

Hint: Reproductions are heavier and colors are harsher than originals.

STARS AND STRIPES

The original name of this pattern is Federal's No.209 and Kokomo's No.209 or Climax. Also known as Brilliant or Late Climax, the design was originally produced about 1900 by the Kokomo Glass Manufacturing Company of Kokomo, Indiana. The Federal Glass Company of Columbus, Ohio, reissued the pattern about 1914.

Stars and Stripes is a simple pattern. Clear vertical, convex panels alternate with thinner, tapered concave panels decorated with diamond cut. The pattern was produced in an extended table service from a mediocre-grade clear nonflint glass. Clear with ruby stain or any other color is rare. Items are round, with the exception of the flat, rectangular confection trays and bowls.

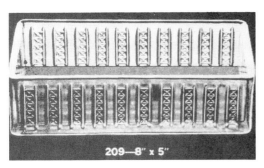

Fig. 349. Reissued No.209 Stars and Stripes clear open confection tray. D.C. Jenkins Glass Co. Circa 1930s. Unmarked.

Fig. 350. Reissue of the Stars and Stripes clear wine. D.C.
Jenkins Glass Co. Circa 1930s. Unmarked.

During the 1930s, the D.C. Jenkins Glass
Company of Kokomo, Indiana, reissued
four items in its No.209 or Stars and
Stripes line. Illustrated in its circa 1933
catalog are the 8-inch by 5-inch clear flat,
open confection tray (Fig. 349), the cordial, the pressed-handle hotel mug, and
the wine (Fig. 350). Each of these items
was made from an original mold in clear
nonflint glass.

Because Jenkins reissues were produced
from original molds, the quality of the glass
is the only appreciable difference between
originals and reissues. Although reissues
are the same weight and height as originals,
they have a distinct grayish cast. Reissues
are not as finely finished as originals (as evidenced by the excessive glass readily seen
on mold lines and edges of the pattern). Because reissues were produced from a lesser
grade of glass, the glass is also bubbly and
contains annealing lines not apparent in earlier items.

Reissues in Stars and Stripes should not
be considered reproductions; they were
merely produced by the original manufacturer from original molds at a later date.

Hint: Stars and Stripes reissues are made
from a lower grade of glass than the originals.
Reproduced items: Bowl, cordial, mug,
wine.

STIPPLED STAR

As a symbol of statehood, it is only natural
to find the star in a variety of pressed-glass
designs. One such pattern, currently known
as Stippled Star, was designed and patented
by William F. Gillinder on March 22, 1870,
under design patent No.3914. Gillinder &
Sons of Philadelphia issued it the same year
as Star.

Stippled Star was originally produced in
an extended table service from a good-quality clear nonflint glass. The design consists
of rows of highly embossed clear stars on a
finely stippled background. Each row of
stars diminishes in size toward the base.
Handles are beautifully applied and crimped.

From 1969 through 1984, the L.G. Wright
Glass Company of New Martinsville, West
Virginia, issued the seven items from new
molds in Stippled Star enumerated in Chart
93. Only three of these items (the No.59-8
fairy lamp, the No.59-5 salt dip, and the
No.59-4 toothpick holder) have contempo-

CHART 93 STIPPLED STAR. L.G. Wright Glass Company, New Martinsville, West Virginia.
CMN: Star.
Mark: Unmarked.
Color Code: A Amber, AM Amethyst, AMB Amberina, B Blue, C Clear, G Green, RBY Ruby.

ITEM	COLOR(S)	YEAR	ORIG	NEW
Creamer. #59-3.	C, G	1969	X	
Goblet. #59-6. 9 oz., 6¼"h.	A, AM, B, C, G, RBY	1968	X	
	AMB	1974	X	
Lamp. #59-8. Fairy.	A, B, G, RBY	1976		X
Salt dip. #59-5. 2"d.	A, AM, B, G, RBY	1968		X
	C	1969		X
Sugar bowl, covered.	A, AM, B, C, G, RBY	1968	X	
Toothpick holder. #59-4. Round, footed, scalloped rim.	A, AM, B, G, RBY	1969		X
Wine. #59-7. 3½ oz., 4½"h.	A, B, C, G, RBY	1968	X	

rary shapes. The remainder are direct copies of original pieces.

Known as Star, Wright reproductions are unmarked and were produced from new molds in clear and contemporary colors (Fig. 351). New items may seem quite confusing. However, upon close examination, you will notice a number of subtle differences. Compared to originals, the stippling on new items is light and even, the stars are much larger, and mold lines are more pronounced. Reproductions are also noticeably thick and heavy and the glass is slick and glossy. The most obvious difference between them is that all the stars on reproductions are equal in size, while those on original items diminish in size toward the base.

You can also distinguish Wright's reproduction goblets from the originals by comparing their measurements. For example, original goblets measure 6 inches high with a diameter of 3¼ inches at the bowl and at the base. In comparison, Wright's reproductions measure 6¼ inches high with a diameter of 3¾ inches at the bowl and 3⅛ inches at the base.

Reproduction goblets also have thicker stems and bases than those of original goblets. And, although the bowls of both goblets each contain four rows of stars, the lowest row on reproductions extends almost to the base where the stem attaches to the bowl.

Fig. 351. Reproduction blue Stippled Star goblet. L.G. Wright Glass Co. Circa 1968. Unmarked.

Hint: Stippled Star items in any color other than clear are reproductions.

STORK

Stork is one of the more puzzling designs in the bird series. It is also known as Clear Flamingo, Crane, Frosted Flamingo, and Frosted Stork. As Ruth Webb Lee points out in her work on pattern glass, the bird more closely resembles a crane than a stork. However, this pattern has been called Stork for so many years that there is little reason to consider a name change.

Stork is a product of the early 1880s. For years it has been attributed to the Crystal Glass Company of Bridgeport, Ohio, which produced a limited number of table pieces from a good-quality clear and clear and frosted nonflint glass.

The design consists of large medallions in which a stork or crane appears in varying positions in the landscape. On many pieces, these medallions are separated by a spray of flowers. Finials are well-sculpted storks.

An interesting addition to the pattern (found on plates, trays, and covered sugar bowls) is the One-O-One border. This border also appears on similar items attributed to the short-lived Iowa City Flint Glass Manufacturing Company of Iowa City, Iowa.

To date, three items have been reproduced in Stork. As late as 1975, the A.A. Importing Company, Inc., of St. Louis, Missouri, introduced the No.PG/1637 Stork oval bread plate illustrated in Fig. 352. These unmarked bread plates were produced from a new mold in clear, clear with

frosted centers, and most likely other contemporary colors. They are 11¾ inches long and carry the customary One-O-One border.

Fig. 353 is a closeup of the new Stork bread plate. When you encounter this plate, you will readily notice that it is heavy and thick and that the design is poorly pressed, exaggerated, and lacks detail. Also, the glass is distinctly yellow and feels slick or oily. The frosting is also light, poorly applied, blotchy, and streaked. The most obvious difference between new and old plates

Fig. 353. Closeup of the A.A. Importing Co., Inc., reproduction Stork bread plate.

Fig. 354. Reproduction Stork No.PG/1638 vaseline spoonholder offered by the A.A. Importing Co., Inc., in 1982. Unmarked.

Fig. 352. Reproduction Stork No.PG/1637 clear and frosted oval bread plate offered by the A.A. Importing Co., Inc. Circa 1975. Unmarked.

is the small One-O-One border and lettering on reproductions.

By 1982, A.A. Importing introduced the 5¼-inch-high spoonholder (No.PG/1638) in clear and vaseline. Both the bread plate and the spoonholder were imported from Taiwan or Korea. Like reproduction bread plates, this spoonholder is also unmarked and was produced from a new mold (Fig. 354). This reproduction is a good copy of the original. However, it is also thick and heavy and shares the same discrepancies as the bread plate.

In 1977, the Summit Art Glass Company of Akron, Ohio, issued the No.540 Stork goblet in amber, blue, and clear. At the same time, the L.G. Wright Glass Company of New Martinsville, West Virginia, issued its

No.77-114 Stork goblet in clear. Both reproduction goblets were produced from new molds and, like new bread plates and spoonholders, are noticeably heavy. The design is also exaggerated and the glass is noticeably slick.

Although Wright reproductions are not permanently marked, Summit goblets are pressed with a "V" within a circle and originally carried a gold and black paper label. By June 1978, the Summit Stork goblet had been discontinued in all colors.

Hint: Stork reproductions are heavy, the frosting is harsh, and the pattern detail is poor.

Reproduced items: Bread plate, goblet, spoonholder.

STRAWBERRY

Judging from the many available patterns, a favorite design of the mold maker centered around the fruit motifs, which adorned much of the pressed-glass tableware throughout the nineteenth century. It is with little wonder, then, that John Bryce designed the Strawberry pattern, which he patented on February 22, 1870 (design patent No.3855).

Also known as Fairfax Strawberry, Strawberry was first produced by Bryce, Walker & Company of Pittsburgh, Pennsylvania, about 1870 in flint and nonflint glass. Although better known in milk white than in clear glass, limited table services originally were made in both color treatments from a good-quality glass.

This pattern is exciting and vibrant. Large stippled strawberries, vines, and leaves are entwined around the clear bowls and covers of each item, while well-molded strawberries are used as finials. Characteristic of fine old pattern glass, the design is finely detailed and pressed in high relief, as illustrated in Fig. 355. Handles are beautifully applied and crimped. In addition, clear items sparkle brilliantly, while those in milk white often display an opal color.

In the mid-1970s, a number of well-mean-

Fig. 355. Closeup of the original Strawberry pattern designed and patented by John Bryce.

ing glass authors, including Metz, Unitt, and Warman, listed the Strawberry eggcup and goblet as being reproductions in clear and color. We believe that all three authors erroneously listed Inverted Strawberry or Strawberry and Currant goblets and wines (both in production at this time) as the infamous Strawberry eggcup and goblet reproductions. Rather than correcting this error,

Metz and Unitt dropped the Strawberry pattern from reproduction status in subsequent revisions of their books and no further mention was made of either item.

To date, we have been unable to substantiate any reproductions in this pattern. However, a prudent approach to suspect items is to compare carefully detail, quality, and weight.

Hint: Strawberry reproductions are unconfirmed and you should carefully examine suspect items.

Reproduced items: Eggcup, goblet.

STRAWBERRY AND CURRANT

Strawberry and Currant is a popular member of the fruit series of pattern glass. This design was originally known as Dalzell's No.9D and was first issued in the early 1890s by Dalzell, Gilmore & Leighton Company of Findlay, Ohio. Throughout the years, it has also become known as Multiple Fruits or Currant and Strawberry.

Strawberry and Currant was originally produced in an extended table service from a good quality of brilliant, clear nonflint glass. The pattern consists of currants, a pear, and strawberries pressed in high relief against a clear background. The arrangement of fruit varies depending upon the item. This variation is especially apparent on the covered butter dish. Here the straw-

berries are found on the base, while the currant and the pear are on the cover.

About 1940, unmarked reproduction goblets were first seen. These new goblets were available in clear and the contemporary colors of amber, blue, and yellow. As you can see from Figs. 356 and 357, reproductions may be quite convincing. However, upon close observation, you will discover that, because these new goblets were produced from a new mold, the pattern is crude and poorly detailed. The glass is thick and heavy and, unlike the old, displays an obvious newness.

In its 1968 catalog, The L.G. Wright Glass Company of New Martinsville, West Virginia, illustrated three items in Strawberry and Currant: the No.72-5 6½-inch-diameter high-standard open compote with ruffled

Fig. 356. Comparison of the design on original and reproduction Strawberry and Currant goblets. (The reproduction is on the right.)

Fig. 357. Comparison of the design of original and reproduction Strawberry and Currant. (The reproduction is on the right.)

Fig. 359. Comparison of the design of original and reproduction Strawberry and Currant. (The reproduction is on the right.)

rim, the No.77-36 8-ounce, 6½-inch-high goblet (Fig. 358), and the No.77-68 2½-ounce, 4¾-inch-high wine. Each of these reproductions was available in solid amber, amethyst, blue, clear, green, ruby, and vaseline. In addition, the No.77-36 goblet was offered in blue opalescent. In 1969, these items were available in cobalt blue and vaseline opalescent. And in 1971, the goblet was available in amber satin.

Compared to original items in Strawberry and Currant, the foot on reproductions is always smaller. The leaves and stems on reproductions are exaggerated and so highly

Fig. 358. Reproduction Strawberry and Currant No.77-36 clear goblet. L.G. Wright Glass Co. Circa 1968. Unmarked.

veined as to appear stippled. Unlike the well-defined pear and strawberry motifs on old pieces, the pear on new items is ovoid and resembles a long branch. And at the base of the original design is a V-shaped branch that is attached to the leaf directly under the pear. On new items, this branch is a straight line that stops about $\frac{1}{16}$ of an inch from the leaf (Fig. 359). On old items, the currants are large and arranged in a natural cluster; at the base of the bowl there is a clear raised and scalloped solid band. On reproductions, this band is divided into panels that flow to the bottom of the bowl, where the stem attaches. On old items, moreover, the rim of the bowl is smooth and finely molded, while the rim on new items exhibits a noticeable ridge that extends ¼ inch into the bowl.

In the late 1970s, the footed creamer appeared in amber. Although this new creamer has yet to be documented in any known trade catalog, the glass shows all the signs of being a product of the L.G. Wright Glass Company and was most likely produced from the new goblet mold.

Reproductions in Strawberry and Currant are unmarked as to manufacturer. In general, the glass is heavy, slick, and oily, the pattern is exaggerated and poorly pressed, and the foot is smaller than that of originals.

Hint: On Strawberry and Currant reproductions, the fruit and branches are overly exaggerated compared to the originals.

Reproduced items: Creamer, compote, goblet, wine.

SWAG WITH BRACKETS

Swag with Brackets is an interesting design that consists of four equidistant brackets that protrude from the body of most items. Between each pair of brackets is a swagged design suggestive of drapery. On such pieces as the covered butter dish and cruet, each bracket is replaced by a flat, round daisy from which the same drapery hangs. Water tumblers have neither bracket nor drapery. With the exception of the cruet (which is blown), a leaf motif extends upward from the base of each of four feet into the body. The same design is on the cruet, but it rises from a flat base.

Swag with Brackets was originally produced about 1903 in a limited number of table pieces by the Jefferson Glass Company of Steubenville, Ohio. Original colors are opalescent blue, canary, green, white, solid crystal, amethyst, blue, and yellow-green (all plain or gold-decorated).

Prior to 1978, the Crystal Art Glass Company of Cambridge, Ohio, under the direction of Elizabeth Degenhart, reproduced the Swag with Bracket toothpick holder illustrated in Fig. 360. Known as Crystal's Colonial Drape pattern, it was produced from a new mold in amber, amethyst (dark and light), aqua, crystal, cobalt, Crown Tuscan, custard, custard light, forest green, milk blue, milk white, opalescent, ruby, sapphire (dark and light), sunset, taffeta, and vaseline.

After Elizabeth Degenhart died in April 1978, the Crystal Art Glass Company was purchased by Bernard Boyd of Cambridge, Ohio. Known as Boyd's Crystal Art Glass Company, Boyd continued to reproduce the Swag with Bracket toothpick holder under the name of Colonial Drape. Using the same mold as the Degenharts, he offered it in candy swirl, chocolate, delphinium, deep purple, heather, ice green, impatient, lemon

Fig. 360. New Swag with Brackets amethyst toothpick holder. Crystal Art Glass Co. Circa 1975. Unmarked.

ice, Mardi Gras, persimmon, purple variant, rubina, and tinkerbell. Beginning in 1978, each new toothpick holder was permanently embossed with a "B" within a diamond (signifying Boyd).

New toothpick holders are glossy, thick, and heavy and the glass is distinctly slick. Unlike original toothpick holders, which are permanently gilded with gold, reproductions are painted with a bright, shiny gold that peels easily.

The easiest way to determine originals from reproductions is by comparing the serrated tops. On originals, the serrations are smooth and rounded and the tops are slightly flared; on the reproductions, the serrations are extremely sharp and the tops are straight-sided.

To date, there are no known reproduction toothpick holders in opalescent glass.

Hint: Original toothpick holders have smooth, rounded tops compared to the sharp serrated top of reproductions.
Reproduced items: Toothpick holder.

SWAN

Swan is one of the most attractive patterns of the figural series of pressed glass. Also known as Plain Swan, it was designed and patented by D. Barker on

April 18, 1882 (design patent No.12887). Although Swan was first issued about 1882, the original manufacturer is not known.

This pattern was produced in a limited table service from a good-quality clear non-

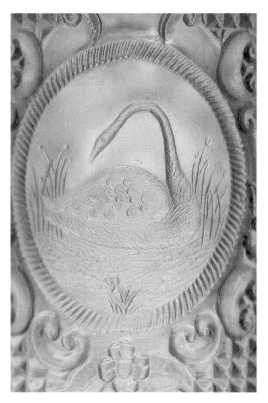

Fig. 361. Closeup of the original Swan pattern designed and patented by D. Barker.

flint glass. Although you may find odd items in amber, deep blue, and yellow, any colored item is rare. As you can see from Fig. 361, Swan is a lovely design of large clear ovals against a fine mesh background. Within each oval there is a well-defined swan with its head facing backward. A similar figure of a swan forms the finials of covered pieces, and handles are pressed.

To date, allegedly only the goblet has been reproduced. In their book *American and Canadian Goblets,* Doris and Peter Unitt picture an unmarked Swan goblet supposedly reproduced in a number of colors. However, without positive catalog identification, this reproduction is impossible to confirm. A prudent approach to purchasing suspect items is to compare carefully detail, quality, and weight.

Hint: Swan reproductions are unconfirmed and you should carefully examine suspect items.

Reproduced items: Goblet.

SYDNEY

Sydney is one of the many geometric patterns in glass design. It is a late pattern consisting of varying cut glass motifs. Fostoria Glass Company of Moundsville, West Virginia, produced this pattern about 1905 in an extended table service in a medium-grade clear nonflint glass.

Sydney is a safe pattern to collect. The only known reproduction is the 5½-inch covered butter dish in milk white illustrated in Fig. 362. The Imperial Glass Corporation of Bellaire, Ohio, produced this butter dish in 1956 as No.1950/59. Imperial's covered butter dish is not as crisply pressed as the original. Although possibly produced from the original mold, this re-

1950/59
5½" Jar & Cover,
(Peanut, Mint, or Butter)

Fig. 362. Reproduction Sydney milk-white covered butter dish. Imperial Glass Corp. Circa 1956. Embossed "IG."

production has a weightiness not apparent in the old.

You need only remember that this pattern was originally produced in clear glass. Milk white or any other color is contemporary. When marked, the new butter is permanently embossed with the Imperial "IG" logo.

Hint: Milk white or any other color is contemporary.

Reproduced items: Butter dish.

TEXAS

Also known as Loop with Stippled Panels, the original name of this pattern is No.15067 or Texas. It was first issued from a good-quality clear nonflint glass by the United States Glass Company of Pittsburgh, Pennsylvania, about 1900 at Factory "B" (Bryce Brothers, Pittsburgh) and Factory "F" (Ripley & Company of Pittsburgh). Original colors are clear, clear with ruby stain, and clear with rose blush (plain or gold-trimmed).

The design consists of a row of large clear loops. The center of each loop is decorated with fine cross-hatching. Finials carry the same design. Handles may be either applied or pressed. Texas was produced in an extended table service in each color treatment (Fig. 363).

In 1962, the Crystal Art Glass Company of Cambridge, Ohio (under the direction of Elizabeth Degenhart), reproduced the Texas individual creamer and double-handled true open sugar bowl. Although it is not known who created the mold for the reproduction creamer, B Mold & Machine of Cambridge, Ohio, created the mold for an open sugar bowl that is compatible to the creamer. Each reproduction was produced in a limited run in amber, amber dark, amethyst, amberina, aqua, blue bell, clear, carnival amethyst, carnival, carnival dark cobalt, cobalt, Cambridge, Crown Tuscan, custard, emerald green, milk blue, milk white, opalescent, peach blo, pine green, red, ruby, sapphire, vaseline, white, and willow blue.

From 1962 through 1972, new items were marked with a hand stamp. From 1972 until Elizabeth Degenhart's death in 1978, reproductions were permanently marked "D"

Fig. 363. Reprint of a United States Glass Co. catalog illustrating an assortment of No.15067 or Texas.

Fig. 364. Reproduction Texas wine in willow blue offered in 1987 by the Degenhart Paperweight and Glass Museum. Embossed with a "D" inside an underlined heart.

Crystal Art Glass Company. He then issued the Texas individual creamer and open sugar bowl in delphinium and changed the mark to an embossed "B" within a diamond (signifying Boyd).

In 1987, the Degenhart Paperweight and Glass Museum, Inc., commissioned the Island Mold and Machine Co., Inc., of Wheeling, West Virginia, to manufacture a mold for reproducing the Texas wine illustrated in Fig. 364. This reproduction was also produced by Boyd's Crystal Art Glass and is permanently marked with a "D" inside an underlined heart. The museum offered two versions of the new wine: those with flared bowls were offered in cobalt blue and willow blue, and those with straight bowls were offered in clear.

Compared to the original items in Texas, reproductions are heavier, the glass is notably glossy and slick, and the design is not as crisply impressed.

Hint: Original items in Texas were never made in solid colors other than clear.

Reproduced items: Individual creamer, individual sugar bowl, wine.

within a heart (signifying Crystal Art Glass). After Degenhart's death, Bernard Boyd of Cambridge, Ohio, acquired ownership of the

TEXAS STAR

Texas Star is an attractive pattern that is part of the clear and frosted grouping of pattern glass. This design is also known as Star Base Swirl, Swirl and Star Base, and Texas Swirl. The Steimer Glass Company of Buckhannon, West Virginia, originally produced an extended table service from a good-quality clear nonflint glass about 1905.

This design is uncharacteristic of Victorian pattern glass. While most patterns are embossed in high relief on the surface of each item, this pattern is embossed into the base. The design is a large stylized star surrounded by smaller stars (Fig. 365). The entire base is machine-ground to produce a clear design under a blanket of frosting. Handles are applied.

Texas Star is a safe pattern to collect because, to date, only the wine has been repro-

Fig. 365. Closeup of the Texas Star design originally produced by the Steimer Glass Co. Circa 1905.

duced. This new wine is unmarked and was produced from a new mold. Made in amberina, clear, and clear with frosted glass, it is exceptionally thick and heavy and the glass is noticeably shiny and slick. The frosting on clear reproductions is comparatively sat-

iny and smooth. Any colored wine is obviously new.

Hint: The frosting on reproductions is smooth; on originals it is coarse.
Reproduced items: Wine.

THISTLE

The thistle has long been a favorite among designers. Its appearance early in the history of pressed glass attests to this fact because thistles adorn some of the earliest pressed flint patterns.

Also known as Early Thistle and Scotch Thistle, Thistle was designed and patented by John Bryce on April 2, 1872, under design patent No.5742. In the same year, Bryce, McKee & Company of Pittsburgh, Pennsylvania, issued the pattern in an extended table service from a good-quality clear nonflint glass.

As stipulated in the original patent papers, the pattern consists of "a Scotch thistle, consisting of the stems, leaves and flowers, so connected and repeated as to form a wreath" covering the article. The design is finely stippled and stands in high relief against an otherwise clear background (see Fig. 366). Handles are beautifully applied, and well-sculpted thistle buds form the knobs of covered pieces.

Fig. 367. Reproduction Thistle goblet in clear with cranberry stained rim. Circa early-1960s. Embossed "R" within a shield mark.

Thistle is a safe pattern to collect. To date, only the goblet has been reproduced (see Fig. 367). New, permanently marked goblets appeared in the early 1960s in clear, amber, blue, and clear with cranberry and ruby stain. Unlike original goblets, which measure $5\frac{5}{8}$ inches high, reproductions are smaller ($5\frac{5}{16}$ inches high). Original goblets have a short, thick stem that flares slightly at the base, while the stem on reproductions is longer, thinner, and more flared. The leaves on originals are long and thin, whereas they are short and chubby on reproductions. The pattern is weaker on reproductions and the thistle bud is more compact.

Reproductions are embossed on the bottom of the base with a clear "R" within a large shield.

Hint: Reproductions are heavier and smaller than originals.
Reproduced items: Goblet.

Fig. 366. Original Thistle clear goblet. Bryce, McKee and Co. Circa 1872.

THOUSAND EYE

The original names for this intriguing pattern are Adam's No.130 and Richards & Hartley's No.103. The design was first produced about 1874 by Adams & Company of Pittsburgh, Pennsylvania, and is characterized by finials and stems composed of three knobs. In 1880, Richards & Hartley of Tarentum, Pennsylvania, also issued Thousand Eye. To distinguish its product from Adams's, Richards & Hartley replaced the three-knob motif with plain stems, scalloped bases, and patterned finials. Both companies continued producing the pattern after they became members of the United States Glass Company in 1891 (Figs. 368 and 369).

Both versions of Thousand Eye were produced from a good-quality nonflint glass in a large and extended table service. Original colors are amber, blue, clear, green, and vaseline. In addition, Richards & Hartley issued a limited number of items in white opalescent.

This design consists of rows of blunt hobnails that diminish in size toward the base. Between each grouping of four hobnails you will also find a small, sharp four-sided diamond. Exceptions to this are the cart-shaped master salt, the covered honey dish, and the syrup pitcher, which do not have the diamonds.

New, unmarked goblets, 8-inch-square plates, cruets, twine holders, and water tumblers appeared as early as 1940 in the original colors of amber, apple green, blue,

canary yellow, and clear. They were followed by reproduction hat match holders, mugs, toothpick holders, and wines.

The Thousand Eye goblet is illustrated in the 1960 catalog of the B&P Lamp Supply Company of McMinnville, Tennessee. This goblet was available in amber, apple green, and blue. As late as 1969, the L.G. Wright Glass Company of New Martinsville, West Virginia, offered the goblet and the No.46 fairy lamp in all the original colors and in the new color of ruby.

Original Thousand Eye goblets are more graceful than the new ones, and the detail is well executed. The bowl on reproductions flares, the hobnail motif is blunt and round, and the diamonds between the hobnails are large. Also, the stem is longer on reproductions, but the knob is smaller (Fig. 370). In fact, the simplest method of differentiating between old and new goblets is to measure the length of the stem. Old stems measure 2⅝ inches from the base of the bowl to the bottom of the foot. Reproductions measure a trifle over 2⅜ inches to a scant 2½ inches. You can find another difference in the edge directly above the upper row of hobnails. In the old, this edge is definitely indented, with a very decided arch. In the new, it is scarcely indented and the arch is not noticeable.

While goblets are the most difficult reproductions to detect, other forms are somewhat easier. On original plates, the eyes are heavy and the corners are carefully exe-

CHART 94 THOUSAND EYE. New Martinsville Glass Company and Viking Glass Company New Martinsville, West Virginia.
CMN: Ancestral.
Mark: Unmarked or paper label.
Color Code: A Amber, AMB Amberina, B Blue, C Clear, CY Canary Yellow, G Green, RBY Ruby.

ITEM	COLOR(S)	YEAR	ORIG	NEW
Bottle, perfume, ball-shaped.	A, AMB, B, CY, G, RBY	1950s		X
	C	1920s		X
Bowl, ivy, 3½"d.	A, AMB, B, CY, G, RBY	1950s		X
	C	1920s		X
Box, puff, covered.	A, AMB, B, CY, G, RBY	1950s		X
	C	1920s		X
Champagne, saucer bowl.	A, AMB, B, CY, G, RBY	1950s		X
	C	1920s		X
Cocktail.	A, AMB, B, CY, G, RBY	1950s		X
	C	1920s		X

ITEM	COLOR(S)	YEAR	ORIG	NEW
Compote.				
Crimped rim.				
5"d., 3¼"h.	A, AMB, B, CY, G, RBY	1950s		X
	C	1920s		X
6"d.	A, AMB, B, CY, G, RBY	1950s		X
	C	1920s		X
Plain rim, 5½"d., 3"h.	A, AMB, B, CY, G, RBY	1950s	X	
	C	1920s	X	
Cordial.	A, AMB, B, CY, G, RBY	1950s		X
	C	1920s		X
Cruet, ball stopper, applied handle.	A, AMB, B, CY, G, RBY	1950s	X	
	C	1920s	X	
Goblet.	A, AMB, B, CY, G, RBY	1950s		X
	C	1920s		X
Hat.				
2"h.	A, AMB, B, CY, G, RBY	1950s	X	
	C	1920s	X	
4"h.	A, AMB, B, CY, G, RBY	1950s		X
	C	1920s		X
Mug.	A, AMB, B, CY, G, RBY	1950s	X	
	C	1920s	X	
Sherbert, single knob stem.	A, AMB, B, CY, G, RBY	1950s		X
	C	1920s		X
Toothpick holder (same as whiskey).	A, AMB, B, CY, G, RBY	1950s	X	
	C	1920s	X	
Twine holder.	A, AMB, B, CY, G, RBY	1950s		X
	C	1920s		X
Tumbler.				
Iced tea.				
12 oz.	A, AMB, B, CY, G, RBY	1950s		X
	C	1920s		X
14 oz.	A, AMB, B, CY, G, RBY	1950s		X
	C	1920s		X
Juice, 5 oz.	A, AMB, B, CY, G, RBY	1950s		X
	C	1920s		X
Old-fashioned, 7 oz.	A, AMB, B, CY, G, RBY	1950s		X
	C	1920s		X
Water, 10 oz.	A, AMB, B, CY, G, RBY	1950s	X	
	C	1920s	X	
Whiskey, 2 oz.	A, AMB, B, CY, G, RBY	1950s	X	
	C	1920s	X	
Vase, crimped rim, 3"d.	A, AMB, B, CY, G, RBY	1950s		X
	C	1920s		X
Wine.	A, AMB, B, CY, G, RBY	1950s		X
	C	1920s		X

CHART 95 THOUSAND EYE. Westmoreland Glass Company, Grapeville, Pennsylvania.
CMN: Thousand Eye.
Mark: Unmarked or paper label.
Color Code: C Clear, CRS Clear with Ruby Stain.

ITEM	COLOR(S)	YEAR	ORIG	NEW
Ashtray, turtle-shaped.	C	1934		X
Basket, 8"l., flat, handled.	C	1934		X

TEM	COLOR(S)	YEAR	ORIG	NEW
Bowl.				
Belled, 11"d.	C	1934		X
Crimped, 11"d.	C	1934		X
Flared, 11"d.	C	1934		X
Triangular.	C	1934		X
	CRS	1960s		X
Two-handled, 10"d.	C	1934		X
	CRS	1960s		X
Box, covered, cigarette, turtle.	C	1934		X
Candlestick.				
Double.	C	1934		X
	CRS	1960s		
Single, 5"h.	C	1934		X
Claret, 5 oz.	C	1934		X
Cocktail, 3½ oz.	C	1934		X
Compote, 5"d.	C	1934		X
Cordial, 1 oz.	C	1934		X
Creamer	C	1934		X
	CRS	1960s		X
Cup and saucer set.	C	1934		X
Goblet, 8 oz.	C	1934		X
Mayonnaise, footed, with ladle.	C	1934		X
Nappy, round, 7½"d., handled.	C	1934		X
Parfait.	C	1934		X
Pitcher, pressed handle.	C	1934		X
Plate.				
6"d.	C	1934		X
7"d.	C	1934		X
8½"d.	C	1934		X
10"d.	C	1934		X
14"d.	C	1934		X
	CRS	1960s		X
Relish, sectioned.	C	1934		X
Salt shaker, footed.	C	1934		X
	CRS	1960s		X
Sauce, flat.	C	1934		X
Sherbert, footed.	C	1934		X
Sherry, 3 oz.	C	1934		X
Sugar, open, handled.	C	1934		X
	CRS	1960s		X
Tumbler.				
Flat.				
1½ oz., Whiskey.	C	1934		X
5 oz., Ginger ale.	C	1934		X
6 oz., Old-fashioned.	C	1934		X
8 oz., Water.	C	1934		X
12 oz., Iced tea.	C	1934		X
Footed.				
5 oz., Ginger ale.	C	1934		X
7 oz.	C	1934		X
9 oz., Water.	C	1934		X
12 oz., Iced tea.	C	1934		X
Wine, 2 oz.	C	1934		X

Fig. 368. Reprints from a United States Glass Co. catalog illustrating an assortment of Richard & Hartley's No.103 or Thousand Eye, including a rare twine holder and two differently shaped toothpick holders.

Fig. 369. Reprint of a Spelman Brothers circa 1885 catalog illustrating an assortment of No.210 or Thousand Eye. (The covered honey does not carry the diamond motif.)

Fig. 370. Reproduction Thousand Eye apple green goblet. Unmarked. New goblets such as this have been offered by the B&P Lamp Supply Company and the L.G. Wright Glass Co. as late as 1960.

cuted. On reproductions, the eyes are impressed lightly and the corners are rounded slightly. Parfaits are modern. The cruets are shaped differently from the old ones and have rounded stoppers. The twine holder is also shaped differently from the original.

During the 1920s, the New Martinsville Glass Company of New Martinsville, West Virginia, issued the Ancestral pattern enumerated in Chart 94. Unmarked and produced from new molds, this design is quite similar to Thousand Eye in that both patterns are composed of rows of hobnail and small sharp diamonds. However, unlike the original Thousand Eye motif, the hobnail and diamond elements on Ancestral are blunt and flat, and items differ in shape. Exceptions are the hat and the flat water tumbler, which are shaped like the originals. During the early 1950s, the Viking Glass Company of New Martinsville, West Virginia, reissued Ancestral from the original molds in solid amber, amberina, blue, canary yellow, clear, green, and ruby.

Another pattern often confused for the earlier Thousand Eye design is known as Hundred Eye (see Chart 95), issued in 1934 by the Westmoreland Glass Company of Grapeville, Pennsylvania. The shapes in this pattern are completely different and the diamonds between the hobnails are three-sided instead of four-sided, like the diamonds in Thousand Eye. Produced in clear or clear with cranberry stain, items in Hundred Eye are not permanently marked.

Reproduction items in Thousand Eye are not permanently marked.

Hint: The diamond points on reproductions are blunt.

THREE FACE

Between 1870 and 1885, increased interest in clear and frosted glass in America culminated in the production of figural glassware. Due to the growing demand for this type of

tableware, it is no wonder that many leading manufacturers of pressed glass turned their attention to what would become some of the most desirable and expensive designs in early American pattern glass. Exemplified in such patterns as Classic, Lion, Three

CHART 96 THREE FACE. Imperial Glass Corporation, Bellaire, Ohio. "Metropolitan Museum of Art Classic Reproductions."
CMN: Three Face.
Mark: "MMA" embossed.
Color Code: CF Clear Frosted.

ITEM	COLOR(S)	YEAR	ORIG	NEW
Candlestick. #G1507A. 9"h., Petal socket.	CF	1980		X
Compote. #G1501E. High standard, open, 6"d., 4½"h.	CF	1985	X	
Cracker jar. #F1320. Covered, 9½"h.	CF	1975	X	
Cake stand. #F1500. High standard, 9½"d., 7¼"h.	CF	1978	X	
Champagne. #F1370. Saucer bowl.	CF	1978	X	
Salt shaker. #F1390. 3"h.	CF	1978	X	

CHART 97 THREE FACE. L.G. Wright Glass Company, New Martinsville, West Virginia.
CMN: Three Face.
Mark: Unmarked.
Color Code: AS Amber Satin, BS Blue Satin, CF Clear with Frosting.

ITEM	COLOR(S)	YEAR	ORIG	NEW
Compote, covered, high standard.				
#65-1. 6"d.	CF	1968	X	
#65-2. 4"d.	CF	1968	X	
Creamer. #65-11. Head under lip.	CF	1969	X	
Goblet. #65-3.	CF	1968	X	
Lamp. #65-4. Oil, plain font.	CF	1975	X	
Salt dip. #65-6. Individual.	CF	1968		X
Salt shaker. #65-7.	AS, BS, CF	1968	X	
Sauce dish. #65-8. Round, footed.	CF	1968	X	
Spoonholder. #65-15. Scalloped rim, footed.	CF	1969	X	
Sugar bowl. #65-12. Covered, footed.	CF	1969	X	
Sugar shaker. #65-14.	CF	1969		X
Toothpick holder. #65-9.	CF	1968		X
Wine. #65-10.	CF	1968	X	

Face, and Westward Ho, no other Victorian pressed glass so embodies the art, talent, and dedication of the designer and mold maker.

Three Face is one of the most exciting patterns in pressed glass. This pattern was designed and patented by John Ernest Miller (mold-shop superintendent with George Duncan & Sons from 1874 to 1891) on June 18, 1878 (design patent No.10727). George Duncan & Sons of Pittsburgh, Pennsylvania, first produced this line in an extended table service from a good-quality clear and frosted nonflint glass (Fig. 371). Although its original name was No.400 or Three Face, it is also known as Three Fates, Three Graces, and Three Sisters.

Fig. 371. Excerpt from an original George Duncan & Sons 1881 glass catalog illustrating the half-gallon Three Face water pitcher.

This delightful pattern consists of three finely sculpted faces that grace finials and stems. Although the remainder of each item is unpatterned, the addition of frosting and sometimes engraving heightened the total effect. Although the history of this pattern is well documented by trade journals in early 1878, little is known of the likeness of the face. Supposedly, this is the face of the designer's wife, Elizabeth Miller, based on family remembrance.

Today, there are many reproductions in Three Face. The first were goblets and 4½-inch sauce dishes, which appeared as early as 1939–40. Next came the 6-inch covered butter dish, and by 1945 all three styles of champagnes and the oil lamp with a scalloped foot and clear, round plain font. All are unmarked and were made from new molds. In her book *The Encyclopedia of Duncan Glass* (p. 95), Gail Krause states that "due to popular demand, the large comport (with or without the cover) was produced again by using a sandcast mold

from a Three-Face comport [compote]. This was done at a brake-shoe company located in Rochester, New York. The mold was assembled at the Washington Mold Company in Washington, Pennsylvania, at the end of the forties." Perhaps this compote is the same limited-edition compote advertised by the Duncan & Miller Glass Company of Washington, Pennsylvania, in the February 1953 issue of *Crockery and Glass Journal,* which according to the ad is "inconspicuously marked to designate it as a replica."

In 1968, the L.G. Wright Glass Company of New Martinsville, West Virginia, issued the twelve items enumerated in Chart 97 and illustrated in Figs. 372, 373, and 374. Like earlier copies, Wright reproductions were made from new molds, and with the exception of the salt dip, sugar shaker, and toothpick holder (which are all contempo-

Fig. 372. New Three Face No.65-3 clear and frosted goblet. L.G. Wright Glass Co. Circa 1971. Unmarked.

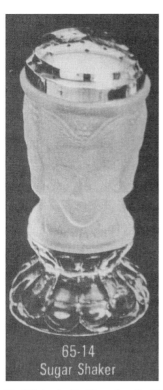

Fig. 373. Look-alike Three Face No.65-9 clear and frosted sugar shaker. L.G. Wright Glass Co. Circa 1971. (Sugar shakers were not originally made.) Unmarked.

Fig. 374. In 1971 the L.G. Wright Glass Co. offered this new No.65-11 Three Face creamer. Like the original, a head can be found under the lip of this copy. Unmarked.

rary), each new item is a direct copy of an original form. Unlike the remainder of this grouping, only the salt shaker was produced in the contemporary colors of amber and blue satin.

A similar toothpick holder was offered by the A.A. Importing Company, Inc., of St. Louis, Missouri. Known as the No.PG/1621 Three Face toothpick holder, it was first imported about 1976. It is 2⅜ inches high and may be easily found in the original color of clear with a satin finish. Although this item is not permanently marked, each replica was originally offered with a paper label that read "A.A. Importing Co., Inc., St. Louis, Missouri—Made in Korea."

Another series of reproductions was commissioned by the Metropolitan Museum of Art in New York City. Beginning in 1975, the museum, in conjunction with the Imperial Glass Corporation of Bellaire, Ohio, in-

troduced the first of several Three Face reproductions (see Chart 96). They were advertised as Imperial's "Metropolitan Museum of Art Glass Reproductions" and were made from a good-quality clear and frosted glass (Figs. 375 and 376). Only the candlestick, which is the base of the footed cake stand with the addition of a candle socket, is not an original form. Typical of Metropolitan glass reproductions, each item is permanently embossed with the "MMA" hallmark.

To date, only one lamp has been reproduced in Three Face. Wright's 10½-inch-high oil lamp with a plain font and a No.1 collar. You can easily detect new lamps by examining the font where the collar is attached. Unlike the sharp, uneven lip of original lamps, the lips on reproductions have been ground and polished smooth. Also, the necks of reproductions have two glass tabs that keep the collar in place.

Presumably, because the original molds for this pattern were destroyed when the

Fig. 375. Reproduction Three Face covered cracker jar by the Imperial Glass Corp. for the Metropolitan Museum of Art. Circa 1975. Embossed "MMA."

Fig. 376. Closeup of the final on the Three Face reproduction covered cracker jar. Unlike originals, the faces on reproductions are lifeless.)

Duncan plant in Pittsburgh burned in 1892, all reproductions are from new molds. Therefore, imitations all share a number of common imperfections. Unlike the smooth, soft, grayish-white frosting of original items, the frosting on reproductions is dull, too white and chalky, and has a coarse, rough texture. Whereas the glass of originals is brilliant and crystal clear, replicas vary from lightly tinged gray to a distinct yellow.

You can see the most obvious difference between old and new items, however, in the detail of the pattern. The design on original items is finely sculpted, as if chiseled from the glass. Here, the facial features are so distinct that they appear lifelike. Each detail is artistically proportioned and unmistakably visible. In contrast, reproductions are

poorly designed. Most conspicuously, the figure's hair, eyes, and nose are blurred and lack the obvious features of the old. On original items, the figure's hair is neatly molded and well defined, whereas on reproductions the hair is not detailed. Moreover, the eyes on replicas range from an Oriental slant to being completely absent. And, unlike the straight, classic nose on original pieces, the nose on reproductions tends to be crooked or misshapen.

As a general rule, reproductions are heavier than originals. Because they were not made from original molds, new items are also larger or smaller than their antique counterparts. Although most replicas are not signed, known marks include those of the Duncan & Miller Glass Company and the Metropolitan Museum of Art.

Hint: Reproductions lack the fine detailing found on originals.

THUMBPRINT

Originally known as Argus, Thumbprint was first produced about 1860 by Bakewell, Pears & Company of Pittsburgh, Pennsylvania, in an extended table service from a good-quality clear flint glass and later from nonflint glass. The pattern is also known as Argus-Thumbprint, Early Thumbprint, Heavy Argus, and Light Argus. Milk white or any other color in flint is rare.

Thumbprint is a simple yet pleasing design that consists of rows of large, elongated thumbprint-like indentations that cover the surface of each item. The glass is a brilliant clear and rings with a fine bell-tone when gently tapped. Due to the various manufacturers, bases, finials, handles, and standards vary. Handles may be either applied or pressed.

As late as 1960, the Imperial Glass Corporation of Bellaire, Ohio, reproduced the 6¼-inch-diameter high-standard covered compote (Fig. 377), the 6¼-inch-diameter low-standard covered compote, and the 4½-inch-diameter round, flat sauce dish in milk-white glass. The high-standard covered compote was offered in doeskin in 1962. In 1963 it was offered in the solid colors of amber, antique blue, ambergio, heather, purple

marble slag, and vaseline, and in 1971 in clear, clear with fired gold, and verde. In 1971, Imperial also added the 8¼-inch-high open compote in the contemporary colors of ambergio, clear, and verde. Each item was produced from a new mold, is permanently embossed "IG," and emulates a known antique form.

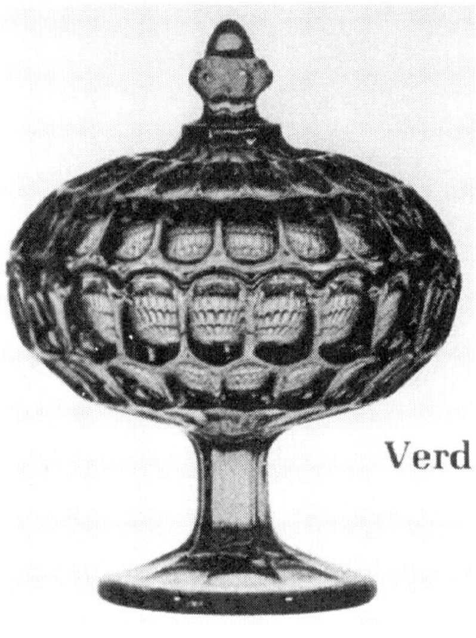

4484 CG
Anniversary Bowl

Fig. 378. Reproduction Thumbprint No.4484 high-standard covered compote. Fenton Art Glass Co. Circa 1962. Unmarked.

Verd

Fig. 377. Reproduction Thumbprint covered high-standard compote. Imperial Glass Corp. Circa 1963. Embossed "IG."

4486 CG
Oval Candy Box

Fig. 379. New No.4486 Thumbprint covered oval candy box. Fenton Art Glass Co. Circa 1962. Unmarked.

CHART 98 THUMBPRINT. Fenton Art Glass Company, Williamstown, West Virginia.
CMN: Thumbprint.
Mark: Unmarked, embossed "OV," or Fenton logo or paper label.
Color Code: CA Colonial Amber, CB Colonial Blue, CG Colonial Green, CP Colonial Pink, CY Clear, CRO Cased Ruby Overlay, EB Ebony, MW Milk White, OR Orange, RU Ruby.

ITEM	COLOR(S)	YEAR	ORIG	NEW
Ashtray, flat.				
#4469. Round, 6½"d.	CA, CB, CG	1964		X
	CP, OR, RU	1967		X
	EB	1968		X
#4476. Oval.	CA, CB, CG	1965		X
	CP	1963		X
#4479. Round, 7"d.	CA, CB, CG, CP	1964		X
Basket.				
#4430. Oval, 6½".*	MI	1960		X
#4434. 8"h.	CA, CB	1969		X
	MI	1969		X
#4437. Handled.*	MI	1960		X
#4438. Ruffled rim, 8½"h., applied crimped clear				
handle.*	CA, CB, CG, CP	1963		X
	EB	1968		X
	MI	1960		X
	OR	1964		X
	RU	1966		X
Bowl.				
Covered. #4486. 3-toed, oval.	CA, CB, CG, CP	1963		X
	MI	1958		X
Open.				
Flat. #4433. Scalloped rim.	CA, CB, CG, CP	1964		X
Low-footed.				
#4423.	CA, CB, CG, CP	1963		X
#4426. Ruffled rim, 8"d.	CA, CB, CG, CP, OR	1965		X
#4427. Ruffled rim, 12"d.*	CA, CB, CG, CP	1963		X
	EB	1969		X
	MI	1960		X
Butter dish, flat, covered.				
#4477. ¼-lb. Oval.	CA, CB, CG, CP, CY	1965		X
#4480. Round.*	MI	1960	X	
Cake stand.				
#4411. Low standard.	CA, CB, CG, CP	1964		X
#4413. Footed, 13"d., 5"h., ruffled rim.*	MI	1958		X
Candleholder.				
#4470. 4"h.	CA, CB, CG, CP, OR	1964		X
	EB, MW	1969		X
#4473. 8¼"h.*	CA, CB, CG, CP	1963		X
	MI	1960		X
#4474. Low.*	MI	1961		X
Candy jar. #4480. Covered.*	MI	1969		X
Candy Box. #4486. Covered, oval, 4-toed.	CA, CB, CG, CP	1965		X
Chalice. #4448. 8"h.	CA, CB, CG, CP, OR	1965	X	
Chip & dip set. #4404. 2-piece; 12"d. plate with rolled				
edges.*	CA, CB, CG, CP	1965		X
	MI	1958		X
Cigarette lighter. #4495.	CA, CB, CG, CP, OR, RU	1967		X
	EB	1968		X

ITEM	COLOR(S)	YEAR	ORIG	NEW
Compote.				
Covered.				
High standard. #4484.*	CA, CB, CG, CP	1963	X	
	MI	1956	X	
Low standard. #4488. 7"d.	CA, CB, CG, CP	1964		X
Open.				
High standard, knob stem.				
#4423. Ruffled rim.	CA, CB, CG, CP	1965		X
#4425. Footed, ruffled rim.	CA, CB, CG, CP, OR	1965		X
	EB	1968		X
#4428. Footed, plain stem.	MI	1958		X
	OR	1971		X
#4429. Ruffled rim.*	CA, CB, CP	1962		X
	CG	1963		X
	EB	1975		X
	OR	1964		X
	RU	1965		X
	MI	1961		X
Low footed, ruffled rim.	CA, CB, CG, CP, OR	1965		X
Creamer. #4403. Pressed handle.*	CA, CB, CG, CP	1963		X
	MI	1958		X
Dish. #4435. Bonbon, 8"d., Flat, round.	CA, CB, CG, CP	1964		X
Epergne. #4401. 3-lily, 4-piece, 9"h. with ruffled rim.*	CA, CB, CG, CP	1964		X
	MI	1958		X
Goblet. #4445. Knob stem, 10 oz.*	CA, CB, CG, CP	1962	X	
	MI	1961	X	
	OR	1965	X	
	RU	1966	X	
Lamp, student with matching shade.				
#1408. 20½"h.	CA, CG, CRO	1966		X
#1410. 19½"h.	CA, CG, CRO	1966		X
Lavabo. #4467. 2-piece, 13½"h.*	MI	1956		X
Pitcher, water.				
#4464. Ice lip, 2-quart.	CA, CB, CG, CP	1964		X
#4465. Plain lip, 34 oz.	CA, CB, CG, CP	1965		X
#4466. Bulbous, applied handle, 60 oz.	CA, CB, CP	1968		X
Planter, hanging.				
#4405.*	MI	1960		X
#4490. 10".*	MI	1960		X
#4497. Square. 4¼"sq., 4"h.*	MI	1969		X
Plate. #4417. Round, 8½"d.	CA, CB, CG, CP	1963		X
	RU	1966		X
Punch set. #4406. 2-piece bowl, 12 cups and ladle. (patterned base; nonpatterned bowl.)	MI	1958		X
Relish. #4416. Four-part, divided, 8½"d.	CA, CB, CG	1966		X
Salt shaker.				
#4408. Bulbous base.*	CA, CB, CG, CP	1963		X
	MI	1958		X
#4409. Footed, tall.	CA, CB, CG	1968		X
Sauce dish. #4433. Flat, scalloped rim.	CA, CB, CG, CP	1964		X
Sherbert.				
#4441.	CA, CB, CG, CP	1962		X
#4443.	CA, CB, CG, CP	1963		X
	RU	1966		X

ITEM	COLOR(S)	YEAR	ORIG	NEW
Sugar bowl. #4403.* Covered, flat.	CA, CB, CG, CP	1963		X
	MI	1958		X
Tidbit set. #4494. Two-tier with 13" and 9"d plates.	MI	1958		X
Tumbler.				
#4442. Water. 12 oz.	CA, CB, CP	1962		X
	CG	1964		X
#4446. Juice, flat, 6 oz.	CA, CB, CG, CP	1965		X
#4449. Iced tea, footed, 13 oz.	CA, CB, CG, RU	1966		X
Vase.				
#4453. Bud, footed, swung. (made from the wine glass)	CA, CB, OR	1963		X
	CG, CP, RU	1965		X
	EB	1968		X
#4454. Footed, scalloped rim. 8"h.	CA, CB, CG, CP, OR	1964		X
#4455. Bud, footed, slender neck.	CA, CB, OR	1965		X
	CG, CP	1963		X
	EB	1968		X
#4456. Bud.*	MI	1960		X
#4459. Bud, footed, 7"h., Pulled scalloped rim.	CA, CB, CG, OR	1966		X
Wine. #4444. 5 oz.	CA, CB, CG, CP	1963	X	
	RU	1966	X	

*Introduced in 1960 in milk white as part of Fenton's "Olde Virginia Glass" line.

Beginning in the mid-1950s, the Fenton Art Glass Company of Williamstown, West Virginia, introduced Thumbprint in milk white as part of its "Olde Virginia" line of glassware. This line was developed by Fenton to meet the needs of large wholesale and catalog houses and consisted of patterns in colors and forms not available as a regular Fenton line. Prior to 1970, items were marked only with a green and white paper label, which read "Olde Virginia Glass Handmade." These labels also pictured a figure of a colonial man and woman. From 1970 to 1979, when the line was completely discontinued, each item was permanently embossed with Fenton's "OV" trademark (an "O" in the opening of a "V").

Today, you can find Fenton offerings of Thumbprint in a seemingly endless variety of contemporary colors and shapes (see Chart 98). Only compotes and two items of stemware (the goblet and the wine) emulate known antique forms (Figs. 378 and 379). Reproductions may seem quite convincing. Although items made prior to 1970 are not permanently marked, this adaptation of the design is typically Fenton in color, design, and quality.

Typical of most reproductions that were produced during the 1960s and 1970s, Thumbprint items are made from a good-quality nonflint glass, while originals were made from flint glass. New items are as heavy as originals but do not resonate when tapped (Fig. 380). Reproductions are thick (which is easily seen at the bottom of the bowls of goblets and tumblers and along the rims of other pieces). Any color other than clear is usually contemporary. Most new items were produced in forms never made originally.

Fig. 380. Contemporary selection of items in Thumbprint offered by Kanawha Glass Co. Circa 1971. Unmarked.

Hint: Thumbprint reproductions are made in nonflint glass in contemporary shapes and colors.

TOKYO

Originally known as No.212, this pattern was first issued by the Jefferson Glass Company of Steubenville, Ohio, about 1904 from a good-quality nonflint glass. Unlike a majority of patterns produced at this time, the design was made in a limited table service. Original colors are clear, solid blue and apple green, and opalescent blue, green, and white (plain or gold-trimmed).

This pattern consists of a row of large clear circles or bull's eyes that is serrated on the outer rim. Between each circle a large stylized fan motif completes the basic design.

Fig. 381 illustrates the only known reproduction in Tokyo. Known as No.8248 or Scroll and Eye, this compote was produced from a new mold by the Fenton Art Glass Company of Williamstown, West Virginia. As early as 1977, Fenton issued this compote in blue opalescent and lime sherbert. In subsequent years, the same mold was used to produce cameo opalescence (1980), French cream (1981), amethyst, country peach, and ruby (1982).

Characteristic of the fine art of glass making, this compote is a good copy of the original. It was produced from a new mold in a fine grade of quality nonflint glass that is clear and brilliant. Fenton's use of color distinguishes this item as contemporary giftware. Although the compote was produced in the original color of opalescent blue, the blue in the reproduction is lighter with less opalescence around the edge of the rim. This compote is also thicker and heavier than the original and the design is in lower relief. Aware of the pitfalls of reproduction glassware, each new compote has been per-

8248 RU
SCROLL & EYE NUT DISH

Fig. 381. Contemporary Fenton Scroll and Eye No.8248 high-standard nut dish, which is a direct copy of the Tokyo open jelly compote. Fenton Art Glass Co. Circa 1978. Embossed Fenton logo.

manently embossed with the company's familiar hallmark.

A similar reproduction compote is known in green opalescent glass. We believe that this unmarked compote was also produced from a new mold because the glass is thick and heavy and the design is smaller and less detailed than the original. The most obvious difference, however, is that the new green is noticeably darker with little opalescent effect.

Hint: Most Tokyo reproductions are permanently marked with Fenton's familiar logo.

Reproduced items: Compote.

TRAIN

The Railroad Train platter commemorates the opening of the Union Pacific, the first transcontinental railroad, which would stretch from the Missouri River to the Pacific Ocean. Produced from a good-quality clear nonflint glass, this platter is 12 inches by 9 inches. Most likely, it was issued by

Adams & Company of Pittsburgh, Pennsylvania, about 1885. In the center of this platter is Engine No.350. Along the clear outside border are four stippled panels embossed with clear, crossed acanthus-like leaves (Fig. 382).

In 1976, the A.A. Importing Company, Inc., of St. Louis, Missouri, offered copies of the Railroad Train Platter as "The Wedding

Fig. 382. Original drawing of the Train platter from the 1885 Spelman Brothers catalog.

Depicts the Completion of the Union Pacific Railway May 10, 1869. Called "The Wedding of the Rails."

Fig. 383. Reproduction amethyst Train platter offered by the A.A. Importing Co., Inc., as late as 1976. Unmarked.

of the Rails" (Fig. 383). Of foreign make and unsigned, these platters were produced in amber, amethyst, and clear glass. They are the same size as the original. However, unlike originals, which are highly sculpted, copies lack descriptive detail. Perhaps the most noticeable defect in reproductions is the perspective of the scene, which shows the shape and size of the train in relation to its surroundings.

On original platters the crossed acanthus-like leaves are sharply pointed and the veining leans in the opposite direction. On reproductions the leaves are blunt and smooth and the veining is straight. The cowcatcher is also shaped differently and is not as sharply defined as the one on the original plate. On originals, two sage bushes appear in the foreground and a finely detailed

branch appears to the right of the platter; on copies, these elements are misshapen or missing. The pebbled surface of the old is finely executed; on the copy, this surface is almost nonexistent.

Reproduction platters are heavier than originals. Clear examples exhibit a definite grayish cast to the glass. New Train platters feel oily and have a slick sheen. The details of the reproduction platter are not as sharply pressed as the originals and the stippling is too evenly placed.

Hint: Train reproduction platters are not well detailed and are heavier than originals.
Reproduced items: Platter.

TREE OF LIFE

Tree of Life is a pattern well known to collectors and dealers. Designed and patented by William O. Davis, it was first issued by the Portland Glass Company of Portland, Maine, about 1870.

This pattern consists of a network of veins pressed in high relief upon a clear ground. Although most items were produced originally from a good-quality non-flint glass, you may find an occasional piece

in flint. You may also find a variety of items, like the celery vase and creamer, fitted into silver-plated holders.

Early variations of Tree of Life were also issued by George Duncan & Sons of Pittsburgh, Pennsylvania, and the Boston and Sandwich Glass Company of Sandwich, Massachusetts. A limited number of items was also produced by Hobbs, Brockunier and Company of Wheeling, West Virginia, about 1888.

The Portland Glass variations have

CHART 99 TREE OF LIFE. L.G. Wright Glass Company, New Martinsville, West Virginia.
CMN: Tree of Life.
Mark: Unmarked.
Color Code: A Amber, B Blue, C Clear.

ITEM	COLOR(S)	YEAR	ORIG	NEW
Bowl, round, open.				
Crimped rim. #60-1. 6"d., 3½"h.	A, B, C	1968		X
Ruffled rim. #60-5. 5½"d., 2½"h.	A, B, C	1968		X
Smooth rim. #60-3. Finger, 4½"d., 3"h.	A, B, C	1968	X	
Compote, eternal-flame stem, high standard.				
Covered. #60-2. 4"h.	A, B, C	1968		X
Open, crimped rim. #60-9. 6½"d., 6"h.	A, B, C	1968		X
Goblet. #60-4. 9 oz., 6½"h., eternal-flame stem.	A, B, C	1968	X	
Relish. #60-7. Flat, leaf-shaped, handled, 8"l., 1¼"h.	A, B, C	1968	X	
Sauce dish. #60-6. Round, 3-toed, 4"d.	A, B, C	1968	X	
Wine. #60-8. 4 oz., 4½"h., eternal-flame stem.	A, B, C	1968	X	

60-2
4" Tall Covered Compote

Fig. 384. Reproduction Tree of Life No.60-2 covered sugar bowl. L.G. Wright Glass Co. Circa 1971. Unmarked. (The eternal-flame finial and stem are characteristic of Wright reproductions.)

60-4
9 oz. Goblet
A, B, C.

Fig. 385. Reproduction Tree of Life No.60-4 goblet. L.G. Wright Glass Co. Circa 1968. Unmarked.

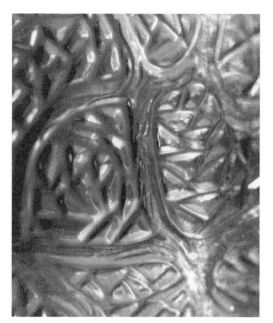

Fig. 386. Closeup of modern-day Tree of Life produced by the L.G. Wright Glass Co. (Unlike the original design, the design on reproductions more closely resembles blunt, smooth triangles.)

Fig. 387. New Tree of Life No.9322 true open compote. Fenton Art Glass Co. Circa 1977. Embossed Fenton logo.

smooth rims with a clear band. The design covers the entire item, including the base and stem. Portland Glass items are sometimes signed either "Davis" interwoven within the design or embossed "P.G.Co." on the base.

The design on the George Duncan & Sons variation covers the entire item except the base and stem. In this variation, items have melon ribbing, finials and standards are a finely molded hand clutching a ball (clear or frosted), bases are ribbed, and stems are conical.

Sandwich items, like those produced by Portland Glass, have a clear band around the rim. Similarly, the design covers the entire item, including bases and standards. The pattern is strongly defined with well-formed branches and stems.

As late as 1968, the L.G. Wright Glass Company of New Martinsville, West Virginia, issued the nine items in Tree of Life enumerated in Chart 99. Each reproduction is unmarked and was produced from a new mold in light amber, blue, and clear

nonflint glass. Each has a contemporary form unlike any known original (Figs. 384 and 385).

As a rule of thumb, Wright reproductions are thick and heavy and have little pattern detailing. Unlike the original design, the pattern is composed of smooth, blunt triangular impressions (Fig. 386). Perhaps the most obvious difference is the use of the "eternal flame" finial and stem, which is characteristic of Wright reproductions. Bases are also patterned or clear and rayed.

In 1977, the Fenton Art Glass Company of Williamstown, West Virginia, produced another version of the Tree of Life pattern. Illustrated in Fig. 387 is Fenton's item No.9322, the true open, footed compote with ruffled rim. This compote, produced from a new mold created by Fenton, was offered in colonial amber, blue, and pink, and in springtime green and wisteria.

The Fenton version of the Tree of Life pattern is dissimilar to items produced by Wright. While Wright used the "eternal flame" standard, the standard on this reproduction is bulbous, patterned, and corresponds to originals produced by the Portland Glass Company. However, Fenton's hand-crimping of the rim distinguishes this compote from the old.

Typically, Fenton compotes were produced from a good-quality clear and colored nonflint glass and are permanently embossed with the Fenton hallmark.

Hint: Reproduction Tree of Life items have poorly designed branches and triangular impressions.

TRIPLE TRIANGLE

Also known as Pillar and Cut Diamond, the original name of this lovely design is Doyle's No.76. This pattern was first issued in an extended table service by the firm of Doyle and Company of Pittsburgh, Pennsylvania, about 1880 from a good-quality clear nonflint glass. Production was continued when Doyle became a member of the United States Glass combine in 1891. At this time, clear with ruby stain pieces were produced and decorated by the Pioneer Glass Company, also of Pittsburgh.

Triple Triangle is an attractive pattern, especially in clear with ruby stain (Fig. 388). The design consists of six intersecting clear bars arranged to produce a rectangle that contains four triangular panels. While the upper three triangles are smooth, each lower panel is filled with tiny sawtooth.

Contrary to popular opinion, Triple Triangle is a safe pattern to collect because only two items have been reproduced. New, unmarked goblets and wines appeared as late as 1983 in clear and clear with ruby stain. Produced from a new mold, they are thicker and heavier than originals. Reproduction goblets and wines are also smaller than the old, the glass is slick or oily, and the pattern appears blurred.

No one should be fooled by reproductions

Fig. 388. Original Triple Triangle wine.

in clear with ruby stain. Compared to the deep, rich ruby on original items, the stain on new items ranges from light cranberry to pale amethyst. All clear items are off-colored and range from a pale yellow to a light gray.

Hint: Staining on reproductions is poorly done and the color is too light.
Reproduced items: Goblet, wine.

TULIP WITH SAWTOOTH

Originally known as Tulip, this pattern was produced by Bryce, McKee and Company of Pittsburgh, Pennsylvania, about 1860 from a good-quality clear flint glass in an extended table service. Milk white, opalescent, or any other color is rare. Later, this pattern was issued in a lesser-quality clear nonflint glass.

This pattern derives its name from the large three-petaled flower that is its chief

Fig. 389. Original Tulip with Sawtooth clear wine. Bryce, McKee & Co. Circa 1860s. (Unlike reproductions, the stem of this original is bulbous and thick.)

TWO PANEL

In the 1880s, the popularity of colored pressed glass tableware soared as a profusion of colors flooded the market. Extended table services were produced in a variety of

decoration. Only a small amount of medium-sized sawtooth fills the open spaces at the base of the flowers (Fig. 389). The glass is brilliant and heavy, although it does not ring with as much resonance as other flint designs. Original stoppers may be patterned or plain, handles are applied, and finials are acorns.

Copies of the Tulip with Sawtooth goblets and wines have been available since about 1940. When old and new ones are placed side by side, you wonder how anyone could be fooled by the reproduction. The old is much thicker and heavier, the knob in the stem is much larger, and the foot is larger and thicker.

Reproductions are not permanently marked.

Hint: Reproductions are smaller, thinner, and lighter than originals.
Reproduced items: Goblet, wine.

color treatments that ranged from varying hues of amber, blue, apple green, and canary yellow to the more elusive shades of amethyst and amberina. Typical of this decade of color is the Two Panel pattern.

Fig. 390. Original Two Panel goblet. Richards & Hartley Glass Co. Circa 1880s.

Fig. 391. Reproduction Two Panel goblet. Circa early-1960s. Unmarked. (Unlike original goblets, there is no ring or band above the knob on reproductions.)

Fig. 392. Closeup of an original Two Panel goblet. Richards & Hartley Glass Co. Circa 1880s.

Fig. 393. Closeup of reproduction Two Panel goblet. Unmarked. (Notice the stem lacks the ring or band above the knob found on originals.)

This pattern, also known as Daisy in Panel or Daisy in the Square, was originally produced as No.25 by the Richards & Hartley Glass Company of Tarentum, Pennsylvania, in the 1880s. Richards & Hartley continued making the pattern after it joined the United States Glass combine in 1891.

Two Panel is an alluring pattern. Shapes are ovoid and the design consists of two plain and two patterned vertical panels. The water tumbler, which has three patterned panels, is an exception. Each panel alternates with one that is filled with tiny squares pressed with small daisies. Finials have a conventional shape and are designed like the patterned panels.

Prior to 1965, new Two Panel goblets and wines appeared in the original colors of amber, blue, clear, apple green, and canary yellow. They are unmarked and were issued from new molds. Compared to authentic goblets and wines, reproductions are heavier, stems are shorter and thicker, the ring or band above the knob is missing, and the colors are pale and washed out. When you compare the patterns, you will quickly notice that reproductions are blunter and the daisy motif is weakly pressed (Figs. 390–393). The reproduction also feels distinctly slick or oily and has a glossy sheen.

Reproduction items in Two Panel are not permanently marked.

Hint: Reproductions are heavier and the stems are shorter and thicker.

Reproduced items: Goblet, wine.

U.S. COIN

U.S. Coin has the unique distinction of being the only pressed-glass pattern to preserve the likeness of six different United States coins: the silver half-dime, the dime, the twenty-cent piece, the quarter-dollar, the half-dollar, and the dollar. With the exception of the half-dime, each coin bears the date of 1892.

The original molds for this pattern were created by the Central Glass Company of Wheeling, West Virginia, in 1891. When Central joined the United States Glass combine in Pittsburgh, Pennsylvania, U.S. Coin was produced by the United States Glass Company as No.15005 or American Coin. After only six months, production was reportedly suspended by U.S. government inspectors on the grounds that using the molds (not the glass) to replicate the coins was illegal. A Spanish coin was therefore substituted for the American coin (see also Columbian Coin).

Also known as Coin, Frosted Coin, and Silver Age, this pattern was originally produced in an extended table service from a good-quality nonflint glass. The glass is brilliant and heavy, and the forms are bold and well suited for this design. The most novel aspect of the pattern is the finial, which is shaped like a stack of coins. Although you most often encounter this pattern in clear glass with clear or frosted coins, you may find rarities in clear glass with amber or ruby-stained coins and ruby-stained glass with clear or frosted coins.

The first reproduction in U.S. Coin was the toothpick holder, which appeared as early as 1935. This new toothpick holder is much heavier, the frosting is exceptionally inferior, and the stars are larger than the original. Whereas the coins on genuine toothpick holders are round and centered, the coins on this reproduction are elon-

gated and reach downward into the curve of the base. In addition, the figures on new toothpick holders are blurred and the word "LIBERTY" is barely visible.

In the mid-1960s, new spoonholders and a second version of the 1892 toothpick were imported by the A.A. Importing Company, Inc., of St. Louis, Missouri. New, unmarked footed spoonholders were offered in clear and vaseline, and toothpick holders were available in clear and clear with gold and silver-painted coins (Figs. 394 and 395). These new spoonholders should fool no one, because original spoonholders were never footed. In like manner, new toothpick holders are heavier than the old, the glass is slick and glossy, old coins were never painted, and the shape of the eagle resembles a young pullet rather than an adult eagle. Both items are illustrated as "Coin" in the 1981 and 1983 catalogs of the Kamei Glass Co., Ltd., of Osaka, Japan, and were imported by A.A. Importing through Nichio Boeki Company, Ltd., of Tokyo.

In 1974, four additional forms in U.S. Coin were introduced to the American market by A.A. Importing: the bread plate, the covered sugar bowl, the paperweight, and the water tumbler. The creamer followed

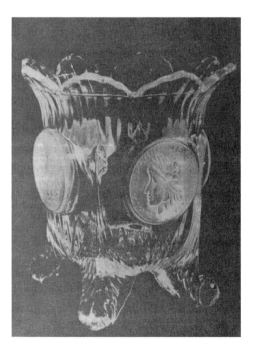

Fig. 394. Reproduction U.S. Coin clear and frosted look-alike footed spoonholder offered by A.A. Importing Co., Inc. Circa 1976. Unmarked. (Footed spoonholders were not originally made.)

Fig. 395. U.S. Coin clear reproduction toothpick holder with frosted coins. Most likely by A.A. Importing Co., Inc. Circa 1974. Unmarked.

"COIN GLASS"

Fig. 396. New U.S. Coin clear and frosted high-standard covered compote and round covered bowl offered by A.A. Importing Co., Inc. Circa 1980. Unmarked.

sometime in 1977 and, one year later, the candlestick, the flat covered bowl, and the high-standard covered compote appeared (Fig. 396). Each is enumerated in Chart 100.

Reproductions can be quite convincing. However, only four of the ten known reproductions (the bread tray, the high-standard covered compote, the covered sugar bowl, and the toothpick holder) conform to known original shapes. Moreover, upon close examination, you can note a number of subtle discrepancies between antique and new pieces.

As mentioned, new bread plates appeared as early as 1974. Although original and reproduction plates share the same general shape, old plates measure 7 inches by 10 inches and are decorated with fifteen coins. Five Morgan dollars appear in the center of the base, two of which are obverse and three reverse. All five coins are arranged so that the top of one coin overlaps the bottom of the next. The arrangement of these five coins is: tail-head-tail-tail-head. Six Liberty half-dollars alternate with four additional Morgan dollars to create the corners and the outer border. When this plate is viewed right side up, the coin configuration on the border is: head-head, tail-tail, head-head, tail-tail, head-tail.

In comparison, new plates measure 8 inches by 10 inches. The Morgan dollar configuration in the base differs from originals in that there are three obverse and two reverse coins that are now on their sides. The arrangement of the coins from left to right changes to: head-tail-head-tail-head. The most obvious difference between old and new plates is on their borders. When held right side up, these reproductions, which

CHART 100   U.S. COIN. A.A. Importing Company, Inc., St. Louis, Missouri.

CMN: Coin.
Mark: Unmarked or paper label bearing the inscription "A.A. Importing Co., St. Louis, Missouri. Made in Japan."
Color Code: C Clear, CF Clear with Frosted Coins, V Vaseline.

ITEM	COLOR(S)	YEAR	ORIG	NEW
Bowl. No.PG/1664. Covered, flat, 6"d., 5"h.	C	1978		X
	CF	1980		X
Bread plate. No.PG/1613. 8" × 10"l.	CF	1974	X	
Candlestick. No.PG/1662. 4"h.	C, CF	1978		X
Compote. No.PG/1633. High standard, covered, 9½"h., 6"d.	C	1978	X	
	CF	1980	X	
Creamer. No.PG/1661. Pressed handle, flat. 4½"h., 4"d.	C, CF	1977		X
Paperweight. No.PG/1614. 2¾"d., 1¾"h.	CF	1974		X
Spoonholder. No.PG/1603. 4¾"h., Footed with scalloped rim.	C, V	1968		X
Sugar bowl. No.PG/1661. Covered, flat, 7"h., 4"d.	CF	1974	X	
Toothpick holder. No.PG/1601.	C, CF	1974	X	
Tumbler, water. No.PG/1645. Flat, 3½"h., 3"d.	C, CF	1976		X

have only Morgan dollars, are configured head-tail, head-tail, head-tail, head-tail, head-tail (Figs. 397 and 398)

New covered sugar bowls appeared at the same time as the new bread plates. Original sugar bowls are 7 inches high with a diameter of 4 inches. The base of old sugar bowls has six half-dollars, the lid has six quarter-dollars, and the finial consists of a stack of six coins. In descending order, these coins are: two dollars, two half-dollars, and two quarter-dollars. Reproduction sugar bowls are also the same size and design as originals. Fortunately, there are some interesting differences. New sugar bowls are heavier than the old, while the glass has an oily sheen. The coins are poorly molded and the frosting is harsh. The most obvious difference, however, is that the dollar coin on the finial is blurred and lacks the fine detailing of the original. On the sides of the finials, the coins lack the fine reeding found on originals and, instead, display a smooth, worn surface.

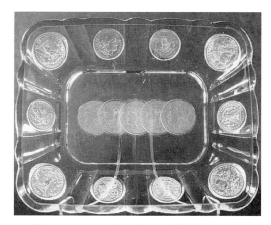

Fig. 397. Reproduction U.S. Coin No.PG/1602 clear and frosted bread plate offered by A.A. Importing Co., Inc. Circa 1974. Unmarked.

Fig. 398. Closeup of coins on the reproduction U.S. Coin bread plate.

Reproduction water tumblers also appeared in 1974. These new tumblers do not resemble original U.S. Coin tumblers, but rather the original silver-dollar bar tumbler, which is always dated 1878 or 1879. Unlike original tumblers, which are 3¾ inches high and 2¾ inches in diameter, reproductions are 3½ inches high and 3 inches in diameter. In addition, old tumblers have six Seated Liberty dimes encircling the base, whereas new tumblers do not. However, the most obvious difference is on the base of each tumbler. Where the base of each authentic U.S. Coin tumbler is plain, the base of reproductions is pressed with an 1892 Morgan dollar.

New covered compotes appeared as late as 1978. Original compotes are 5⅞ inches in diameter and 9¼ inches high. The bowl and lid each have nine quarter-dollars, the stem has six dimes, and the finial is a stack of three Morgan dollars. Although original and reproduction compotes share the same coin configuration, new compotes are 6 inches in diameter and 9½ inches high. However, reproductions have an oily sheen, which is most noticeable at the bottom of the compote bowl. New compotes are also heavier than originals, the detail of the coins is blurred, the frosting is blotchy and poorly done, and the dollar on the finial is barely visible.

Flat covered bowls, like the one illustrated in Fig. 396, also appeared at the same time as the high-standard covered compote. These bowls are often mistaken by collectors and dealers for the covered butter dish. Actually, new bowls are nothing more than the bowl of the compote without the standard. Produced from the same mold as the compote, bowls share the same discrepancies. In fact, the bowl is a new shape that was never made originally.

Unlike other forms, new creamers appeared as late as 1977. Original creamers are the same shape as the spoonholder, or 5⅛ inches high with a 3-inch base diameter. Six quarter-dollars are found on each original creamer. Reproduction creamers, in comparison, are 4½ inches high with a base diameter of 4 inches. New creamers are heavier and larger than the original. The most important difference is that reproduction creamers have six half-dollars instead of six quarter-dollars. The dates on new creamers are barely visible and the detailing is blurred.

Two additional forms were imported by A.A. Importing between 1974 and 1978: the 4-inch-high candlestick and the paperweight. Both, available in clear with frosted coins, are strictly contemporary.

Reproductions in U.S. Coin share a number of common discrepancies. New items are heavier than originals, the glass has a slight bluish tint with an oily sheen, and the

detail on reproductions is blurred and not as crisply molded. The date on all reproductions is 1892 and often is barely visible. The frosting is harsh, and the pieces are poorly done. On many pieces, coins are either partially frosted or the frosting is so poorly applied that it appears an inch above the coin motif.

Reproductions are not permanently marked but may carry the original paper label from A.A. Importing Company, Inc.

Hint: Reproductions have poorly detailed coins and the frosting is harsh.

VERMONT

Also known as Honeycomb with Flower Rim, Vermont Honeycomb, and Inverted Thumbprint with Daisy Band, the original name of this pattern is U.S. Glass No.15060 or Vermont. The United States Glass Company of Pittsburgh, Pennsylvania, produced this pattern as part of its state series about 1899.

Original colors are blue, clear, clear with amber or ruby stain, custard (enamel decorated), and emerald green (gold trimmed). Most items have three splayed feet. Finials are created by three similar feet, which hold a solid glass ball.

This design consists of a band of daisies around the rim of most items. (An exception is the salt shaker, on which the band of daisies is placed lower down on the rim to produce room for the cover.) Each item is adorned by a honeycombed optical effect

that is pressed from the inside. Each foot is a long, flowing leaf that sweeps back upon itself from where it is attached to the body. Handles are a similarly designed leaf whose base terminates into a foot.

In 1965, the Crystal Art Glass Company of Cambridge, Ohio (under the direction of Elizabeth Degenhart), introduced the reproduction Vermont toothpick holder. Known as Crystal's Forget-Me-Not, this reproduction is 2½ inches high and was produced from a new mold created by the Island Mold and Machine Company of Wheeling, West Virginia. These toothpick holders were produced on a limited run in more than 140 contemporary colors (see Chart 102). Until 1972, they were not permanently marked. After this time, however, Crystal permanently embossed each with "1972" and a "D" within a heart (signifying Degenhart).

After the death of Elizabeth Degenhart in 1978, Bernard Boyd acquired the Crystal

---

CHART 101 VERMONT. Boyd's Crystal Art Glass Company, Cambridge, Ohio.
CMN: Forget-Me-Not.
Mark: "B" in a diamond, embossed.
Color Code: Frosty Blue/Orange, Pumpkin Slag, Tomato Creame, Tropical Green, Tropical Green Slag, White Creame, Winter White, Zak Boyd Slag, Sand Piper, Elizabeth Slag #3, Pineapple, Mardi Gras, Ice Green, Impatient January Slag, Leprechaun, Magic Marble, Opaline Blue, Opaline Blue Slag, Pink Champagne, Purple Variant, Redwood, Robin Egg Blue, Root Beer, Rubina, Russett Green, Sugar Plum, Tangerine, Apple Green, Apple Green Slag, Avocado/Red, Candy Swirl, Chasm Blue, Dawn, Deep Purple, Flame, Frosty Blue, Heather.

ITEM	COLOR(S)	YEAR	ORIG	NEW
Toothpick holder.	All Colors	unknown		X

CHART 102   VERMONT. Crystal Art Glass Company, Cambridge, Ohio.

CMN: Forget-Me-Not.

Mark: Unmarked or, beginning in 1972, embossed "D" in a heart.

Color Code: Amber Dark, Amber Light, Amberina, Amethyst Dark, Amethyst Light, Amethyst with White, Angel Blue, Antique Blue, Apple Green, April Green #1, April Green #2, Aqua, Baby Blue Slag, Baby Green, Baby Green Slag, Baby Pink Slag, Bernard Boyd's Ebony, Bittersweet Slag, Bloody Mary #1, Bloody Mary #2, Bluebell, Blue Bird #2, Blue Fire, Blue Fire Opal, Blue Green, Blue Jay, Blue Marble Slag, Blue & Crystal Slag, Blue & White, Bluina, Brown, Buttercup, Buttercup Slag, Cambridge Pink, Canary, Caramel Dark, Caramel Light, Carnival Cobalt, Carnival Crown Tuscan, Carnival Dark Cobalt, Chad's Blue, Champagne, Charcoal, Chartreuse, Chocolate, Chocolate Creme, Cobalt, Cobalt Light, Concord Grape, Crown Tuscan, Crystal, Custard, Custard Slag Dark, Custard Slag Light, Daffodil #1, Daffodil #2, Dapple Gray Slag Dark, Dapple Gray Slag Light, Delft Blue, Delft Blue Slag, Dichromatic, Dogwood, Gray Slag Light, Elizabeth's Lime Ice, Emerald Green, End of Blizzard, Fog, Forest Green Dark, Forest Green Light, Frosty Jade, Gold, Grape, Gray Green Slag, Gray Slag Dark, Gray Slag Light, Green, Heatherbloom, Heliotrope Dark, Heliotrope Light, Henry's Blue, Honey, Honey Amber, Ivory #1, Ivory #2, Ivory Slag, Ivorene, Jabe's Amber, Jade, Lavender Blue, Lavender Green Slag, Lavender Marble Slag, Lemon Opal, Milk Blue, Milk Blue Opalescent, Milk Blue Slag, Milk White, Mint Green, Mint Green Slag, Mulberry, Misty Green, Old Lavender, Opalescent, Opalescent Slag, Opalescent with Marigold Trim, Orchid, Peach Clear, Peach Opaque, Peach Blo, Pearl Gray, Periwinkle, Persimmon, Pigeon Blood, Pine Green, Pink, Powder Blue Slag, Red, Red White & Blue Slag, Rose Marie, Royal Violet, Rubina, Ruby, Sapphire, Shamrock, Smoky Heather, Snow White, Sparrow, Sparrow Slag, Spring Green, Spring Green Slag, Taffeta, Teal, Tomato, Twilight Blue, Unique Blue, Vaseline, Violet #1, White Opalescent Slag, Willow Green, Wondor Blue, Zack Boyd Slag.

ITEM	COLOR(S)	YEAR	ORIG	NEW
Toothpick holder, 2½"h.	All Colors	1965	X	

Art Glass Company and continued production of the Vermont toothpick holder. He also added more than 35 new colors (see Chart 101) to this line and changed the mark to an embossed "B" within a diamond (signifying Boyd).

The easiest way to detect Crystal Art Glass toothpick holders is by carefully examining the feet (Fig. 399). As you will discover, there are ten plumes on the feet of original toothpick holders and only nine on reproductions. In addition, the shank of the foot on old items is longer and thicker than on new ones. And, while reproductions have a single row of beading, the originals have a double row.

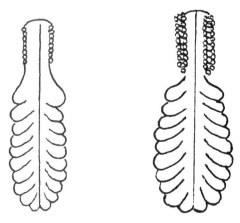

Fig. 399. Comparison of design on feet of original and reproduction Vermont toothpicks. (The reproduction is on the left.)

Fig. 400. New Vermont toothpick holder in amberina. Kanawha Glass Co. Circa 1975. (Characteristic of Kanawha reproductions is the hobnail motif, which does not adorn the body of originals.)

In 1969, the Pilgrim Glass Corporation of Ceredo, West Virginia, issued a similar toothpick holder in the Vermont pattern. Known as Pilgrim's No.452, they are unmarked and were produced from a new mold. Examples are documented in blue milk glass and vaseline, and undoubtedly other colors were used. Like original toothpick holders, those produced by Pilgrim have a honeycombed body.

In 1970, the Kanawha Glass Company of Kanawha, West Virginia, issued still another reproduction of the Vermont toothpick holder, known as Hobnail. Like other reproductions, this one was produced from a new mold. From 1970 through 1978, these toothpick holders were offered in amber, amberina, and end-of-day glass, although other colors were undoubtedly used. Characteristic of Kanawha toothpick holders is the hobnail body, which does not appear on originals (Fig. 400).

As a general rule of thumb, new toothpick holders are heavier and thicker than originals. Colors are contemporary, artificial, and harsh in comparison to old pieces. Original toothpick holders are 2½ inches high, while reproductions are 2⅝ inches high.

Hint: Original toothpick holders are 2½ inches high.

WEDDING RING

Wedding ring is a heavy, brilliant pattern of the 1860s and has been known by this name for many years. Where and by whom this lovely pattern was originally produced remains uncertain. Also known as Double Wedding Ring, it was first issued from a fine-quality clear flint glass in a limited number of forms in both a light and a heavy version. Typical of the period, handles are beautifully applied.

Wedding Ring is an interesting design that makes effective use of a chain of large clear interlocking circles. This chain covers the entire decorated surface of each item. Often mistaken for the Single Wedding Ring, a much later pattern produced in nonflint glass, Wedding Ring produces a lasting belltone resonance when gently tapped.

As late as 1969, the L.G. Wright Glass Company of New Martinsville, West Virginia, issued the five items in Wedding Ring enumerated in Chart 104. Each item is unmarked and was produced from a new mold in both contemporary and original colors. Only the No.11-2 9-ounce goblet (Fig. 401) and the No.11-7 5-ounce wine have an original form. Wright reproductions were produced from nonflint glass and will not produce a belltone when tapped.

Fig. 401. Reproduction Wedding Ring No.11-2 clear nonflint goblet. L.G. Wright Glass Co. Circa 1971. Unmarked. (Typical of Wright copies are the rayed bases found on the goblet and the wine.)

A second reproduction of the Wedding Ring goblet was produced in the mid-1970s by the Old Sturbridge Village Museum in Sturbridge, Massachusetts. Also known as Wedding Ring, this goblet was produced from a new mold by the Imperial Glass Cor-

CHART 103   WEDDING RING. Dalzell-Viking Glass Company, New Martinsville, West Virginia.
CMN: Wedding Ring.
Mark: Unmarked or clear acetate label.
Color Code: C Clear, B Blue (Pale), P Pink.

ITEM	COLOR(S)	YEAR	ORIG	NEW
Goblet.	C, B, P	1989	X	
Plate, 6"d.	C, B, P	1989	X	
Sherbert, footed.	C, B, P	1989		X
Sugar bowl, covered.	C, B, P	1989	X	
Toothpick.				
Squatty.	C, B, P	1989		X
Tall.	C, B, P	1989		X

CHART 104   WEDDING RING. L.G. Wright Glass Company, New Martinsville, West Virginia.
CMN: Double Wedding Ring.
Mark: Unmarked.
Color Code: A Amber, AM Amethyst, B Blue, C Clear, COB Cobalt Blue, G Green, RBY Ruby.

ITEM	COLOR(S)	YEAR	ORIG	NEW
Goblet. #11-2. 9 oz., 6¼"h.	A, AM, B, G, RBY	1968	X	
	C	1977	X	
	COB	1969	X	
Salt dip. #11-8. Round, flat. Individual.	A, B, G, RBY	1968		X
	AM	1984		X
Sherbert. #11-5.	A	1984		X
Toothpick holder. #11-6. Round, flat	A, AM, B, G, RBY	1968		X
Wine. #11-7. 5 oz., 5½"h.	A, B, G, RBY	1968	X	
	C	1977	X	
	COB	1969	X	

poration of Bellaire, Ohio. Because it, too, was made from nonflint, the glass will not produce a belltone. Old Sturbridge Village reproductions are permanently embossed "OSV" and originally carried a paper label; they are documented in clear and in the contemporary colors of blue or ruby.

In the late 1980s, the Dalzell-Viking Glass Company of New Martinsville, West Virginia, issued a third series of items in Wedding Ring (see Chart 103). Also known as Double Wedding Ring, they were produced from new molds. Unlike the Sturbridge and Wright reproductions, new goblets by Dalzell were made from flint glass and produce a fine belltone. Although items are not permanently marked, each Dalzell-Viking reproduction originally carried a clear acetate label printed "Dalzell-Viking Glass Co." in black block letters.

When you examine new Wedding Ring items, you will notice a number of interesting discrepancies. Although any contemporary color or shape is obviously new, clear items are entirely too bright. That is, the glass glistens or shines with a brilliance that is not apparent in original items. Although reproductions may produce a belltone resonance, new items are lighter in weight than their antique counterpart. The design is also smaller and thinner and, unlike the round circles of antique forms, the circles on reproductions are noticeably elongated.

Hint: Original Wedding Ring items were made in clear flint glass.

WESTWARD HO

Westward Ho is a good example of the numerous clear and frosted designs popular from 1870 to 1885. Like other members of the elite family of figural designs, this pattern embodies the apex of the Victorian mastery of pressed-glass making. Although the theme of Westward Ho is uniquely American, its allure is universal.

The original name of this ware is Pioneer. Also known as Tippecanoe, the line was designed by the German mold maker Jacobus and was first issued in 1879 by the firm of Gillinder & Sons of Philadelphia. Although made in a complete table service from a good-quality clear and frosted nonflint glass, Westward Ho is dissimilar to standard tableware lines of this time in that it includes a number of innovative forms, such as the footed sauce dish and the covered marmalade jar.

Westward Ho is an interesting pattern. Befitting its name, this design is reminiscent of pioneer America and depicts a frosted scene of buffalo, a large log cabin, and deer set against a Western prairie. Each of these elements is exquisitely detailed and crisply molded, and upon all covered pieces a figure of a crouching or kneeling Indian forms the finial.

Today, Westward Ho is often considered unsafe to collect. Spurred by others' misunderstandings of the so-called "great reproduction craze of the 1940s," many collectors and dealers tend to judge all pieces of this pattern as new. As convenient as such suppositions may appear, so are they equally untrue. While a number of classic patterns has been copiously reproduced, knowledge is the most effective weapon against defrauding yourself.

Reproductions in Westward Ho appeared as early as 1936. The first was the goblet, followed somewhat later by the 4-inch sauce dish and the new oil lamp (Fig. 402), made from the contemporary goblet mold. By 1940, this list had been expanded to include the small oval low-footed compote, the round, covered high-standard compote, the water pitcher, and the 4½-high wine.

The most widely reproduced item in this

Fig. 402. Closeup of clear and frosted Westward Ho reproduction oil lamp. Unmarked. Although collectors and dealers have often been taken by such lamps, you need only remember that lamps are strictly contemporary.

pattern remains the goblet. In 1936, clear 8-ounce goblets by the Westmoreland Glass Company of Grapeville, Pennsylvania, were illustrated in the catalog of Paul Thomas of Parkesburg, Chester County, Pennsylvania. By April 1940, Westmoreland had begun advertising them in blue opaque, clear, and milk-white glass (Fig. 403) in *House and Garden* magazine. A month later, a similar ad for clear goblets was placed in *House Beautiful* by Bloomingdale's in New York City. Comparable ads followed in *Crockery and Glass Journal* and *China, Glass and Decorative Accessories,* and by February 1964 goblets appeared in Brandywine blue, golden sunset, and laurel green.

In 1979, Westmoreland was commissioned by the Gateway Carnival Glass Club of Troy, Illinois, to produce the Westward Ho goblet in purple carnival glass. Limited to an edition of 1,000 pieces, each item was permanently signed "Gateway Carnival Glass Club, 1979" and embossed with the Westmoreland trademark.

When Westmoreland closed in 1984, the

Fig. 403. Reproduction milk-white Westward Ho goblet. Westmoreland Glass Co. Circa 1952. Unmarked.

mold for the Westward Ho goblet was purchased by the Plum Glass Company of Pittsburgh, Pennsylvania. Today, Plum produces this goblet in cobalt blue.

Interestingly, all reproduction goblets

have not been produced domestically. In 1953, Glasscrafts and Ceramics, Inc. (formerly Czecho-Slovak Glass Products Company), of Yonkers, New York, imported a similar goblet in clear, unfrosted glass.

The most prolific manufacturer of Westward Ho reproductions, however, is the L.G. Wright Glass Company of New Martinsville, West Virginia, which produced the nine items listed in Chart 105. As you can see from this chart, only the No.66-12 low-footed water tumbler and the No.66-7 low-standard covered compote (sauce dish with cover) are new forms; the remainder of this list corresponds to original forms. From as late as 1968, this assortment has been available in the original color of clear and frosted glass and has often confused collectors and dealers (Figs. 404, 405, and 406).

Because of the number of apparent discrepancies in reproductions, we emphatically state that all Westward Ho copies have been made from new molds. This is perfectly obvious when you consider the quality, the design, the workmanship, and the size of each new item.

Dissimilar to original items, which are

CHART 105   WESTWARD HO. L.G. Wright Glass Company, New Martinsville, West Virginia.
CMN: Westward Ho.
Mark: Unmarked.
Color Code: CF Clear and Frosted.

ITEM	COLOR(S)	YEAR	ORIG	NEW
Butter dish. No.66-8. Covered, footed.	CF	1969	X	
Celery vase. No.66-11. Footed, scalloped rim.	CF	1969	X	

Compote, covered.
 High standard, round.
  No.66-2. 6"d.
 Low standard.
  Oval.
   No.66-1. 6"l.
  Round.
   No.66-6. 5"d.
   No.66-7. 4"d.
	CF
	
	CF
	
	CF
	CF
		1968
		
		1968
		
		1968
		1969
			X
			
			X
			
			X
			
				X

Creamer. No.66-9.	CF	1969	X	
Goblet. No.66-3.	CF	1968	X	
Sherbert. No.66-4. Footed.	CF	1968	X	
Sugar bowl. No.66-10. Covered, footed.	CF	1970	X	
Tumbler. No.66-12. Water, low circular foot.	CF	1969		X
Wine. No.66-5.	CF	1968	X	

Fig. 404. Reproduction Westward Ho No.66-2 clear and frosted 6-inch-round high-standard covered compote. L.G. Wright Glass Co. Circa 1971. Unmarked.

Fig. 405. Reproduction clear and frosted Westward Ho No.66-1 6-inch-long low-standard oval covered bowl. L.G. Wright Glass Co. Circa 1971. Unmarked.

Fig. 406. Reproduction clear and frosted Westward Ho No.66-6 5-inch-round low-standard covered compote. L.G. Wright Glass Co. Circa 1971. Unmarked. (This compote is actually the footed sauce dish with a sugar-bowl lid.)

crystal clear with a smooth, gray-white frosting, early reproductions are slightly yellow. Moreover, the frosting is chalky, dry, and dead white with a coarse, harsh texture that is absent on the old. Although the quality of the frosting on later copies was somewhat improved, frosted portions remained blotchy or irregular, and the glass takes on the greenish cast most often associated with L.G. Wright reproductions.

The differences between old and new items are further seen when you consider the design. Original items are crisply molded and the pattern (which is in high relief) is exceptionally detailed (Fig. 407). This realism is found throughout the old Westward Ho line and is exemplified in the figures of the buffalo, the deer, and the Indian-shaped finial. Whereas the animals on reproductions are dull, lifeless and undetailed, those found on originals are vibrant, lifelike, and well designed. And, unlike copies, the animals' hair on old pieces is distinct and readily visible. Another

Fig. 407. Original clear and frosted Westward Ho goblet. Gillinder & Sons. Circa 1879.

discrepancy is in the shape of the deer's mouth, which is always a visible, straight closed line on old items. However, on reproductions, the mouth is either partially open or entirely blurred.

On those items that are covered, the most obvious difference is in the finial. On old pieces, finials are beautifully molded, look carved rather than pressed, and become spirited and lively when placed under strong light. Here, the intricate details of a noble American Indian reflect the pride, skill, and workmanship of the finest mold maker. This is particularly true of the figure's face and stature, which are always animated and lifelike. In contrast, the finials on reproductions are poorly designed, poorly molded, and lifeless with little, if any, detail. For example, the figure's face is devoid of all expression, ill-defined, and blurred. Upon his head is a poor representation of a headdress, minus the three dominate plumes found on originals (see Fig. 405).

In general, Westward Ho reproductions are always heavier than originals. This may be accounted for by the thickness of the glass, the use of new molds, and the pressing process employed. Because this pattern was originally made only in clear with a frosted finish (and rarely in clear), any colored item is modern.

Westmoreland glass was not permanently marked until after 1949, when the company introduced its familiar "WG" logo. Plum Glass Company items have a paper label and Wright pieces are not marked.

Hint: Reproductions have poor pattern detail and frosting is harsh.

WHEAT AND BARLEY

Appropriately named, Wheat and Barley is a member of that group of pressed glass popular during the color years of Victorian pressed tableware. The original name of this pattern is Duquesne and the design was first issued in the 1880s by Bryce Brothers of Pittsburgh, Pennsylvania. Later, when Bryce became a member of the United States Glass combine in 1891, it continued making the pattern at its factory.

Wheat and Barley was originally produced in an extended table service from a good-quality nonflint glass in amber, blue, canary yellow, and clear. The pattern consists of highly embossed clusters of wheat and barley suspended against a paneled background. Plates, which lack the paneled background, are exceptions to this design.

Only one item has been reproduced in Wheat and Barley. Illustrated in Fig. 408 is the new goblet, which first appeared prior to 1990. These goblets are unmarked and are documented in amber, blue, clear, and canary yellow. They were issued from a new mold and are heavier than originals. In addition, the colors are harsh and artificial, and the design is blurred and poorly pressed.

Fig. 410. Closeup of the amber original Wheat and Barley goblet. Bryce Brothers. Circa 1880s. (Unlike reproductions, the leaves on originals are well formed and heavily stippled.)

Fig. 408. Reproduction amber Wheat and Barley goblet. Unmarked.

As you can see by comparing Figs. 409 and 410, reproduction goblets differ considerably from original goblets. Compared to the original goblets, which have finely detailed sprigs of wheat and barley tied around a short knotholed branch, the sprigs on reproductions are not detailed and the knot that ties them resembles a ship's wheel. Additionally, the leaves on old goblets are serrated, smooth, and paired naturally, while the veining and stippling are realistic. Although the leaves on reproductions are also serrated, they are blunt and irregular, while the veining and stippling are overly exaggerated.

When you examine a new goblet, you will also notice an excessive amount of glass within the base of the bowl. In comparison, the bowls of old goblets are thin and have an indentation at the bottom of the bowl that drops into the stem.

Reproduction goblets are not permanently marked.

Fig. 409. Closeup of the amber reproduction Wheat and Barley goblet. (Notice how the knot resembles the shape of a ship's steering wheel.)

Hint: On reproduction goblets, the knot joining the sprigs resembles a ship's steering wheel.

Reproduced items: Goblet.

WHEAT SHEAF

The wheat motif is one of the more popular plant designs from the nineteenth century. Our Victorian ancestors used this figure in almost every medium, including furniture, silver, china, and glass. One of the most well-known versions of this design is Wheat Sheaf. It was first produced during the 1870s in an extended table service in a good-quality clear nonflint glass by Hobbs, Brockunier & Company of Wheeling, West Virginia. The pattern was originally produced in clear, but rare items are known in amber, blue, and yellow. Today, Wheat Sheaf is considered scarce because it is seldom seen outside of bread plates, goblets, and pitchers.

Today, many glass scholars feel that round bread plates are not a part of the original Wheat Sheaf pattern. The design on these round plates consists of a centered sheaf of wheat surrounded by an inner border of clear ribs. Above this ribbing is a large stippled outer border embossed in clear lettering, "GIVE US THIS DAY OUR DAILY BREAD." The original Wheat Sheaf pattern has the wheat motif, but there is never any ribbing or stippling. Original round plates were produced in 10- and 11-inch sizes.

As late as 1973, the Imperial Glass Corporation of Bellaire, Ohio, issued the Sheaf of Wheat bread plate illustrated in Fig. 411 for Old Sturbridge Village, Sturbridge, Massachusetts. This new tray is 10 inches in diameter and was known as Imperial's No.6503 or Old Sturbridge Plate. These plates were produced in a good-quality clear nonflint glass from a new mold and are permanently marked "OSV" (signifying Old Sturbridge Village).

Reproduction plates are heavier and thicker than originals. In addition, the stippled border is coarse, exaggerated, and resembles large dewdrops. On original plates, the border is well defined and the stippling more closely resembles diamond point. The top of the wheat sheaf in the center of the plate consists of large dewdrops. On originals, this area is much smaller and resembles a large diamond-point design.

A second Wheat Sheaf bread plate is illustrated in Fig. 412. It is 11 inches long and classified as a fooler because it has no origi-

Fig. 411. Reproduction Wheat Sheaf clear bread plate by the Imperial Glass Corp. for the Old Sturbridge Village Museum. Embossed "OSV."

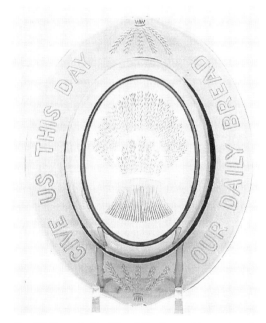

Fig. 412. Reproduction Wheat Sheaf emerald green bread plate. Circa 1980s. Unmarked.

nal counterpart. Typical of most reproductions, this plate is unmarked, heavy and thick, and oily and glossy.

Hint: Reproduction bread trays are thick and heavy.

Reproduced items: Bread tray.

WILDFLOWER

The original name of this lovely design was listed as No.140 by Adams & Company of Pittsburgh, Pennsylvania. One of the more popular patterns of the floral group, Wildflower was first issued by Adams about 1874 in a large and extended table service from a good-quality nonflint glass. Original colors are amber (light and dark), apple green, blue, clear, and canary yellow. After 1891, when Adams became Factory "A" of the United States Glass Company, also of Pittsburgh, the pattern was reissued (Fig. 413).

Wildflower consists of six-petaled flowers, leaves, berries, and a single stem. Each of these elements is finely stippled, pressed in high relief, and horizontally arranged upon a single stem to decorate the other-

wise plain midsection of items. A band of finecut above this floral motif and another band of narrow fluting below complete the design (Figs. 414, 415, and 416).

For more than half a century, Wildflower reproductions have caused endless confusion among collectors and dealers. As early as 1936, copies of the goblet, the 10-inch-square plate, and the tumbler entered the market. Unmarked, each item was produced from a new mold in all the original colors. Compared to original items, early reproductions are poorly molded, colors are harsh and artificial, the glass is excessively heavy, and the fluting around the base is narrow. Most notably, reproductions are poorly stippled, and the size of the design can vary on the same item.

In 1968, the L.G. Wright Glass Company of New Martinsville, West Virginia, produced the eight items enumerated in Chart 108. Only the No.67-10 10½-inch-high, covered stick-candy jar and the No.67-2 5½-inch-high, low-footed covered compote are contemporary in shape. The other forms are antique (Fig. 417).

As you can see from Fig. 418, Wright reproductions can be quite convincing. Like earlier copies in this pattern, Wright chose to use the original colors. To this color scheme, the company added the contemporary colors of amethyst, ruby, and vaseline opalescent. Because individual forms were intermittently produced by the Fenton Art Glass Company and others, each item was not made in all colors. Produced from new molds, Wright reproductions are unsigned

Fig. 413. Reprint of a United States Glass Co. catalog illustrating an assortment of Wildflower. (Note that original pieces are always lightweight and evenly stippled.)

Fig. 414. Spelman Brothers 1885 wholesale catalog illustration of the original Wildflower table set.

CHART 106   WILDFLOWER. Crystal Art Glass, Cambridge, Ohio.
CMN: Wildflower.
Mark: Embossed "D" in a heart.
Color Code: A Amber, AM Amethyst, AMB Amberina, AG Apple Green, BB Bluebell, BM Bloody Mary, BV Blue Variant, C Clear, CH Chocolate, COB Cobalt, CP Cambridge Pink, CS Candy Swirl, CT Crown Tuscan, CUS Custard, DP Deep Purple, EG Emerald Green, ELI Elizabeth's Lime Ice, F Flame, FG Forest Green, G Green, HEL Heliotrope, HA Holly Amber, HG Holly Green, IG Ice Green, MB Milk Blue, MW Milk White, NG Nile Green, OP Opalescent, P Peach (Clear), PB Peach Blo, PC Pink Champagne, PER Persimmon, PNK Pink, PNKL Pink (Light), PV Purple Variant, RD Red, RM Rose Marie, RBY Ruby, SAP Sapphire, TB Twilight Blue, V Vaseline, WB Willow Blue.

ITEM	COLOR(S)	YEAR	ORIG	NEW
Candleholder, footed. Sauce dish with center holder.	A, AM, AMB, BB, COB, CT	1971		X
	EG, MG, OP, PG, RBY	1971		X
	PV, SAP	1971		X
Dish, candy, covered, footed.	A, AM, AMB, AG, BB, BM	1971		X
	BV, C, CH, COB, CP, CS	1971		X
	CT, CUS, DP, EG, ELI, F	1971		X
	FG, G, HEL, HA, HG, IG	1971		X
	MB, MW, NG, OP, P, PB	1971		X
	PC, PER, PNK, PNKL, RD	1971		X
	RBY, SAP, TB, V, WB	1971		X

CHART 107   WILDFLOWER. Mosser Glass, Incorporated, Cambridge, Ohio.
CMN: Wildflower.
Mark: Unmarked or embossed "M" or "M" within a circle.
Color Code: CT Crown Tuscan, RBY Ruby.

ITEM	COLOR(S)	YEAR	ORIG	NEW
Candy jar, covered, stick.	CT	unknown		X
	RBY	1989		X
Compote, covered.				
High standard.	CT	unknown	X	
Low standard.	CT	unknown	X	
Creamer, pressed handle.	CT	unknown	X	
Salt, master, oblong, flat.	CT	unknown	X	
Sugar bowl, covered.	CT	unknown	X	

CHART 108   WILDFLOWER. L.G. Wright Glass Company, New Martinsville, West Virginia.
CMN: Wildflower.
Mark: Unmarked.
Color Code: A Amber, AM Amethyst, B Blue, C Clear, G Green, RBY Ruby, V Vaseline, VO Vaseline Opalescent.

ITEM	COLOR(S)	YEAR	ORIG	NEW
Creamer. No.67-3. Pressed handle, footed, 3"d., 5½"h.	A, B	1968	X	
Compote. No.67-2. Low standard, covered, 4"d., 5½"h.	A, B, C	1968		X
Goblet. No.67-5. 8 oz., 6"h.	A, B, C, RBY, V	1968	X	
	VO	1969	X	
Jar, No.67-10. Stick candy, covered, 3¾"d., 10½"h.	A, B, C	1968		X
Salt dip. No.67-7. Master, flat, rectangular.	A, AM, B, C, G, RBY	1968	X	
Sauce dish. No.67-9. Round, footed, 4"d., 2¾"h.	A, B, C	1968	X	
Sugar bowl. No.67-4. Covered, footed, 4"d., 7¾"h.	A, B	1968	X	
Wine. No.67-12. 2½ oz., 5"h.	A, B, RBY, V	1968	X	
	VO	1969	X	

Fig. 415. Spelman Brothers 1885 wholesale catalog illustration of the original Wildflower turtle-base salt, which has not yet been reproduced.

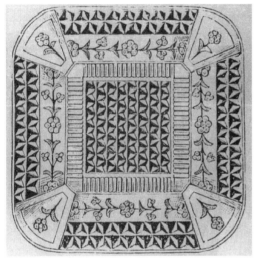

Fig. 416. Excerpt from a United States Glass Company catalog illustrating the large Wildflower plate.

Fig. 417. Reproduction Wildflower creamer and covered sugar bowl. L.G. Wright Glass Co. Circa 1968. Unmarked.

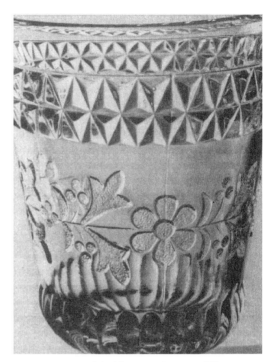

Fig. 418. Closeup of the blue reproduction Wildflower goblet. (When you examine new goblets, you will notice that the stippling is blotchy and poorly applied.)

and share the same poor molding, harsh and artificial color, and excessive heaviness as earlier copies. Here, too, the most notable differences on reproductions are found in the poor quality of stippling and the size of the design.

New goblets are excessively heavy and thick. On original goblets, a distinct indentation goes into the stem. Ordinarily, this area is too thick and even on reproductions. However, this rule of thumb does not always apply to all new goblets. Typical of most reproductions, those by Wright are heavy and thick and the finecut borders are smooth or blunt. Tumblers are also thicker at the bottom than originals.

While reproductions by L.G. Wright Glass are troublesome, two items of little concern appeared in 1971. Crystal Art Glass of Cambridge, Ohio (under the direction of Elizabeth Degenhart), introduced two new forms in Wildflower; the low-footed covered candy dish and the low-footed candleholder with center insert. Both items are contemporary and were produced from new molds created by the Island Mold and Machine Company of Wheeling, West Virginia. From 1971 until Degenhart's death in 1978, both items were produced in the original colors of amber, apple green, and clear and in the assortment of contemporary colors enumerated in Chart 106. For the general shape of this new covered candy dish, Crystal adopted the original round, footed sauce dish. Then, by adding a matching patterned lid, it produced a miniature copy of the low-footed compote. Candlesticks were created by adding a socket to the center of this open candy and eliminating the cover. Although the candleholder was never signed, many of the new covered candy dishes were marked on the inside bottom of the bowl with a "D" in a heart (signifying Degenhart).

At least two additional contemporary glasshouses produced copies of this pattern. In 1985, the Summit Art Glass Company of Akron, Ohio, issued the No.593 Wildflower bell. This bell was produced from a new mold in amberina, cobalt, morning glory, evergreen, mulbury, mulbury iridized, and rubina and is strictly contemporary. When signed, these bells are permanently marked with a "V" within a circle (signifying the Summit Art Glass Company). In addition, Mosser Glass, Inc., of Cambridge, Ohio, was producing from new molds the five items enumerated in Chart 107 as late as 1981. As you can see from this listing, only one item (the covered stick-candy jar) is contemporary in shape. The remainder of this grouping corresponds to original forms. Like those issued by Wright, Mosser reproductions were produced in a number of contemporary colors, including Crown Tuscan and ruby. When signed, Mosser reproductions are permanently embossed with either an "M" or an "M" within a circle.

Hint: Reproduction items have poorly molded vines and flowers and pieces are heavier.

WILD ROSE WITH BOWKNOT

Originally known as Sultan, this pattern was produced by McKee Brothers of Pittsburgh, Pennsylvania, about 1902. Original color production included chocolate and clear (plain or frosted with cold-enamel decoration). A toothpick holder is also known in decorated custard.

Wild Rose with Bowknot was originally produced from a good-quality nonflint glass in a limited number of table pieces. The design consists of vertical panels of highly embossed wild roses against a smooth background. Above and below each panel is a large C-scroll, and on either side of each rose is a panel containing a stylized bowknot (Fig. 419). This pattern is also similar to another McKee pattern, Wild Rose with Scrolling, which was made only in the four-piece child's miniature table set.

The Fenton Art Glass Company of Williamstown, West Virginia, experimented in using old designs with contemporary shapes and colors. About 1961, it issued the six items in Wild Rose with Bowknot that are

Fig. 419. Butler Brothers April 1902 catalog illustration of the original Wild Rose with Bowknot pattern.

enumerated in Chart 109. This line was produced exclusively in cased color combinations and milk white. Each item was produced from a new mold and, although unsigned, originally carried a paper label. In 1976, Fenton issued the No.2807 student lamp in custard, milk white, and opaque blue as part of its "Olde Virginia Glass" line.

CHART 109 **WILD ROSE WITH BOWKNOT. Fenton Art Glass Company, Williamstown, West Virginia.**
CMN: Wild Rose with Bow Knot.
Mark: Unmarked, embossed "OV," or paper label.
Color Code: AG Apple Green, BG Opaque Blue, C Coral, CT Custard, HA Honey Amber, MI Milk White,
PB Powder Blue, WR Wild Rose. (All in cased "overlay" colors.)

ITEM	COLOR(S)	YEAR	ORIG	NEW
Lamp. #2807. Student.	BG, CT, MI	1976		X
Pitcher. #2865. Water, 32 oz., applied handle.	MI	1961		X
Salt shaker. #2806.	MI	1961		X
Syrup jug.	AG, C, HA, PB, WR	1960		X
Vase, bulbous.				
#2855. 5"h.	AG, C, HA, MI, PB, WR	1961		X
#2857. 7½"h.	AG, C, HA, MI, PB, WR	1961		X
#2858. 8"h.	MI	1961		X

Like other items in this line, each piece was permanently marked with the company's "OV" insignia (an "O" within the opening of a "V"). The entire line was completely suspended in 1979.

Wild Rose with Bowknot is a safe pattern to collect. No one should confuse the new Fenton adaptations for old. A simple rule to remember is that no original item was made in cased or milk-white glass. Also helpful is a general knowledge of the original shapes used by McKee and the modern shapes used by Fenton.

Hint: Wild Rose with Bowknot was never made originally in cased or opaque colors.

WISCONSIN

One of the state patterns Wisconsin is also known as Beaded Dewdrop or Prism; it was officially called No.15079 by the United States Glass Company of Pittsburgh, Pennsylvania. This pattern was first issued about 1903 in an extended line of tableware from a good-quality clear nonflint glass.

This design consists of a connected row of large, heavily stippled vertical panels, each containing a slightly thinner clear panel. In addition, a row of tiny dewdrops outlines each stippled panel, while a C-scroll faces downward above each arch. Many items are also decorated with beaded rims and a band of small dewdrops placed above the central design.

To date, only the toothpick holder has been reproduced in Wisconsin. In 1962, the Crystal Art Glass Company of Cambridge, Ohio, introduced new 2¼-inch-high by 2⅜-inch-diameter toothpick holders from a contemporary mold owned by the B&P Lamp Supply Company of McMinnville, Tennes-

see. Known as the Witch's Pot or Kettle, this toothpick holder was issued in clear and a rainbow of contemporary colors, including avocado, red, candy swirl, heather, ice blue, ice green, impatient, frosty blue slag, peach whisper, redwood, royalty, rubina, smoke, and tropical green. Due to a reported dispute, this mold was returned to B&P Lamp and, in 1971, Elizabeth Degenhart had a similar mold (without lugs or side handles) made by the B Mould & Machine Company of Cambridge, Ohio (Fig. 420). From 1972 until Degenhart's death in

Fig. 420. New clear Wisconsin toothpick holder. Crystal Art Glass Co. Circa early 1970s. Embossed "D" within a heart.

April 1978, new toothpick holders were permanently marked with a "D" within a heart (signifying Degenhart).

After Degenhart's death, Bernard Boyd of Cambridge, Ohio, purchased the company and renamed it Boyd's Crystal Art Glass, Inc., and continued production of the Wisconsin toothpick holder. At this time, the mark was changed to an embossed "B" within a diamond (signifying Boyd).

At least two other contemporary toothpick holders are known. Throughout the 1980s, the Guernsey Glass Company of Cambridge, Ohio, produced similar toothpick holders without the side handles. They are unmarked and were also made from new molds in clear glass. As late as 1982, another copy of the toothpick holder was imported from Taiwan. Unlike those produced by Crystal Art Glass and Guernsey, imported reproductions are covered and come in the contemporary colors of amberina, clear, cobalt blue, green, pink, and purple slag. Contemporary imports are unmarked and carry only a small label printed "Made in Taiwan."

In general, new toothpick holders are heavy and slick or oily. The glass is exceptionally bubbly, and those produced in clear are often grayed or amethystine. The design is also different on reproductions: the beads are larger and slightly misshapen and the stippling is even compared to originals. In addition, original toothpick holders were made with handles or lugs. Only early Crystal Art Glass reproductions have handles, but the glass is of an inferior quality.

Hint: Handleless Wisconsin toothpick holders are reproductions.

Reproduced items: Toothpick holder.

YALE

Also known as Ball and Fan or Turkey Track, the original name of this lovely pattern is Crowfoot. Designed and patented by Julius Proeger on August 30, 1887 (design patent No.17675), this design was first issued by McKee Brothers of Pittsburgh, Pennsylvania, in the late 1880s.

Yale was produced in an extended table service from a good-quality clear nonflint glass. The design consists of rows of clear convex circles that are adorned on the lower right side with an impression of a five-pointed fan. The glass is clear, brilliant, and, although nonflint, heavy.

Only two items, the goblet (Fig. 421) and the high-standard cake stand, have been reproduced in Yale. As late as 1960, new, unmarked goblets flooded the market in amber, blue, and clear and undoubtedly in other colors. New goblets are 6 inches high with a 3-inch-diameter base. Reproductions are poorly finished and have excessive glass along mold lines and rims. Unlike original goblets, the bowls of new goblets turn slightly inward. In addition, noticeable straw

Fig. 421. Reproduction light blue Yale goblet. Unmarked.

lines, color deformities, and telltale signs of foreign manufacture differentiate new goblets from old ones.

Copies of the high-standard cake stand quickly followed in amber, blue, and opalescent white. Reproductions are heavy and thick and the poorly pressed pattern is faint in many of the circles.

Remembering that Yale was not produced originally in color will prevent you from mistaking the new colored goblet and the cake stand for the old.

Reproductions are not permanently marked.

Hint: Any color other than clear is a reproduction.

Reproduced items: Cake stand, goblet.

Appendix

GLASS COMPANIES

Adams & Co. Established in 1851 in Pittsburgh, PA, as Adams, Macklin & Co. The name was changed to Adams & Co. in 1861. Became Factory "A" of the United States Glass Company in 1891.

Anchor-Hocking Glass Co. Founded in 1905 by Isaac J. Collins, L.B. Martin, and L. Philip Martin et al. in Lancaster, OH, as the Hocking Glass Co. In 1969, the name was changed to Anchor-Hocking Corp. In 1970, the firm purchased the Phoenix Glass Co. of Monaca, PA. Still in business today.

Atterbury & Co. Founded in 1859 as Hale, Atterbury & Co. by Thomas Bakewell Atterbury in Pittsburgh, PA. In 1865, the name was changed to Atterbury & Co.; by 1893 the name was changed to Atterbury Glass Co., and in 1894 the factory closed.

Bakewell, Pears and Co. Founded in 1808 as Bakewell & Ensell, in Pittsburgh, PA. Became Bakewell, Pears & Co. in 1844. Reorganized in 1880 as Bakewell, Pears & Co., Ltd. In 1882 the factory was sold. First factory in America to produce flint glass.

Bartlett-Collins Glass Co. Founded in 1903 by George F. Collins and R.H. Thomas in Coffeyville, KY. In 1907, the firm was purchased by Premium Glass Co. In 1912, the factory was moved to Sapulpa, OK. When H.U. Bartlett joined as a partner in 1915, the name was changed to Bartlett-Collins Glass Co. Still operating today.

Beatty, A.J., & Sons. Founded in 1845 as Beatty & Stillman in Steubenville, OH, by Joseph Beatty, Sr., and Edward Stillman. Became Factory "R" of the United States Glass Company in 1892. (*See* Tiffin Glass Co.)

Beatty-Brady Glass Co. (*See* Indiana Glass Co.)

Bellaire Goblet Co. Founded in 1876 in Bellaire, OH, and moved to Findlay, OH, in 1888. Became Factory "M" of the United States Glass Company in July 1891.

Boston and Sandwich Glass Co. Founded in 1825 in Sandwich, MA, by Deming Jarves as the Sandwich Mfg. Co. In 1826 the company incorporated as the Boston & Sandwich Glass Co. In 1858, Jarves resigned to establish the Cape Cod Glass Co. By January 1, 1887, the plant was closed by a workers' strike and never reopened under original management.

Boston Silver Glass Co. Founded about 1857 by Alonzo E. Young and John W. Haines in East Cambridge, MA. Operated as late as 1873.

Boyd's Crystal Art Glass Co. (*See* Crystal Art Glass Co.)

Bryce Brothers. Founded in 1850 as Bryce, McKee & Co. by James Bryce, brothers John P. and Robert D. Bryce, and Fred M. McKee in Pittsburgh, PA. In 1854, William T. Hartley and Joseph Richards joined as partners and the name was changed to Bryce, Richards & Co. When Hartley and Richards detached themselves from the firm and William Walker joined, the name was changed to Bryce, Walker & Co. In 1882, the firm was reorganized as Bryce Bros. and in 1891 became Factory "B" of the United States Glass Co.

Bryce, Higbee & Co. Founded in 1879 as the Homestead Glass Works by John Bryce, Charles K. Bryce, Joseph A. Doyle, and John B. Higbee in Pittsburgh, PA. In 1907, the firm went out of business.

Bryce, McKee & Co. (*See* Bryce Brothers.)

Bryce-Richards Glass Co. (*See* Bryce Brothers.)

Bryce, Walker & Co. (*See* Bryce Brothers.)

Burlington Glass Works. Founded in 1874 by Edward Kent and Alfred Miles in Hamilton, Ontario, Canada. Until 1881, the firm specialized in lamps and chimneys. In the mid-1880s, the firm expanded into table glassware. In 1885, the firm was bought by the Hamilton Glass Co. (also of Hamilton, Ontario) and in 1897 the factory was closed.

Cambridge Glass Co. Founded in 1900 by the National Glass Co. of Pittsburgh, PA. By 1907, economic depression forced National Glass into bankruptcy and the factory was sold to Arthur J. Bennett. In 1954, the factory was closed and in 1960 the Imperial Glass Co. purchased the Cambridge name and molds.

Campbell, Jones & Co. Founded in 1865 by James W. Campbell, John Davis, Jenkin Jones, and John F. Loy by occupying the idle Shepherd Co. in Pittsburgh, PA. When James Campbell withdrew in 1885, the firm was reorganized as Jones, Cavitt & Co., Ltd. In 1891, the plant was destroyed by fire.

Cape Cod Glass Works. Founded in 1858 by Deming Jarves and James D. Lloyd in Sandwich, MA. Upon the death of Jarves in 1869, the factory was closed and later sold to Dr. R.C. Flowers and later to George L. and Sewall Fessenden and Charles W. Spurr.

Central Glass Co. Founded in 1863 as Oesterling & Hall by Andrew Baggs, Peter Cassel, Roy Combs, William K. Elson, John Henderson, Henry James Leasure, and John Oesterling in Wheeling, WV. In 1864, the name was changed to Oesterling & Henderson Co. and by 1867, the firm was renamed the Central Glass Co. Became Factory "O" of the United States Glass Co. in 1891.

Challinor, Taylor & Co., Ltd. Founded 1883 by David Challinor and David Taylor. Formally established as a limited partnership in Tarentum, PA, in 1885. Became Factory "C" of the United States Glass Company in 1891. The plant was destroyed by fire in 1893.

Clevenger Brothers. Founded in 1929 in Clayton, NJ by Henry Thomas (Tom), Lorenzo (Reno), and William Elbert (Allie) Clevenger, who had apprenticed at Moore Brothers' Clayton Glass Works, Clayton, NJ. Earliest pieces were free-blown. By 1934, molds were introduced and items were mold-blown. Still in business today.

Columbia Glass Co. Founded in 1886 in Pittsburgh, PA. Became Factory "J" of the United States Glass Company in 1891. The plant closed in 1893.

Co-Operative Flint Glass Co. Founded circa 1869 as the Beaver Falls Cooperative Glass Co. in Beaver Falls, PA, by Thomas B.A. David and William F. Modes. In 1879, former McKee Brothers workers formed the Co-Operative Flint Glass Co., Ltd. In 1908, the name changed to the Co-Operative Flint Glass Co. The plant closed in 1937.

Crystal Art Glass Co. Founded in 1947 by John and Elizabeth Degenhart in Cambridge, OH. Initially, the firm produced paperweights but, after 1964, produced reproduction glass. Upon the death of Elizabeth Degenhart in 1978, the company was sold to Bernard Boyd.

Crystal Glass Co. Founded in 1888 by Ed Muhleman and Addison Thompson et al., who purchased the LaBelle Glass Co. plant in Bridgeport, OH. By 1899, it became part of the National Glass Co. and the name was changed to the Crystal Glass Works.

Curling, Robertson & Co. Founded in 1827 as the Fort Pitt Glass Works by Robert B. Curling and William Price in Pittsburgh, PA. In 1828, Henry Higbee and Curling's two sons (William and Alfred B.) joined the firm, and the name was changed to R.B. Curling & Co. When Higbee withdrew in 1834, the name was changed to R.B. Curling & Sons. In 1835, Morgan Robertson became involved with the firm and the name was changed to Curling, Robertson & Co. By 1867, George W. Dithridge joined the firm and the name was changed to Dithridge & Son. When Edward Dithridge, Sr., died in 1873, son George acquired ownership of the business, which was reorganized and renamed Dithridge & Co. By 1901, the firm was purchased by the Pittsburgh Lamp, Brass and Glass Co.

Dalzell, Gilmore & Leighton. Founded in 1883 as Dalzell Bros. & Gilmore in Wellsburg, WV, by Andrew C., James, and William Dalzell and E.D. Gilmore. In 1883, the firm leased the idle Brilliant Glass Works located in Brilliant, OH, and commenced operation. By 1888, the firm agreed to move to Findlay, OH, with the promise of free gas and a free site and the name was changed to Dalzell, Gilmore & Leighton. In 1899, the firm joined the National Glass Co. and operated as Dalzell, Gilmore & Leighton Glass Works. By 1902, the plant was closed.

Dalzell-Viking Glass Co. (*See* New Martinsville Glass Mfg. Co.)

Doyle & Co. Founded in 1866 by William Beck, Joseph Doyle, and William Doyle et al. in Pittsburgh, PA. Became Factory "P" of the United States Glass Co. in 1891.

Duncan, George & Sons. Established in 1874 by George A. Duncan, Sr., in Pittsburgh, PA, by purchasing Ripley & Co. with his two sons, Harry B. and James E., Sr., and his son-in-law Augustus H. Heisey. Became Factory "D" of the United States Glass Company in 1891. In May 1892, the factory was destroyed by fire and U.S. Glass decided not to rebuild.

Duncan & Miller Glass Co. Founded in 1892 by James E. Duncan, Sr., Harry B. Duncan, and John Ernest Miller as George Duncan's & Sons in Washington, PA. In December 1900 the firm was incorporated and renamed Duncan & Miller Glass Co. in Washington, PA. The plant closed in 1955.

Duncan Glass Co. (*See* Duncan & Miller Glass Co.)

Federal Glass Co. Founded in 1900 by George and Robert Beatty, James Bracken, W.C. Bracken, and John Kuntz, Jr., in Columbus, OH. By 1958, the firm became the Federal Glassware Division of the Federal Paper Board Co., Inc., of Montvale, NJ. The plant closed in 1980.

Fenton Art Glass Co. Founded 1905 in Martins Ferry, OH, by John W. and Frank L. Fenton. A new factory was built in Williamstown, WV, in 1906. Still operating today.

Fostoria Glass Co. Founded in 1887 by Lucian B. Martin and W.S. Brady in Fostoria, OH. The factory opened in 1888. In 1891, the factory in Fostoria was closed and moved to Moundsville, WV. The factory closed in 1986.

Gillinder & Sons. Founded in 1861 as Franklin Flint Glass Works by Thynne Gillinder in Philadelphia, PA. In 1863, Edwin Bennett joined the firm as a partner and the name was changed to Gillinder & Bennett. When Bennett retired in 1867, William Gillinder's sons, James A., Sr., and Frederick R. joined the firm and the name was changed to Gillinder & Sons. In 1888, the pressed-glass division was moved to Greensburg, PA. In 1891, this division joined the United States Glass Co. as Factory "G."

Guernsey Glass Co. Founded in 1970 in Cambridge, OH, by Harold Bennett, owner of the Cambridge Glass Museum. Produced handmade reproduction glassware.

Higbee, John B., Glass Co. Founded in 1897 by John B. Higbee, Oliver J.W. Higbee, and R.G. West in Bridgeville, PA. In 1913, the firm declared bankruptcy for sixty days. The plant recovered throughout 1914 but closed in 1918.

Hobbs, Brockunier & Co. Founded as Barnes, Hobbs & Co. by James B. Barnes and John L. Hobbs in 1845 in South Wheeling, WV. The company was also known as the South Wheeling Glass Works. The name was changed to Hobbs, Barnes & Co. in 1849. By 1863, the firm was reorganized and the name was changed to J.H. Hobbs, Brockunier & Co., later known as Hobbs, Brockunier & Co. At this time, William Leighton, Jr., joined the firm and a year later invented his lime-glass formula. The firm was dissolved in 1887 and reorganized in 1888 as Hobbs Glass Co. In 1891 it joined United States Glass Co. as Factory "H."

Imperial Glass Corp. Founded in 1901 in Bellaire, OH, by J.N. Vance, Edward Muhleman, and James F. Anderson as the Imperial Glass Co. Due to construction, the plant began pressing glass in 1904. By 1931, the company was forced into bankruptcy but continued under court-appointed receivers and the name was changed to the Imperial Glass Corp. In 1972, the firm was purchased by Lenox, Inc., and operated as the New Imperial Corp. In 1982, the company was sold to Merrimac Industries Corp. of Minneapolis, MN, and filed for bankruptcy. By 1984 the company was sold to Consolidated Stores of Columbus, OH, and the Lancaster Colony Corp.

Indiana Glass Co. Founded 1895 by George Beatty and James C. Brady, who purchased

the idle A.J. Beatty & Sons factory in Steubenville, OH, from the United States Glass Co. Joined the National Glass combine in October 1898 as the Beatty-Brady Glass Works. Incorporated as the Indiana Glass Co. in 1909. By 1955, the company merged with the Lancaster Lens Co. of Lancaster, OH, and became the Lancaster Glass Corp. In 1962, Indiana Glass became a part of the Lancaster Colony Corp.

Indiana Tumbler and Goblet Co. Established as the Greentown Glass Works in Greentown, IN, in 1893 and incorporated in 1894 by David C. Jenkins, Jr., David C. Jenkins, Sr., Thomas Jenkins, Lewis Jenkins, Jr., and Charles Miller, Jr. In 1899, it became a member of the National Glass Co. combine and became known as the Indiana Tumbler & Goblet Works. By 1900, Jacob Rosenthal joined the company as glass chemist and superintendent. In 1903, the factory was destroyed by fire.

Jeannette Glass Co. Founded on June 20, 1898, by Joseph W. Stoner, W.A. Huff, and associates in Jeannette, PA. By 1971, the name was changed to the Jeannette Corp. Still operating today.

Jefferson Glass Co. Founded in Steubenville, OH, in 1900 by Harry Bastow, Grant Fish, George Mortimer, and J.D. Sinclair. About 1906, A.G. Frohme and George L. Caldwell became owners and decided to relocate the plant in Follansbee, WV. In 1907, the firm was incorporated in Follansbee and the Steubenville plant was sold to the Imperial Glass Co. The factory was permanently closed in the early 1930s.

Jenkins, D.C., Glass Co. Founded in Kokomo, IN, in 1900 as the Kokomo Glass Mfg. Co. by David C. Jenkins, Sr., Addison Jenkins, and David C. Jenkins, Jr. In 1905, the plant was destroyed by fire and reorganized in 1906 by David C., Jr., and his son Addison as the D.C. Jenkins Glass Co. By 1932, the company was bankrupt.

Jones, Cavitt & Co. (*See* Campbell, Jones & Co.)

Kamei Glass Company, Ltd., Osaka, Japan. Producers and exporters of pressed glass, including reproductions in Croesus and U.S. Coin.

Kanawha Glass Co., Kanawha, WV. Contemporary manufacturer of pressed glassware and novelties. Later relocated to Dunbar, WV. Prior to 1986, the company closed and was sold to Raymond Dereume and moved to Punxsutawney, PA, where the name was changed to Raymond Dereume Glass, Inc.

Kemple, John E., Glass Works. Founded in 1945 by John E. Kemple in East Palestine, OH, to produce reproduction glassware. In 1956, the plant was destroyed by fire and in 1957 a new plant was constructed in Kenova, WV. Upon Kemple's death in 1970, the plant was closed.

King, Son & Co. Founded as the Cascade Glass Works in 1859 in Pittsburgh, PA, by Johnson, King & Co. In 1864, the name was changed to Johnson, King & Co., and in 1869 to King, Son & Co. By 1884, the company was reorganized as King, Son & Co., Ltd. In March 1888, the firm incorporated as the King Glass Co. In 1891, the firm joined the United States Glass Company as Factory "K."

Kokomo Glass Mfg. Co. (*See* D.C. Jenkins Glass Co.)

LaBelle Glass Co. Founded in 1872 in Bridgeport, OH, by Andrew H. Baggs, E.P. Rhodes, and F.C. Winship. By 1886, Harry Northwood was employed as a designer, metal worker, and plant manager. After being destroyed by fire in 1887, the plant was reopened in January 1888, but by April 1888 it was bankrupt.

Lancaster Colony Corp. Founded in 1908 as the Lancaster Glass Co. by Wallace Graham, Lucian B. Martin, and Fred Von Stein et al. in Lancaster, OH. In 1923, Hocking Glass gained control of the firm. In 1933, Hocking gained control of Lancaster Glass and both Hocking and Lancaster became part of the Anchor-Hocking Glass Corp.

Libbey Glass Co. Due to labor unrest and prohibitive fuel costs, by 1888 the New England Glass Works (then owned by Edward Drummond Libbey, son of William L. Libbey) was moved to Toledo, OH, and the name changed to W.L. Libbey & Son Co., Proprietors, New England Glass Works. By 1892, the name was changed to Libbey Glass Co. In 1983, the firm operated in Toledo as the Libbey Glass Division of Owens-Illinois Glass Co.

Lyon, J.B., & Co. (*See* O'Hara Glass Co.)

McKee & Brothers. Founded in 1850 as F. & J. McKee (also spelled M'Kee) in Pittsburgh, PA, by Frederick and James McKee. In 1853, the name was changed to McKee Brothers (also known as McKee & Brother), and in 1860 the name changed to McKee & Brothers. In 1888, the plant was moved to Jeannette, PA. In 1899, the firm joined the National Glass combine and operated as McKee & Bros. Glass Works. In 1903, the plant was badly damaged by flooding and in 1904 was leased to McKee-Jeannette Glass Co. In October 1908, McKee Glass Co. was created and in 1910 the company was reorganized. The Thatcher Mfg. Co. purchased the company's assets in 1951, and in 1961 the Jeannette Glass Co. of Jeannette, PA, acquired Thatcher's interests in McKee. In 1962, Jeannette occupied the McKee site and "McKee" disappeared from the name.

Model Flint Glass Co. Founded in 1888 as the Novelty Flint Glass Co. in Findlay, OH, by A.C. Heck, A.L. Stephenson, A.L. Strasburger, and W.C. Walters. By 1893, the plant was moved to Albany, IN. In 1899, the firm joined the National Glass Co. and operated as the Model Flint Glass Works. By 1902, National abandoned the plant, which eventually was sold to David McLloyd in 1908.

Mosser Glass, Inc. Founded 1971 by Thomas Mosser in Cambridge, OH, to produce reproduction novelties and tableware. Still operating today.

National Glass Combine. Chartered in Harrisburg, PA, in July 1899 as the National Glass Co., this was the second largest glass combine in the United States and consisted of Beatty-Brady Glass Works, Canton Glass Works, Central Glass Works, Crystal Glass Works, Cumberland Glass Works, Dalzell, Gilmore & Leighton, Fairmont Glass Works, Greensburg Glass Works, Indiana Tumbler & Goblet Works, Keystone Glass Works, Model Flint Glass Works, McKee & Bros. Glass Works, Northwood Glass Works, Ohio Flint Glass Works, Riverside Glass Works, Robinson Glass Works, Rochester Glass Works, Royal Glass Works, and the West Virginia Glass Works.

New England Glass Co. Incorporated on February 16, 1818, by Amos Binney, Daniel Hastings, Deming Jarves, and Edmund Munroe et al. in East Cambridge, MA. By 1827, the firm was involved in producing pressed glass; by 1852, it was thought to be the largest glass factory in the world. In 1875, competition, the cost of fuel, and the refusal to adopt the new soda-lime glass forced the company into bankruptcy and sale by 1877. In 1878, the plant was leased to William L. Libbey. In 1880, the firm was named the New England Glass Works, Wm. L. Libbey & Son, Proprietors. Because of labor unrest and fuel costs, by 1888 a plant was established in Toledo, OH, and the name changed to W.L. Libbey & Son Co., Proprietors, New England Glass Works, and the factory in Cambridge, MA, was closed. (*See* Libbey Glass Co.)

New Martinsville Glass Mfg. Co. Founded in 1900 as the New Martinsville Glass Mfg. Co. in New Martinsville, WV, by Mark Douglas, David Fisher, and G.W. Motheny. By 1937, the plant was bankrupt. In 1938, the firm was purchased by William Schultz and Carl Williams et al., and the name was changed to the New Martinsville Glass Co. In 1944, G.R. Cummings purchased all stock and the name was changed to the Viking Glass Co. By 1986, the company was purchased by Kenneth Dalzell (president of the defunct Fostoria Glass Co.) and the name was changed to the Dalzell-Viking Glass Co. Still in business today.

Northwood Glass Works. Founded in 1888 by Henry Helling and Harry Northwood et al. in Martin's Ferry, OH. By 1889, the firm was referred to as the Northwood Glass Co. In 1893, the plant was moved to Ellwood City, PA, and the name was changed to the Northwood Glass Co. In 1895, rumors circulated that the firm would go back to Martin's Ferry, and by 1896 bankruptcy was filed in Ellwood City. At this time, the plant was closed, and the firm was moved into the bankrupt Indiana Glass Co. plant in Indiana, PA. Known as the Northwood Co., the plant operated with Northwood as manager and Northwood's brother Carl as traveling salesman. In 1899, the Northwood Co. joined the National Glass Co. combine and operated as the Northwood Glass Works in Indiana, PA. After leaving the National Glass combine in January 1902, Northwood acquired and refurbished the abandoned Hobbs, Brockunier & Co. plant in Wheeling, WV, which it acquired from the United States Glass Co., and changed the name to H. Northwood (&) Co. In 1905, the name was changed to Harry Northwood Glass Co. In 1918, Northwood died, and a few years later the plant was closed.

O'Hara Glass Co. Known as the O'Hara (Flint) Glass Works circa 1852, by 1875 the name was changed to the O'Hara Glass Co., Ltd. In 1891, the firm became Factory "L" of the United States Glass Co. and was sold in 1893 to Park Bros. & Co.

Ohio Flint Glass Co. Originally founded by some of the stockholders of the Buckeye Novelty Glass Co. of Bowling Green, OH. In 1891, the Buckeye plant was purchased by the Ohio Flint Glass Co., and in 1892 Ohio Flint was operating out of the old Buckeye plant. In 1893, Ohio Flint moved to Dunkirk, IN, and was in operation by mid-year. Ohio Flint was completely destroyed by fire in February 1899 and a new plant was rebuilt in Lancaster, OH. By November 1899, the new Lancaster plant was functional. In 1900, Ohio Flint joined the National Glass Co. combine and operated as the Ohio Flint Glass Works. In 1904, the plant was leased by the National combine to the original Ohio Flint Glass Co. By 1907, Ohio Flint was declared bankrupt and by December of that year the plant was closed.

Pairpoint Mfg. Co. Established by Thomas J. Pairpoint in 1880 in New Bedford, MA. In 1894, the company merged with the Mount Washington Glass Co. In 1900, the name was changed to the Pairpoint Corp. In 1938, the company was sold to J. & B. Kenner, Inc. In 1939, the firm was sold to Robert Gundersen and the name was changed to Gundersen Glass Works until 1952, when the name changed to the Gundersen-Pairpoint Glass Works. In October 1957, the factory was re-sold to Robert Bryden and became known as the Pairpoint Glass Co., Inc., and was moved to East Wareham, MA. In February 1958, the company became known as the Pairpoint Glass Co., an importer of glassware from Spain. In 1970, Bryden reopened the factory in Sagamore, MA, where it still operates today.

Phoenix Glass Co. Founded in 1880 in Phillipsburgh, Beaver County, PA, by Andrew Howard and William I. Miller. The plant was destroyed by fire and rebuilt in 1884 and 1893. By 1970, the firm was purchased by the Anchor-Hocking Corp.

Pilgrim Glass Co. Founded in Ceredo, WV, in 1949 by Alfred Knobler, the company is a contemporary manufacturer of handmade pressed glass. In 1986, the firm introduced cameo glass. Still in operation.

Plum Glass Co. Located in Pittsburgh, PA, the company is a contemporary manufacturer of pressed glass, including a number of classic patterns produced from original Westmoreland molds.

Portland Glass Co. Founded in 1863 in Portland, ME, by John B. Brown and J.S. Palmer et al. The plant was destroyed by fire in 1867 and rebuilt in 1868. By 1870, the firm was reorganized as the Portland Glass Works. The company closed in 1873.

Richards & Hartley Glass Co. Founded as the Richards & Hartley Flint Glass Co., in Pittsburgh, PA, in 1865 by William T. Hartley, Joseph Richards, and John Wilson. In 1884, the firm moved to Tarentum, PA, and the name was changed to the Richards & Hartley Glass Co. In 1891, the firm joined the United States Glass Company combine and became Factory "E." In 1893, the plant was closed by United States Glass Company, and in 1894 it was sold to Henry K. Brackenridge, who, in turn, sold it on a second deed to the Tarentum Glass Co.

Ripley & Co. Founded in 1865 in Pittsburgh, PA, by Thomas Coffin, Nicholas Kunzler, Daniel C. Ripley, Sr., Jacob Strickler, and John Strickler. Became Factory "F" of the United States Glass Company in 1891.

Riverside Glass Works. Founded in 1879 in Wellsburg, WV, by Charles N. Brady, John Dornan, and J.E. Ratcliffe. By 1886, the plant had been destroyed by fire; it was rebuilt the following year. In 1899, Riverside joined the National Glass combine. As late as 1904, National leased the Riverside plant to a stock company and the name was changed to the Riverside Glass Co. In 1911 the plant was sold by National to the Ohio Valley Brass Co.

Smith, L.E., Glass Co.   Founded in 1907 in Jeannette, PA, by Louis E. Smith and Thomas E. Wible et al. for the purpose of decorating tableware. In 1909, the firm purchased the bankrupt Anchor Glass Co. plant in Mount Pleasant, PA, for the purpose of producing glassware rather than purchasing it. The plant was destroyed by fire in 1913 but was quickly rebuilt. In 1920, Smith purchased a second plant, the Greensburg Glass Co. plant in Greensburg, PA. As early American pattern-glass reproductions became popular throughout the 1940s, Smith engaged in producing this type of glassware. In 1975, Owens-Illinois, Inc., of Toledo, OH, purchased Smith, which continued to function as a wholly owned subsidiary company.

St. Clair Glass Works, Inc.   Founded in 1938 in Elwood, IN, by John St. Clair and sons: Bob, Ed, Joe, John, and Paul. John, Sr., died in 1958, and Joe began to experiment with pressed glass. In 1964, the factory was destroyed by fire but was rebuilt. In 1971, the factory was sold, and by 1974 Joe repurchased the original factory. In 1977, the molds were sold to the Summit Art Glass Co. of Mogadore, OH.

Steimer Glass Co.   Founded in 1900 in Buckhannon, WV, as the Valley Glass Co. by J.T. Ballentine, Davis M. McCloskey, T.C. Steimer, and John K. Tener. By May 1904, the name was changed to the Buckhannon Cut Glass Co. and by September 1904 was changed again to the Steimer Glass Co. In September 1906, the firm closed.

Summit Art Glass Co.   Founded in 1972 by Russell and Joanne Vogelsang in Akron, OH. In 1977, the Vogelsangs purchased a number of molds from the St. Clair Glass Co., and the plant was moved to Mogadore, OH. In 1984, the plant was moved to Rootstown, OH. Still in operation today.

United States Glass Co.   Established in 1891 in Pittsburgh, PA, this was the largest pressed-glass combine and consisted of thirteen manufacturers. By August 1891, two additional factories were added, and in 1892, three more, totaling eighteen in all. Factories were assigned a letter of the alphabet as follows: "A" (Adams & Co.); "B" (Bryce Bros.); "C" (Challinor, Taylor & Co.); "D" (George Duncan & Sons); "E" (Richards & Hartley); "F" (Ripley & Co.); "G" (Gillinder & Sons); "H" (Hobbs Glass Co.), "J" (Columbia Glass Co.); "K" (King Glass Co.); "L" (O'Hara Glass Co.); "M" (Bel-

laire Glass Co.); "N" (Nickel Plate Glass Co.); "O" (Central Glass Co.); "P" (Doyle & Co.); "R" (A.J. Beatty & Sons); "S" (A.J. Beatty & Sons); and "T" (Novelty Glass Co.). By 1938, only the plant in Tiffin, OH, and the two plants in Glassport, PA, were operational, and the central offices were moved from Pittsburgh to Tiffin, OH. In 1955, the Duncan & Miller division was created; equipment and molds were acquired from the Duncan plant in Washington, PA. By 1963, the United States Glass Co. had filed for bankruptcy.

Valley Glass Co.   (*See* Steimer Glass Co.)

Weishar Enterprises.   Wheeling, WV. Family-owned business that has been producing pressed glass and molds for the industry since the early 1900s. In 1960, Joseph J. Weishar produced numerous molds for the Moon and Star pattern and in 1988 produced Moon and Star in miniature.

Viking Glass Co.   (*See* New Martinsville Glass Co.)

Westlake Ruby Glass Works,   Columbus, OH. Contemporary decorators of reproduction pressed glass. Still operating today.

Westmoreland Glass Co.   Grapeville, PA. (*See* Westmoreland Specialty Co.)

Westmoreland Specialty Co.   Founded in 1889 in Grapeville, PA, by George M. Irwin, Charles H. West, and George R. West. By 1924, the name had been changed to the Westmoreland Glass Co. In 1981, the firm was acquired by David Grossman Designs, Inc., of St. Louis, MO. In 1985, the company was permanently closed.

Wheaton Glass Co.   Established in 1888 in Millville, NJ, by Dr. Theodore Carson Wheaton. Initially the company produced blown pharmaceutical bottles and scientific glassware. As late as 1980, the firm operated as Wheaton Industries, engaging in the production of pressed glass and pressed-glass reproductions.

Windsor Glass Co.   Founded in 1886 in Pittsburgh, PA, by A.M. Bacon and R.B. Brown. The factory was destroyed by fire in May 1887 and rebuilt in September of the same year. The plant closed in 1890.

Wright, L.G., Glass Co.   Founded in the 1930s in New Martinsville, WV, by Lawrence G. Wright, this company was a brokerage house and not a manufacture of pressed glass. Through the years, Wright specialized in the creation of reproduction glassware that he had made in contemporary glass factories from original and new molds made to his specifications. When Wright died in 1969, business affairs were continued by his wife. Today, the company still operates under the direction of Wright's niece.

MANUFACTURERS' MARKS

Embossed mark.
Boyd's Crystal Art
Glass Co., Inc.,
Cambridge, OH.

Paper label.
Cambridge Glass Co.,
Cambridge, OH.

Hand stamp.
Crystal Art Glass Co.,
Cambridge, OH.

Embossed mark
or hand stamp.
Crystal Art Glass Co.,
Cambridge, OH.

Paper Label.
Duncan & Miller Glass Co.,
Washington, PA.

Paper Label.
Duncan & Miller Glass Co.,
Washington, PA.

Paper Label.
Duncan & Miller Glass Co.,
Washington, PA.

Paper Label.
Duncan & Miller Glass Co.,
Washington, PA.

Paper label.
Fenton Art Glass Co.,
Williamstown, WV.

Paper label.
Fenton Art Glass Co.,
Williamstown, WV.

Embossed mark.
Fostoria Glass Co.,
Fostoria, OH, for
the Henry Ford Museum,
Dearborn, MI.

Paper label.
Fostoria Glass Co.,
Fostoria, OH, for
the Henry Ford Museum,
Dearborn, MI.

Paper label.
Imperial Glass Corp.,
Bellaire, OH.

Paper label.
Imperial Glass Corp.,
Bellaire, OH.

String tag.
Stamm House Victorian Glass
by Imperial Glass Corp.,
Bellaire, OH. Circa 1965.

Embossed mark.
Imperial Glass Corp.,
Bellaire, OH.

Paper label.
Indiana Glass Co.,
Dunkirk, IN.

Paper label.
John E. Kemple Glass Works,
East Palestine, OH.

Paper label.
John E. Kemple Glass Works,
Kenova, WV.

Paper label.
L.E. Smith Glass Co.,
Mount Pleasant, PA.
Circa 1958.

Paper label.
L.E. Smith Glass Co.,
Mount Pleasant, PA.
Circa 1963.

Paper label.
L.E. Smith Glass Co.,
Mount Pleasant, PA.
Circa 1953.

Paper label.
L.E. Smith Glass Co.,
Mount Pleasant, PA.
Circa 1970.

Paper label.
Tiffin Glass Co.,
Tiffin, OH.

Paper label.
Viking Glass Co.,
New Martinsville, WV.

Embossed mark.
Westmoreland Glass Co.,
Grapeville, PA.
After 1940.

Embossed mark.
L.G. Wright Glass Co.,
New Martinsville, WV.

Glossary

Acid Etching. The process of coating the surface of a glass object with a protective resin, wax, or similar resistant material, then cutting a design into this coating, exposing the glass surface. Applying acid or acid vapor, which is corrosive to glass, etches the glass surface.

Annealing. The process of slowly cooling hot glass to prevent internal stresses and possible fractures. This process also strengthens newly formed glass, which otherwise would be too brittle.

Batch. The mixture of raw glass ingredients combined in proportion to a prescribed glass formula.

Belltone. The resonant sound flint glass makes when gently tapped.

Bone Ash. The material added to a batch of glass for the purpose of creating an opalescent effect when the glass is reheated.

Camphor Glass. White, semi-opaque glass.

Cap Ring. That part of the pressing mold on top of the base mold and surrounding the plunger, thus centering the plunger and controlling the flow of hot glass into the cavity of the mold.

Cased Glass. A type of glass usually consisting of two or more layers of glass, such as those containing a clear outer surface and an opaque inner layer.

Chocolate Glass. Glass with a chocolate color sometimes referred to as caramel glass, developed in 1900 by Jacob Rosenthal at the Indiana Tumbler & Goblet Co.

Clambroth Glass. A name given to a type of smoky, semi-opaque glass resembeling the color of clam broth.

Cold-Paint Process. The application of paint to the surface of glass to produce a decorative effect not requiring reheating; thus the glass is easily susceptible to pealing and wear.

Color-Stain Process. The process of coloring glass with a chemical, such as cadmium oxide, whose true color matures or develops at high temperature. The least expensive method of coloring glass. Unlike the cold-paint process, stained colors are permanently embedded into the surface of the glass.

C-Scroll. A decorative element fashioned in the form of a stylized "C."

Custard Glass. Opaque or translucent near-yellow to off-white colored glass usually having uranium florescence under long-wave ultraviolet light.

Embossed. Raised or protruding, not recessed.

Enameling. The technique of decorating glassware either permanently under extreme heat or nonpermanently by the cold-paint process. (*See* Cold-Paint Process.)

Engraving. The technique of decorating glass by manipulating its outer surface against small rotating copper wheels to produce a design of varying depth.

Etching. (*See* Acid Etching.)

Fenton. The word "Fenton" within a circle. Embossed trademark of the Fenton Art Glass Company of Williamstown, West Virginia. First used in 1970, then altered in the 1980s to include an "8" below the word "Fenton," and in the 1990s to include a "9" below "Fenton."

Fiery Opal. The glowing pale blue tinge of some opaque white glass appearing where the glass is thinnest and observed by holding the item up to a strong light.

Finial. The knob fastened to the top of an article or the handle on top of a cover or lid.

Firepolishing. The process of reheating an article after it has been cast to obliterate mold marks, tool marks, or rough edges and to add brilliance to newly pressed glass. Originally referred to as "flashing."

Flint Glass. A type of glass containing lead oxide as a principal ingredient, thus producing a bell-toned resonance when gently tapped.

Fooler. Not a reproduction, but the adaptation of an antique design to a contemporary form. Also known as a look-alike.

Frosted Glass. The matte finish on clear glass produced by acid-etching or sandblasting.

Frosting. A gray-dull finish produced by exposing glass to potassium fluoride and hydrofluoric acid, or produced by the process of sandblasting.

Gilding. The gold decorative color on glass usually produced by applying brown oxide of gold and firing the glass.

Gilt Trim. Covered with gold, or of the color of gold.

HFM. Embossed hallmark of the Henry Ford Museum in Dearborn, Michigan.

Hydrofluoric Acid. An aqueous solution of hydrogen fluoride (HF), which attacks silica and silicates, used in frosting and etching glass.

IG. Embossed logo of the Imperial Glass Corporation of Bellaire, Ohio.

Intaglio. Refers to the deep, sunken design of pressed glass. Recessed rather than raised.

Iridescent. Having or exhibiting a play of colors producing rainbow effects.

K. Embossed hallmark of the John E. Kemple Glass Works of Kenova, West Virginia.

KW. Embossed hallmark of the Wheaton Glass Company of Millville, New Jersey.

Lime Glass. A type of nonlead glass used for pressing, ordinarily consisting of bicarbonate of soda (rather than soda ash), lime, and silica as its principal ingredients.

Look-alike. (*See* Fooler.)

Machine-Ground Frosting. The process of decorating a section of glass with a matte or coarse gray surface by pressing the article against an abrasive wheel.

Marble Glass. A type of glass, also known as slag, produced by combining two different colors of molten glass and then reheating to a temperature suitable for pressing. For example, mixing opaque white and purple glass will produce the variegated marble effect known as purple or marble slag.

Milk-White Glass. (*See* Opaque White Glass.)

MMA. Embossed hallmark of the Metropolitan Museum of Art, New York City.

N. Underlined "N" within a circle. Embossed logo used by Northwood Glass Company of Indiana, Pennsylvania.

Near Cut. Embossed logo used by the Cambridge Glass Company of Cambridge, Ohio.

Opalescent. Transparent glass created by adding calcium phosphate to the glass mix. Upon pressing, the article is air-cooled and reheated to a cherry-red color, at which point desired portions strike a milky-white color caused by the presence of the heat-sensitive calcium phosphate.

Opaque Glass. A nontransparent glass produced by adding coloring agents to the formula, which add density to the glass produced.

Opaque White Glass. The correct name of the glass more commonly known as milk glass or opal glass.

Packer's Glass. Glass containers produced specifically to hold edibles such as candy, jelly, or mustard.

Pearl-like. Having a luster similar to a pearl. Luminous, lustrous, or radiant.

PG. Hallmark of the Plum Glass Company of Pittsburgh, Pennsylvania, embossed within the shape of a keystone.

Pontil Mark. The scar or rough surface at that point on the bottom of a blown or pressed-glass item where that item had been removed from the pontil rod. Such marks are frequently ground and polished, producing a less visible circular, concave impression.

Pres Cut. Embossed logo used by McKee Brothers of Pittsburgh, Pennsylvania.

Punty. Also known as a pontil or punty rod. The iron rod employed in gathering molten metal for pressing. Also used for holding hot pressed items for additional hand-finishing.

Resonance. The auditory vibration or ring associated with lead glass, produced by gentle tapping.

Sandblasting. The process of decorating portions of the surface of glass by sand propelled by compressed air, producing a frosted or matte finish.

Satin Finished. A finish on glass, produced by hydrofluoric acid, suggestive of satin, especially in its smooth, lustrous appearance and sleek touch.

Scratch Mark. (*See* Straw Mark.)

SI. Embossed hallmark of the Smithsonian Institution, Washington, DC.

Sick Glass. A condition in glass caused by the presence of moisture or cleaning agents reacting with the alkali in the glass, usually eroding the inner surface of the object and resulting in a cloudy appearance.

Slag. (*See* Marble Glass.)

Shear Line. (*See* Straw Mark.)

SM. Embossed mark of the Sandwich Glass Museum of Sandwich, Massachusetts.

Souvenir Glass. Small clear with color-stained glass items such as goblets, toothpick holders, and wines intended for sale at carnivals, fairs, and resort areas, usually engraved with names, dates, and events.

Staining. (*See* Color-Stain Process.)

Stippling. The background of small closely spaced depressed glass dots surrounding a pattern's design, often imparting a silvery metallic luster or shine.

Straw Mark. A blemish or scratch-like fissure on pressed glass appearing on that portion of the item's surface that has come in contact with the plunger of the press. Also known as a shear line.

Turn. The amount of glassware produced within a specified amount of time, usually in four to six hours.

V. "V" within a circle. Embossed hallmark of the Summit Art Glass Company of Mogadore, Ohio.

W. Underlined "W" within a circle. Embossed logo of the L.G. Wright Glass Company of New Martinsville, West Virginia.

WG. Embossed hallmark of the Westmoreland Glass Company of Grapeville, Pennsylvania.

Bibliography

CONTEMPORARY GLASS CATALOGS AND PRICE LISTS

A.A. Importing Co., Inc., St. Louis, MO.
Catalog No.33, "Bicentennial, Spring–Summer." 1976.
Catalog No.34, "Early Bird Edition," 1976.
Catalog No.35, 1977.
Catalog No.36, 1978.
Catalog No.38, "Early Bird Edition," 1979.
Catalog No.40, "Early Bird Edition," Fall 1980.
Catalog No.41, "Spring–Summer," 1980.
Catalog No.42, "Early Bird Edition," 1981.
Catalog No.44, "Early Bird Edition," 1982.
Catalog No.45, 1982.
Catalog No.47, 1983.

Clevenger Brothers Glass Works. Illustrated Sales Brochure. Undated.

Duncan & Miller Glass Company, Washington, PA.
"Genuine Duncan: The Loveliest Glassware in America." 1943.
Price List No.143, 1943.

Fenton Art Glass Company, Williamstown, WV.
"Baker-Smith's Salesman's Photographs." 1937–1951.
"Catalog Pages and Photographs of the 1930's." 193[?].
"Fenton's New Shapes and Colors for 1940."
January–July 1940 Catalog.
"Fenton's New Creations in Art Glass." 1941 Catalog.
July 1, 1941, Price List.
"Fenton's New Creations in Art Glass." 1942 Catalog.
"New 1943 Creations." 1943 Catalog.
1948 Catalog.
January 1, 1949, Price List.
"Introducing Tiara in Crests and Overlays." 1949 Catalog.
"Authentic Fenton Handmade." 1950 Catalog.
1950 Price List.
"New Item Illustrations, 1950–1952." Catalog.
1951 Illustrated Sales Brochure.
1951 Catalog Supplement.
"Your New 1953–1954 Catalog: Handmade Fenton Glass." 1953.
"Handmade Fenton Glass: Our 50th Year." 1955 Catalog.
July 1955 Catalog Supplement.

"How We Make a Good Line Even Better; Being a Catalog of New Shapes and Colors Handmade in the Age-Old Manner." January 1956.
1956 Catalog Supplement.
"America's Finest Art Glass in Color, An Ancient Art Still Unchanged." 1956 Catalog.
"An Ancient Art Still Unchanged." 1958 Catalog.
July 1961–1962 Catalog.
"Fenton: America's Finest Glass in Color." 1960 Catalog.
"Fenton: America's Finest Glass in Color." July 1961–1962 Catalog.
January 1, 1962, Catalog Supplement.
July 1, 1962, Catalog Supplement.
January 1963 Catalog.
July 1963 Catalog Supplement.
January 1964 Catalog Supplement.
July 1964 Catalog Supplement.
January 1965 Catalog.
January 1966 Catalog Supplement.
"Fenton: The Wonderful World of Handmade Glass." 1967 Catalog.
1968 Catalog Supplement.
July 1968 Catalog Supplement.
January 1969 Catalog.
1969 Lamp Supplement.
July 1969 Catalog Supplement.
January 1971 Catalog.
July 1971 Catalog Supplement.
January 1973 Catalog.
July 1973 Catalog Supplement.
"Two Year Catalog, January, 1977 through December, 1978."
July 1977 Catalog Supplement.
January 1978 Catalog Supplement.
July 1978 Catalog Supplement.
July 1979 Catalog Supplement.
1979–1980 Catalog.
January 1980 Catalog Supplement.
June 1980 Catalog Supplement.
November 15, 1980, Catalog Supplement.
December 14, 1980, Catalog Supplement.
1981–1982 Catalog.
1982 Catalog Supplement.
January 1982 Catalog Supplement.
1983 Catalog Supplement.

"Fenton Classic, a Continuing Celebration in Fine Glass." 1985–1986 Catalog.
"Two Year Catalog January 1985–December 1986." Catalog.
1985–1986 Catalog.

Fostoria Glass Company.
"Handmade Flint Glass Reproductions from the Henry Ford Museum Collection by Fostoria." 1967 Catalog.
January 1, 1972, Eastern Price List Catalog.
1974 Price List.
January 1, 1974, Eastern Price List Catalog.
1982 Catalog.

Glasscrafts & Ceramics, Inc., Yonkers, NY.
1953 Catalog.
1953 Price List.

General Merchandise Company, Milwaukee, WI.
Wholesale Catalog No.76

Haley, K.R., Glassware Co., Inc., Greensburg, PA. 194[?]–195–[?] illustrated sales brochure.

Imperial Glass Corp., Bellaire, OH.
"Imperial Photo Notebooks." 1930's–1970's.
Imperial Catalog Pages. 1936–1940.
Imperial 195–[?] Sales Brochure.
General Catalog No.53. 1953[?].
"Imperial's Vintage Milk Glass: Handmade in Olden Manner." 1953–1955.
"Notebook assembled by E.C. Kleiner." 1956–1958.
"Price List No.58." 1958.[?].
1960 Catalog.
Catalog No.66A. 1966 Catalog.
Supplement One to Catalog No.62. "Our 60th Year." 1964.
1966 Catalog.
1971 Catalog.
"Handcrafted Imperial Glass." 1972 Catalog.
"Imperial Hand Crafted Glass by Lenox." 1973–1980.
1977 Catalog.
"Imperial Glass by Lenox." 1978 Catalog.
1980 Catalog.
"Imperial Glass: An American Handcrafted Tradition." 1982 Catalog.
Catalog "F". Undated.

Indiana Glass Company, Dunkirk, IN.
1964 Catalog.
1965 Catalog.
1966–1968 Advertising Brochures.
1967 Catalog.

Jeannette Glass Company, Jeannette, PA.
1956 Catalog.
"An Exciting New Line for 1958." 1958 Catalog.
1966 Catalog.
July 1, 1966, Price List.

Jenning's Red Barn, Inc., New Martinsville, WV.
1978–1980 Catalog.
Undated catalog.

Kamei Glass Company, Osaka, Japan.
1981 Catalog.
1983 Catalog.

Kanawha Glass Company, Dunbar, WV. 1980–1981 Catalog.
1974 Catalog.
1975 Catalog Supplement.
1976 Catalog.
Summer 1976 Catalog Supplement.
"No.78 Catalog." 1978.
1978 Catalog.
"1978 Catalog Supplement."
1980–1981 Catalog.

Kemple, John E., Glass Works, Kenova, WV.
"Kemple Glass: Authentic Antique Reproductions," 1967[?] Catalog.

Levay Distributing Company, Edwardsville, IL.
1983 Price List.

Libbey Glass Company, Toledo, OH. "1981 Pacesetter Catalog."

Mosser Glass, Inc., Cambridge, OH. 1976 Catalog.

Summit Art Glass Company, Akron, OH. 1977 Sales Brochure.

Smith, L.E., Glass, Mount Pleasant, PA.
January 1, 1968, Price List.
1975 Catalog.
January 1, 1975, Price List.
"American Heritage Crystal Collection." 1982 Catalog.
1982 Catalog.
January 1, 1982, Price List.

Summit Art Glass Company, Ravenna, OH.
1985 Catalog.
1985 Wholesale Price List.

Tiara Exclusives, Dunkirk, IN.
"Happy Tenth Anniversary Tiara." 1980 Catalog.
1981 Catalog.

Viking Glass Company, New Martinsville, WV.
"Original Photographs." 1966–1979.
"Jewels of Light: Treasured American Glass." 1972 Catalog.
1974 Catalog.
1976 Catalog.
1983 Catalog.
1984 Catalog.

Westmoreland Glass Company, Grapeville, PA.
"Westmoreland's Handmade 'Old Quilt' Pattern." 1955 Catalog.
1955 Catalog.
1967 Catalog.
1974 Catalog Supplement.
"Treasured Gifts." 1976 Catalog.
1983 Catalog.

Wright, L.G., Glass Company, New Martinsville, WV.
  1969 Master Catalog.
  1969 Supplement to Master Catalog.
  1970 Supplement to Master Catalog.
  1971 Supplement to Master Catalog.
  1972 Supplement to Master Catalog.
  1978 Supplement to Master Catalog.
  1979 Supplement to Master Catalog.
  1980 Supplement to Master Catalog.
  1982 Supplement to Master Catalog.

CONTEMPORARY MUSEUM, MAIL ORDER, AND TRADE JOURNALS

American Heritage Collection.
  1980 Mail-Order Catalog.
  1981 Mail-Order Catalog.

Clymer's of Bucks County, Nashua, PA. Mail-Order Catalog, 1974.

Crockery and Glass Journal.
  February 1959.

Down's Collector's Show Case.
  1984 Mail-Order Catalog.

Gift and Art Buyer.
  January 1963.
  July 1961.

Gifts and Decorative Accessories.
  July 1966.

Metropolitan Museum of Art, New York, NY.
  1971 Catalog.
  1975 Catalog.

  1976 Catalog.
  1977 Catalog.
  Spring 1978 Catalog.
  Christmas 1978 Catalog.
  Christmas 1979 Catalog.
  Christmas 1980 Catalog.
  Christmas 1981 Catalog.
  Fall 1982 Catalog.
  Christmas 1984 Catalog.
  January 1985 Catalog.
  1986 Catalog.
  1987 Catalog.

Smithsonian Institution, Washington, DC.
  Fall 1978 Catalog.
  Spring 1978 Catalog.
  Fall 1979 Catalog.
  Fall 1981 Catalog.
  Fall 1984 Catalog.
  Summer 1982 Catalog.

REFERENCE BOOKS

Belknap, E. McCamly. *Milk Glass.* New York: Crown Publishers, 1949 (fifth printing).

Bickenheuser, Fred. *Tiffin Glassmasters.* 2 Volumes. Marietta, OH: Antique Publications, 1979, 1981.

Bredehoft, Neila M.; George A. Fogg; and Francis C. Maloney. *Early Duncan Glassware. Geo. Duncan & Sons, 1874–1892.* Saint Louisville, OH: Authors, 1987.

Ferson, Regis F., and Mary F. Ferson. *Yesterday's Milk Glass Today.* Greensburg, PA: Chas. H. Henry Printing Co., 1981.

Florence, Gene. *Degenhart Glass & Paperweights.* Cambridge, OH: Degenhart Paperweight and Glass Museum, Inc., 1982.

Hammond, Dorothy. *Confusing Collectibles: A Guide to the Identification of Contemporary Objects.* Revised Edition. Des Moines, IA: Wallace-Homestead Book Co., 1979.

———. *More Confusing Collectibles.* Wichita, KS: C.B.P. Publishing Company, 1972.

Hartley, Julia Magee, and Mary Magee Cobb. *The States' Series Early American Pattern Glass.* Lubbock, TX: Authors, 1976.

Heacock, William. *Fenton Glass: The First Twenty-Five Years.* Marietta, OH: O-Val Advertising Corp., 1978.

———. *Fenton Glass: The Second Twenty-Five Years.* Marietta, OH: O-Val Advertising Corp., 1980.

———. *Fenton Glass: The Third Twenty-Five Years.* Marietta, OH: O-Val Advertising Corp., 1989.

Herrick, Ruth, M.D. *Greentown Glass.* Grand Rapids, MI: Author, 1959.

Jenks, Bill, and Jerry Luna. *Early American Pattern Glass, 1850–1910: Major Collectible Table Settings.* Radnor, PA: Wallace-Homestead Book Co., 1990.

Krause, Gail. *A Pictorial History of Duncan and Miller Glass.* Washington, PA: Author, 1976.

———. *The Encyclopedia of Duncan Glass.* Hicksville, NY: Exposition Press, 1976.

Lechler, Doris, and Virginia O'Neill. *Children's Glass Dishes.* Nashville, TN: Nelson Publishers, 1976.

Lee, Ruth Webb. *Antique Fakes and Reproductions.* Northboro, MA: Author, 1950.

———. *Early American Pressed Glass, Enlarged and Revised.* Northboro, MA: Author, 1931, 1933. (Thirtieth Edition, 1946.)

———. *Victorian Glass Specialities of the Nineteenth Century.* Wellesley Hills, MA: Lee Publications, 1944.

Lindsey, Bessie M. *American Historical Glass.*

Rutland, VT: Charles E. Tuttle Co., 1967. (Second Edition.)

Lucas, Robert I. *Tarentum Pattern Glass.* Tarentum, PA: Author, 1981.

Measell, James. *Greentown Glass: The Indiana Tumbler & Goblet Company.* Grand Rapids, MI: Grand Rapids Public Museum, 1979.

Metz, Alice Hulett. *Early American Pattern Glass, Volume I.* Chicago: Author, 1958.

Peterson, Arthur G., Ph.D. *Glass Salt Shakers: 1000 Patterns.* Des Moines, IA: Wallace-Homestead Co., 1970.

———. *Glass Patents and Patterns.* DeBary, FL: Author, 1973.

———. *400 Trademarks on Glass.* Tacoma Park, MD: Author, 1968.

Pyne Press (Ed.). *Pennsylvania Glassware, 1870–1904.* New York: Charles Scribner's Sons, 1972.

Shuman, Susan W., and John A. Shuman III. *Lion Glass.* Boston: Branden Press, 1977.

Smith, Don E. *Findlay Pattern Glass.* Findlay, OH: Author, 1970.

Stuart, Anna Maude. *Bread Plates and Platters.* Hillsborough, CA: Author, 1965.

Unitt, Doris, and Peter Unitt. *American and Canadian Goblets,* 2 Vols. Peterborough, Ontario, Canada: Clock House, 1970. (Second Edition, 1974.)

———. *American and Canadian Goblets, Volume Two.* Peterborough, Ontario, Canada: Clock House, 1974.

Viking Glass Company. *Beauty in Glass from Viking.* New Martinsville, WV: Viking Glass Company, 1967.

Warman, Edwin G. *Milk Glass Addenda.* Uniontown, PA: E.G. Warman Publishing Co., 1959. (Second Edition, Enlarged & Revised.)

Welker, John, and Elizabeth Welker. *Pressed Glass in America: Encyclopedia of the First Hundred Years, 1825–1925.* Ivyland, PA: Antique Acres Press, 1985.

Index of Company Names

Index of Pattern Names